32 Battalion

32 Battalion

The Inside Story
of South Africa's
Elite Fighting Unit

PIET NORTJE

ZEBRA

Published by Zebra Press
an imprint of Struik Publishers
(a division of New Holland Publishing (South Africa) (Pty) Ltd)
PO Box 1144, Cape Town, 8000
New Holland Publishing is a member of Johnnic Publishing Ltd

www.zebrapress.co.za

First published 2003
Published in paperback 2004
Reprinted in 2006 (twice) and 2007

5 7 9 10 8 6 4

Publication © Zebra Press 2003
Text and maps © Piet Nortje 2003

Cover photographs © AFP PHOTO/Pedro UGARTE and Piet Nortje

PUBLISHING MANAGER: Marlene Fryer
MANAGING EDITOR: Robert Plummer
EDITOR: Marléne Burger
PROOFREADER: Ronel Richter-Herbert
COVER AND TEXT DESIGNER: Natascha Adendorff-Olivier
TYPESETTER: Monique van den Berg
INDEXER: Robert Plummer

Set in 10.5 pt on 13.5 pt Minion

Reproduction by Hirt & Carter (Cape) (Pty) Ltd
Printed and bound by Paarl Print, Oosterland Street, Paarl, South Africa

ISBN 978 1 86872 914 2

Log on to our photographic website www.imagesofafrica.co.za for an African experience

He which hath no stomach to this fight
Let him depart
But we in it shall be remembered.
We few, we happy few, we band of brothers.
He today that sheds his blood with me
Shall be my brother.

SHAKESPEARE: *Henry V*, Act 4 Scene 3

Contents

Photographs between pages 158 and 159

List of maps and illustrations

Preface

MY ENTIRE ADULT life has been that of a soldier, almost half of it spent with one of recent history's most unique fighting units. In 1989, surrounded by veterans and serving members of 32 Battalion, it occurred to me that someone really ought to preserve for posterity the tale of how a ragtag band of foreign freedom fighters became the South African Army's best fighting unit since the Second World War.

Four years later, that same unit had become a political punchbag, consigned to the trash heap by the last apartheid government as soon as this became politically expedient. By then Colonel Jan Breytenbach, founding father of the Buffalo Soldiers, had published two books on the subject, but the first, *Forged in Battle*, dealt almost entirely with the role played by what was then known as Bravo Group during *Operation Savannah*, the former SA Defence Force's highly successful 1975 campaign against the communist-backed MPLA in Angola. His second book, *They Live by the Sword*, covered the period up to 1989, but contained largely anecdotal material, Breytenbach having transferred out of the unit in early 1977. On the eve of disbandment, therefore, the story of a unit unlike any other in the SADF remained untold.

In early 1993, during informal discussions with two former 32 Battalion officers – Commandant Werner Sott, outgoing OC 7 SA Infantry Battalion, and his successor, Commandant Daan van der Merwe – I ignored the first rule of military service and volunteered to compile the unit's story. They informed me that someone had already been approached to do so, but I nonetheless began collecting every scrap of information I could find. Towards the end of that year, a staff paper by Major Wally Vrey, entitled 'The History of 32 Battalion', landed on my desk, and

I raised anew the need for a published account, only to be told yet again that one was already in the pipeline.

By January 1998 there was still no sign of either the promised history or the unnamed chronicler. Five years had elapsed since the unit ceased to exist, and my fears were mounting that vital information and verifiable facts would soon be lost forever. I turned to Brigadier General Eddie Viljoen, the battalion's longest-serving commanding officer, who not only immediately offered his assistance, but also sound advice on how I should proceed. Armed with the blessing of all former commanding officers and mindful of the need to thoroughly document everything I wrote, given the controversy surrounding South Africa's role in the conflict of the past and 32 Battalion's contribution in particular, I was eager to begin. But operations in which 32 Battalion was involved were still classified, and without access to official records and documents the book I envisaged would be stillborn.

As a serving member of the SA National Defence Force, I had to obtain authorisation from the chief of the SA Army before I could start mining the wealth of information contained in 2 319 files – all stamped 'Top Secret' – at the Department of Defence's Documentation Centre in Pretoria. From November 1999 to April 2002, the contents of those files were gradually declassified and shaped into the unexpurgated story of an unconventional unit's war.

During the same period, I sent 1 309 e-mail messages to former members of 32's leader group, inviting personal accounts and recollections, photographs and anecdotes, and ran a website for some six months to solicit contributions from those who had moved abroad. The response was so disappointing – only seven people answered my e-mails – that I decided, in the end, to ignore everything except the official records and my own experiences.

The result may shock some and will certainly surprise others. Most of what appears in this book has never before been made public, and much of it will be news even to those who served with 32 Battalion at various times between 1976 and 1993. Some of the names on these pages have featured prominently in media reports in recent years for reasons that have nothing at all to do with the battalion, and should in no way be construed as a reflection on the unit. Equally, those whose names are not given in full should not be regarded as anything but victims of incomplete records and inadequate memories. Despite exhaustive inquiries, it has simply not been possible to identify some individuals by more than rank and surname, and no disrespect is implied or intended by the omissions.

Of special note to readers are the chapter headings, taken from the English translations of songs traditionally sung by members of 32 Battalion on the eve of battle, on the parade ground or on many a long journey home to loved ones. The power and poignancy of these simple lyrics speak for themselves.

As a career soldier, I know only too well the value of teamwork, and I am sincerely grateful to the following for their unfailing help, motivation and support: Wally Vrey, Steve de Algera and Rene Geyer (without whom I could never have waded through the thousands of documents perused), Johannes 'Groenie' Groenewald (for information on Nova de Marco), Eddie Viljoen (for identifying photographs and incidents, especially during 1976 and 1977), Louis Bothma, Fires van Vuuren, Sam Heap, IG van Rooyen, Mark Craig and Nelson Fishbach; Marléne Burger, my editor, without whose knowledge and sage suggestions this book might never have seen the light.

Special thanks to my wife Mariana and our children Ruanne and Mariné. During the past five years their support never wavered and they have cheerfully tolerated both my travels throughout South Africa to gather information and the endless hours spent at the computer, even though there must have been times when they felt nothing mattered as much as 'his book'. Without your love and understanding, there would have been no book, but you are and always will be my most important concerns.

Finally, those expecting to find within these pages the definitive account of major military operations carried out by the SADF from 1975 will search in vain. What they will discover instead is the extent of a single unit's contribution to every major campaign, from *Savannah* to *Packer*, over a 13-year period during which the unsung heroes of 32 Battalion were never far from the front lines – the story of a band of brothers who spilled their blood together, shed it for South Africa and were truly forged in battle.

PIET NORTJE
MTUBATUBA
MAY 2003

Abbreviations

ANC: African National Congress
APLA: Azanian People's Liberation Army (armed wing of the PAC)
BDF: Botswana Defence Force
Bn: battalion
COSATU: Congress of South African Trade Unions
CP: Conservative Party
CSI: Chief of Staff Intelligence
FAPA: Força Aérea Popular de Angola (People's Air Force of Angola)
FAPLA: Forças Armadas Populares de Libertação de Angola (People's Armed Forces for
    the Liberation of Angola)
FNLA: Frente Nacional de Libertação de Angola (National Liberation Front for Angola)
FRELIMO: Frente de Libertação de Moçambique (Liberation Front for Mozambique)
GOC: General Officer Commanding
IFP: Inkatha Freedom Party
JMC: Joint Monitoring Commission
MI: Military Intelligence
MK: Umkhonto we Sizwe (Spear of the Nation – the ANC's armed wing)
MPLA: Movimento Popular de Libertação de Angola (Popular Movement for the
    Liberation of Angola)
OAU: Organisation of African Unity
OC: Officer Commanding
PAC: Pan Africanist Congress
PLAN: People's Liberation Army of Namibia (SWAPO's armed wing)
PWV: Pretoria–Witwatersrand–Vereeniging metropole

SAAF: South African Air Force
SADF: South African Defence Force
SADFI: South African Defence Force Institute
SAI: South African Infantry (corps or battalion)
SAP: South African Police
SDU: Self-Defence Unit (paramilitary group trained by MK to enforce ANC control of black townships)
SWA: South West Africa
SWAPO: South West African People's Organisation
SWATF: South West African Territorial Force
TRC: Truth and Reconciliation Commission
UDF: United Democratic Front
UNITA: União Nacional para a Independéncia Total de Angola (Union for the Total Independence of Angola)
USSR: Union of Soviet Socialist Republics

1

If you walk this way, we can win

THE CIVIL WAR IN ANGOLA

AS THE WINDS of change buffeted colonial Africa during the late 1950s and early 1960s, storm clouds were gathering over territory claimed by Portuguese seafarers four centuries before. By April 1974, when a military coup toppled Marcello Caetano's repressive Lisbon regime, Angola stood on the brink of a civil war that would rage for 30 years. Spawned by the nationalist aspirations and ethnic loyalties of that country's indigenous peoples, the conflict would be fuelled by American economic interests on the one hand, Soviet expansionism on the other.

The military junta led by General António de Spínola in Lisbon had begun withdrawing Portuguese armed forces from Angola soon after seizing power, setting 11 November 1975 as independence day for the colony. But attempts to draw the three main political factions into a coalition that would serve as a transitional government were short-lived. By October 1975, at least 1 500 combat-ready Cuban troops had been despatched from Havana to boost the ranks of Agostinho Neto's Marxist and largely urban-based Movement for the Liberation of Angola (MPLA). Formed in Luanda in December 1956, the MPLA enjoyed the support of both the Organisation of African Unity (OAU) and the independent front-line states of Zambia and Tanzania as the first post-colonial government of Angola. But as Moscow shipped tons of arms and squadrons of military advisers to the MPLA, Washington began throwing millions of dollars at the uneasy alliance between Holden Roberto's National Front for the Liberation of Angola (FNLA) and Jonas Savimbi's National Union for the Total Independence of Angola (UNITA). The Central Intelligence Agency entered the fray by funding a covert programme to boost the FNLA's ranks with foreign mercenaries.

Many MPLA cadres had been trained in Morocco and Algeria, and on 1 August

1974, the MPLA announced the formation of the People's Armed Forces for the Liberation of Angola (FAPLA). Within two years, FAPLA had been transformed from lightly armed guerrilla units into a national army capable of sustained field operations.

Since 1962, the FNLA had found support within the Bacongo tribe, thousands of whose members had fled across the northern border to Zaire (the former Belgian Congo) to escape the bloody civil strife. Roberto's chief ally was his brother-in-law, President Mobutu Sese Seko, who had allowed a 15 000-strong army to train and prepare for war in a mountain stronghold straddling the border of Zaire and Angola in the coffee-rich province of Uige. UNITA was formed when Savimbi broke away from the FNLA in 1964, travelling to communist China for military training and becoming a disciple of Mao Zedong. His constituents were Angola's rural peasants, and from the day UNITA was formed until Savimbi was killed in 2002, his was primarily a bush war. On the eve of independence, UNITA claimed the allegiance of about 40 per cent of the population and controlled many of Angola's rich, food-producing central and southern provinces, allowing Savimbi to regulate the flow of food to the rest of the country. On 1 August 1975, UNITA formally declared war on the MPLA.

The FNLA had been waging a sporadic guerrilla campaign against coffee plantations, communication lines and villages in northern Angola since the end of 1961, in accordance with the principles of revolution advocated by Roberto's friend, Frantz Fanon. Considered one of the twentieth century's most important exponents of anti-colonial revolution, Fanon believed that in Africa, true liberation had to start with the peasants, and that the shackles of a colonial past could be broken only by total revolution, which demanded absolute violence.

In 1968, the FNLA opened an eastern front, crossing the Cassai River from a base at Nzilo II, near the Katangese mining town of Kolwezi, to establish a presence in the Lunda province, from where marauders moved east, west and south.

On 15 January 1975, a ceasefire was signed by the Portuguese, FNLA, MPLA and UNITA, but the ink on the accord was barely dry before the MPLA was plunged into a leadership struggle between Neto and Daniel Chipenda, which culminated in Chipenda quitting the movement, taking with him some 2 000 well-trained soldiers. But the Alvor Agreement, as it was known, made provision for only the three existing political factions, and Chipenda failed to gain recognition for his breakaway group. On 13 February, an MPLA attack on Chipenda's headquarters left at least 20 combatants dead and drove his splinter group out of Luanda. Within two weeks, Chipenda joined the FNLA as deputy secretary general, extending the movement's sphere of influence to the Kuanyama tribe in the southern and south-eastern regions of Angola, where cadres occupied several abandoned Portuguese military bases, as well as to towns on the west coast.

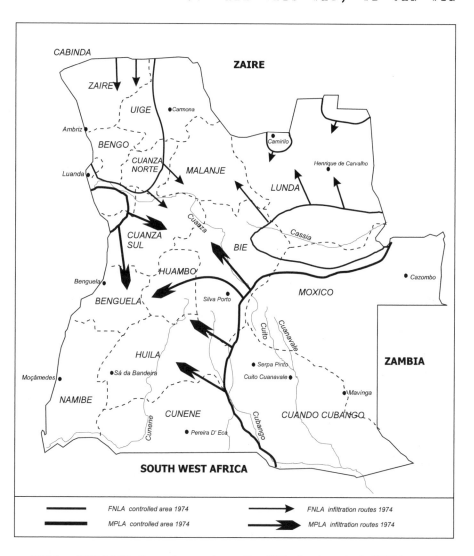

FAPLA and FNLA infiltration and areas of operation, 1974, showing extent of MPLA control

Thanks to financial support from America and a measure of military training by communist China, the FNLA had little problem recruiting members. A report from Luanda at the time noted that 'FNLA soldiers have a neat uniform, modern arms, good pay and allowances, efficient transport and their discipline and behaviour are excellent'. On 28 February 1975, an FNLA delegation approached the South African embassy in London seeking support in the form of weapons. The initial request was for 40 to 50 medium-calibre artillery pieces, with ammunition. A month later, Chipenda met with South African Defence Force (SADF) representatives at Rundu, on the southern bank of the Kavango River, promising FNLA action against the South West African People's Organisation (SWAPO) in return for funding and weapons from Pretoria. With some 3 000 troops deployed at Serpa Pinto, Ninda, Cuito Cuanavale and Luena, Chipenda was firmly in control of southern Angola, and became the first of the SADF's allies to declare communism a common enemy.

With approximately 15 000 troops to the MPLA's 6 000 and UNITA's meagre 1 000, the FNLA's military superiority was evident even in Luanda, the MPLA's political stronghold, where some 6 000 FNLA soldiers had been deployed. Control of the capital lay at the core of repeated bloody clashes between FNLA and MPLA forces from March to July 1975, with a series of ceasefires being breached amid mounting rumours that the FNLA was running out of money due to overspending on military vehicles and equipment. Simultaneously, an economic crisis in his own country demanded Mobutu Sese Seko's full attention, and his support for Roberto and Chipenda began to wane just as Soviet satellite states increased their aid to the MPLA.

The remaining Portuguese security forces were unable to stem the fighting in towns and cities north of Luanda, and a ceasefire brokered by Portugal's Minister of Foreign Affairs, Melo Antunes, held for a mere four days in May before renewed fighting broke out in the districts of Cuanza Norte, Malanje and Cabinda.

After a month-long truce, the MPLA launched its final assault on the FNLA in Luanda on 9 July, just one day after Odinga Odinga, the FNLA commander in the Cuando Cubango province, had turned to the SADF for assistance. Like Chipenda earlier, he vowed to use the 300 troops he had at Mpupa, 60 km north of Angola's border with South West Africa, against SWAPO insurgents. He also informed Brigadier Dawie Schoeman, Officer Commanding 1 Military Area, that the MPLA was slowly but surely driving the FNLA out of towns in southern Angola.

By 12 July, the MPLA was also gaining the upper hand in Luanda, totally destroying the FNLA's headquarters and driving Roberto's forces into a defensive position at São Pedro da Barra. Six days later, an FNLA counter-offensive saw fighting break out in Luanda's northern suburbs, while the MPLA attacked FNLA-held towns such as Salazar, Malanje, Henrique de Carvalho and Sá da Bandeira. By 24 July, the FNLA had recaptured the town of Caxito, 60 km north of the capital, but they never again took control of Luanda. Now better armed, trained and organised than their traditional and once stronger rivals, the MPLA scored one victory after another, capturing the southern towns of Lobito, Benguela, Moçâmedes, Pereira D'Eca and Luso, and launching attacks on UNITA strongholds as well.

On 5 August, Schoeman despatched a staff officer, Commandant Philip du Preez, to Pretoria with a request that badly needed weapons be shipped to the FNLA forces at Mpupa. The request dovetailed with a fact-finding visit to the Operational Area by then South African Defence Minister PW Botha, who authorised Operational Order 8/75, issued on 28 August by the South African Army, in terms of which the FNLA was to be given whatever support was needed to halt the MPLA's advance.

South Africa had been marginally involved in the Angolan melée since 1966, when SWAPO began using the southern region of the Portuguese colony as a springboard for terror attacks in neighbouring South West Africa. Now, with all of Angola engulfed in an internecine struggle for political supremacy, the SADF had embarked on a campaign that would presage a full-scale conventional war against highly trained Cuban troops, armed with some of the most advanced weaponry Russia's arsenals could offer.

SWAPO was founded in Cape Town in 1958 as the Owamboland People's Congress by Herman ya Toiva, Andries Shipanga, Jac Simmons – a communist – and Ben Burak. Sam Nujoma assumed leadership of the organisation when ya Toiva was arrested the following year, and the name SWAPO was adopted in 1960. Up to the end of 1962, SWAPO members received no foreign military training, but a number of them were schooled in Marxism, trade unionism and politics at institutions in the former USSR. From 1963, however, military training began in earnest at the Kongwa base in Tanzania, while some cadres were sent further afield to countries such as Egypt, North Korea, Yugoslavia, Ghana, Algeria and China.

When the organisation's leaders fled into exile in Tanzania during November 1963, a military wing, the People's Liberation Army of Namibia (PLAN) was set up, and following a vigorous recruitment drive the first guerrilla infiltration of South West Africa was recorded in 1969, three years after Nujoma had identified targets in the erstwhile German protectorate as:

- Police stations, strategic and military installations;
- Prominent individuals; and
- White farmers.

While Nujoma himself served as supreme military commander, Dimo Hamambo was appointed commander of the armed forces. Following the Portuguese withdrawal in 1974, SWAPO set up several training bases in Angola, the ideal host country for PLAN because of its proximity to South West Africa. From 1975 guerrillas underwent training in Zambia, and in 1976, 80 cadres travelled to Cuba for specialised training in sabotage techniques. By 1978, SWAPO had a functional military structure in place, and while early training and equipment were of inferior quality, by the middle of the 1980s PLAN had been moulded into a well-organised army.

From its headquarters in the Zambian capital of Lusaka, SWAPO controlled

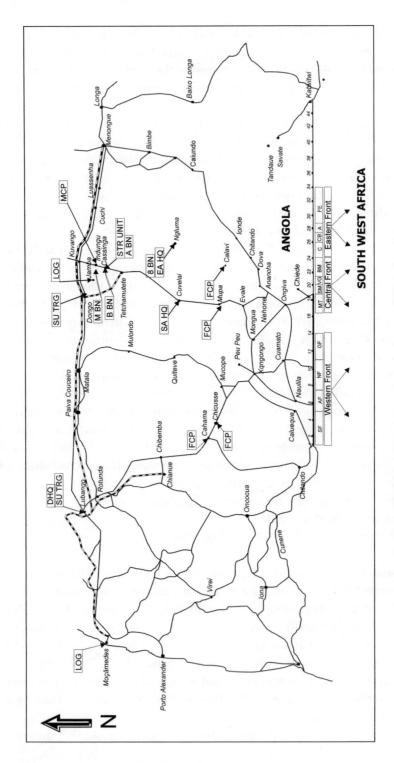

Traditional SWAPO deployments and areas of responsibility in Angola

both the internal political wing and the external activities of PLAN, but operational command was exercised from the Angolan town of Lubango, allowing close liaison with the MPLA/FAPLA and Cuban surrogate forces.

Strategically, PLAN deployed its troops in south-western Angola across the widest possible front, with regional detachments of about 80 men each, as well as semi-conventional battalions spread over an area marked in the north by Dongo, in the east by Menongue, in the west by Porto Alexandre and to the south by the border with South West Africa.

The 460-km border runs from the Cunene River in the west to the Kavango River in the east, and in the mid-1970s consisted of nothing more than a poorly constructed wire fence with tracks on either side. Survey beacons were situated at 10-km intervals along the fence, with Beacon 1 at the Cunene and Beacon 46 at the Kavango River.

PLAN's Western Front was controlled from headquarters at Cahama and a Military Command Post (MCP) in the Chicusse area, with four detachments – SF, AF, NF and GF – operating east and west of the Cunene River as far as Beacon 14.

Another four detachments – MT, SM, VG and BM – covered the Central Front, their area of operations stretching from Beacon 17 to Beacon 24, with headquarters in the vicinity of Cuvelai and an MCP at Mupa.

On the Eastern Front, the traditional headquarters were in the Ngluma and Puturunhanga area, the MCP in the vicinity of Dova, Nehone and Catala, the Operational Area of detachments C, CB, A and FE falling between Beacon 24 and Beacon 34.

The semi-conventional battalions were deployed further north. East of Cassinga, the 250 soldiers of Alpha Battalion faced UNITA along the Cubango River. Bravo Battalion was responsible for operations against UNITA in a 50-km area running from north of Cassinga to the south-western corner, though some elements of the 300-strong force operated as far south as Anhanca, Evale and Nehone.

The 300 men of Moscow Battalion were responsible for the area north of Cassinga, towards the hamlet of Jamba (not the town of the same name that would later serve as UNITA's headquarters), and north-east towards the MCP at Indungo. An element was also deployed in the Mulave and Mulolo areas south of Cassinga. SWAPO's 8th Battalion was deployed in the Ngluma area, with some of the 500 members operating against UNITA around Nehone, Catala and Dova.

The 100-strong 10th Battalion carried out reconnaissance from its headquarters in the Cunene area for the MCP in the areas of Cuvelai, Vinte Sete and Mpupa. A strike unit of some 130 men stationed north of Cassinga was armed with artillery and anti-aircraft guns, while bases at Lubango and Dongo were home to a special unit established in 1979 and were used to prepare guerrillas for the annual infiltration of white farming areas in South West Africa.

The 1st Mechanised Brigade – total strength 2 500 – operated against UNITA north of the Moçâmedes–Menongue railway line, with traditional deployment of the first battalion at Andulo, the second at Nharea and the third in the area of Matala/Dongo. Initially, PLAN stationed liaison officers at FAPLA units, but from the middle of 1980 the lines between the two armies began to blur, and SWAPO's forces came to depend increasingly on the support and protection afforded by the well-established FAPLA bases.

From the outset, PLAN fighters were armed by the Soviet Union, China and Cuba. As the relationship with FAPLA strengthened, the Angolans provided support in the form of heavy weaponry such as artillery and occasionally even tanks, but the customary armaments used by PLAN were the following:

- Light weapons: 7,62-mm Tokarev pistol; PPSh 41 sub-machine gun; VZ 23/24/25/26 carbine; AK assault rifle (all variants); RPD machine gun, PKM machine gun; 9-mm Makarov pistol.
- Heavy weapons: 12,7-mm DSHK 38/46 machine gun; 23-mm ZU23 and 14,5-mm ZPU 1 anti-aircraft gun (both also utilised in a ground role); 30-mm M55 tri-barrel gun.
- Rocket launchers: 40-mm RPG 7 anti-tank/personnel rockets; 82-mm B10 recoilless gun (also used against personnel); 122-mm DKZ B rocket launcher (single tube of the BM 21); SA 7 'Grail' man-portable surface-to-air missile system.
- Mortars: 60 mm and 82 mm.
- Mines: The complete range of TM anti-tank mines; POM Z, PMN, PMD 6 anti-personnel mines.
- Hand grenades: F1, RGD 5, RG 4 and RG 42.

On 21 August 1975, UNITA declared itself the FNLA's ally against the MPLA. To ensure that weapons supplied to the FNLA by South Africa were properly utilised, the SADF decided to provide training to their new-found comrades in arms, and Commandant Jan Breytenbach, a founder member of the SADF's Special Forces, was assigned to the task. He reported to Rundu, headquarters of 1 Military Area – which until March 1976 comprised the entire South West African Operational Area, including Owamboland, Kavango and the Caprivi Strip – on 29 August, and immediately set about devising a training programme in conjunction with high-ranking FNLA officers.

The choice of Breytenbach for this covert and extremely sensitive task was almost inevitable. A career soldier, he was no stranger to unconventional military operations and had earned a reputation for getting the job done, no matter what the odds. A veteran of the 1956 Suez crisis, when he was an officer in the Royal Naval Fleet Air Arm, as well as the Rhodesian bush war, Breytenbach was one of four SADF members who had spent several months in the breakaway Nigerian state of Biafra in 1969, training rebel forces as part of a highly classified and little known South African initiative.

Intended to warn President Julius Nyerere against continued support of communist-backed liberation forces, Breytenbach had also led a daring assault by the SADF's fledgling Special Forces on strategic installations in the Tanzanian capital of Dar es Salaam in 1972. His exploits were all the more remarkable given his family ties, since his brother Breyten, a renowned poet, painter and writer, was a vociferous opponent of apartheid, jailed for seven years in 1975 after being found guilty of terrorism.

A blunt man whose disdain for military bureaucracy often verged on insubordination, Breytenbach was at his happiest in the bush, far from the pen-pushers, and engaged in the unorthodox warfare at which he excelled. Involved in counter-insurgency operations from a remote base in the Caprivi since 1970, he was the perfect candidate to train the FNLA troops.

In a 3 September letter to Brigadier Jannie Geldenhuys, Director Operations at SA Army headquarters, Breytenbach made it clear that the desired objectives could not be achieved simply by training and arming the FNLA, and strongly recommended that SADF officers be deployed to command and control future operations. 'I personally think,' wrote Breytenbach, 'that the success of operations depends on good low level command and control, which means white South African control, also to be exercised over logistical support.' This had also been the request of the FNLA, Breytenbach reported. 'Even before we could suggest it, they requested that we should support them not only with training, but also with the physical planning and control of operations.'

By the end of August, the MPLA was in control of 11 of the 16 district capitals, but Breytenbach was of the opinion that the first trained FNLA battalions could be used to capture towns such as Moçâmedes, Sá da Bandeira and even Lobito from the MPLA and, after securing them, move on to take towns such as Nova Lisboa and Silva Porto.

On 24 September, the SADF launched a four-phase plan to assist the FNLA and UNITA, spearheaded by Task Force Zulu, which consisted of a battalion of Bushman soldiers drawn from the Caprivi and 1 000 FNLA troops. Alpha Group was led by Commandant Delville Linford, while Bravo Group fell under Breytenbach's command. Over the next three months, in what became known as *Operation Savannah*, the South African-led forces would cut a swathe through a vast expanse of Angola occupied by FAPLA, engage Cuban surrogate forces in battle for the first time and advance rapidly to the very heart of FAPLA country – Novo Redondo – before being ordered to pull back.

Because FAPLA was a conventional army, it was broken up into brigades along lines similar to those of Warsaw Pact motorised rifle regiments. The combat element comprised three motorised infantry battalions, a tank company of ten T54 or T55 tanks and a mixed artillery battalion. Support elements included a reconnaissance company with PT76 tanks and BRDM 2 armoured personnel carriers, and a company or platoon of engineers. The strength of the brigades varied, but was generally around 1 900. Each motorised infantry battalion had three companies of three platoons, using BTR 60 armoured cars or trucks in some cases. The three infantry companies had the usual support weapons – light machine guns, RPG 7s and 60-mm mortars.

Each battalion had four support elements: a platoon with six 82-mm mortars; an anti-tank platoon with either six Sagger anti-tank missile teams or B10 recoilless guns; a grenade launcher platoon with six AGS 17s; and an air defence platoon with three SA 7 teams and four 14,5-mm ZPU 1 anti-aircraft guns.

The artillery battalion generally had six batteries: two with six 122-mm D 30 howitzers each; two with four 76-mm guns each; and one with eight 122-mm BM 21 multiple rocket launchers and six 120-mm mortars.

Additional tanks, air defence and artillery were deployed as needed. FAPLA's tactical groups were usually multi-battalion forces smaller than brigade strength, formed for a specific operation or task. All the weapons available to SWAPO were also used by FAPLA, along with the following:

General weapons: 30-mm AGS 17 grenade launchers; 57-mm anti-aircraft guns; SA 9 'Gaskin' surface-to-air missile systems; 76-mm guns; 120-mm mortars; 122-mm BM 21 multiple rocket launchers and BM 14 rockets.

Armour: PT76 tanks; T34 and T54/55 tanks; BRDM 2 armoured scout cars; BTR 60 armoured personnel carriers with 14,5-mm gun.

During *Operation Savannah*, the SADF and its Angolan allies faced the full range of firepower available to FAPLA and its foreign surrogates. Task Force Zulu was in the vanguard of the campaign, covering 3 159 km of Angolan territory in 33 days and engaging in 14 full-scale battles and 21 skirmishes, which left 210 of the enemy dead, 96 wounded and 56 taken prisoner.

But as the war escalated, the SADF's direct involvement deepened, with Zulu soon being joined by other task forces, such as Foxbat, Orange and X-Ray. At first light on 12 December 1975, it fell to Foxbat to engage a 1 000-strong infantry battalion, including many Cubans, in one of the hardest and most decisive battles of the campaign. Masterful use of the SADF's artillery won the day, and when the battle at Bridge 14 was over, at least 400 of FAPLA's troops were dead, including Commandant Raul Diaz Arguelles, commander of the Cuban expeditionary force. Four South Africans were killed in action and a number of SADF soldiers were awarded the Honoris Crux, the highest decoration for gallantry under fire. Among them was Sergeant Danny Roxo, who single-handedly killed 11 men, four of them Cubans, and would go on to become one of the legendary members of 32 Battalion.

Although FAPLA was the enemy throughout *Operation Savannah*, it was never 32 Battalion's primary target. However, by acting as SWAPO's flank guard and hosting the guerrillas in their bases, FAPLA troops were regularly on the receiving end of action by 32 Battalion in support of UNITA. Despite their overwhelming firepower, numerical and weapons superiority, FAPLA invariably came off worst from encounters with 32 which, until 1986, had access only to small arms, light machine guns, RPG rockets, 40-mm M79 grenade launchers, and 60- and 81-mm mortars. In the wake of *Operation Savannah*, Bravo Group was involved in fighting against FAPLA until the middle of 1976. After withdrawing from the Cuando Cubango province, 32's first action against SWAPO was during *Operation Cobra* in 1976 – and for the next decade, 32 Battalion would wage relentless war against the organisation's armed wing, PLAN.

What they did, and how they did it, would earn this unconventional group official recognition as the best fighting unit in the South African Army since World War II. But in August 1975, when he first laid eyes on the ragtag assembly that would form the nucleus of his beloved 'Buffalo Soldiers', what Commandant Jan Breytenbach saw was 'the most unwarlike body of troops' he had ever met.

2

I want to be a soldier

EARLY DAYS AND EARLY BATTLES

WHEN PRETORIA AUTHORISED the training of FNLA troops by the SADF, Commandant Jan Breytenbach sprang into action without delay. In the absence of any communication links between 1 Military Area headquarters at Rundu and Odinga Odinga's base at Mpupa, 60 km to the north in Angola, Breytenbach's first step was to find out exactly what he had let himself in for. On 30 August, he flew to Mpupa in a Piper Aztec piloted by Commandant Jules Moolman of the South African Air Force. Also in the party were Major Coen Upton and FNLA luminary Daniel Chipenda's brother-in-law Pelissa, an Italian who had travelled to Rundu from his game farm near Mpupa in mid-July to enlist SADF support on behalf of the FNLA, and who was well acquainted with Odinga Odinga.

The situation in Angola was extremely fluid, with control of towns, even entire areas, changing hands on a regular basis, and little or no intelligence at all reaching Rundu. With no way of establishing in advance whether or not Mpupa was still under FNLA control, the aircraft landed only after first flying over the base to confirm that a flag visible from the air was indeed that of the SADF's new-found allies. The conditions that met them on the ground were appalling. An official report compiled by Breytenbach at the time records:

The approach was through a minefield of human excrement, several hundred metres wide, through which one had to step very gingerly indeed in order not to fall foul of these anti-personnel devices. Millions of flies swarmed everywhere and the stench was all pervading. Papers, old and empty beer bottles, plastic containers and all sorts of rubbish were littered everywhere in the camp itself.

Pelissa, acting as interpreter, informed Odinga that Breytenbach was now in command of his troops, and would arrange for them to receive food, clothes and ammunition. Odinga, in turn, informed Breytenbach that a parade had been hastily convened. The motley collection of FNLA fighters was called to attention and ordered to present arms. Odinga and Breytenbach exchanged the customary salute, the men were ordered to stand at ease and the base commander launched into a speech in Portuguese, of which Breytenbach could understand not a single word. As suddenly as it had begun, the speech ended, the troops drew to attention and presented arms once more. Odinga saluted Breytenbach again, and solemnly informed him: 'You are now in command of Chipenda's FNLA in southern Angola.'

From within the ranks came a chorus of 'FNLA Oyez' and 'Viva Carpenter' as Breytenbach – whose code-name for covert Angolan operations was Carpenter – contemplated what he would later describe as 'without a doubt the scruffiest, most underfed, worst armed and most unwarlike body of troops I had ever seen in my life'.

Some of the men lined up before him were clad in brightly coloured pants and equally lurid shirts. The headwear of choice appeared to be baseball caps, and a fair number sported sunglasses. Few of them had any footwear to speak of. Most were barefoot, their feet and legs pockmarked with suppurating ulcers caused by malnutrition.

But as Breytenbach's aircraft took off after the march past, Odinga Odinga and his *commandantes* waved them a cheerful farewell, their gestures doubtless enlivened by visions of maize meal by the bag, meat by the ton, pristine camouflage uniforms and brand new rifles trundling in from Rundu the very next day.

However, it was not until 15 September, two weeks later, that Breytenbach and a group of SADF instructors returned with truckloads of the rations the troops would need to build up their physical strength for the war that was surely coming. By the time training equipment, the first consignment of green jungle fatigues and R1 rifles arrived shortly afterwards, the FNLA troops had been organised into two rifle companies, a mortar platoon, an anti-tank section and a machine-gun platoon.

The mortarists and machine-gunners were issued with World War II British Sten sub-machine guns. The 12 mortars, of the same vintage, had three-inch barrels and a maximum range of 1 000 m. The machine guns were .303 Vickers with cloth belts.

Corporal Frans van Dyk was put in charge of the mortar platoon, while Corporal Vingers Kruger took command of the machine-gun platoon. The two rifle companies were under command of Captain Jack Dippenaar – with two corporals, Nel and Retief, as platoon leaders – and Lieutenant Connie van Wyk, initially assisted by Corporal Mechie van der Merwe and later also by Sergeant Robbie Ribeiro.

The FNLA *commandantes*, who had hitherto acted as company and platoon commanders by default but were largely ignorant about the art of warfare, were relegated to the position of platoon sergeants. Those who refused to accept the lesser appointments were summarily discharged and evicted from the base.

The priority was instruction in weapons and attack. Anything else would have to wait until circumstances allowed. Breytenbach had been given a mere 14 days to prepare his troops for battle, and neither he nor his instructors could spare time for anything else. However, he appointed a troop named Domingos, and later Odinga Odinga himself, as the nominal camp commandant, to clean up the highly unsanitary conditions, take care of rudimentary administration and ensure that the troops were fed.

Despite the drastically abbreviated schedule, early training proved to be a nightmare. The FNLA cadres were not only raw, they were physically unfit, and there were not nearly enough uniforms or weapons to go around. Each day began with a cross-country run, followed by weapons training until 10h00, section, platoon and company drills until noon, a siesta to escape the worst heat until 15h00, more drills until 18h00, supper and a night training session. It was a punishing schedule, but the rewards became noticeable as both the energy and stamina of the troops increased.

As more and more FNLA recruits found their way to Mpupa, a third company, Charlie, was established under command of Almerindo Marao da Costa – universally known as Marao – and two other Portuguese, Danny Roxo and Silva Sierro, as platoon commanders. Each company was still one platoon leader short.

Shortly after training began in earnest, Daniel Chipenda, FNLA party secretary Kombuta and a mysterious American who claimed his name was Cameron, paid a flying visit to Mpupa. Cameron told Breytenbach he would have no difficulty arranging delivery of enough weapons, ammunition, clothing and rations for 1 000 men for a period of six months, assuring the SADF officer that the Mpupa airstrip was ideally situated for a clandestine shuttle service by C130 aircraft from Zaire under maximum security conditions.

After their meeting the fledgling FNLA battalion gathered on the parade ground, where Chipenda delivered an impassioned speech, promising a new dawn for Angola, death to all FNLA enemies, freedom of speech and religion, and a capitalist society. Then he and his companions flew north in their Piper Aztec. The enigmatic Mr Cameron was neither seen nor heard from again, and the promised support never materialised.

Early in October 1975, about half of the troops were sent to Serpa Pinto, where another FNLA training camp had been set up, leaving some 270 men behind at Mpupa. Within days, the intelligence officer conveyed a report that UNITA troops garrisoned at Cuangar planned to invade the town of Calai. The

UNITA commander at Cuangar, Johnny Katala, was also an officer in SWAPO and had been extending SWAPO's influence in the Kavango area, just across the river in South West Africa. The overwhelmingly pro-FNLA residents of Calai were terrified that they would be rounded up and massacred should Katala succeed in taking the town.

Despite being authorised only to train rather than deploy his troops, Breytenbach despatched Captain Jack Dippenaar's Bravo Company to defend Calai, and despite the reprimand this move earned him when it was reported to Brigadier Schoeman, decided to leave them in place after visiting Calai himself, just in case UNITA went ahead with the planned attack. At the same time Breytenbach stepped up the pace of training at Mpupa, focusing particularly on the newly formed Charlie Company and the anti-tank platoon. Less than a month after launching the FNLA training programme, Breytenbach was ordered to

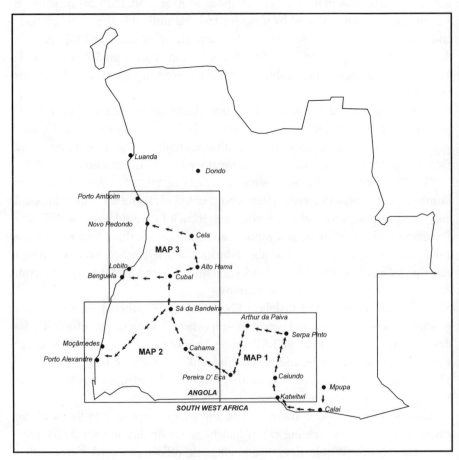

The advance of Task Force Zulu during *Operation Savannah*.
Details of Battle Group Bravo's operations appear on maps 1 to 3

report to SADF headquarters at Rundu, where he learned from Colonel Koos van Heerden, Officer Commanding 73 Motorised Brigade, that a new task force, Zulu – comprising battle groups Alpha and Bravo – had been formed, and would invade southern Angola one week later to seek out and destroy the MPLA forces.

On 24 September the South African government had approved a four-phase plan of support for the FNLA and UNITA. Phase 1 had entailed the provision of assistance to maintain control of areas already held by the opposition forces. Now it was time to launch Phase 2, aimed at gaining control of the south-eastern corner of Angola, including the towns of Sá da Bandeira and Moçâmedes. Phase 3 would be the taking of Benguela, Lobito and Novo Redondo, while the final phase would see a major push against FAPLA. The task force was under command of Van Heerden, with Commandant Delville Linford leading Battle Group Alpha, made up of Bushmen stationed at Alpha Base in the Caprivi.

The Caprivi is a narrow strip of land some 30 km wide and 400 km long, extending from the eastern corner of Namibia's border with Angola to the north and Botswana to the south. Since September 1974, the SADF had secretly been housing and training a few hundred Bushman refugees who had sided with the Portuguese military in Angola. Hunted down and wantonly slain by the various black factions as the entire country became a battlefield, the defenceless hunter-gatherers migrated south, finding refuge – and a totally new way of life – as fully fledged members of the SADF. Throughout the Angolan conflict the Bushmen proved invaluable allies, particularly because of their uncanny natural tracking skills. Along with their wives and children, they were housed at the specially constructed Camp Alpha, later renamed Omega, in the eastern Caprivi.

Task Force Zulu's second battle group, Bravo, would be under Breytenbach's command, and would comprise his three companies of FNLA troops. The entire expedition was to be conducted in a way that would allow the SADF 'plausible deniability' – all signs of South African involvement had to be hidden, with troops wearing non-specific or former Portuguese uniforms and using Portuguese G3 and Belgian-made FN rifles. Their vehicles would be Land Rovers or vegetable trucks bought from Angolan refugees.

While Battle Group Alpha was preparing on the airfield at Rundu, the troops still at Mpupa were moved to Calai to rejoin Charlie Company and consolidate Battle Group Bravo.

To disguise the fact that the operation had originated on South West African soil, the attack on Pereira D'Eca, capital of the Cunene province, would not be a direct assault from Owamboland, but via a circuitous route along the Cubango River to Caiundo, then westwards past Nehone before turning south to the target. From Rundu/Calai a vehicle track ran along both sides of the river to Katwitwi, and it was on this track that Task Force Zulu's headquarters element and Battle

Group Alpha set off from Rundu at 14h00 on 14 October 1975. Simultaneously, Battle Group Bravo departed from Calai on the Angolan side of the river. A large group of Portuguese refugees had been housed in a camp at Katwitwi, and as the convoy passed through the town at 22h00, they turned out in force to line the streets and cheer the soldiers on their way. At a point some five kilometres north of Katwitwi, where the two river tracks converge, Bravo spent the night, moving out at first light for Caiundo, which they reached at midnight on 15 October – only to find that the road they were scheduled to follow to Nehone was still under construction, and could not be used to advance on Pereira D'Eca. Breytenbach and an FNLA commander named João set off to reconnoitre an alternative route to the north via Serpa Pinto, which was found to be readily accessible. Battle Group Bravo followed, bypassing the town before turning west, much to the chagrin of the troops, who had envisaged a triumphant parade through what was, after all, not only the first town to be 'liberated' by the FNLA, but also the capital of the Cuando Cubango province and seat of Daniel Chipenda, who was even then disporting himself in the former Portuguese governor's palatial residence.

After spending the night at Cuchi, Battle Group Bravo turned south on 17 October, Breytenbach leading the way in his cut-down Land Cruiser. Some 76 km from Cassinga, Breytenbach was still not sure if his group had already penetrated enemy territory, as despite UNITA having declared itself the FNLA's ally, pockets of Savimbi's forces encountered along the route had seemed unfriendly, though not openly hostile. After passing the mining town of Tetchamutete to the west, it was evening before the convoy approached Cuvelai, noting as they crossed the bridge across the river that the street lights in the town were on, which seemed incongruous. The lead company deployed on the river bank, while Breytenbach took Corporal Nel and his platoon across the bridge to assess the situation. They were met by an unarmed UNITA lieutenant, who said he had come to escort them to his commander's headquarters, just south of the town in the old Portuguese *quartel*. As Breytenbach and his men followed the UNITA officer along the main street, the lights suddenly went out and all hell broke loose, with machine-gun fire pouring out of buildings on the left-hand side. As they hit the dirt, Breytenbach shouted an order for Nel's men to return fire. Fortunately, the hidden UNITA troops were firing high, but so were the men of Bravo, and the thatched roofs of several buildings were soon ablaze. It was obvious that Bravo would have to mount a counter-attack and clear the *quartel*, but they would first have to silence the UNITA machine gun. Breytenbach ordered a white Portuguese troop to destroy the machine gun with a 3,5-inch rocket launcher, but both his attempts were hopeless failures. Breytenbach and Nel ordered their men to attack, and when they failed to respond, they bodily grabbed troops by the seat of their pants and scruff of their necks and ran them towards the *quartel*, dropping them into a favourable attack position before racing back to pick up another pair of reluctant warriors. Eventually the message got through to the remaining troops and the platoon formed an assault line, sweeping forward through the *quartel*. UNITA fired a few shots, followed by some 60-mm mortar rounds that were hopelessly wide of the mark, then fled into the bush beyond and around the village. Evidently, news that the FNLA and UNITA were now on the same side had not yet filtered through to all Savimbi's men in the field.

Breytenbach brought up the rest of his battalion and was informed by Sergeant Danny Roxo that there was a UNITA headquarters ten kilometres down a side road. A furious Breytenbach ordered Roxo to destroy the UNITA post. By this time, Bravo had been joined by Colonel Koos van Heerden and his field headquarters, which included a UNITA liaison officer. When Roxo returned and reported that the UNITA headquarters had been vacated, Van Heerden signalled to Rundu: 'First elements were attacked by UNITA upon arrival. Compliments returned. No losses.'

Neither side had suffered any casualties, and that night the men of Battle Group Bravo slept warmly by the still smouldering fires in the *quartel* of Cuvelai. The next morning, with no intelligence on enemy deployments at their disposal, Bravo Group moved out, Lieutenant Connie van Wyk's B Company, with Corporal Oupa van Dyk's mortars under Van Wyk's command, in the vanguard. Van Wyk took the lead Sabre – a Land Rover fitted with armoured plates on either side and a mounted 7,62-mm machine gun – followed by two more Sabres, each fitted with 30-calibre Brownings, and one of his platoons.

As they approached Mupa (not to be confused with the town of Mpupa), short bursts of machine-gun fire from Van Wyk's Sabre signalled a contact. Immediately ahead was a ten-seater Land Rover, the doors flung open as the occupants ran for the bush. A sweep through the village revealed nothing of interest. The convoy passed through several more villages without incident before slowing down as it reached the outskirts of Evale, where Bravo ran into a well-laid ambush.

Van Wyk came under sudden heavy fire from the thick scrub to the left, just metres away from the road, before an RPG 7 rocket slammed into the side of his vehicle. Fortunately, it failed to detonate, and Van Wyk returned fire furiously, standing upright and totally exposed in the back of the Sabre as he raked the bush with his 30 Browning, pinning down the enemy long enough to allow the second Sabre and lead platoon to move up and cover his flank. Breytenbach sped forward in his Land Cruiser to assess the situation, while Vingers Kruger brought up two more Land Cruisers, each carrying two mounted Vickers machine guns, and began pumping bursts into the ambush site. Then Breytenbach ordered Corporal van Dyk to lay down mortar fire in the bush ahead of Van Wyk's vehicle, to prevent FAPLA reinforcements coming to the aid of the ambushers. Suddenly, a fierce firefight, which sounded considerably more ferocious than the initial contact, broke out some distance down the road behind them. Jack Dippenaar's Alpha Company was deployed to the rear on both sides of the road, covering both the left and right flanks, but until then had not fired a single shot. The shooting had to be coming from Charlie Company, furthest back in the convoy, but no radio communication was getting through. Realising that FAPLA was trying to box them in, Breytenbach decided to first clear the way ahead, then go to the aid of the rearguard. With the remainder of Van Wyk's company he launched a swift flanking attack, sweeping through a hamlet where only a few inhabitants remained. An RPG 7 rocket launcher lay discarded on the outer perimeter of the village and the bloody bodies of some FAPLA fighters were sprawled deeper in the scrub, but the firing had stopped.

Breytenbach realised he could no longer hear the sound of gunfire from the rear of the convoy either, and was still unable to reach Charlie Company by radio. Fully expecting that they had been overrun by FAPLA, he drove through Dippenaar's company to the rear. The first group he encountered was that of Van Heerden's field headquarters. Next, he located an abjectly apologetic Sergeant Marao, whose men, with a mere four days of training under their belts, had hit the deck at the first sound of gunfire, half of them taking cover on one side of the road, the rest on the opposite side. In their untrained ignorance they had then proceeded to open fire on one another, each believing themselves to be under attack by FAPLA.

The firefight left three FAPLA dead and three members of Bravo wounded, one of whom subsequently died despite being given the best medical treatment available.

When the column moved out Van Wyk again took the lead, and some five kilometres further, on sighting a FAPLA flag waving over what turned out to be Evale, Bravo laid down mortar fire and Van Wyk unleashed the combined firepower of his Sabres. When Dippenaar's company moved up to clear the buildings lining both sides of the road, FAPLA had already gone, leaving behind some ammunition, hand grenades and 20 MPLA uniforms.

On Sunday 19 October, Task Force Zulu advanced via Nehone to within five kilometres of Pereira D'Eca, and moved into position for the pending assault. Battle Group Alpha would attack the southern section of the town and despatch troops down to Santa Clara, on the South West African border, to secure the area and link up with another South African battle group making its way into Angola from Owamboland. Van Wyk and the eight Vickers machine guns mounted on a truck were deployed with Alpha as part of the stopper group that was to keep the main road to Forte Roçadas open.

Bravo would attack Pereira D'Eca from the north, clear the kimbo and secure the airfield some eight kilometres to the west, along the road to Forte Roçadas.

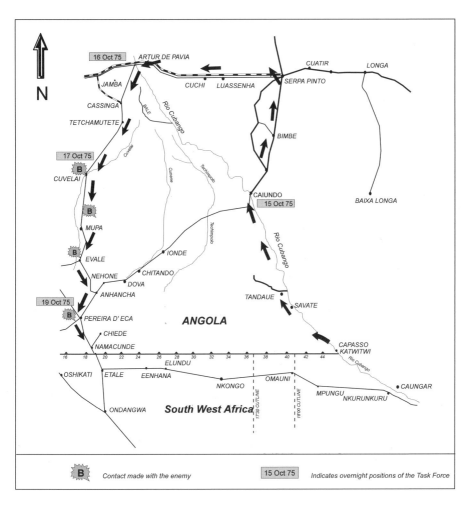

MAP 1: Battle Group Bravo's advance from the assembly point at Calai to Pereira D' Eca

Breytenbach used Alpha Company to attack the northern sector of the town and Bravo Company to clear the kimbo, holding Charlie Company in reserve until it would join Alpha Company in securing the airfield. Van Dyk's mortar platoon supplied support.

The mortar attack on the Portuguese *quartel*, held by the MPLA, began at 13h15. In the counter-bombardment, one Bravo soldier was killed and five wounded. One Alpha member was also wounded.

Alpha Company ran into the MPLA's main defensive position three kilometres south of the town. The MPLA had clearly expected any attack to come from this direction, and although the Bushman soldiers deployed exactly as they had been trained to do once the firing began, the truck carrying the mounted machine guns

21

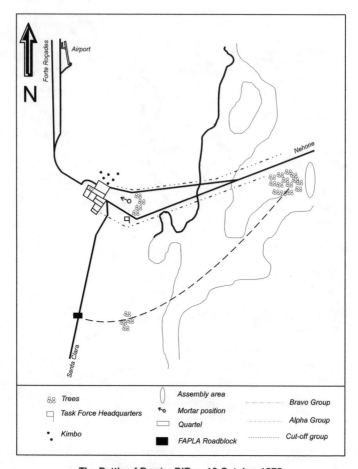

The Battle of Pereira D'Eca, 19 October 1975

got stuck in a freshly ploughed field, and was of little use. While Bravo's companies pushed through to the airfield without encountering too much resistance, Van Wyk made slower progress through the sprawling maze of mud and tin shanties. He had great difficulty keeping his men in any kind of formation, especially once the town's inhabitants began emerging from their homes to welcome their liberators.

Task Force Zulu had anticipated that the town would be defended by between 300 and 400 MPLA soldiers, but actually had to contend with less than half this number, who quickly abandoned any attempt at defence and fled into the surrounding bush.

While Pereira D'Eca was being attacked, and despite not being authorised to do so, a group of soldiers from 2 SA Infantry Battalion under the command of Commandant Boy du Toit launched a successful assault on Forte Roçadas.

Breytenbach, ordered to the town by Brigadier Schoeman, duly reported to Task Force Zulu headquarters that South African troops were in control. In line with a decision taken meanwhile by the South African authorities to send armoured cars into Angola, Du Toit was ordered to detach his 81-mm mortar group and his armoured car squadron to Task Force Zulu.

The advance to Sá da Bandeira resumed on 21 October, Battle Group Alpha leading the way past Humbe and Chama before veering off near João de Almeida to clear the towns and villages west of the main road, while Bravo Group proceeded to João de Almeida. At 13h00, a few kilometres from the town, they made contact with a small group of the enemy, who wasted little time vanishing into the bush, to be followed shortly afterwards by those of their comrades who had remained in the town itself. By 15h00, Task Force Zulu had occupied João de Almeida – but further north, the MPLA was engaged in strengthening its defences at Sá da Bandeira.

When Battle Group Bravo moved out of João de Almeida on the morning of 23 October, an FNLA platoon under command of Sergeant Danny Roxo stayed behind to prevent any enemy advance from Task Force Zulu's rear. Skirmishes during the previous nine days had removed the element of surprise from the column's advance, and the men of Bravo were alert to likely ambushes as they traversed the mountainous terrain punctuated with cuttings that offered ideal cover for the enemy. The first attack came from infantry with light anti-armour rockets and missiles, and was easily repulsed. The next attack, however, was heavier, requiring a bombardment by the armoured cars as well as the firepower offered by all the machine guns, including those mounted on the flatbed truck, and the three-inch and 81-mm mortars. In sharp contrast to their shabby performance at Cuvelai, the FNLA troops engaged the enemy with gusto, yelling and shouting as they charged through the MPLA line, emptying their magazines at point-blank range into their frankly stunned opponents.

It was a landmark firefight, not only because it offered the first clear sign that Battle Group Bravo was capable of functioning as a well-oiled war machine, but because the victors were able to capture two 82-mm recoilless guns with ammunition and a single tube 122-mm rocket launcher with five projectiles. This was the first time anyone in Task Force Zulu had seen the deadly weapon, but it didn't take long for Breytenbach's men to start using it to great effect against the enemy! The next ambush had been set up where the road from Cangolo joins the main route south-east of Rio Grande. The enemy position was easily overrun, with FAPLA suffering one dead, three wounded and three prisoners of war. When their comrades fled, they left behind four shot-out vehicles and a large supply of ammunition.

The column came to Rotunda as the sun was setting. The few buildings that made up the village were loosely scattered on the high ground, and these were swiftly raked with mortar and machine-gun fire before two companies, supported by armoured cars, moved in on either side of the main road to Sá da Bandeira to clear the area. FAPLA left in a hurry, and as dusk settled over the village Bravo took up defensive positions for the night. Later that evening Commandant Linford and Battle Group Alpha joined them, just in time to witness an uncoordinated and spiritless counter-attack by FAPLA troops who had obviously been despatched from Sá da Bandeira to retake Rotunda. Two FAPLA vehicles were soon burning on the main road, thanks to the armoured cars, while Corporal Kruger's machine-gunners played their role well, firing long bursts at FAPLA's gun flashes. Unfortunately, one of Kruger's men took a fatal shot to the head during the exchange.

Still later that night, Battle Group Bravo received its final briefing for the attack on Sá da Bandeira, the largest town in southern Angola. According to intelligence reports, 122-mm rocket launchers were deployed on Monte Cristo, a hill over-looking all entrances to the town, which was surrounded by FAPLA bases and minefields. Van Heerden thus decided the primary objective should be for Breytenbach's group to take the airport, some five kilometres out of town, while the rest of Task Force Zulu held back in reserve. Linford, meanwhile, was to move Alpha Group around the town to the north and prevent the enemy fleeing towards Humpata and Moçâmedes.

Bravo Group moved out after breakfast, and at 15h00 the armoured cars began bombarding the airport control tower and adjacent buildings. Only light resistance had been anticipated at the airfield, but as the guns fired again and again, not a single shot was returned. However, as Sergeant Robbie Ribeiro's infantry company surged forward to occupy the buildings, small-arms fire crackled from the entire length of the airfield perimeter, where FAPLA had dug in. One of Ribeiro's Portuguese troops went down almost immediately, shot in the stomach, while the rest of his men hit the dirt and began returning fire furiously. When the enemy fire showed no sign of abating, Ribeiro called up the four armoured cars, which opened up with their coaxial machine guns, even their main guns at times, as Ribeiro and his men systematically cleared the enemy positions from one end of the airfield to the other.

Eventually the firing died down, and Ribeiro and his men trotted back with a group of prisoners. Eighty-four dead FAPLA were collected from positions around the airfield, but later more bodies were discovered in the long grass.

With the airfield secured, the main attack on the town could proceed as planned. As they reached the outskirts of Sá da Bandeira, the companies and armoured cars of Bravo Group spread out, the infantry lines soon being swallowed up among the buildings while the armoured cars rumbled from cover to cover behind them,

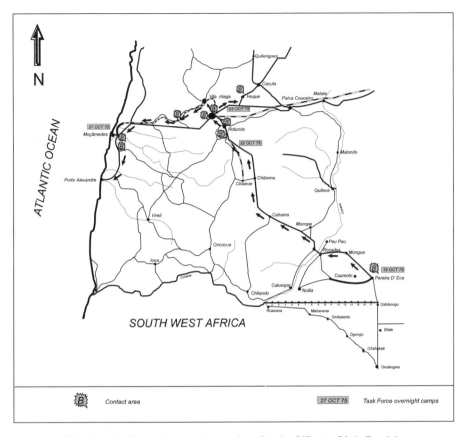

MAP 2: Battle Group Bravo's advance from Pereira D'Eca to Sá da Bandeira

poised to fire at the first sign of resistance. Just ahead of Breytenbach's Land Cruiser, a 90-mm gun boomed and a civilian vehicle burst into flames. It had been speeding to the airfield and narrowly missed colliding with the Eland as it rounded a corner. Two of the occupants, a Portuguese man and a woman, were killed, while a second man was pulled alive from the wreckage by the troops.

Without meeting any resistance, Bravo Group cleared their designated sector, regrouping at the former Portuguese artillery barracks from where they observed truckloads of FAPLA troops fleeing northwards. On the morning of 24 October, Bravo attacked the old Portuguese infantry *quartel*. The initial bombardment by the mortar platoon did little damage, as the distance was too great and the bombs fell short of their targets, but the noise alone was enough to send the enemy running from the building, and several FAPLA soldiers were taken prisoner and locked up in the town cells. The three infantry companies and armoured cars never even had to enter the battle.

The real prize of capturing Sá da Bandeira became evident once the firing stopped. Apart from seven perfectly serviceable aircraft, Task Force Zulu commandeered the contents of several warehouses crammed with weapons, ammunition, battle fatigues, boots and other equipment. Every soldier was issued with at least two sets of camouflage fatigues, a groundsheet and a pair of boots. The mortar and machine-gun platoons were overjoyed to be given brand new PPSh carbines, as they had never really taken to the Stens.

Operating from the old artillery barracks, Bravo Group set about consolidating their position, carrying out sorties in the direction of Hoque, east towards Serpa Pinto and down the old road and railway mountain pass as far as Vila da Arriaga. At Hoque, Jack Dippenaar's company ran into a bloody fight with FAPLA, and even though his men emerged victorious, Breytenbach divined that the entire battalion seemed to be losing heart for the battle. He gained the strong impression that Chipenda's faction of the FNLA felt they had done what was required of them, and would be quite content to carve out a future in the prime piece of Angola that had been liberated, leaving the MPLA and UNITA to squabble over the rest of the country.

The SADF had a somewhat different perspective, however, and Van Heerden's next objective was the coastal town of Moçâmedes. It was crucial that the task force take control of the harbour to prevent it from being used to ship FAPLA reinforcements and equipment down from the north. What Van Heerden did not know was that, in addition to both FNLA and MPLA forces, the port also still housed a Portuguese unit. All Portuguese forces had been confined to barracks since May, pending repatriation after independence, but a group of senior left-wing officers in Luanda had previously been instrumental in supplying the MPLA with arms and equipment, and no one could be sure where the loyalty of the remaining troops would lie.

On 25 October, Van Heerden received reports that fighting had broken out between the MPLA and FNLA, and that the MPLA had gained the upper hand, deploying three artillery pieces at the entrance to the town.

On the morning of 27 October, Task Force Zulu began to advance on Moçâmedes from two directions: Battle Group Bravo moving down the mountain through Vila da Arriaga – pausing briefly to cut the telephone line – and Battle Group Alpha taking the route via Humpata. Between Vila da Arriaga and Caraculo, Bravo made contact with FAPLA, killing nine and capturing eight, including *Commandante* Xieta, who had played a key role in the battle for Sá da Bandeira.

The next morning, Task Force Zulu again ran into FAPLA, dug in on both sides of the main road into Moçâmedes, and had to first clear the way before entering the port, the armoured cars in close support. Despite meeting fierce resistance, Dippenaar's company captured FAPLA's headquarters, which held a vast quantity of firearms, ammunition and clothing, but it was Lieutenant Connie van Wyk's group that hit the jackpot. After clearing the docks of all enemy troops, they found warehouses packed to the rafters with equipment and hundreds of spanking new pick-up trucks, several MAN tipper trucks and some earth-moving equipment parked on the quayside. The vehicles were swiftly added to the convoy.

Lieutenant van Wyk took a column eight kilometres south to Porto Alexandre, but found no sign of the enemy.

On the second day in Moçâmedes, Bravo Group moved into the barracks formerly occupied by a Portuguese parachute battalion, which had simply melted away without incident when the battle for the town began. The men of Bravo spent the night at the golf club and clay pigeon shooting range before getting back to business. Leaving Charlie Company under the command of Sergeant Marao to secure the town and the province of Huila, Breytenbach and the rest of Bravo Group returned to Sá da Bandeira, occupied meanwhile by two more FNLA companies under the command of Commandant Frank Bestbier.

The old artillery barracks once again served as a temporary base, and by 31 October Bravo was ready to resume the advance to the north and join forces with Battle Group Alpha. Lieutenant Connie van Wyk led Alpha Company and a troop of armoured cars east to secure the route to Nova Lisboa, setting up a roadblock about ten kilometres from Catengue on the road to Caimbambo. All traffic was stopped. Civilians were prevented from travelling any further and the majority of FAPLA soldiers surrendered immediately. Those unwise enough to try to escape were gunned down, and when Breytenbach arrived he found four stark naked FAPLA prisoners of war digging graves, some 20 of which already held bodies.

Among the dead was an MPLA paymaster, who had been carrying bags full of escudos. The money was used to buy fresh meat and vegetables for the troops, the task force having spent the last of its own cash a few days before.

Breytenbach's orders from Van Heerden were to attack FAPLA in the area between Catengue and Nova Lisboa in order to clear the way to Benguela. On the morning of 4 November, both Alpha and Bravo companies swung into action with armoured cars in support. Van Wyk and his group would join up with them en route.

As they neared Caimbambo, members of the interim government's police force warned Breytenbach that a group of about 20 FAPLA fighters had taken up position east of the town. Breytenbach sent Van Wyk with a platoon and two armoured cars to surprise the group, approaching them from the road that ran south around Caimbambo, while the rest of Bravo proceeded according to plan.

When Major Toon Slabbert brought his yellow camouflaged armoured car to a halt in the main street, he was more than a little taken aback to be greeted with

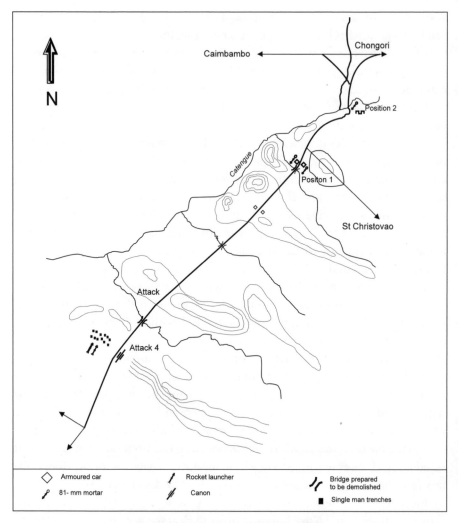

The Battle of Catengue, 2 November 1975

enthusiasm by a FAPLA *commandante*, who had mistaken the convoy for a Cuban unit, and paid for his error by being summarily arrested. All hell broke loose as FAPLA soldiers appeared from every direction, to be met by a hail of fire from Bravo's infantrymen and armoured cars that left 12 FAPLA dead.

Dippenaar had been sent to scout the area west of the town, and several loud explosions from that direction sent Bravo's troops running for cover into the nearest buildings. It took a fair amount of yelling and cursing by Breytenbach and Slabbert to get the frightened troops back onto the armoured cars and headed west to go to Dippenaar's aid as mortar bombs, B10 anti-tank guns and the dreaded multiple-barrel BM 21 'Stalin Organ' rained down shells and rockets on the town. From a distance of 500 m, Bravo's Eland armoured cars pumped 90-mm rounds into the high ground where the B10 was placed.

Dippenaar, who had taken cover behind a baobab tree, reported that he had run into heavy enemy fire at close range as soon as he and his troops crossed a bridge. On inspection, they found that the bridge had been packed with explosives, and had it not been for the fact that the firing circuit was damaged by enemy fire, Dippenaar and his men would have been cut off from the rest of Bravo.

It was obvious that FAPLA was well dug in, and a frontal assault appeared out of the question. Van Heerden ordered Battle Group Alpha to make a wide flanking manoeuvre that would take them some 20 km behind the FAPLA lines, while Battle Group Bravo – reinforced by Charlie Company and an 81-mm mortar platoon fresh out of Danie Theron Combat School, which had arrived from Sá da Bandeira in the interim – would launch the attack. Meanwhile, Connie van Wyk was engaged in his own battle against the FAPLA group some eight kilometres east of the town.

Because of terrain restrictions a full frontal attack turned out to be the only solution after all. The 81-mm mortars opened up with a sweeping bombardment on the enemy's mortar and B10 positions. When the FAPLA guns fell silent, the infantry moved in, supported by the armoured cars. Breytenbach's headquarters followed close behind.

Slabbert's Elands had little trouble neutralising the B10 and machine-gun positions, and Breytenbach switched Alpha Company from the left to the right side of the road, thus using his more experienced troops to attack the highest point of the enemy's terrain. Captain Grobbie Grobbelaar and Charlie Company were to attack the high ground to the right of the road.

The mortar bombs continued to rain down on the enemy positions, along with 90-mm shells from the armoured cars, as the two infantry companies advanced to the intermediate high ground, pausing once to allow the vehicles to close up. Suddenly, the firing tempo increased dramatically. Charlie Company stumbled on an unexpected trench system, which resulted in some heavy fighting before they could break through and reach the top of the hill. Dippenaar's company had better luck, capturing their objective with little resistance, but almost immediately came under attack from the rear. Somewhere in the dense bush, FAPLA had regrouped and was fighting back at close range.

Dippenaar launched a counter-attack with Alpha Company, but it was obvious that they did not have enough firepower. Most of the armoured cars were in a cutting and in no position to offer effective support, leaving only the Vickers machine guns available. Corporal Kruger dismounted both machine guns from the Land Rovers and the soldiers physically manhandled them into position to afford fire support. The battle tipped in Bravo's favour when the flatbed truck on which another eight Vickers were mounted, turned sideways and poured one burst of fire after another into the enemy ranks.

Among the captured weaponry were B10s and 12,7-mm heavy machine guns. Of great value was a FAPLA battle map, showing all the enemy's deployments and battle plans – but there was also a disturbing piece of intelligence indicating that the enemy had accurately projected Task Force Zulu's anticipated route and advance, as well as the overall military plan of all the forces involved.

Several dead Cubans were found, mostly sprawled behind crew-served weapons. Cubans had also manned the FAPLA command post, and the captured battle map was annotated in Spanish rather than the Portuguese which might have been expected. This was the first evidence that FAPLA had Cuban advisers right down to battalion level, and offered some explanation for the surprisingly extensive defensive position, consisting of a double trench system about 800 m long. It was estimated that up to 1 000 FAPLA troops had been engaged, and Battle Group Bravo was justifiably proud of having had the temerity to attack and defeat them with only two infantry companies and eight armoured cars. The battle started at 08h00 and continued all day until about 18h00. Bravo casualties were astonishingly light, with only a few soldiers suffering light wounds and one having his lower jaw shot away.

The next morning, Breytenbach sent Van Wyk into Caimbambo with Bravo and Charlie companies and a troop of armoured cars to clear the town of any FAPLA remnants. As they moved up the main street, excited Angolans waved at them from the verandahs of their houses, but Breytenbach was totally nonplussed when a senior FAPLA commander rushed towards him, saluted and planted a kiss of greeting on both his cheeks. The FAPLA man realised his error almost immediately, but neither he nor the soldier with him had the chance to use their AK47s before being disarmed. As the mopping-up operation got under way, the hapless FAPLA commander found himself feeding Corporal van Dyk the coordinates needed to drop mortar bombs with deadly accuracy on the FAPLA troops trying to escape along predetermined routes. Bravo Group later established that hundreds of FAPLA soldiers, many wearing civilian clothes, had been in Caimbambo en route to the front lines at Nova Lisboa, and like his comrade the day before, the FAPLA officer who had kissed his way into captivity had mistaken the new arrivals for Cuban reinforcements.

The battle group pushed on to Cubal, approaching from the south in the late afternoon. The main road to Nova Lisboa bypassed Cubal on the eastern side, and FAPLA was reported to be concentrated on the southern perimeter, facing the river, with a headquarters in the southernmost building on the main street.

Breytenbach's strategy was to send two vehicles carrying troops charging down the street bordering the southern edge of the town. When the troops debussed, their allocated close-support armoured cars peeling off with them, the assault force would shake out in extended line format. The remaining armoured cars would open fire on the headquarters. Van Dyk and his men would deploy just beyond the bridge to provide mortar support as needed, while Kruger's task was to head for the northern sector and deploy his machine guns to cut off the escape route to Nova Lisboa.

The armoured cars flattened the FAPLA headquarters without drawing a single shot. The streets were empty, the houses appeared deserted. Later, however, frightened residents emerged from their homes to relate tales of terrible atrocities inflicted on them by FAPLA troops.

The sound of mortar fire sent Breytenbach rushing to the bridge, where he found Van Dyk's men in high spirits, the ground between their base plates and the bridge strewn with FAPLA dead, trucks slewed haphazardly across the road. It seemed the FAPLA contingent assigned to the defence of Cubal had left earlier in the day and travelled south to join up with another group, but had been ordered to turn around and return to hold Cubal. By the time they arrived, Bravo was already in control of the town.

Sadly, a day of easy triumph ended in a tragic mistake.

Breytenbach despatched Captain Grobbelaar, two armoured cars and one company to explore the road south-east of Cubal, where a FAPLA group was rumoured to be. After they had left, and on his own initiative, Captain James Hills sent out two Land Rovers mounted with Vickers machine guns with Van Dyk and Kruger – both promoted in the field to sergeant in the meanwhile – in command. About two kilometres out of Cubal, at a place called Cassiva, the road forked, and while Grobbelaar's group had driven south-west, the two Land Rovers went in the opposite direction.

As Grobbelaar's group was returning they ran into an ambush, the enemy opening fire from a house as the vehicles passed. The troops debussed and took cover behind the Land Rovers, but almost immediately came under fire from the south-east as well. A single 90-mm shell lobbed by an armoured car destroyed the house, but another hit one of the Land Rovers by mistake. Both Van Dyk and Kruger were seriously wounded by 'friendly fire' and had to be casevaced to Rundu. The Vickers and mortar platoons were heartbroken at the loss of their leaders. Replacements were eventually flown in, but they never developed the same rapport with the troops as Van Dyk and Kruger had built up, and in time Breytenbach disbanded the mortar platoon and divided the troops up among the rifle companies.

On the morning of 5 November, Battle Group Bravo returned to Catengue and by 15h00 was on the move towards Benguela, spending the night in the *quartel* south of the city.

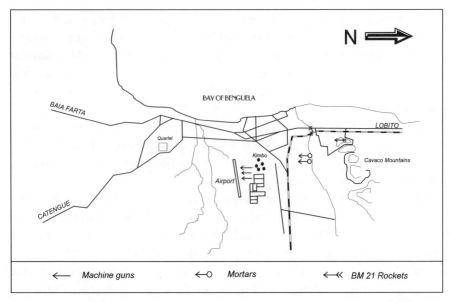

The Bay of Benguela, showing positions of FAPLA's mortars, machine guns and multiple rocket launcher

Van Heerden had wanted Bravo Group alone to clear Benguela, but Breytenbach pointed out that this was simply too tall an order for a single battalion, proposing as an alternative that he bypass Benguela on the eastern flank and take up a position on the high ground dominating the city to the north. While a patrol ventured out to reconnoitre a way around the town, Battle Group Alpha engaged the enemy in a furious battle centred on the airfield. Breytenbach sent reinforcements in the form of a troop of armoured cars and a platoon of infantry, and joined Delville Linford at his command post in one of the airport buildings, which was under constant bombardment from a BM 21, located on the high ground north of the city.

When the reconnaissance patrol returned with the news that flooded rivers made any advance around Benguela impossible, Breytenbach and Linford decided to launch a phased attack, with Bravo securing the shanty town and area around the cemetery, where they could deploy their mortars in support of the main assault on the city itself. Breytenbach ordered Dippenaar not to waste time fighting house to house, but to move as swiftly as possible along the entire length of the main street and attack the Cuban BM 21 positions. Grobbelaar and Charlie Company would clear the southern sector, but the chief objective was to capture the high ground to the north.

Bravo Group launched the attack towards midday, and met little resistance in the shanty town. As soon as the 81-mm mortars found their range, the Cubans rapidly withdrew, and by sunset on 6 November Benguela was in the hands of

Task Force Zulu. By the time the column reached Lobito, the next town to the north, it had already been evacuated by the enemy.

Four days of frustration followed as the task force waited for the South African government to decide whether or not the advance should continue. Zulu had moved so rapidly, often faster than the enemy could withdraw, that FAPLA was constantly kept off balance and denied sufficient time to prepare proper defensive positions. The four-day hiatus while the politicians made up their minds could provide the enemy with just enough time to make any further advance far costlier in terms of casualties.

During this time, Breytenbach also had another problem to contend with. His FNLA troops demanded a meeting with their political leader to clarify their role in the ongoing conflict. Chipenda was duly brought in to address their concerns, but this would be the last time the FNLA soldiers of Battle Group Bravo saw or heard from him. Finally, word came that Task Force Zulu was to proceed. Bolstered by the addition of a 140-mm G2 artillery troop that equipped them to take on the Russian-made BM 21s for the first time since the expedition was launched, the battle groups set off for Novo Redondo. Alpha led the way, and despite running into some heavy fighting along the way, by the evening of 16 November, FAPLA had been driven north of the Queve River, and Novo Redondo secured. Bravo's next orders were to move up the coastal road and take Porto Amboim. Battle Group Alpha was to find and take the bridge across the Queve River to the east in preparation for an assault on Quibala, from where the road would lead straight to the Angolan capital of Luanda.

On reaching the bridge spanning the Queve River at its widest point near the Atlantic coastline, Breytenbach took a small patrol of four armoured cars and one infantry platoon to probe FAPLA's reaction. Halfway across the bridge they came under heavy rocket and mortar fire, and were forced to retreat to the low hills that fringe the southern limit of the floodplain. During a furious battle between Captain Smokey Bouwer's artillery and FAPLA's BM 21s, three of the enemy's five rocket launcher positions were destroyed, but so was the bridge, closing off any hope of Bravo reaching Porto Amboim. Breytenbach withdrew to Novo Redondo and sent out scouts to probe for an alternative crossing further upstream. The only possibility was north of Vila Nova de Celes, but that bridge, too, had been blown up.

Task Force Zulu's northern advance had ground to a halt, and on 19 November, Battle Group Bravo and Zulu's headquarters were ordered to the central front to reinforce Foxbat, the UNITA task force engaged in battle around Cela and Santa Comba. Foxbat had been forced to withdraw rapidly from Ebo after FAPLA cunningly led them into a trap while fording a stream that had come down in flood. Battle Group Bravo was urgently required to set up an intermediate position on which Foxbat could fall back.

Moving towards Cela via Lobito and Alto Hama, Bravo continued north past Santa Comba before turning west and taking up defensive positions on the high ground offered by a long range of hills, facing westwards some ten kilometres off the main road to the north. The secondary road along which Foxbat was withdrawing ran around the northern flank.

Foxbat soon appeared and sped past the defensive position. Bravo prepared to engage the enemy, but nothing happened. Patrols sent out on two different routes found no sign of an enemy in pursuit, but gruesome evidence of their handiwork awaited at the side of the road opposite the northernmost point of the defensive position.

As Foxbat raced towards the safety of Cela, civilian trucks carrying FNLA infantry had detached from the column, halting where they were found, awash with blood and laden with dead and seriously wounded. To his horror, Breytenbach realised that most of the casualties were men from his old Charlie Company, which he had left behind in Moçâmedes, and from a company commanded by Captain Jock Harris.

Charlie Company's commander, Sergeant Marao, had been shot through both legs and was lying on a stretcher. Sergeant Sierro told Breytenbach that Marao had crawled several kilometres on his hands and knees to safety.

The trucks had been ambushed by the Cubans, who waited until Foxbat's armoured cars had passed through the kill zone before attacking the infantry trucks. More than 80 men from Charlie Company were killed that day, the Cubans cold-bloodedly executing the wounded where they lay. Marao would have been among the dead had he not been able to crawl away unseen.

Breytenbach appointed Sierro commander of what was left of the company, and the surviving wounded were evacuated to the hospital at Cela.

Following the retreat from Ebo, Colonel Blackie Swart replaced Van Heerden as officer commanding Task Force Zulu, bringing with him SADF infantry, 140-mm guns and additional armoured cars. His first action was to plan a left-flanking manoeuvre via a route that would bypass Ebo, with Bravo Company being detached to Foxbat while Alpha and Charlie companies took up defensive positions on high ground facing north towards the river.

The plan had to be aborted, however, when Swart was unable to use Foxbat's UNITA troops for the attack, since they hastily withdrew from the battle zone each time the enemy BM 21s opened fire. Swart was forced to devise another plan, which involved crossing the Nhia River over a small but well-constructed bridge behind a hill code-named Top Hat.

Because the bridge was not visible from Bravo and Foxbat's positions, Swart ordered Breytenbach to send out a patrol on 27 November to establish whether, in fact, it was still intact. If it could be used to make the crossing, the battle group

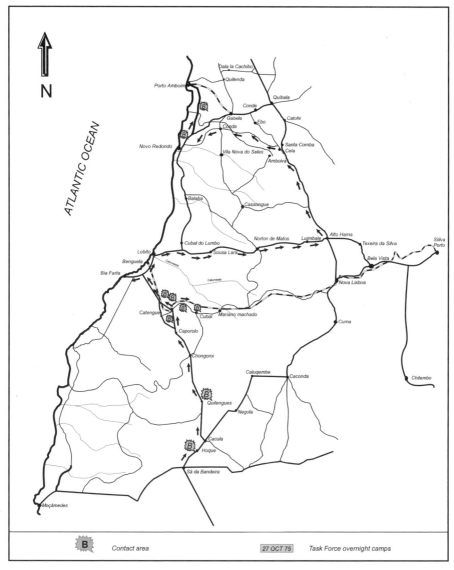

MAP 3: Battle Group Bravo's advance from Sá da Bandeira to Benguela and
the northernmost penetration of Angola before being ordered to withdraw

could launch a frontal attack on FAPLA from the road to Quibala, instead of trying
to outflank them from the west.

Unbeknown to the South Africans, however, FAPLA had occupied Top Hat on
the opposite side of the river, and launched a blistering attack on Sergeant Danny
Roxo's platoon, which had been ordered to go out with four armoured cars to
inspect the bridge.

The commanders could hear heavy machine-gun and mortar fire, but could not see what was happening. After a while, however, Breytenbach saw two Elands retreating at high speed, and stopped them to get a situation report. He was not pleased to learn that these were the only two armoured cars that had accompanied Roxo's patrol, and even less happy that they had abandoned the infantrymen in mid-battle. He immediately ordered the Elands back into action, but they were unable to get closer than about 1 000 m due to the enemy bombardment intensifying and threatening not only the armoured cars, but Breytenbach's own soft-skinned command vehicle.

Suddenly, through the smoke, Breytenbach saw his infantrymen making their way back along the road, walking in single file and apparently unperturbed by the shells falling all around them. The Eland commanders refused to go forward to pick up the men, and it was left to Roxo and his platoon to make their way on foot to the waiting vehicles and clamber on board so that they could return to base.

Roxo's report was not good. Not only had the bridge been demolished, but two of his men were missing in action, presumed captured. They had indeed been taken prisoner, but later that night managed to escape from the cells they were being held in at Catofe, a tiny village just beyond the bridge, and only when they rejoined their unit did the full story of what had happened at Top Hat emerge. The platoon had ridden the two armoured cars to a turn in the road, where Roxo dismounted and, telling his men and the armoured cars to cover him, walked off alone to inspect the bridge. Having established that it no longer existed, Roxo was making his way back when a Cuban troop suddenly appeared in his path. Roxo shot him, and all hell broke loose. He had passed through a Cuban ambush on his way to the river, but they held their fire, expecting the rest of his platoon to follow. When this did not happen, they waited until he returned and opened fire on him anyway. It was a decision that cost them dearly. Not only did Roxo survive the ambush, he took out no less than 11 enemy – including four Cubans – in the process, thus firing the first shots in what, over the ensuing days, would be one of the modern SADF's finest hours – the Battle of Bridge 14.

Only later did Breytenbach learn that while Roxo was inspecting the bridge, the two men who were taken prisoner had gone off into the bush to round up some stray cattle for the pot, and had been left behind when the patrol hastily withdrew under fire.

By early December, after several weeks of combat, the men of Bravo were severely battle fatigued, and some of them were seriously ill as well. Malaria had taken a heavy toll among the leader group, with captains Dippenaar and Grobbelaar, Lieutenant Connie van Wyk and others being casevaced to South Africa for treatment. Breytenbach requested permission from Brigadier Dawie

Schoeman to withdraw the entire battle group to somewhere further south for a spell of well-earned rest and recuperation.

Schoeman refused, his sole concession being an offer to replace the entire white leadership echelon with newly arrived platoon leaders. Breytenbach declined the offer. Having already detected that the troops had difficulty accepting new-comers who had replaced the platoon and company commanders struck down by malaria, he knew they would never trust an entirely new group of leaders. Nor, he believed, would any new commanders be able to build the necessary rapport with the physically spent and mentally exhausted troops, whom they would almost certainly view as inferior fighting men, having no inkling of how well they had actually performed under South African command.

In fact, red lights were flickering in several quarters regarding South Africa's further political and military involvement in the Angolan conflict, and there was a very real danger that Battle Group Bravo would be left leaderless and abandoned to its own devices if the SADF leader group withdrew. The FNLA's own leaders had long since deserted the cause, with Chipenda nowhere to be found and Holden Roberto on the verge of admitting defeat and seeking political asylum in Tunisia.

When Breytenbach was formally ordered to withdraw and return to South Africa, he refused, as did all his officers and non-commissioned officers (NCOs). The stalemate lasted three weeks, and it was Schoeman who blinked first, finally granting Breytenbach permission on 5 December to replace Bravo Group's companies with UNITA troops, and withdraw from the battle zone.

Three days later, Battle Group Bravo began the trek southwards in 12 vehicles, passing Nova Lisboa and stopping at Serpa Pinto. All along the route, troops were dropped off to make their way home. By the time the convoy reached Katwitwi, the trucks were all but empty – but every troop had been instructed to report to mustering points at Calai, Cuangar, Vila Nova da Armada and Mpupa by mid-January 1976.

When Breytenbach left Angola it was with every intention of returning, armed with a fresh mission for the ragged group of men he and his officers had begun to mould into a formidable fighting machine.

3

Buffalo is our home

PUTTING TOGETHER A UNIT

LISBON'S PROPOSED INDEPENDENCE day – 11 November 1975 – found Angola in chaos. The economy had long since collapsed, thousands of refugees had fled their homes, the civil war had escalated as foreign interests turned it into an international issue, and Portugal had washed its hands of the whole debacle. The MPLA stepped into the power vacuum, declaring itself the ruling party and Agostinho Neto president of the troubled land. In February 1976, both the Organisation of African Unity and the United Nations recognised the MPLA's position – but the FNLA and UNITA had no intention of abandoning the armed struggle.

By the end of January, *Operation Savannah* was history and all conventional SADF forces had been withdrawn from Angola – but it would be another 13 years before South Africa's official involvement in the bloody conflict ended.

True to his word, Jan Breytenbach – promoted to colonel in the interim – returned to Mpupa as planned to gather the remnants of Battle Group Bravo and start turning the FNLA's bush warriors into a full-blooded fighting unit. He was convinced that the only way to save South West Africa from a civil war such as the one that had engulfed post-colonial Angola, was to keep SWAPO – and its MPLA hosts – from gaining an unchallenged foothold north of the Cunene River.

Since the FNLA was already the dominant force in southern Angola and enjoyed the support of the local population, it made sense to Breytenbach – still acting under his original mandate to train the FNLA troops – that they should serve as a buffer between the communist-backed FAPLA and the SADF deployed in the South West African Operational Area.

At its height, Battle Group Bravo had consisted of a mere 270 troops, but when Breytenbach arrived at Mpupa, he was met by several thousand men, women and children. A fair number of the original Bravo members had not returned after their leave, but in Breytenbach's absence, after losing a major battle against UNITA at Serpa Pinto, the FNLA had been pushed steadily south by Savimbi's forces. Abandoned by their political leaders, Holden Roberto and Daniel Chipenda, the main body of FNLA soldiers naturally gravitated to Mpupa, with smaller groups scattered throughout southern Angola, and Breytenbach realised that the first step to achieving his objective was to bring all the members of this fragmented force under his command.

The flood of Angolan refugees had become a major problem for the South African authorities, with large concentrations of mostly FNLA supporters at both Ondangwa and Chitando. On 5 February, Brigadier Ben de Wet Roos, Officer Commanding 2 Military Area, issued orders to 101 Task Force to relocate them to Savate. The Officer Commanding 1 Military Area fully expected that following the exodus two days later in ten 10-ton trucks, hundreds of former FNLA soldiers and their dependants would find their way to Mpupa, and he was proved right.

On 13 February, Breytenbach began selecting the top candidates from the horde of potential soldiers at his disposal. Those who did not make the cut were sent to refugee camps at Calai. As before, SADF Special Forces operators formed the leader group.

One by one, battalion headquarters staff began arriving at Rundu, the Cape Town Highlanders providing both the first intelligence officer, Major Chuch Chambers, and his successor, Major Pat Tate.

On 16 February, Breytenbach received word that a well-organised FNLA battalion had arrived at Chitando after fighting their way south. It didn't take him long to persuade their commander, Kiote, that his men should join Bravo. Commandant Sybie van der Spuy and Staff Sergeant Mike Tippet were sent to Savate to start training a group of half-starved FNLA troops living with their families under the command of Geraldo, while Sergeant Major Willy Ward was despatched to Vila Novo da Armada, where he enlisted another group, under the command of Zaire.

Breytenbach set up his 'headquarters' in a shack at Rundu, from which he not only commanded Bravo Group operations in the Cuando Cubango province as far north as Mavinga until early 1977, but waged an ongoing battle within the SADF to obtain the necessary logistical support for what were now South Africa's major allies in Angola. An urgent request for 100 Unimog 4×4-type vehicles to Major General Constand Viljoen, at the time General Officer Commanding 101 Task Force and later Chief:SADF, resulted in the delivery of only ten, despite SADF Chief General Magnus Malan being advised that 'only that type of vehicle can operate within the assigned area of responsibility and due to extreme extent of area, trained elements must be given a high degree of mobility to be effective'.

On 24 February, hoping to ensure that Bravo Group would become an indispensable SADF asset – just in case the South African politicians decided to pull the plug on their allies – Breytenbach sent General Viljoen a letter formally proposing the utilisation of friendly guerrilla forces in southern Angola. 'This headquarters,' he wrote, 'believes that as a result of the internationally-forced withdrawal to the South West African border, the military and political situation in South Angola has deteriorated to such an extent that it presents a critical threat.'

His motivation must have impressed the right people in high places, as just two days later 101 Task Force Administrative Headquarters received a signal containing guidelines to provide logistical support for 1 000 men. However, a surprise element of the order was that Bravo Group was to be issued with PPSh carbines instead of R1 rifles. As an SADF unit in embryo, it had been expected that they would receive the standard FN or R1 infantry rifles.

On 22 March, Breytenbach was authorised to relocate trained members of Bravo Group from Mpupa to the western Caprivi. Elements on operational deployment against FAPLA and the Cubans in the Cuando Cubango province were excluded from the move to Pica Pau – Portuguese for woodpecker – which was nothing more than a clearing in the bush on the east bank of the Kavango River.

The only accommodation available to the soldiers and their families was hopelessly too few 15 × 15 feet tents dating from World War II, or makeshift shelters made from branches and whatever else they could lay their hands on in the surrounding area. There were no tools or equipment of any kind, but by 27 March the move was complete, and even though it was still known as Bravo Group, that became the official date on which the SADF's newest and most unconventional unit was born. But it would take another 17 months, and two more moves, before 32 Battalion found a permanent home at Buffalo Base.

Into the wilderness of the western Caprivi came Warrant Officer Piet Slade as base sergeant major and Major Peter Rose as commander. He would be succeeded first by Major Charlie Hochapfel and later still by Major Gideon Rousseau.

Even before the move to Pica Pau, the SA Army chief had authorised the issuing of basic rations to all members of Bravo Group, along with monthly payment from a special fund of R5 per private, R10 per lance corporal and R15 per corporal. Military red tape being traditionally slow to unroll, however, the first payday was not until June.

Breytenbach had also tried, before the move from Mpupa, to obtain basic equipment for his men. Winter was approaching, and on 23 March he sent a signal to 16 Maintenance Unit at Grootfontein, reiterating a list of supplies he had requisitioned earlier, but which had not been delivered. In no mind to mince words over yet another bureaucratic bungle, Breytenbach ended his signal: 'In the meantime, the members of Bravo Group have done their part with the minimum

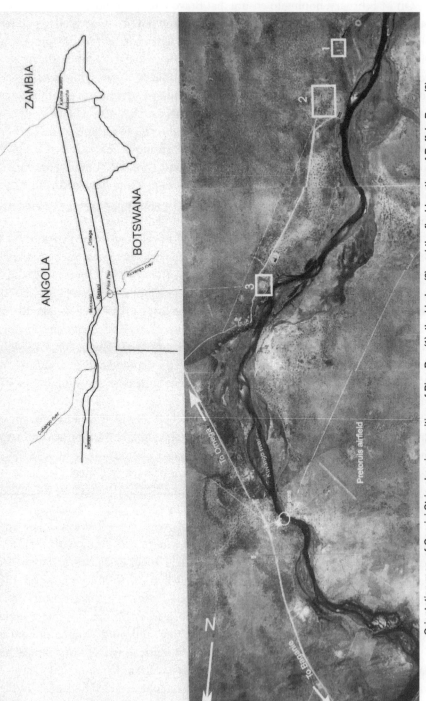

Orientation map of Caprivi Strip showing position of Pica Pau (1), the kimbo (2) and the final location of Buffalo Base (3)

of equipment and logistical support. The wives and children of the soldiers are living in unspeakable conditions, yet we expect them to display a positive attitude. What is the possibility that we, as South Africans, can show the people of Bravo Group that they can trust us to carry out requests for logistic support as a matter of utmost urgency? Not one troop has even received a blanket or sleeping-bag.'

On the purely military side, one of the earliest steps was transformation of the FNLA rank structure, which seemed to be largely confined to *commandante* and sergeant. On 30 March, Major Rose ordered the removal of all FNLA insignia and the troops were assigned SADF ranks according to their seniority in the FNLA. Most of those who qualified became sergeants, with a few appointed as corporals. Only José Francisco qualified for the rank of lance corporal.

Breytenbach's signal about the lack of basic bedding for the troops marked the start of a relentless campaign to gain full recognition for Bravo Group as a military unit. On 4 April, under the heading 'Motivation of ex-FNLA/UNITA troops', Breytenbach set out a few home truths in a letter to General Viljoen. Since the FNLA had collapsed as a political movement, its soldiers no longer had a cause for which to fight, and Breytenbach argued: 'We must therefore substitute something else for the FNLA/Angolan political ideals. This can be achieved, I believe, by building a unit-based esprit d'corps [*sic*] among the black troops. We should not lose sight of the fact that the troops in question come from various tribes and parts of Angola.' Outstanding training, Breytenbach suggested, was the key, but this could only be achieved by 'the white instructors becoming part of the unit – identifying fully with it by actually being posted to the unit'.

The issue of apparel was also addressed: 'Until recently, we have been supplying an FNLA or UNITA army with whatever we could lay our hands on. This can no longer be the case, as the ex-FNLA force now being trained by us, is seen as an integral part of the SA Army.'

And then there was the question of a suitable name. Bravo Group, wrote Breytenbach, should be changed to something more descriptive. 'One possibility, which would both accurately describe the unit and serve to camouflage its guerrilla activities, is the Frontier Guard, or *Grenswag* in Afrikaans. In time to come we could introduce the 1st, 2nd etc. Frontier Guard battalions.'

The minimal rate of pay was another consideration. On an average of R10 a month, the troops had to feed and care for their families, and Breytenbach suggested that remuneration be brought in line with that of the Bushman Battalion based at Alpha, whose members were receiving 'something like R35 a month plus rations for themselves and their families'.

But the most pressing concern was the living conditions at Pica Pau. If the troops were to be turned into fully motivated fighting men, 'we must house them in a well constructed camp and quarters of which they can be proud and which can be kept clean and tidy in a manner befitting soldiers'.

Four days later, the first sign that the SADF was in earnest regarding the integration of Bravo Group came in the form of approval for almost all Breytenbach's proposals. He had until 25 April to submit a detailed planning order and motivation, but he beat this deadline by ten days. In a staff paper entitled 'Organisation and training of a black force – Operation Budgie', Breytenbach set out the plan that would form the basis of organising and training the unit. Every aspect of personnel, logistics and training was covered, and the plan deviated from accepted infantry concepts in only two regards: there would be two battalions, each consisting of three rifle companies and a support company, and a Sabre squadron would fall under control of Special Forces Headquarters.

While the battle to equip the unit continued, deployment of guerrilla groups in the Cuando Cubango province proceeded, but before long, fresh problems demanded attention. The cohabitation of the soldiers and their families was not working well, and troops who had completed their basic training were moved to a new position, west of Pica Pau. Construction of a mess facility and bar had begun, and the rest of the base was already in the planning stage, but a new training ground had to be found, as the area around Pica Pau was not big enough. A new base was set up to the east and quickly became known as Dodge City, under the command of Major John Hooley, a Citizen Force member of the Cape Town Highlanders. Towards the end of 1976 and during early 1977, pseudo-operators from Bravo Group were trained at Dodge City to infiltrate the ranks of SWAPO in Owamboland.

A team of SA Army engineers – Colonel Frik van Rheede van Oudtshoorn, Colonel Ken Henry and project leader Colonel Faan Grobbelaar – was appointed to construct a base modelled on the relatively cheap but effective 'Huhnerleiter' shelters system designed by the SADF's Commandant Ivor Olën. Building began on the nucleus of 29, which would offer accommodation as well as an administrative complex and operations room. On 18 May, in terms of Command Directive No. 15/76 ops 34, issued by 101 Task Force, Breytenbach was formally appointed Officer Commanding Bravo Group, and for the first time the unit's responsibilities were spelled out as follows: 'The primary aim of Bravo Group is to deny SWAPO an area of 50 kilometres north of the South West African border by means of clandestine operations, and to be available for any task inside South West Africa if needed.'

Breytenbach fired his next salvo in the battle for equipment on 27 May in the form of a personal letter to Commandant Piet Moolman, Director Army Equipment, in which he pleaded for uniforms, webbing and 'bigpacks' for the troops fighting in Angola, who were making do with whatever they could lay their

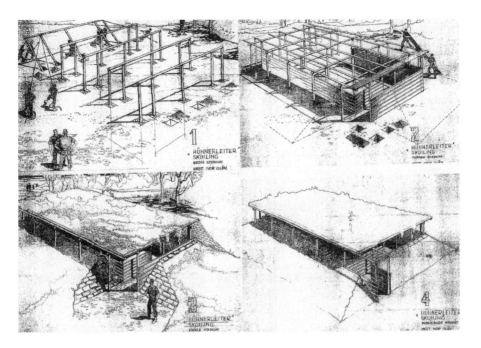

Construction of Huhnerleiter shelters

hands on. Fortunately, Moolman had visited Pica Pau earlier and seen for himself what the conditions were, but despite his best efforts it was not until 21 July that the first consignment of web belts, bigpacks, sleeping-bags and water bottles arrived. But at least it was a start.

Construction of the shelters was progressing well, despite the additional work required by orders from Breytenbach that they were not to be built at ground level, but sunk 1,5 m into the ground to offer better protection against attack. Once equipment began arriving the planning schedule had to be amended, since without proper storage facilities the completed shelters had to be used on a temporary basis as stores rather than to house the troops, but this was a small price to pay for the long-awaited and much needed supplies. Additional personnel also arrived, Commandant Gert Nel being appointed second-in-command and Major Eddie Viljoen from the Rustenburg Commando being attached to the unit.

By June, the area of operations had been extended from the Cuando Cubango province to central Angola, creating extremely long logistical lines which, coupled with support that was erratic at best, made it all but impossible to supply troops deployed up to 500 km from Pica Pau. The solution was to turn over the Omauni base in 2 Military Area – Owamboland and Kaokoland – to Bravo Group as a forward operational base. On 27 July, command of the base was formally handed to Major Viljoen by the incumbent Griqualand East Commando, which returned to South Africa. A platoon of mounted soldiers remained behind temporarily.

Although some supplies were sent from Rundu to Nkurunkuru and then to places such as Savate and Tandaue, by 17 August Omauni was the chief source of logistical support for:

- A command group and troops at the base itself, consisting of 14 white and 57 black members, as well as 32 mounted soldiers.
- Two companies deployed on the Angolan cutline between beacons 22 and 31, consisting of 32 white personnel, including 27 paratroopers detached from 2 Military Area, and 142 black troops. One white and 27 black troops were on leave at Pica Pau.
- The Tandaue group of two white and 113 black members, of whom 61 were on leave at Pica Pau.
- The Savate group – two white and 130 black members undergoing training.

Their available weaponry included AK47 or G3 rifles, an 81-mm mortar and 15 60-mm mortars, and five light machine guns.

The rest of Bravo Group was deployed as follows:

- Call sign 39B at Luenge – five white and 123 black soldiers.
- Call sign 20B at Rito – four white and 472 black soldiers.
- A total of 41 white and 290 black members at Pica Pau, including 88 on leave.

Dependants in the Pica Pau village numbered 226 women and 201 children, along with 151 refugees – 31 men, 27 women, 41 children and 52 Bushmen.

Rations were received on a weekly basis from Rundu, and Warrant Officer Piet Slade was placed in charge of distributing them to the non-combatants.

As the deployed guerrillas moved deeper and deeper into Angola, not even Omauni was close enough to re-supply them, and an additional logistics base – promptly named Donkey – was set up west of Chana Ohikik and south of Beacon 38, with Staff Sergeant van Heerden of 15 Maintenance Unit in charge. By December, the need for another operational base in the vicinity of Beacon 27 had become a priority. On a visit to Eenhana, Breytenbach and Viljoen learned that a base known only by its radio call sign, CN, was situated some 15 km north-east of Elundu and seven kilometres south of the border. Occupied at the time by a platoon from 3 SA Infantry Battalion, it was reallocated to Bravo Group, with all equipment except personal kit remaining behind when the 3 SAI platoon left. In addition to ammunition, this gave Bravo a significant number of extra machine guns, vehicles and radios. A Citizen Force officer, Commandant Eddie Wesselo, was placed in command.

During the construction phase at Pica Pau, the black troops continued to live in tents pitched close to the river. The white leader group began building their own quarters, which became known as 'sparrow nests', from whatever materials they could scrounge, ranging from thatch grass cut along the river banks to old sheets of corrugated iron.

With the arrival of Major Ken Greef as logistics officer, clear signs of military order became visible, to the extent that Gert Nel informed the group that a new name, Cheetah, would henceforth be used, and that suggestions for a distinctive unit beret and shoulder badge would be welcomed. The name found little favour with the men, and was never really used.

But the fledgling unit suffered a severe setback in November, when the onset of the rainy season resulted in all the shelters flooding and the equipment stored in them being destroyed. This was the unfortunate result of Breytenbach's order that the shelters be sunk into the ground, rather than built on the surface and reinforced with sandbags. When General Viljoen heard of the disaster, he ordered the demolition of all the shelters, with the exception of one which for some reason had not been affected. Thousands of rands had already been spent on building the base, and a year later there was still no accommodation for the troops.

The entire plan had to be revised, and early in January 1977 authorisation was granted for Project Carpenter, which would entail the erection of prefabricated wooden Warren huts in the kimbo. The first phase would see the building of 355 houses, 45 ablution blocks and a shop. Meanwhile, the unit had been organised into companies, platoons and sections, and the tent town accordingly divided along company lines. On 8 January the unit was upgraded to a battalion group because of its size. An infantry unit normally consists of only three rifle companies, whereas the newly named 32 Battalion had seven and a headquarters element.

Recruiting of fresh troops was an ongoing process, and on 21 February the first official discharges took place, Sergeant E Chimbanda and Rifleman F Hipi being found unfit for military duty. A sure sign that 32 Battalion had finally gained recognition as an element of the SA Army was the allocation to each member of a force identity number, which differed from those of the regular SADF only in respect of the suffix, SP – for 'Soldado Preto', the Portuguese for black soldier. Critics could argue that this reflected the racist attitude of the armed forces, but it should be remembered that at the time, black soldiers – let alone Portuguese-speaking ones – were virtually non-existent in the SADF. It has been suggested that 32 Battalion was a pioneer of desegregation and that in fact no form of 'apartheid' was practised within the unit, but that is not entirely true. Separate amenities for 'whites' and 'blacks' existed at all bases used by 32 Battalion – but on the battlefield, and during deployments, no form of discrimination on grounds of race was ever practised.

At the end of January, Breytenbach had returned to Pretoria to attend a staff officer's course, and Gert Nel assumed command of the unit. On 4 February, 32 Battalion was granted permission to move into the recently vacated headquarters of 1 Military Area. The Regimental Sergeant Major, Pep van Zyl, wasted no time, and by the middle of April a spanking new mess and recreation facility, complete with thatched roof, had been erected close to the corrugated iron headquarters buildings.

On 23 February, approval was granted for an increase in remuneration from R65 to R85 a month. As more and more members joined the battalion, Commandant Nel introduced colour-coded epaulettes in order to keep track of the constant human traffic between the base and the kimbo. Yellow indicated that the wearer was on official leave, transit camp residents wore green, brown denoted troops already assigned to rifle companies, and blue was reserved for headquarters personnel such as drivers, cooks and storemen.

Since all the former FNLA members were in South West Africa illegally, and did not enjoy refugee status, the process of obtaining residence permits for them was set in motion on 29 February, with a target completion date of 30 April. On 6 March, the CN base was handed back to Elundu, from where all 32 Battalion operations were to be run in future. By 1 April, all the rifle companies had a full leader group for the first time. They were:

- Alpha Company: second lieutenants Des Burman, H Fourie and H Rademeyer (platoon commanders); corporals Eduardo João, J Segunda and A de Abreu (platoon sergeants).
- Bravo Company: second lieutenants R Griessel and S Kriel, Sergeant L Hearn (platoon commanders); corporals J Appolinario, D Antonio and A de Veira (platoon sergeants).
- Charlie Company: sergeants C Oosthuizen, K Kelly and S Gericke (platoon commanders); corporals L Francisco, B Mudongo and L Joni (platoon sergeants).
- Delta Company: second lieutenants D de la Rey, H Louw and P Fourie (platoon commanders); corporals F Ndala, M Munongo and M Angola (platoon sergeants).
- Echo Company: second lieutenant J de Beer, candidate officers P du Plooy and J van Tonder (platoon commanders); corporals V Banezol, M Eduardo and A Leiti (platoon sergeants).
- Foxtrot Company: lieutenants J Henrico, J Scholtz and C van der Westhuizen (platoon commanders); corporals A Abreuo, KK Miguel and C Domingos (platoon sergeants).

The formal organisation of platoons within the rifle companies contributed greatly to the smooth running of the unit. However, the black platoon sergeants still lacked the experience to be truly effective in combat, and for a period from the end of 1977 white NCOs with the rank of temporary sergeant replaced and mentored the black soldiers until they were ready to assume their full responsibilities.

With the various military and operational duties finally settled into an accepted rhythm, attention began to turn to the social side of life, including romance. The first wedding at Pica Pau was that of Rifleman H Cruz, in April 1977, complete with an 'official' wedding car – possibly the first time that a brown army Land Rover had ever served in this role! Warrant Officer Mark Kanganjo had been a schoolteacher before the war, and on his own initiative began running informal classes for the children living in the kimbo. This prompted Commandant Nel to set up a proper school, which opened at the end of April with Kanganjo as the principal, seven Portuguese teachers and 74 pupils. Tuition was offered up to Standard 5 in Portuguese, their mother tongue.

On 12 April, the R460 000 needed for Project Carpenter was authorised and the first Warren huts were delivered on 11 May. However, negotiations with the building contractor, LTA, were still in progress, and they would not be able to start erecting the kimbo houses or new bungalows at what had been known as Buffalo Base since 7 March, until later in the year.

As it happened, the SA Army chief issued an order on 5 July that the entire unit, including the kimbo, was to move at least 50 km further south of the Angolan border within six weeks, as it was feared that FAPLA could attack Buffalo, believing that it housed UNITA soldiers. By 19 July, four possible alternatives had been identified: North or West Bushmanland, the south-western Kavango, including the Mangeti region south of Owamboland, Abenab mine near Tsumeb, or 'somewhere' in South Africa. Ten days later, South African prime minister John Vorster visited the unit, and on being told of the pending relocation, rescinded the order there and then. No country, said Vorster, was going to dictate to him where to place his forces, and 32 Battalion would stay exactly where it was.

The critical housing problem was alleviated for a while by a 'gift' of 60 more vintage tents from Natal Command, which had just been issued with new and larger models, but, welcome as they were, the hand-me-downs were already in an advanced state of disrepair.

In October, Commandant Nel was authorised to erect quartermaster stores, and Major Gideon Rousseau was appointed base commander. A well-known artist, he designed and supervised construction of a permanent facility, including two dining halls and a kitchen, which became known as Tretchi's mess and replaced the existing makeshift facility under tarpaulin.

Breytenbach's final administrative battle before taking leave permanently of the battalion had dealt with formal recognition and organisation. Even though its numbers far exceeded those of a normal infantry battalion, he had proposed a structure including a headquarters component, rifle companies and a support company. On 29 August, Commandant Nel received a telex from 101 Task Force Logistical Section that included the following:

2. Col van Heerden (Army HQ) confirms that the org of 32 Bn was finally approved and accepted by the minister on Monday 29 Aug 1977.
3. Congratulations – at last!

The official approval provided the impetus needed to proceed with reorganisation of the various elements, including the headquarters company. Nel took it upon himself to appoint suitable candidates as tailors, plumbers, builders and carpenters, as it was self-evident that the unit would have to rely on its own resources for maintenance and essential services. By the time LTA moved onto the site to start building the Warren huts, members of the unit had already made most of the building blocks needed for the foundations.

With their wives and children living in the nearby kimbo, it was inevitable that some of the troops would be drawn into domestic conflict from time to time. On 29 September, a simmering dispute over the amount of influence exercised by some families turned violent when an anti-personnel mine was planted at the entrance to one of the tents in the kimbo. The husband's departure for the base at 03h00 passed without incident, but when his wife left the tent somewhat later, she tripped the mine and was badly injured.

Even more serious, from an operational point of view, was the discovery that certain individuals were not only regular visitors to a FAPLA element deployed at Mucusso, but were sharing information with them. A full investigation resulted in the discharge of 15 troops found guilty of subversion and collaboration with the enemy.

The importance of Omauni as both a logistics and operational base led to the existing airstrip being upgraded, with a tarred landing zone for helicopters added in October. By Christmas 1977, Buffalo Base was a hive of construction activity and 32 Battalion was well on the way to maturity. An operational analysis requested by the Chief:SADF for submission to the prime minister on 29 December reflected an impressive combat record. From December 1976 to December 1977, the unit had accounted for no less than 187 enemy fatalities, in exchange for 12 of their own, with 66 wounded.

The figures were an early sign of the remarkable performance for which 32 Battalion became renowned. The next best 'kill ratio' for the same period was that of 101 Special Unit, which was responsible for 12 enemy dead and one taken prisoner.

Whether it was these figures that impressed Pretoria, or whether the bureaucratic machine simply became better oiled, 32 Battalion saw a marked improvement in support from January 1978. Just four days into the new year, four ten-ton Magirus Deutz vehicles arrived that could be used to ferry troops from Buffalo to Omauni for deployment. Having lost their training area around Dodge City to the engineers, the terrain east of the kimbo was officially designated the battalion's training area on 14 March. On 6 April, ten Buffel landmine-resistant armoured personnel carriers were added to the fleet of ageing Unimogs.

The troops were still armed with a wide selection of weapons, including FN and AK47 rifles, PPSh carbines and whatever else they were able to loot from the enemy, and in an effort to standardise, 500 South African-made R1s and 300 Russian AK47s were issued on 17 July. Companies deployed in South West Africa were issued with the R1s, while those operating inside Angola got the AKs, although some members of the leader group preferred to carry R1s, even on special operations. With the rifles came six Bedford trucks and two Land Rovers. Someone, it seemed, had at last awakened to the fact that 32 Battalion could not fight a war with determination alone.

The needs of the soldiers' families were not neglected either. By the end of September a new and bigger school had been constructed, and suitably qualified South African National Servicemen were being drafted to Buffalo Base as teachers. While accommodation was still under canvas for the most part, the leader group set about making their 'sparrow nest' houses more habitable, building their own hot water systems and installing showers and even hand basins.

Because of the danger of crocodiles, swimming or bathing in the Kavango River was strictly prohibited, but, inevitably, there were those who ignored the rule. One of them was Second Lieutenant RN Brits, a National Service teacher, who was taken by a crocodile on 14 November. His body was never recovered.

Around mid-1978, the need for an effective reconnaissance capability became imperative, and Commandant Nel obtained approval to set up a 'recce' wing, hand-picking 45 junior leaders from the School of Infantry at Oudtshoorn to undergo a physical selection process by the Regimental Sergeant Major (RSM), Sergeant Major Pep van Zyl. Seven officers and seven non-commissioned officers made the grade: second lieutenants Stef Naude, Theuns Marais, Willy Botha, Zack Garret, Frans Fourie, Chris Pool and Billy Botes, along with corporals Kevin Fitzgerald, Dirk (Daisy) Loubser, Gavin Monn, Pieter Nortje – the author of this book – Mike Kiley, Thabo Maree and Kevin Veenstra.

A smattering of lance corporals and troops already serving in 32 Battalion also joined the reconnaissance wing, and after initial training at Buffalo Base, the entire group was sent to Omauni at the end of December for advanced training and to launch their operations. They fell under the command of Staff Sergeant Blue Kelly, with Sergeant Ron Gregory as the second-in-command.

Despite the fact that 32 Battalion was becoming a textbook example of Breytenbach's early conviction that by building esprit de corps, a ragtag mob could be shaped into a proud and highly effective unit, it was no more immune to the problem of troops going absent without leave (AWOL) than any other military group. Sometimes the offenders would return after a few days, others were never seen again. In the case of 32, however, the problem was dealt with internally, never reported to higher authority, and those who came back were suitably punished.

But on 23 November, that situation changed after headquarters learned via diplomatic channels that a group of 15 had gone AWOL to Botswana in February – following a heavy battle at Chana Mamuandi, where 11 soldiers were killed and 40 wounded – and joined up with Angolan refugees who had fled to Botswana in 1968 and 1976. The 32 defectors had told their comrades they were tired of war and wanted no further part of it, and after their presence in Botswana became known, the SADF issued orders that all further AWOL cases were to be reported to headquarters.

Over the next few months, other unconventional practices within 32 Battalion would also be regulated, and it soon became apparent that full recognition by the SADF carried the price tag of universal military formality.

The arrival of Commandant Deon Ferreira – call sign Falcon – as Officer Commanding 32 Battalion at the beginning of 1979 marked the first major change. Previously, the OC had concentrated on the day-to-day running of the unit, leaving Major Eddie Viljoen to focus on the military operations. But Ferreira was a soldier's soldier, and he took personal control of operations from the start. By July he had persuaded the generals that all future deployment of 32 Battalion should be confined to Angola, and that other units should be used in the South West Africa Operational Area. From August, it thus became possible for companies to be deployed for five weeks at a stretch, returning to base for five weeks of rest and any further training they might need, then going back to the bush for another five-week stint. This regular pattern was interrupted only when an ongoing operation required the troops involved to stay out for as long as the battle demanded, or until they could be relieved.

A consistently high kill ratio had become a trademark of the unit, and the troops were justifiably proud that the superior skills they had acquired, equipped them to inflict far greater losses on the enemy than they suffered themselves. However, every fatality within the ranks of 32 was felt by all the members.

Ferreira – who died in 2002, only months after retiring from the 'new' SADF as a lieutenant general and Chief of Joint Operations – introduced the concept of 'butterfly' operations, a search-and-destroy tactic applied with particular success against SWAPO's Far East Detachment.

A temporary overnight base would be set up for three infantry companies, a tactical headquarters and a number of Alouette helicopter gunships. One company was assigned to defend the base, while the others would be lightly armed at all times and on constant standby for action. The commander would identify and evaluate possible enemy locations for attack, and at first light Puma helicopters carrying the fireforce would follow the gunships to the target area, seeking out the enemy from the air. When spotted, the gunships would provide covering fire while the Pumas flew in to disgorge the ground forces. The Alouettes would remain in position to provide supporting fire, while the Pumas withdrew until called back to pick up the troops and proceed to the next contact.

A high degree of fitness was demanded of troops taking part in these operations, as they had to hit the ground running, but the results were spectacular. In just the first five days of a tactical trial period, 84 SWAPO were killed. These operations also saw the forging of strong and lasting bonds between 32 Battalion and the SA Air Force helicopter pilots.

With Ferreira himself running operations, Major Viljoen took care of administration, and signs of his involvement soon began to show. A bungalow complex known as the 'Palácio Regimental' served as the commanding officer's living quarters and guest house for several years, the sickbay was finally completed and National Service doctors arrived to tend to both the troops and their families. A small clinic was also set up in the kimbo and run by a trained SADF nursing sister. By the end of Ferreira's first year at Buffalo Base the troops had their own mess, canteen and kitchen, while private unit funds were used to finance construction of an officers' bar opposite the Tretchi's mess, which was officially opened by Lieutenant General Jannie Geldenhuys, Chief of the Army, in early 1980. The occasion would be one of few reasons for celebration in a year that would take a heavy toll on 32 Battalion.

The new decade ushered in a dark period for the SADF's 'Buffalo Soldiers'. The emphasis was now firmly on operations, with Ferreira – or Falcon – spending much of his time in the field, either directing events from a tactical headquarters or at the front lines with his men, but 1980 would also see important developments in the structure of the unit.

Since mid-January 1979, the reconnaissance group at Omauni had been divided into teams, each consisting of a white second lieutenant as leader, a corporal as second-in-command and three riflemen. Staff Sergeant Blue Kelly, head of the 'recce group', insisted that team members share accommodation, five to a tent, regardless of rank. Inevitably, this gave rise to problems, not only in regard to command and control, but in terms of maintaining discipline. Kelly's refusal to separate the ranks sparked serious friction with the officers, and led to his transfer and replacement by Lieutenant Willem Ratte.

Buffalo Base had been established inside a game reserve, and hunting of any kind was strictly prohibited. However, the lucrative trade in illegal ivory proved too much of a temptation for some, and in August Rifleman E Makau was sent to prison after being convicted by a civilian court of being in possession of two elephant tusks. The incident left an ugly blot on the battalion's copybook.

But the most traumatic event of the year was the loss of 16 members, killed in action during *Operation Tiro-a-Tiro*, also known as *Savate* (see Chapter 8).

In the run-up to Zimbabwean independence, Rhodesian bush war veterans – black and white – had flooded the ranks of the SADF's Special Forces, bringing with them considerable experience of counter-insurgency and guerrilla warfare. Those who found their way to 32 Battalion were from the white leader group, and were assigned to the various rifle companies. Most of these former Rhodesians were involved in *Savate* on 21 May, when three rifle companies overran an entire FAPLA brigade. It was an outright military victory, to be sure – but at such a high cost in human lives to 32 Battalion that the date was observed annually thereafter as Savate Day, in remembrance of those who died.

Even though more than five years had passed since Commandant Jan Breytenbach first set foot at Mpupa, the very existence of 32 Battalion remained one of the SADF's best-kept secrets, known in January 1981 to only a handful of people, even within the military. Since the student riots in June 1976, the eyes of the international community had been firmly fixed on the violence-wracked southern African sub-region, with PW Botha's government facing mounting pressure not only to relinquish Pretoria's 60-year mandate over South West Africa, but also to scrap apartheid and put an end to white minority rule in South Africa.

Covert security force operations formed the cornerstone of Botha's 'total war' against the communist-backed 'freedom fighters' whose targets, more often than not, were civilian – or 'soft'. With Angola having been acknowledged by the world as a sovereign independent state under MPLA rule, particular care was taken to keep the SADF's continued support of anti-communist forces in that country from becoming public knowledge.

One man's betrayal was about to change that, however, and cast a shadow of infamy over 32 Battalion that would have far-reaching consequences.

On 30 January 1981, Corporal Trevor John Edwards, a British citizen who joined the battalion after leaving the Rhodesian Army, went AWOL. He made his way via Lusaka to the United Kingdom, and in an interview with the *Guardian* newspaper, accused the unit of committing brutal atrocities against Angolan citizens. One of his mildest claims was that '32 Battalion of the South African Defence Force is a military conjuring trick, manned by 1 200 soldiers who were supposed to have been killed by Cubans in 1975, led by mystery officers from a base which officially does not exist'.

This was the first time the unit's existence had been revealed – even to South

African taxpayers who had unknowingly funded 32 since 1975 – and the fallout was extensive. As military and political correspondents from both the South African and foreign media clamoured for the right to visit the unit and conduct their own investigations, and an official task force was appointed to probe Edwards's claims of atrocities, the SADF's official response was 'no comment'. But as the international media branded members of the unit 'psychopaths', 'murdering desperadoes' and 'mercenaries', it became clear that something would have to be done to counter the storm of negative publicity.

At the time, only selected South African journalists, who had been granted security clearance in order to qualify as accredited military correspondents, were allowed access to SADF facilities, particularly in the Operational Area. The system has been severely criticised as a form of censorship, and some of those who agreed to be vetted before being allowed to visit military bases and attend confidential and generally off-the-record background briefings about the security situation were later denounced as apartheid spies. But the truth is that most of them simply wanted to write the stories that most often dominated the news in South Africa, and accepted that the system was the price they had to pay.

Foreign journalists were a different matter. Convinced that the accreditation process was part of an orchestrated propaganda exercise, only a handful of international correspondents succeeded in penetrating the war zone. In the wake of the Edwards accusations, however, Stephen Glover of London's *Daily Telegraph* became the first foreign journalist granted access not only to Buffalo Base on 26 February, but also to a platoon tracking SWAPO guerrillas who had attacked a South African base two weeks before.

In an article published shortly afterwards, Glover portrayed the situation in both a balanced and an accurate manner, arriving at the following conclusion:

It is easy to see why the South African government wished to keep quiet the existence of this crack unit, although it still vehemently denies that they are mercenaries. Either way, it goes without saying that the credulousness of many of those who believe the stories of atrocities in respect of 32 Battalion is proportionate to their hatred of South Africa. If the war is to be resolved not only in the bush but in the editorial columns of international newspapers, then South Africa may have made a mistake in giving life to 32 Battalion.

Military correspondents from South African newspapers were also introduced to the unit for the first time, and reported that Edwards was not only a drunk and a troublemaker who had been the subject of repeated disciplinary action, but that along with all other soldiers in the Operational Area, he had been required to sign a special undertaking that no brutalities would be committed against 'innocent civilians'. In light of Edwards's claim that he had deserted and run to the media because he could 'no longer stand the killing of defenceless Angolans', an angry Deon Ferreira told reporters he wanted Edwards back, so that he could be tried for murder 'if he has one shred of evidence to prove his accusations'.

Far less widely reported was an attempt by the MPLA government to cash in on the Edwards affair, which backfired when another deserter, Rifleman José Ricardo Belmundo, failed to confirm any allegations of atrocities.

Belmundo had gone AWOL before Edwards, but he was officially listed as dead, based on reports from some of his friends about an incident in Rundu. In fact, he had crossed into Angola at Calai and handed himself over to FAPLA, and when the Edwards storm broke, he was paraded at a media conference in Luanda as a witness to 'the crimes of the racist and apartheid regime of South Africa'.

According to the official 13-page record of his media debut, obtained by the author from the Angolan authorities in 2002, Belmundo appeared as he had before the Commission of Inquiry, wearing his South African Army uniform with buffalo insignia. It was explained by Lieutenant Colonel Ngongo, FAPLA Intelligence and Reconnaissance Division, that in view of the recent revelations by British mercenary Trevor Edwards, the Angolan authorities had decided it was an opportune moment to present Belmundo to the press and public. Belmundo, an FNLA member up to 1975 and subsequently a captain in 32 Battalion, had 'surrendered to the Angolan people'.

Sporting three miniature buffalo heads rather than the customary SADF captain's insignia of three stars, Belmundo happily supported claims that 32 Battalion was home to mercenaries, was an ally of UNITA and was actively deployed inside Angola, and that he had been promoted through the ranks to captain. However, he could not confirm a single accusation of atrocities or brutal treatment of civilians. As for his elevated rank, the reality is that no black Portuguese troop was commissioned as an officer until 1986.

The footnote to the Edwards debacle was eventually written when an American television crew was allowed to spend time with 32 Battalion both in the base and in the field at the end of April – but the glare of adverse publicity that had exposed the unit's existence resulted in all future operations being clouded by suspicion, and caused administrative headaches that would plague commanding officers for as long as the unit existed.

With the need for utmost secrecy removed, troops were allowed to spend their annual leave outside the perimeters of Buffalo Base for the first time. This had a dramatic effect on both the tally of soldiers who went AWOL and the number of dependants who moved into the kimbo. Unmarried troops returned from leave with women whose ethnic origins were anathema to the traditional Angolan clans, and friction among the kimbo residents increased. From 1981 onwards it was never possible to determine exactly how many civilian dependants 32 Battalion was taking care of, as every time Sergeant Major Carl Roza tried to carry out a census, the illegal residents simply hid in the bush until the count was over.

The first families had already moved into their newly built quarters, laid out in squares of eight units each with a communal ablution block in the middle. The houses were small, many consisting of only three rooms, and at the request of the occupants a special agreement was reached by which the contractor would add a kitchen at an additional cost of R500, to be paid by the troops themselves. However, the quality of the work was well below standard, and the contractor left the site with much of it unfinished. In due course, this would become a serious bone of contention within the unit, as the majority of those concerned had paid for their kitchens in advance.

With the Rhodesian bush war over, 1982 saw a major influx of white foreigners of various nationalities into the SADF. Most were assigned to Military Intelligence, but as soon as they learned of the existence of 32 Battalion's reconnaissance group, they clamoured to be transferred to what was still the SADF's most unconventional unit. In February a group of 29 volunteers, ranging in rank from lance corporal to lieutenant, and in nationality from American (Lieutenant Verduin) and Puerto Rican (Corporal Nelson Fishbach) to Israeli (Corporal Karu) and New Zealander (Sergeant Major Phill Kearns), arrived to start their training.

A diary kept by Fishbach, the Puerto Rican, describes their introduction to 32 as follows:

18 February 1982 – Today we left for SWA. We arrived in Rundu where the headquarters of 32 Battalion Buffalo Regiment is located. There, we received some of our kit and my AK47 and left at 17h00 for Omauni, where the 32 Bn recce base is located, a 250 km journey to a base that is only 16 km from Angola. We arrived at 21h30 and all the base personnel were afraid of us because they received such bad reports on us that they thought we were going to tear the place apart. What they didn't know was that we were as afraid as they were.

19 February 1982 – Today we put our tents up, cleaned our AK47s and were divided into groups. They showed us the base: 100 m × 100 m with a 50 Cal. And 30 Cal. Heavy machine-guns on the walls, bunkers all around the perimeter walls with openings to shoot out, mortar pits at different places in the base. We also have a big pink pig with 10 little ones of the same colour. A donkey, geese, two dogs (one a Basset hound) and a monkey that always rides on the big dog's back or hangs from his neck and gets into everything. The latrines are divided for blacks and whites. Mess hall also divided. Underground 'pub' with lots of plaques on the walls of the former members of the unit that served and left, and also a real skull of a SWAPO terrorist still with dry gum between its teeth. Green beret on and a collar of 50 Cal rounds belt. This skull or head was brought back from operation Protea in Aug 81.

What a first impression! The skull was indeed that of a SWAPO guerrilla, shot dead by a member of the Home Guard during the attempted abduction of a local headman, Silas, and which served as a macabre reminder to everyone frequenting the bar that the enemy was never far away.

The battalion had now been in existence, albeit in various guises, for six years, and although a number of SADF members had moved on, the unique character of 32 had forged bonds that they had no wish to break. Jan Breytenbach had been more than vindicated: it was indeed possible to merge disparate groups whose loyalty was first and foremost to their unit rather than any cause or country. Early in 1982, former members of the leader group established the 32 Battalion Association, which never lacked support, and in later years operated from its own building in Voortrekkerhoogte – now Thaba Tshwane – home of the military in Pretoria.

At Buffalo, the close proximity in which raw recruits and battle-hardened soldiers lived proved highly unsatisfactory, and on 9 March Lieutenant Groenie Groenewald set up the Nova de Marco facility, where trainees would live while learning the skills they would need to survive a war that showed every sign of escalating into a full-scale conventional confrontation.

On 13 March, 32 Battalion found itself in the media spotlight once more, but this time it was due to the spectacular success of the aptly named *Operation Super* (see Chapter 8), which left 201 SWAPO – and three members of the battalion – dead, and totally destroyed a guerrilla base 22 km inside Angola. Tons of Soviet-made equipment, much of it still in crates, was captured or destroyed as well.

Lieutenant Peter Waugh, a trained cavalry officer, had joined the unit in January, and by 1 April had made a case for adding an equestrian wing to the recce group in order to achieve a swifter response time in support of Project Spiderweb, which drew the local population into reporting SWAPO infiltration through the Kavango province.

During April the first companies finally moved into their newly built quarters, complete with full ablution facilities, hot running water and electricity. The company stores, too, could at last be managed properly.

On 12 May a message was received that tribal headmen from the entire area around the base were on their way to Omauni to retrieve their cattle, claiming ownership of half the herd that had been at the base since 1977. The two members assigned to look after the livestock vehemently denied this, insisting that all 52 cattle had come from the herd originally brought out of Angola with the FNLA families.

On the morning of 15 May, the headmen duly arrived, some from as far afield as Elundu, 150 km away. Civilian affairs officers and Commandant Ferreira were also present, and with all the cattle herded into a kraal, the headmen began selecting animals which they swore had gone missing as far back as 1977. None of the animals bore an identifying brand, and it was evident that the headmen had no way of proving ownership, but for the sake of peaceful coexistence and the underlying hearts-and-minds doctrine of wooing the local population, Ferreira allowed the headmen to leave with 42 head of cattle. The mystery of where those cattle actually came from was never solved.

When the Chief:SADF decided to return black veterans of the Rhodesian bush war to the various SADF units that had originally recruited them, a group of 37 who had been absorbed by Military Intelligence was left in limbo, with no unit they could rejoin. On 30 November, Commandant Viljoen was authorised to add these 'orphans' – complete with brand new AK47s, RPD machine guns and RPG 7 rocket launchers – to the recce group at Omauni.

The group included former Selous Scouts and paratroopers, but the majority had served in the Rhodesian African Rifles. From day one they had difficulty accepting the strict discipline and routine of the recce group, arrogantly insisting that they were already well trained, and far from having to learn anything from the South Africans, could probably teach them a thing or two. Willem Ratte, by now a captain, not only proved them wrong, but probably took some pleasure in showing them that their previous experience left room for a great deal of training. After their first operation with the recce group, 36 of the former Rhodesians resigned and quit the army. Only Rifleman O Mfumu stayed on as the group's Morse Code signaller.

Negotiations began for the South African Defence Force Institute (SADFI) to take over the unit shop in the kimbo, the sole source of funds for use exclusively by 32 Battalion. A compromise was reached whereby SADFI would manage the shop, but the sale of all cigarettes and alcohol would remain in the hands of the unit. Not only would this ensure continued contributions to the unit fund, but it would allow better control over the sale of alcohol, which was strictly controlled and limited to a few beers a day per family.

The unit funds were used to provide non-essential facilities, such as the community hall, on which construction began during the year.

The era of the Falcon ended on 31 December, and Ferreira was replaced as

Officer Commanding by his former second-in-command, Commandant Eddie Viljoen. The Chief of the Army had issued a directive that the unit's logistical and financial affairs were to be a priority, and Viljoen introduced Project Logfin, headed by logistical officer Major Jan van der Vyver, to deal with the problem.

The new SADFI shop opened in early 1983 as planned, offering a far greater range of products than the little unit shop had been able to supply. Some of the soldiers' wives even found employment as cashiers, creating a number of two-income families for the first time.

The community hall was opened on 26 March by Deon Ferreira, by then a colonel and Officer Commanding Sector 20 of the Operational Area. It was used for numerous activities, a regular disco being one of the most popular.

By now, the unit had been in existence long enough for members to start hankering after traditions. Except for the cemetery south of the kimbo, there was no shrine within the base at which tribute could be paid to those who had given their lives. Commandant Viljoen's suggestion that plaques bearing the names of all the fallen be mounted on a Tree of Honour near the Palácio Regimental found great favour.

Among the most important visitors to the base during 1983 were members of the State Security Council, who were thoroughly briefed by Viljoen about the unit's functions and operational tactics, and they left with an extremely positive attitude towards 32 Battalion. Perhaps they were assessing the unit's ability to join forces with UNITA in the conventional battles against FAPLA that were surely coming.

Operations inside Angola were directed from a tactical headquarters at the Ongiva airfield, staffed by 32 Battalion personnel when needed. The tactical HQ commanders rotated every two to three months, and were incapable of grasping 32's unique operational strategy, which inevitably gave rise to clashes between the company and HQ commanders. Viljoen was authorised to establish a 32 Battalion tactical HQ at Ionde, and the task fell to his second-in-command, Major Boela Niemand. The HQ was operational by the end of March, and was named Fort Boela in his honour.

As the war dragged on, individual members of the inaugural Citizen Force leader groups had returned to the unit periodically to serve their compulsory three-month camps. Early in 1983, Viljoen succeeded in having all those who had served with 32 since inception placed in a 'pool', so that he could rely on receiving men who had already proved their mettle. The first group of seven reported for duty between 4 May and 1 July, and were assigned to the rifle companies for deployment during *Operation Snoek* (see Chapter 9). They had not lost their soldier's instincts back in civilian life, and made a useful contribution during operations, but had a hard time adapting to the introduction of formal military rules and regulations. Since January, as part of the long-term plan to fully integrate

32 into the SADF, much had changed, and 'old-timers' did not always take well to the less casual conditions. In a debriefing report, the mid-year intake noted especially that it was 'not nice' that separate bars had been set up for ranking and non-ranking officers, and said they missed the original all-ranks facility. Since it seems extremely unlikely that these men were never exposed to any other military unit, they ought to have been familiar with the universal non-fraternisation rule. One can but surmise that for some, at least, one of the great attractions of 32 in the early years was the very lack of strict but standard military procedures. Perhaps they had hoped that the unconventional practices, born of necessity, would remain in force for ever more.

The unit's intelligence capability suffered a severe blow on 28 June with the cancellation of Project Spiderweb, introduced in 1981 by Willem Ratte in far-eastern Owamboland. It had proved an enormous success, as can be seen in Chapter 8, but the high command had spoken, and with the exception of Ohikik, detached troops were withdrawn from all the strong points, leaving the area south of the Chandelier road open to SWAPO once again.

Of the white leader group of former Rhodesians who had arrived in 1981, only Sergeant Major Phill Kearns of New Zealand, Sergeant KD Clark (American), Corporal Terry Kotze (Zimbabwean) and Corporal Dave Gardener, another 'Kiwi', were still around, having enlisted for another year in mid-1982. On 1 August 1983, a signal from headquarters informed Kearns that the newly elected left-wing government in New Zealand had severed all diplomatic ties with South Africa, and that unless he and his countrymen returned home within two weeks, their citizenship would be revoked. Gardener promptly heeded the call, but Kearns refused, staying with 32 for the remaining six months of his contract.

Amid the earnest business of waging war, soldiers will always find time for a little light relief, and it was no different for the men of 32. Since Eddie Viljoen – then still a major – had joined the unit in 1976, it had become a tradition that newcomers and selected visitors were made the butt of practical jokes. In August, it was the turn of Staff Sergeant Bancroft, the newly appointed personnel officer. On a routine visit to Omauni, he found himself in the middle of an ambush as he approached the entrance to the base.

With no inkling that this was a mock attack, albeit with carefully controlled real explosives, the hapless desk jockey was scared out of his wits, and insisted on completing his administrative tasks as soon as possible so that he could return to the relative safety of Rundu before the day was out. The punchline was a signal from Captain Ratte to Colonel Viljoen, recommending that Bancroft should receive a medal. Viljoen played along beautifully, sending an answering signal that claimed: 'On returning yesterday, the very dusty member's words were: "War is hell".'

On 8 September, the SADF's Quartermaster General finally granted authority for 32 Battalion to purchase its own colours – a major step towards creating the unique identity that is the pride of any military unit. It had taken six years, but the Buffalo Soldiers were about to be acknowledged as bona fide members of the South African Defence Force.

Sadly, the year ended on a tragic note when Major van der Walt, a founder member, was killed, and his wife and children injured in an accident on Christmas Day while driving to Rundu.

The SADF's covert support for the FNLA had always been a double-edged sword. By supplying the Angolans with the means to fight their communist-backed enemies, South Africa could take its own war on terrorism into areas that would otherwise have been immune to its influence. But by 1984, the conflict wracking most of southern Africa loomed so large on the international geopolitical agenda that the rules were about to change dramatically.

Since 1980, South Africa had launched several major operations against SWAPO bases in Angola. By 1983, a proposal was on the table for complete withdrawal of all SADF forces from Angola in return for a guarantee from President José Eduardo dos Santos (who had succeeded Neto when he died in 1979) that the areas vacated would not be filled by Cuban or SWAPO troops. The signing of the Lusaka Agreement in 1984 finalised the deal, which would be overseen by a Joint Monitoring Commission (JMC). All SADF troops were to be out of Angola by 1985.

With its operational area at the heart of the dispute, 32 Battalion found itself in the invidious position of having to operate side by side with the very enemy most of its members had been fighting since 1973. The years of hard work invested in turning a ragged FNLA mob into a highly disciplined army had more than paid dividends. Had it not been for the military professionalism they had assimilated, the JMC would have been a disaster from the start. As it was, the difference between the performance of 32 Battalion and that of FAPLA was undeniable.

Because of the size to which the unit had grown, the post of Officer Commanding had been upgraded to that of colonel, which brought Viljoen a well-earned promotion. In April 1984, the unit's ceremonial dress, including the black and white stable belt, was officially approved – but just as 32 was poised to claim the just rewards of its hard-won battle honours, politics began chipping away at its infrastructure.

The tactical headquarters at Ionde was the first casualty, with evacuation of Fort Boela starting on 18 March. Two days later, all equipment had been moved back to Buffalo Base. The buildings and a limited amount of supplies were handed over to UNITA.

The 32 'recce wing' had never fitted into the accepted infantry battalion matrix, and now orders were issued to disband it. Since this coincided with the establishment of a Special Forces component for the restructured South West African Territorial Force, the members were given the choice of joining SWATF or returning to Buffalo Base. Only six white members opted to stay on, and on 9 May the Omauni base was formally handed over to SWATF's new Special Forces – including Captain Ratte.

Within just a few months, the realisation had sunk in that depriving 32 of its own intelligence wing was a huge mistake, and Major Peter Waugh was recalled to rectify the situation. By 12 November the 'recce unit' was back in business, but this time members were detached to each company rather than operating as a separate entity.

As always in a military situation, 1984 found death on active duty. One of 32's founding members, Sergeant Major Carl Roza, was buried with full honours in Pretoria on 9 April. Three kimbo residents were killed and another 61 wounded when a social event turned into a tragedy. The community had made good use of the hall opened the year before, and a regular disco was one of the most popular activities. At 23h30 on 14 July, while the disco was in full swing, someone threw two high explosive hand grenades into the packed hall. Those responsible were never found, but the general belief was that they must have been covert SWAPO or FAPLA infiltrators. The senseless attack and fatalities served only to strengthen the resolve of 32 members against their sworn enemies.

If 1984 had placed undue demands on the men involved in the JMC, 1985 would offer more than enough reason for their chests to swell with pride. At an official parade on 27 August, 32 Battalion became the first SA Army unit to be presented with its colours in an Operational Area. The flags and banners that would be displayed on all future ceremonial occasions arrived soon afterwards.

Among those on hand to salute the unit for the first time were rookies whose training had begun in mid-1984. Although the average strength of a three-platoon company was 90 instead of the usual 140 men, it was decided to reactivate Hotel Company, disbanded in 1979, and staff it with the unblooded troops. It took only one operational deployment to show what the old hands already knew – the best chance of success in the field lay in a combination of youth and experience. Hotel Company was disbanded – again – at the end of August, and the members were assigned to the other companies.

On 12 September a freak accident claimed the life of Major van der Vyver, the logistics officer. While supervising the loading of a C130 for a night re-supply drop to troops deployed at Mavinga, he inexplicably ran straight into the aircraft's spinning propeller, dying instantly.

A definite high point of the year was the opening of the Forte Club on 15 June. Because 32 Battalion headquarters was situated inside the Sector 20 military base, all facilities were shared. This had led to numerous altercations in the bar, and Colonel Viljoen had finally ordered that 32 should get its own facility, built under the supervision of Sergeant Major Carl Kolbe. Visitors to the unit during the year included a group of American opinion-formers – probably gathering ammunition to whip up support for UNITA when they returned home – and members of the SADF's Generals and Admirals Club. But however pleasant the 1985 social calendar was, it was merely a scene-setter for the celebrations that would mark 32 Battalion's tenth birthday.

Festivities over the weekend of 27 March 1986 began with a unique trooping of the colour. Not only was this the first time 32 Battalion's colours had gone on public display, it was the first parade of its kind ever held in the Operational Area and the first time UNITA officers, led by deputy commander Brigadier Nzau Puna, had attended an SADF event in full military regalia. It was one of the battalion's proudest moments, and included the commissioning of the first black Angolan candidate officers by Lieutenant General Ian Gleeson, the SADF's Chief of Staff. The nine men who left the parade ground with elevated rank that day were second lieutenants AJ Andre, J Appolinario, D Augusto, DA Correia, D Da Sousa, TT de Abreu, J Germano, M Kanganjo and D Stephanie.

The rest of the weekend was filled with sport and family events, the highlight being a boxing tournament umpired by Piet Crous, the 1984 World Boxing Association cruiserweight champion.

But even as the toasts were drunk and congratulations handed out, the battalion was getting ready to go to war on an unprecedented scale. The visits by the State Security Council and the influential Americans had been followed by preparations for what could only be a major conventional offensive. The build-up continued throughout 1986, with 32 Battalion expanding to include a squadron of Ratel 90 anti-tank armoured cars, an anti-aircraft troop of 20-mm guns mounted on Ystervark (porcupine) vehicles, and an artillery troop of Valkiri Multiple Rocket Launchers (MRLs).

Developed in record time by Armscor engineers, the Valkiri was South Africa's answer to the dreaded Stalin Organ. The 24 vehicle-mounted tubes could rain down 127-mm rockets each weighing 60 kg at a rate of one per second, over a range of more than 20 km. For the first time, the Buffalo Soldiers would have a highly effective antidote to the Russian-made 'Red Eye' they had come to hate.

With the hardware came the more than 200 personnel who made up what became known as the Support Group, headed by Permanent Force senior leaders and National Servicemen as junior leaders. For the first time, white conscripts and black Angolans would fight side by side under the banner of 32 Battalion.

The Support Group moved into their newly constructed accommodation next to the Echo Company lines in August, with additional personnel arriving throughout the year, along with more logistical vehicles than 32 Battalion had ever seen! Technical support became a full-time requirement, and Commandant Jan Griessel, the senior technical officer, was transferred to manage the light workshop troop. Although the new weapons had been tested extensively during military exercises, this was the first time they would be deployed operationally. Not unexpectedly, various teething problems occurred, but these were swiftly rectified by Armscor engineers assigned to the task.

Armscor experts also arrived in May, along with paint specialists from Plascon, to design special camouflage for the vehicles and weapons systems. Because it would be deployed deep inside Angola, the hardware had to be invisible from the air, and traditional camouflage patterns were not ideally suited to the terrain.

Within the unit, it was an open secret that the massive build-up was aimed at providing support for UNITA, and that this would be no series of guerrilla skirmishes, but a major conventional war. Since 8 February, members of the reconnaissance teams had been withdrawn from their respective rifle companies to once again serve as a team under Major Waugh, specifically tasked to monitor both UNITA and FAPLA operations in the third and sixth regions – an area stretching from the South West African border to 100 km north of Mavinga, and from the Zambian border to 150 km west of Menongue. When necessary, 155-mm G5 field guns were attached to units from 61 Mechanised Battalion and 4 SA Infantry Battalion, proving their superiority over anything the enemy could roll out, particularly during operations *Southern Cross* and *Alpha Centauri* (see Chapter 10).

The threat of air attack dictated that a guided ground-to-air missile system be added to 32's 14,5-mm and 20-mm anti-aircraft guns, and an SA 7 anti-aircraft missile system was added to the Support Group. From 4 June to 4 July, an SA 9 anti-aircraft missile system was also brought in, and although full training on the system was given it was never deployed with 32, though it was later used by Special Forces.

Amid the serious business of preparing for war, no one lost sight of the 'important' issues, and on 21 June, 32's inaugural RSM, Sergeant Major Pep van Zyl, officially opened the Shuva Club, a bar for the junior NCOs. As the year drew to a close, construction began on a new transport park for the fleet of vehicles that seemed to increase daily, and Colonel Viljoen took his leave of the battalion, having been transferred to Sector 10. The new year would see a new commander, Colonel Jock Harris, at the helm.

Harris had a rather more relaxed style of command than his predecessors, and among the early signs that 32 Battalion was entering a new era were two decisions that proved extremely popular, but were fraught with hidden problems. The first was the abolition of controls over the amount of alcohol individuals could buy. With access to liquor unlimited for the first time in the unit's history, alcohol abuse – and all its accompanying evils – soared.

In April, Harris granted authority for soldiers to bring civilian vehicles onto the base. Parking was provided close to the main gate, and vehicles remained barred from the kimbo. The problem was that few of the Angolan troops had any driving experience, let alone licences, and the 250-km road between Buffalo and Rundu became a death trap, with numerous accidents and dozens of fatalities.

A major concern arose when intelligence reports from Windhoek indicated that some of the Portuguese members of the unit were clandestinely recruiting Angolans to desert and go home. The former FNLA leader Daniel Chipenda had become an MPLA government collaborator, and it was thought that he might be trying to rebuild his personal power base. But although the reports were investigated, no proof of the claims was found.

In 1987, the SADF had a severely limited anti-tank missile capability in the form of the Milan system, so it came as a pleasant surprise that 32 was the first unit to receive the new-generation ZT3 system – the first four Ratel infantry combat vehicles equipped with 127-mm anti-tank missiles, developed under the code-name Project Mongol and delivered to the unit on 19 February. Towards the end of the SADF's involvement in the Angolan war, the system would be used to great effect during operations *Hooper* and *Packer*.

By March there could no longer be any doubt that 32 Battalion was destined for deployment with UNITA in the Mavinga area. On 10 March, *Operation Castillo* was launched to test the battalion's combat readiness and commit a battle plan to paper. From this date on, equipment of every description was shipped into Buffalo daily.

For some months past it had been obvious that the source of new recruits in the immediate vicinity had been exhausted. Any further enlistments would have to come from within the ranks of UNITA, but this was never authorised, and the diminishing numbers led to disbandment of Alpha Company on 31 March, with members being reassigned to bring the remaining companies – some of which were operating with as few as 75 men – up to full strength. All available manpower was needed, as from January the unit was involved on virtually a full-time basis in operations in and around Cuito Cuanavale.

In late September, 32 received an unexpected bonus in the form of a rebel leader from the tiny island of São Tomé, a largely forgotten casualty of communist expansion in Africa. In January 1985, a group of ten former politicians from the island had travelled from Portugal to Gabão and launched a movement against the communist regime in São Tomé e Principe. Six months later, they led a group of 100 former islanders to Cameroon, from where they intended waging their armed struggle.

However, the São Tomé government learned of their plans and placed enormous pressure on Cameroon to evict them. On 9 April 1986, 76 of the rebels set sail for

Walvis Bay in a 17-m fishing boat, arriving 21 days later and approaching the South African authorities for support and assistance in pursuit of their goal. They were detained at the Rooikop military base while waiting for their leaders to arrive from Portugal, but when they failed to do so, the detainees were declared illegal immigrants and sent to prison on 12 March 1987. Eventually, one of the leaders did arrive in South Africa and entered into negotiations for the release of his men.

It was he who turned up at Buffalo Base in late September, offering the services of his followers, who were not only native Portuguese speakers, but had no family encumbrances. He left the Caprivi to continue negotiating with the South African authorities at Walvis Bay, and although it would take another six months, eventually succeeded in having the group released. In May 1988, 53 of them returned to Buffalo to undergo military training. The remaining 21 returned to São Tomé.

In many ways, 1987 had been a year of change for 32 Battalion, and there was one more to come. After just 12 months as Officer Commanding, Colonel Harris was to be replaced by Colonel Mucho Delport.

When Delport and the new RSM, WO1 Tallies Botha, arrived in January, it was to a virtually deserted base, with every available member operationally deployed. By 15 July this was still the case, with troops as far afield as the Cunene province, where three companies – Bravo, Charlie and Golf – were actively involved in the last Joint Monitoring Commission set up prior to Namibia becoming independent.

On 8 August, with all the pieces of the political puzzle finally in place and independence for South West Africa just 18 months away, a ceasefire was declared, and to all intents 32 Battalion's war was over.

By the beginning of December the unit had reverted to its original structure of infantry companies, and the Support Group had returned to South Africa. The Forte Club was officially handed over to 320 Forward Air Control, since 32 Battalion headquarters was moving to new premises on the northern side of the Rundu base, and the unit was split into two operational groups, with Colonel Delport the commander-in-chief.

Operational Group 1, under command of Major Louis Scheepers, consisted of Delta Company (under command of Lieutenant Villiers de Vos), Echo Company (under command of Lieutenant Wouter de Vos) and Foxtrot Company (under command of Captain Wally Vrey).

Operational Group 2 was commanded by Major Phillip le Roux and comprised Bravo Company (under command of Captain Keith Evans), Charlie Company (under command of Captain Jo Maree) and Golf Company (under command of Captain William Schickerling).

Even though the word had been out since August that 32 Battalion would not be calling Buffalo Base 'home' for very much longer, the year-old town council that now ran affairs in the kimbo decided to formally honour the man who had started it all by officially naming the settlement Vila Breytenbach. But the writing was on the wall. The unit was to be relocated to Pomfret, an abandoned asbestos mining town in the barren Northern Cape, and by May 1989 footprints in the sand would be the only testimony to 32 Battalion's 12-year sojourn in the Caprivi.

4

The way of Buffalo

TRAINING AND LEADERSHIP

FROM THE OUTSET, training was a priority for the unit, even though in its earliest form it was informal, on a strict need-to-know basis and specifically designed to prepare Battle Group Bravo for *Operation Savannah*. From 1976, the training programme became steadily more regimented and aimed at raising the level of expertise among the former FNLA fighters to that of the regular SADF.

Circumstances dictated that training take place on a decentralised basis at Savate, in and around Mpupa and north of Dirico, while Dodge City – later renamed Chetto – was used to train pseudo-operators, though not for sustained periods. At Buffalo the training area lay some 24 km east of the main base and stretched as far as the Botswana border. In addition to combat training, instruction was also given to medical orderlies, chefs, drivers and administrative staff.

By the end of 1982, 300 fresh troops were needed to bring the unit up to full strength, and Sergeant Major Carl Roza, the chief clerk, was given the task of finding suitable recruits among the civilians living in and around Rundu. Because of the unique nature of 32's work, no existing military doctrine covered the requirements, and after much deliberation the following criteria were applied, which remained valid until the very last intake of recruits:

- Age: Between 18 and 23.
- Physical fitness: Must be able to run a 2,4-km time test in 15 minutes, do 20 push-ups and 40 sit-ups without interruption.
- Literacy: Must be able to read, write and speak Portuguese.
- Must have an identity document.
- Must have at least a grade 6 school qualification.

The educational requirement was very often judged on merit, as the majority of recruits originally came from Angola, where they had not had access to any normal schooling since 1975.

On the first day of recruitment at Rundu, more than 500 willing candidates turned up. Even after those who fell outside the age requirements had been weeded out, some 400 remained, divided into three distinct groups: the peasants, barefoot and clad in shorts and T-shirts; the fashion-conscious, wearing the high-heeled shoes and bell-bottom pants so popular at the time, along with colourful Kavango shirts and dark glasses; and the intellectuals, neatly dressed in suits and toting suitcases with extra clothing.

For the running test, candidates were allowed to remove only their shoes, and surprisingly, some of those who shed 10-cm heels covered the distance in a mere nine minutes. The physical selection did little to reduce the numbers, and a group of 380 were told by a Portuguese instructor that this was their last chance to accept the following conditions: on successful completion of a seven-month training cycle, recruits would be enrolled as members of the SADF. While in training they would have no holidays or leave and would not be paid, but would be provided with food and clothing. On completion of training, recruits would be given seven days' leave, and their first salaries would be paid one month after officially joining the SADF. Military apparel would be worn at all times during training, and civilian clothes would only be returned to recruits at the end of the seven-month period.

Not even these harsh conditions were enough to dissuade large numbers of candidates, and Sergeant Major Roza returned to Buffalo with 360 hopeful rookies in tow.

The training curriculum, based on normal infantry principles, comprised the following:

- Week 1: Physical and mental induction, including running, marching and up to 48 hours' sleep deprivation.
- Week 2–16: Basic training and introduction to military discipline, rank structure, rules and regulations, drills, musketry, bushcraft and fieldcraft, buddy aid (first aid), map reading, signals (radio).
- Week 17–19: Platoon weapon training on 7,62-mm GPMG (LMG), later the SS 77 60-mm patrol mortar; M79 (later the 40-mm MGL) RPG 7 rocket launcher; hand grenades; pyrotechnics; Claymore mine. The emphasis was on practical and tactical use. Not for these recruits the luxury of expending hundreds of rounds on the shooting range. Once they had mastered the basics, small groups with loaded weapons would move out in an extended line, and on a signal from the instructor, empty their weapons at a designated target. It was imperative that operational use of their weapons become second

nature from the start, and by conclusion of this phase each recruit would have shot at least 10 000 rounds of light machine-gun ammunition, between 20 and 30 RPG 7 grenades, and have tossed at least 20 M26 hand grenades.

- Week 20–25: Section, platoon and company battle drills, with emphasis on practical firing, movement and tactics. After four or five dry runs, all drills included live ammunition. By the end of the period, recruits would have taken part in at least 50 section or platoon attacks.
- Week 26–30: Counter insurgency (COIN), including patrol tactics and formations, obstacle crossing, temporary bases, ambushes, vehicle movement and drills, immediate action and helicopter drills. For COIN training, recruits moved deeper into the bush, operating from a temporary base under actual conditions they would encounter before long.

For the seven months of training the daily routine varied little, starting at 04h00 with reveille and cleaning of the base. Inspection was followed by three hours of drills, brunch and another five hours of instruction, with an hour of physical training – which might include a 20-km run – to end the working day. After supper, from 18h00 to 19h00, recruits had three hours to themselves before lights out at 22h00. On Saturdays and public holidays, training ended at noon, with the rest of the day being spent on maintenance of the base and surrounding area. There was no training on Sundays, when church services were held as far as possible and afternoons were set aside for laundry and other personal chores.

Because they were all volunteers, recruits could withdraw from the programme at any time, but over all the years of 32's existence, only 25 did so. At least some of their tenacity can be attributed to the strong motivation offered by the instructors, normally sergeants who had served in the FNLA and been with 32 from the start, and who never missed an opportunity to impart to the recruits the history of both the war and the unit, along with stirring tales of the adventures and victories of those who had paved the way for the newest generation of fighting men.

Discipline was strictly enforced, and any infraction during training earned a recruit a once-only warning. Repeat offenders were summarily discharged, but this happened surprisingly seldom. During 32's lifespan there were four intakes, the last in 1985, by which time it was all but impossible to find enough Portuguese-speaking recruits to fill the ranks, and the unit was forced to revert to English as its chief language. This opened the door for members of various South West African ethnic groups to join 32 as well, and in 1985, 18 recruits were also drawn from the kimbo at Buffalo Base – the sons of fathers who had been with the unit since 1976 and were now old enough to follow in their footsteps. Having grown up in a military environment, these youngsters were excellent candidates and rapidly became NCOs.

The high point for the recruits was the passing-out parade, when they returned to Buffalo Base for the first time in seven months and were issued with their equipment and berets before being assigned to the various rifle companies.

The 1982 intake started training in February under the watchful eyes of sergeants Appolinario, Fermino, Mussole and Amorim. Lieutenant Groenie Groenewald was placed in overall charge of the training by Commandant Deon Ferreira, whose sole guideline was: 'You are responsible for training the recruits.'

Initially housed in tents adjacent to the company lines, the recruits spent what little free time they had socialising with the old hands, sharing their liquor and enraptured by their war stories. Groenewald soon recognised that this fraternisation could lead to serious disciplinary problems, and had the recruits move their tents some distance away. But the socialising continued, and on the morning of 9 March, after a particularly raucous weekend, Groenewald issued orders for all the recruits to pack their gear and move to Lekkerhoekie, a section of the training terrain east of the base. Since there was no transport they had to move on foot, carrying all their equipment, including the metal trunks in which they stored their possessions.

Groenewald and Sergeant Appolinario went ahead on a motorcycle to scout out a suitable location for a new camp. While debating the merits of possible sites under a big tree on the edge of the Kavango River floodplain, halfway between Lekkerhoekie and Kelly's Triangle, the first recruits made their appearance in the distance. Groenewald and Appolinario realised that they had to make up their minds fast, or the recruits would realise that they didn't actually have a plan in place.

Appolinario suggested that they establish the base right where they were, but Groenewald pointed out that the site could be cut off from the only access road during the rainy season. Appolinario countered that the recruits could cut a new road to the north, and the decision was taken just as the first heavily laden recruits reached the tree.

It was a long and tiring day, but by the end of it defensive trenches surrounded the chosen site and a large section of the bush around the tree had been cleared with machetes and spades. Perhaps it was the memory of their 24-km march from Buffalo that morning, completed in less than four hours and carrying full kit, that spurred the recruits to action.

As night fell the instructors gathered round a fire under the big tree to discuss the next day's programme, and decided to name the new base Novo de Marco, the Portuguese for 9 March.

Over the next three months, all 'free time' was spent building the facilities. With no logistical support such as vehicles or additional tools, the work teams went on foot into the bush to cut poles and grass with which to erect huts and bungalows. Only natural materials from the immediate environment were used, though in later years various improvements and sturdier structures were added, and the base remained in use until 1989.

Selection of the leader group was one of the most important facets of 32 Battalion's success. Originally hand-picked from among white Permanent Force (PF) members, it later became necessary to introduce National Servicemen as junior leaders – platoon commanders and sergeants. Black Portuguese members played an important role in the leader group as well, some up to platoon sergeant level, but there were never enough of them to fill all the slots.

National Servicemen had to volunteer to serve in the battalion, and were admitted only after a year of training at the School of Infantry at Oudtshoorn. It was absolutely crucial that the right men be chosen for the job. These newly qualified second lieutenants and corporals would be required to command and lead veterans of the war, some of them with up to ten years of hard guerrilla fighting under their belts, and rank alone would not command their respect or guarantee their cooperation. Personality and the ability to interact with the men were as important as natural leadership abilities when it came to choosing the junior leader group, and the selection process was tough.

Over a five-day period at Buffalo, small groups of volunteers were subjected to rigorous physical and mental testing, and only those who made it through the first 120 hours would qualify for further training. At the first sign of undue stress, candidates were withdrawn from the programme and returned to their original units. Those who made it all the way through were as well prepared for war as any man can ever be.

For the first five days the men were divided into teams of five or six, each team being issued with a medical bag and five cans of food. Each man was given five rounds of ammunition to be used in self-defence against possible enemy or wild animals, and two 81-mm mortar bomb canisters filled with cement, which had to be carried for the entire period, bringing the total weight each man bore for five days to 35 kg.

Over a 24-hour cycle, the junior leaders had to exit the training area on a forced 20-km march against time that would bring them to a point in the bush marked only by a compass bearing. On arrival they would be told the rendezvous point had been moved another five kilometres, and that they had only enough time to reach it if they ran the full distance. If they made it that far, they would be given a ten-minute rest period before being sent off to yet another point, some ten kilometres further, carrying a six-metre telegraph pole per group, and again racing against the clock. The next step was to cross the Kavango River and report to a designated point for food – only to find on arrival that there was no food, just a note ordering them to yet another point. While their instructors sat around a campfire, enjoying a splendid meal, the junior leaders had to await further orders in a temporary base close by, tired, wet and hungry. By 21h00 they would be allowed to sleep – only to be rudely awakened at 03h00 to start the whole routine again!

The training was brutal – but it was designed to save lives. If potential junior leaders could not get through this five-day programme, statistics showed they would survive no more than eight weeks of deployment.

After selection week came cadre training, a week of intensive instruction in basic spoken Portuguese, unit customs and traditions, operational medical assistance – including the insertion of intravenous drips and administering injections – navigational skills, foreign weapons and enemy tactics, vehicle movement and drills, and battle drills. At the end of this week, the junior leaders were assigned to the rifle companies for operational deployment under the supervision of an old hand who was nearing the end of his National Service.

The introduction of the reconnaissance wing ushered in a whole new training era for 32. Instruction was given by Special Forces operators, and members were required to complete certain Special Forces training. The first selection of candidates took place in November 1978, when 45 volunteers – second lieutenants and corporals who had graduated from the School of Infantry – placed their fate in the hands of the RSM, Sergeant Major Pep van Zyl.

Much like the junior leaders, the candidates were divided into four-man groups and issued with a rubber bag containing 25 litres of water and four tins of food – which had to last them five days. They were also given B22 military radios and call sign charts. Before first light the teams were instructed to pack all their equipment into their bigpacks and report to headquarters, where they were blindfolded, loaded onto two trucks and driven into the bush for about 40 minutes.

Just as dawn began to break the trucks stopped, and the teams were each given a map and a compass. Their only instructions were: 'Figure out where you are and report to the designated point within three hours. If you don't make it in time, you can pack your bags and leave.'

They had been dropped west of the Kavango River, close to the Botswana border, and in order to reach the designated point some 20 km away, would have to cross the crocodile-infested river. The entire group of 45 made it in time!

The routine was repeated the next day, with no one being allowed to sleep. The morning of the third day started just outside the main gate at Buffalo, and required a 30-km forced march in the direction of Omega Base. Thinking they could both beat the system and demonstrate initiative, the majority of the group hitched a ride on a civilian truck travelling towards Katima Mulilo – but they had not bargained on the RSM waiting for them halfway along the route!

The 'shortcut' not only resulted in the course being extended by a day, but inspired Pep van Zyl to *really* turn the pressure on.

The next march was back to the Botswana border, and across the Kavango River again. By this time, both the mental and physical strain was starting to show. Water was no problem, but the food had long since been eaten. There was thus great relief on arrival at the next rendezvous point to find the RSM and unit caterer Sergeant Jumbo Tato waiting with five freshly baked loaves of bread and tea for everyone – just as soon as a 60-minute physical training session had been completed.

The enjoyment was short-lived. The bread was studded with foul-tasting anti-malaria tablets and the tea had the distinct flavour of diesel fuel! As anyone who ever trained under him knows only too well, Sergeant Major Pep van Zyl was a man of infinite imagination when it came to toughening up his troops.

Following their 'refreshments', the recruits faced a 25-km stretch to Bagani bridge before turning back to the turn-off to Omega. Brave hearts were broken that day, and by the end of it almost 50 per cent of the group had withdrawn from the course.

The final ordeal, on what was now day six of the course, was a night march from Omega to Buffalo carrying the ubiquitous six-metre telegraph poles. By first light, those who had made it finally qualified for a well-deserved meal, and sleep.

This was the only time recce wing members had to undergo such gruelling selection. Thereafter, only experienced members of the battalion, with at least a year of operational experience, were accepted by the recce wing for specialist training over several weeks, which included minor tactics, bushcraft and survival, signals, advanced field medicine, foreign weapons, demolition, small boats, advanced map reading and reconnaissance tactics.

In 1980, authority was granted for members of the recce wing to undergo parachute training at 1 Parachute Battalion in Bloemfontein, and two years later some members completed a minor tactics course at Special Forces School in the Dukuduku Forest near Mtubatuba, in what is now KwaZulu-Natal.

As the role of air support during attacks on enemy bases became more important, the recce wing had to become proficient in forward air control, and along with some members of the rifle companies received training in this area at Ondangwa in 1983 – the first time a course of this nature was presented in the Operational Area. Later, after resettlement at Pomfret, recce wing members also learned 'hot' extraction techniques and how to abseil out of helicopters. They also acquired the skills of house penetration and clearing.

As the nature of the conflict moved towards a conventional rather than primarily a guerrilla war, the Support Company needed to become more mobile, and both the 106-mm anti-tank guns and the Milan missile system had to be mounted on Unimog vehicles. In 1983, successful tests under the supervision of the School of Infantry's Captain Dawid Lotter, the SADF's anti-tank warfare expert, led to retraining in mobile support.

In 1984, responsibility for all training was assigned to Captain Daan van der Merwe, Lieutenant Leon Myburgh and Sergeant Major Piet Nortje (the author). The following year, Commandant Eddie Viljoen brought training in line with that presented throughout the SADF, and for the first time outside instructors were brought to Buffalo Base to present courses in such diverse disciplines as platoon command, air supply and waitering.

Since so much else about 32 Battalion differed from any other unit within the SADF, especially in the early years, it was hardly surprising that special demands were also made on the successive commanders and RSMs, and that some individuals who might have qualified for such posts in every other way simply lacked the right temperament or attitude for the job. Not only was this a unit in which the primary spoken language was Portuguese rather than Afrikaans or English, it also came with a complete town and community, numbering close on 5 000 souls, to manage. In the midst of a war zone it was not unusual for the OC to play the role of peacemaker between rival families still waging a domestic vendetta dating back to their former lives in Angola, or for the RSM to act as marriage counsellor when the strains of military life took their toll on couples.

In its choice of senior leaders, 32 Battalion was generally fortunate, drawing men with the ability to set aside personal ambition for the sake of the group as a whole, and whose reward lay in the combined success and achievements of the unit rather than individual glory – though a stint with 32 certainly did no harm to their future military careers. Here are brief pen pictures of those who led 32 Battalion from womb to tomb.

OFFICERS COMMANDING
1975–1977: Commandant (later colonel) Jan D Breytenbach, also known as Carpenter or Brown Man. His military career started in the tank corps in 1950. In 1955 he joined Britain's Royal Navy as a navigator and took part in the 1956 Suez campaign. On rejoining the SA Army in 1961 he became a paratrooper, and was a founder member of the South African Special Forces. After leaving 32 Battalion, he went on to found 44 Parachute Brigade and led the airborne assault on Cassinga on 4 May 1978 – the largest operational parachute drop since World War II.

1977–1978: Commandant Gert Nel, on whose shoulders the task fell of consolidating the unit put together by Breytenbach and preparing it for full incorporation into the SADF. His term ended with a transfer to 2 Military Area as commanding officer.

1979–1982: Commandant Deon Ferreira. The mere mention of his call sign – Falcon – on radio intercepts by the enemy was enough to send them into a panic. He revolutionised the unit's operational tactics and obtained official authority for members to deploy deep inside Angola. From June 1982, he served as Officer Commanding Sector 20.

1982–1987: Commandant (later colonel) Eddie Viljoen, Ferreira's second-in-command, had served continuously in the unit from 1976, bar a year during which he attended a staff officer's course. He was given the nickname of 'Fanagalo' by the black troops due to his superb command of the bastardised lingua franca of the goldmines. Among the rest of the members he was known as Big Daddy, but his operational call sign was Echo Victor. Viljoen was instrumental in launching 32 Battalion on the road to full regimental status, and during 1986, with the addition of the Support Group, he became OC of the third largest unit in the SA Army. At the end of that year he was transferred to Oshakati as Senior Staff Officer Operations: Sector 10.

1987: Colonel Jock Harris, who had first become involved with Battle Group Bravo during *Operation Savannah*. He introduced a number of changes to the social structure of the unit, and left to command all the South African forces involved in the final conventional phase of the Angolan war.

1988–1993: Colonel Mucho Delport, whose first responsibility was to prevent the western sector of Angola becoming the conduit for a Cuban invasion of South West Africa. He led the battalion during relocation to Pomfret, and served as OC until 32 Battalion was disbanded in March 1993.

REGIMENTAL SERGEANTS MAJOR

1976–1978: WO1 Pep van Zyl, a legend within the South African military even before his appointment. He was responsible for instilling discipline in the unit, and was closely involved in the building of Buffalo Base and the unit headquarters at Rundu. He went on to become RSM of 1 Reconnaissance Commando in Durban.

1979–1981: WO1 Lars Ueckerman, the first RSM to take part in a major offensive with the unit, namely *Operation Tiro-a-Tiro*, better known as *Savate*. He played a key role in conveying front-line casualties to evacuation points during this operation. At the end of 1981, Sergeant Major Ueckerman accepted a senior post in the South African Medical Service.

1982: WO1 PW van Heerden, former Special Forces, was the first RSM stationed at Buffalo Base, his predecessors having been housed at the Rundu headquarters. A specialist in various fields, he was transferred back to Special Forces after just one year.

1983–1985: WO1 Faan Joubert, former Parachute Battalion, was RSM when the unit was awarded its colours and was in charge of the first SADF colours parade in the Operational Area. He was also responsible for the convoy that took part in the first top secret operation in 1984, *Forte*. On leaving the unit, he was promoted to Brigade Sergeant Major.

1985–1987: The most controversial appointment of an RSM was that of the author, WO2 Piet Nortje. Only 25 years old at the time, he was given a temporary promotion to WO1, which was approved by Major General Georg Meiring, Officer Commanding SWATF, when not one of the ranking sergeants major to whom the post was offered was willing to accept it. Nortje had been with the unit since 1978, spoke Portuguese fluently, had extensive operational experience and, according to his OC, Colonel Viljoen, was the best candidate for the job. In 1986 it fell to him to arrange the trooping of the colour parade for the unit's tenth birthday, and a year later he transferred out of the unit but continued to pursue a military career.

1988–1991: WO1 Tallies Botha barely had time to catch his breath before plunging into action with the unit. Later, it was his task to resettle the unit at Pomfret – a challenge equal to any combat he had seen – before being transferred to the Army Gymnasium.

1992–1993: The last RSM of 32 Battalion was WO1 Tienie Geldenhuys, whose final sad duty was to ensure that the ceremonial disbandment parade went off without a hitch. Thanks to the professionalism of not only Geldenhuys, but those who went before him, it did.

5

I like the trumpet

SYMBOLS AND TRADITIONS

EVEN THOUGH OTHER SADF units and regiments could boast far longer histories and much grander traditions, by August 1976, 32 Battalion was ready to take its place alongside them with pride. Both on the battlefield and in the corridors of power, the unit had fought hard for recognition, and the natural next step was to acquire the symbols of success.

In the military milieu, insignia of rank automatically command respect, but it is the emblems of identity that evoke pride in those who wear them and, in the case of units that have earned the title of 'elite', inspire awe among their peers. The two most visible signs of belonging are the beret badge and shoulder flashes, and Jan Breytenbach was determined that those worn by 32 Battalion would be as distinctive as the unit itself.

At the time, infantry units were denoted by a springbok head pinned to their berets. For 32, a buffalo was chosen, not only in honour of the vast herds of animals that roamed the Caprivi where the unit was formed, but in recognition of the fighting spirit the men of Buffalo Base shared with this fearless and most dangerous of wild animals. The unit motto, too, reflected the raw grit that became synonymous with the battalion: *Proelio Procusi – Forged in Battle*.

All symbols had to be heraldically correct, and while the SA Army division that was responsible for making sure the symbols were correct had no problems with the proposed badge, it took several attempts to finalise a shoulder flash. Designs submitted by unit members ranged from a human skull pierced with a dagger to a broken AK47. Eventually, Commandant Breytenbach instructed Major Pat Tate, who had some artistic talent, to draw a large and unmistakeably rude sign involving a clenched fist. No sooner had the sketch arrived in Pretoria than a furious Major General Constand Viljoen telephoned the unit, telling the unfortunate Major Eddie Viljoen, who happened to take the call, in no uncertain terms what he thought of Breytenbach's irreverent suggestion.

In the end the design came from an employee in the heraldry section, and featured a black background with six silver arrows crossed. The background acknowledged that the majority of unit members were black Angolans, and the arrows represented the six indigenous tribes from which they came – the Ganguela, Kuangali Buskussu, Bacongo, Lunda Chokue, Ovibundo and Kimbundu.

Both badge and shoulder flash were officially approved on 23 March 1977, and the unit was authorised to start wearing the insignia from 30 November.

UNIT COLOUR, BANNERS AND FLAGS

'In the first battle of Bull Run (1861) the raw Confederated troops were rallied under heavy fire by General Joseph Johnstone, the Commander-in-Chief, who stood with the Colour in his hand until the men gathered quickly in rank and file. The Archduke Charles at Aspen (1809) led his young troops to the last assault with a Colour in his hand.'

Ceremonial Manual of the SA Army

The significance of the colour to any fighting unit can never be overestimated. It is the ultimate symbol of pride, the flag around which troops rally both in battle and in victory, the final tangible link between those who live to fight another day and their fallen comrades. For 32, obtaining the much-prized unit colour proved far more difficult than the insignia exercise had been. At the initiative of Colonel Eddie Viljoen, a design was supplied by the Quartermaster General on 8 August 1983, and an insurance company agreed to sponsor the manufacturing costs up to an amount of R3 000. But the colour flag had to be made in London, and as the result of a series of bureaucratic bungles and genuine misunderstandings, by late 1984 no order had been placed with the manufacturers, Toye, Kenning and Spencer, and the original design had somehow been lost. However, on 27 August 1985, 32 Battalion finally became the first SADF unit to receive its colour while serving in the South West Africa Operational Area, when SA Army Chief Lieutenant General Jannie Geldenhuys officially presented the rifle-green colour, fringed with black and gold, with a silver buffalo head and two crossed arrows. On 1 March 1992, battle area distinctions for SWA/Angola, SWA/Zambia and battle distinctions for Eheke, Cassinga/Chetaquera, Mulemba/Molala, Xangongo/Ongiva, Mavinga I, II and III, Cuito Cuanavale and Calueque were added to the colour.

The next step in the identity process was to acquire flags and banners for the various sub-units, and Colonel Viljoen invited company commanders to submit their suggestions by the end of May 1985. The recce group operating out of Omauni was way ahead of him, however, since Captain Eeben Barlow and Staff Sergeant Kevin Sydow had come up with a distinctive design for parachute wings two years before. The design failed to gain heraldic approval, however, and was only ever displayed internally, but those wings became one of the most treasured symbols of service in 32 Battalion. Only members of the recce group who had proved themselves in at least four operations were presented with the wings, which had a nutria background bordered in scarlet, to symbolise the blood shed in battle, and the buffalo head, pierced with a green dagger – the universal Special Forces symbol, depicted in green to indicate the newness of this particular group – superimposed on yellow bat wings, symbolising the fact that the recce group worked almost exclusively under cover of darkness.

When the recce wing was reactivated in 1986, Major Peter Waugh designed a new banner featuring a bat in flight, while Colonel Viljoen and RSM Nortje created a battalion banner with a rifle-green background and the unit badge embroidered on a black shield.

The headquarters banner, designed by Sergeant Major FL Smith, depicted a clenched black fist pierced by a white lightning bolt, and bore the slogan 'We Serve'. When the unit relocated to Pomfret, the headquarters company was replaced by a larger element, the Support Wing, and the banner was redesigned in 1991.

The rifle companies adopted the following banners:

- Alpha: A fish eagle in flight, designed by Lieutenant Leon Myburgh, symbolising this winged inhabitant of the area around Buffalo, poised to attack its 'invisible' prey, the fish in the Kavango River.
- Bravo: A leopard against a red background, designed by Lieutenant Shawn Ward, symbolising readiness to attack at any time, and the blood of fallen comrades.
- Charlie: A rhinoceros against a dark blue background, designed by Captain Frank Kranenberg, symbolising strength.
- Delta: A dragon rampant inside a large D, designed by Sergeant TT de Abreu and Corporal Peter Williams, symbolising inviolability.
- Echo: An elephant head, designed by Captain Neil Walker and Sergeant Dume Stephanie, in recognition of the herds – numbering up to 100 – that wandered through the company lines daily on the way to the river to drink.
- Foxtrot: A lion's head, allegedly designed by Sergeant Dave Yates, but uncannily similar to the one depicted on cans of a well-known brand of beer, symbolising the king of the jungle.
- Golf: A stylised skull and crossbones featuring the unit's crossed arrows and a camouflage beret on the skull, designed by Sergeant Gawie Venter.

- Hotel: A cobra poised to strike, against a sky-blue background, designed by Lieutenant Mac McCallum, symbolising the power of even the newest 'baby'. Unfortunately, due to Hotel Company being disbanded soon after it was formed, no official photograph of this banner exists. When 32 was disbanded, both the banner and the flag mysteriously disappeared, only to emerge in 1993 as those of Delta Company, 7 SA Infantry Battalion, to which a large number of former 32 members had transferred.

The Support Company missed the deadline for submission of designs, and it was not until late 1986 that approval was finally granted for a banner depicting a scorpion, bearing the motto *Agressivos, Rapidos, Potentes, Precisos*. The banners of 321 Infantry Battalion (Operational Group 1) and 322 Infantry Battalion were designed by Commandant Thinus van Staden, and incorporated the existing designs of the companies that served in them.

UNIFORMS

When Jan Breytenbach assumed command of Daniel Chipenda's fighting men in 1975, what passed for uniforms more closely resembled a biblical coat of many colours. Those from the north had green jungle fatigues, but the rest had gone to war in anything from lurid cotton shirts to threadbare vests. Almost all were barefoot.

By the end of *Operation Savannah*, each man had acquired some form of uniform, either from warehouses abandoned by the enemy or 'donated' by prisoners. When Battle Group Bravo moved from Mpupa to Pica Pau in 1976, they were still wearing this motley collection of apparel, and it was not until the end of that year that each member of the unit was issued with at least one set of SADF 'browns' – the standard nutria battledress. Initially, all they received were pants, shirts, web belts and bush hats, but early in 1977 bush jackets and pullovers were added. In April a consignment of old SA Police camouflage uniforms arrived and were used for special operations by the companies that deployed inside Angola. The next batch of camouflage clothing was of the type used by the Portuguese armed forces in Angola, but only 90 sets were available and these were stored at Omauni base for use on covert operations.

A variety of footwear remained in use until late in 1982, with many troops preferring their own over the standard SADF boots with which they were all issued.

When it came to battledress, improvisation was the order of the day. The first bigpack used was a clandestine model scrounged from somewhere deep inside the army stores, after which packs designed for use by Special Forces in the early 1970s, consisting of a bag and wire A-frame, were used until early 1979. A mixture of military and homemade webbing served the purpose. Because of the shape of the AK47 magazine, a special pouch was designed in 1978, but the troops found it to be totally impractical in the bush, and made their own chest webbing, in which the magazines fit snugly. The standard webbing and magazine pouches for the R1 rifle were judged the most comfortable under operational conditions.

The recce wing made use of the widest possible range of uniforms from as early as 1979, including those of FAPLA, the Chinese rice-pattern camouflage used by SWAPO, the standard mustard-coloured SWAPO uniforms, the green worn by the Cubans, the dark green of UNITA, and certain specially designed apparel reserved for highly clandestine operations.

In late 1976, Breytenbach launched a campaign for a beret that distinguished the unit from the standard dark green infantry beret. He settled on a camouflage pattern similar to that used by the police, and although it was never heraldically approved, nor even officially authorised, Major General Constand Viljoen gave Breytenbach the nod, and the first berets arrived on 24 February 1977, and were made available to the troops at R3 each.

But it became virtually impossible to acquire any more of these berets, and it was only in 1979, when Commandant Deon Ferreira became Officer Commanding, that he assigned Major Eddie Viljoen to pursue the matter. By that time, 32's in-house tailor was improvising berets from camouflage shirts.

In due course, a consignment of new berets did arrive, but the camouflage pattern differed from the original. Ferreira decided that the berets would be worn while the search for the correct material continued, and in 1983 rolls of the original fabric were located and the berets became more uniform.

In early 1979, 32 received a consignment of battle jackets, courtesy of Special Forces. These were the first battle jackets designed for the SA Army, made of thick padded canvas, which made them hot, heavy and uncomfortable. The design was quickly changed and later jackets proved far more wearer friendly.

The biggest change came late in 1979, when Commandant Ferreira success-fully negotiated a unique summer and winter pattern camouflage uniform for the unit, consisting of pants, long-sleeved shirts, bush jacket, pullover, cap, canvas boots and standard webbing. The battledress included chest webbing and a bigpack based on the civilian H-frame hiking backpack, with several additional pouches. Both the bigpack and the chest webbing were of a dark green waterproof canvas. In 1981, battle jackets with numerous pouches were issued for use during Butterfly operations.

These items – along with the conventional 'browns' worn around the base – made up a troop's entire wardrobe until 1984, when a specially designed camouflage bigpack and battle jacket were added.

With the unit finally equipped to look like the soldiers they had become, thoughts naturally turned to the more formal ceremonial dress required in terms of SADF policy. The first item, a black and white stable belt with buffalo head buckle, was first worn by unit members at the Pretoria funeral of Sergeant Major Carl Roza on 9 April, although it was not officially approved until October.

Next came a simple black silk cravat with the white buffalo head embroidered on it. Bakelite shoulder and sub-unit flashes were manufactured, and it was not until the unit relocated to Pomfret that any major changes were made to reflect the fact that the unit now fell under Northern Cape Command. At the same time, the camouflage uniforms were withdrawn and the unit reverted to the standard SADF 'browns'.

PARADES AND HONOURS

The SADF *All Arms Drill Manual,* 1971, defines the purpose of drills as follows:

> to develop in the individual soldier that sense of instinctive obedience which will assist him at all times to carry out his orders. That the foundation of discipline is based on drill has been proven over and over again. Good drill, well rehearsed, closely supervised, and demanding the highest precision is an exercise in obedience and alertness.

Needless to say, the first lesson learned by 32 Battalion was how to drill in squads, but it was not until 1977 that ceremonial drills were added to the curriculum. Because the unit never had a brass band, the men marched to the cadence of their own voices, lustily singing the simple but evocative lyrics they had brought with them from Angola. As the unit developed, new songs were added to the repertoire, acknowledging incorporation into the SADF, the move to Pomfret, and their homesickness for the country they had loved and lost.

Up to 1985, no conventional military music was heard during any routine 32 Battalion parade or function – only these traditional songs, accompanied by the thunderous stamping of feet. Sung in a mixture of Portuguese and indigenous Angolan languages, each song had a special meaning and was rendered when the occasion demanded. It was not unusual to hear a company belting out a stirring battle hymn while marching or running from one point to another, but the most moving times were those immediately before deployment, when the soldiers sang poignantly of leaving their loved ones behind to take part in a fight from which they might not return alive. The original versions are pure poetry, and lose much in translation, but both appear at the back of this book and should give readers a fairly good idea of why these songs, almost childlike in their simplicity, were so near to the hearts of men fighting a brutal war.

The first time a military band took part in a 32 Battalion ceremonial parade was on 9 June 1981, when Lance Corporal Feliciano Costa received the Honoris Crux medal (silver) from President PW Botha.

Because its members were in the front lines throughout the Angolan conflict – 66 cross-border operations between 1976 and 1987 – 32 Battalion racked up an exceptional number of battle honours, particularly given its brief lifespan, and medal parades were a feature of unit life from as early as 1979, when the first Pro Patria medals were presented during a parade at Buffalo. The parade at which Lance Corporal Costa was honoured was the first in the Operational Area at which the SADF's highest award for bravery was presented, and the first at which medals were handed out by anyone other than the Officer Commanding. The SWATF military band took part in this parade, but the final march past and leaving of the parade ground were to the familiar accompaniment of the unit's a capella singers.

Over the years, the unit received many letters and signals from high-ranking SADF officers and political leaders commending their military prowess. The most prized symbol of recognition was a gold plaque, presented on Christmas Day in 1984 by General Jannie Geldenhuys, engraved with the words: *32 Battalion has the best fighting record in the SA Army since World War II – Keep it that way.*

Individual members of the unit were rewarded with medals and decorations for their loyalty and courage under fire on a regular basis. Each of these awards was hard-earned and duly appreciated by the recipients, but the entire unit shared in the pride of 32's 13 Honoris Crux winners. These men, and the exceptional acts of bravery they performed, are:

Lieutenant Connie van Wyk: On 18 October 1975, Van Wyk led Battle Group Bravo's advance on Pereira D'Eca, travelling in a Land Rover. The enemy had laid several ambushes along the route, and at the second of the day, an RPG 7 rocket hit his vehicle, but failed to detonate. The attack was repulsed, but 15 minutes later Van Wyk's group came under fire for the third time, again with RPG 7s. A sizeable enemy force manoeuvred between Van Wyk and the rest of the column, cutting him, and the one troop with him, off. They nevertheless succeeded in making their way back to the main force and launched a mortar attack on the enemy. Later, during the advance to Benguela, Van Wyk, Alpha Company and a troop of armoured cars were ordered to secure the road to Nova Lisboa. Some ten kilometres from Catengue, en route to Caimbambo, Van Wyk set a roadblock, with a single armoured car and an 82-mm recoilless gun the only visible hardware, all other vehicles being hidden in the bush flanking the road. A black FNLA troop was positioned on high ground to observe the road to Caimbambo. Van Wyk's group manned the roadblock for three days, and when they withdrew, they left the graves of 26 guerrillas behind. On 22 May 1979, Van Wyk was killed in an operation against SWAPO.

Sergeant Danny Roxo: Details of his one-man mini-war at Top Hat in December 1975, which left 11 enemy, including four Cubans, dead, are described in Chapter 2. Born in the mountains of northern Portugal, as a young man Roxo became a professional hunter and safari guide in Mozambique's Niassa Province. When the war against FRELIMO began in 1964, he formed his black trackers, gun bearers and a few hunting friends into a personal militia, armed by the Mozambican authorities, who paid him a bounty for every guerrilla killed. A ruthless opponent, Roxo was given the name of the White Devil by FRELIMO. He and his followers were actively involved in the bloody September 1974 uprising in Mozambique, following the announcement that Lisbon had capitulated and agreed to hand over power to Samora Machel, president of FRELIMO. Little is known about Roxo's movements after the withdrawal of Rhodesian forces from Mozambique in November 1974, but it is likely that he joined company with them, or with the South African recces fighting covertly under their flag, subsequently making his way across the continent and taking up arms in Angola. Roxo was killed on 2 September 1976, while serving with 32 Battalion (see Chapter 6).

Warrant Officer 2 Willy Ward: The daring capture of 70 hostile UNITA soldiers and 13 French mercenaries on the road between Vila Nova da Armada and Baixa Longa in early 1976, is described in full in Chapter 6.

Major Eddie Viljoen: In February 1978, he was commanding a company of five platoons tasked to destroy a SWAPO base. To reach their objective, they had to undertake a 30-km forced march. On arriving at the target, the group split in two, one consisting of two platoons, the other of three. With the larger group, Major Viljoen skirted the northern side of a shona that lay between them and the enemy base. A local guide who had accompanied them led the smaller group into an ambush on the southern side of the shona. As soon as firing broke out, Major Viljoen led his group forward to assist them, only to be caught in the ambush himself. The enemy force of at least 200 SWAPO was armed with RPG 7 rocket launchers as well as 60- and 82-mm mortars firing at pre-selected targets. Despite being offered air support by helicopter gunships, Viljoen refused, fearing they could be shot down. He and his men fought their way out of the ambush and, even though he was wounded, he continued to lead his men in a running battle over a distance of seven kilometres until they could be safely extracted by helicopter.

Lance Corporal Feliciano Costa: On 22 April 1979, an 11-man reconnaissance patrol made brief contact with the enemy 16 km inside Angola and exchanged fire, with no losses on either side. Some time afterwards, the enemy was sighted making their way to a waterhole, and the patrol laid an ambush for them. During the ensuing firefight, Costa's RPD machine gun was smashed, one of his comrades killed and five others wounded. Despite this, he managed to kill two of the enemy by lobbing hand grenades about ten metres in front of his own position. With a large group of enemy in pursuit, the patrol withdrew to lay a fresh ambush on their own tracks. Carrying the body of their dead comrade, they made slow progress, and as the enemy closed in, Costa – who no longer had a weapon – 'borrowed' a white phosphorous grenade and two M26 hand grenades from his comrades. Despite the lack of cover, he began moving to meet the enemy head on. As soon as he spotted them, he lobbed the phosphorous grenade into their midst, setting at least five men alight immediately. Those who came to their aid also suffered serious burns. Costa then threw the two hand grenades, and the rest of his patrol opened fire on the enemy, killing most and forcing the survivors to retreat.

Corporal Eduardo João: On 29 November 1979, while acting platoon sergeant with Delta Company, 32 Battalion, and shortly after a contact with SWAPO, Corporal João heard what sounded like a stick breaking. He motioned his troops to wait and went forward to investigate. He spotted a wounded SWAPO and decided to take him prisoner for interrogation, but as he approached the man, a hidden SWAPO force opened fire and Corporal João ordered his men to attack. A 60-mm mortar bomb exploded in front of him, and he was temporarily blinded by the debris. As soon as he regained his sight he set off in pursuit of the 'wounded' SWAPO, chasing him for 200 m through dense bush. Cornered near a kraal, the SWAPO guerrilla opened fire, and João sustained a bullet burn across his chest. Having twice endangered his own life in order to take his quarry alive and extract vital information from him, João realised he would not be able to do so, and shot the SWAPO guerrilla in the head.

Second Lieutenant Petrus Nel: Towards the end of 1981, SWAPO had set up a new infiltration route to the Kaokoveld, and it was decided to attack their transit camp at Cambeno, 40 km north of the Cunene River. Puma helicopters ferried the assault force to the area, but as they were lifting off, Lieutenant Nel realised that the enemy were just 50 m from the landing zone. The gunships opened fire while the ground troops scrambled to consolidate their position. A fierce firefight broke out, with Lieutenant Nel's position being attacked on both flanks simultaneously. He called for air support but none was available. He and two of his troops then charged the enemy head on in a bid to give the rest of the assault force a chance to regroup. During this action, Lieutenant Nel was killed, and was awarded the Honoris Crux decoration posthumously.

Corporal Victor Dracula, Rifleman Bernardo Domingos: After Second Lieutenant Nel was killed, Corporal Dracula assumed command. He realised that he had to recover Nel's body in order to retrieve the only available radio. He and Domingos made two attempts to reach their dead commander, but were beaten back by heavy enemy fire at point-blank range. On their third attempt, despite having to cross some 40 m of open terrain under sustained fire, they succeeded.

Dracula called in air support and launched a ground attack that routed the enemy, leaving at least 17 of them dead.

Major Hannes Nortmann, Sergeant Rihan Rupping: During the attack at the Lomba River on 13 September 1987, a group of T54 tanks, manned by a combined FAPLA/Cuban force, broke through the defence line and into the midst of a troop of Ratel 90 armoured vehicles. During a brief exchange of fire, one of the T54s was shot out at a distance of only 20 m. Three of the Ratels were surrounded and cut off when they got stuck in enemy trenches. Their crews bailed out, and all the remaining enemy tanks were destroyed by the Ratels that were still mobile, manoeuvring behind the tanks and firing on them from the rear. In the process, however, another Ratel got stuck in the trenches. The only way to recover the vehicle was to pull it out with the recovery vehicle under command of Sergeant Rupping. While approaching the crippled Ratel, more enemy tanks appeared and opened fire on the vehicle in the trench. Major Nortmann and Sergeant Rupping proceeded under heavy fire and managed to hook the recovery vehicle's tow cable to the stranded Ratel. As they drove away, the tank fire intensified and the Ratel was hit, killing the entire crew. Nortmann and Rupping succeeded in towing the damaged vehicle to safety, so that the bodies of all crew members could be recovered.

Captain Petrus van Zyl, Lieutenant Tobias de Vos: During *Operation Modular* on 11 November 1987, an attack was launched on FAPLA's 16th Brigade. An Olifant main battle tank had been disabled in the middle of an enemy minefield and could not be recovered. To avoid the crippled tank falling into enemy hands, Captain van Zyl, seconded from Echo Company to UNITA as a liaison officer, and Lieutenant de Vos, platoon commander, Echo Company, decided to try to extract it with the help of a recovery vehicle. They succeeded, under heavy fire, but on reaching the safety of their own lines were informed that one crew member was missing, presumed wounded. Van Zyl and De Vos then re-entered the minefield and located the missing man. While helping their wounded comrade back to their own lines, the group encountered an enemy patrol, which Van Zyl swiftly disposed of. The man they had rescued, survived.

From 1976 to the middle of 1983, operations were the mainstay of 32 Battalion, and apart from personal expressions of gratitude or congratulations by a senior officer, the rewards were few. As a more tangible token of appreciation, Commandant Eddie Viljoen introduced specially designed merit certificates for exceptional performance by individuals. The unit, too, received various awards, including a silver platter presented by two civilians, Alexander and Christopher Brits, in appreciation of the work done by the unit in the field of urban deployment in KwaZulu-Natal during the troubled early 1990s. Engraved on the plate are the words: 'To the men and women from 32 BN especially 322 Infantry Battalion, you generate faith and trust in the human race. Many thanks.'

The first medal parade at Pomfret took place on 27 March 1991, and a year later Major General FS Mulder, Inspector General of the SA Army, presented unit members with six Pro Patria, 920 Southern Africa, 1 046 General Service, 41 Meritorious Service (bronze, ten years) and two Chief:SADF Commendation medals – 2 015 in all, the largest number ever handed out at a single 32 Battalion parade. It was on this memorable occasion that General Mulder stated: '32 Battalion ranks among the great fighting units, not only in South Africa, but in the world.' Ironically, just 12 months later, the SADF would bow to political pressure and the unit would cease to exist.

But, amid the controversy that raged over deployment of 32 Battalion in areas wracked by some of the worst violence in the run-up to the 1994 elections, singular honours continued to be heaped on the men of Buffalo.

The custom of granting the freedom of the city to a military unit or regiment dates back to feudal times, and has come to symbolise the confidence of the civilian population in the chosen force, which then has the right to march through the town or city concerned 'with drums beating, colour flying and bayonets fixed'. It is an honour neither given nor taken lightly, and it was bestowed on 32 Battalion by no less than two local authorities within six months.

On 21 September 1991, the East Rand city of Kempton Park afforded the battalion this honour, followed on 3 April 1992 by the Northern Cape town of Vryburg. Sadly, the unit never had the chance to exercise the right of entry to either town, as it was disbanded before this could happen.

CUSTOMS AND TRADITIONS

Monuments and ceremonies to commemorate the dead are as much a part of military tradition as saluting, and 32 Battalion was no different than any other unit in this regard.

The unveiling of a military monument is both a solemn and a sacred ritual, even in the heart of the African savannah, and on 25 May 1985, the Tree of Honour was officially declared 32 Battalion's memorial to the dead at a dignified parade presided over by Lieutenant General Georg Meiring. For as long as the unit was based at Buffalo, the tree served as the pivot of all memorial services.

After *Operation Forte*, Colonel Viljoen instituted a formal tradition as part of the official opening of the Forte Club. Every Permanent Force officer who served with the unit was given a pewter beer tankard with a glass bottom. These mugs were never allowed to leave the premises of the club, even if the officer transferred to another unit. It was only when 32 Battalion was disbanded that the owners were finally allowed to take their tankards home.

Although the tankards could be used at any time, and hung permanently over the bar in the club, it was when members paid tribute to a fallen comrade that they played their most important role.

Since the death of Honoris Crux recipient Second Lieutenant Petrus Nel during *Operation Super* in 1981, the haunting song 'Ride to Agadir', composed by Mike Batt, had been adopted as the unit's personal funeral dirge. Long before he was killed in action, Nel had made it known that if he ever had a military funeral, he wanted this music played instead of the traditional funeral march. His wish was honoured, and the song became part of 32's unique final tribute to its dead.

When an officer died, his colleagues would gather at the bar and fill their mugs with their beverage of choice for a last toast to the fallen man. The closest friend of the deceased would then deliver a short eulogy, after which 'Ride to Agadir' would be played, and one of the officers present would ceremonially smash the glass bottom of the dead man's tankard, using a miniature hammer specially made for this purpose. A black ribbon was then tied around the tankard before it was hung in its customary place. In due course, a bronze plate bearing the name of the fallen soldier would be mounted over the tankard. After the move to Pomfret the tankards were no longer hung in the bar, but placed in a glass display cabinet.

As an extension of this tradition, similar mugs, engraved with the dates 27 March 1976 – 26 March 1993 were specially made and broken at a private ceremony following the formal disbandment parade in 1993. It was a fitting way to mark the untimely death of a proud battalion whose credo since early 1977 had been Honesty, Loyalty, Justice.

Until late in 1984, the only remembrance day marked by the unit was 21 May – Savate Day. In time, successive commanding officers added other significant dates to the calendar, though not all were observed with full parades or wreath-laying ceremonies. In chronological order of the years in which the events they commemorate took place, 32 Battalion's special days were:

* Founders Day – 27 March (1976)
* Eheke Day – 27 October (1977)
* Mamuandi Day – 8 February (1978)
* Savate Day – 21 May (1980)
* Super Day – 13 March (1982)
* Forte Day – 11 March (1985)
* Lomba Day – 13 September (1987)
* Resettlement Day – 1 June (1989)

In addition to ceremonial parades on special occasions, the men turned out weekly for a battalion parade. In the early years these were something of a shambles, but from 1986 they were executed with fine military precision, and towards the end a full ceremonial parade by 32 Battalion was known to be something of a showpiece. Even though they were first and foremost combat troops rather than parade ground performers, the members took as much pride in the pomp and symbolism of a change of command ceremony as they did in winning the day on the battlefield, and never were they more impressive than during the disbandment parade at Pomfret on 26 March 1993. As they marched from the parade ground singing lustily, the words of their song, 'Luta ate oa fim', brought a lump to many a battle-hardened throat: 'Fighting till the end, Fighting till the end, We are going to fight until the end, Combatants of Buffalo.'

Because of its situation in the bush and the basic facilities available, 32 Battalion came late to the military custom of formal dinners, which were an annual event at the Rundu headquarters from 1985, though the first such event at Buffalo Base was not until 1990.

The secrecy that shrouded the battalion's operations and a lack of accommodation limited the invitation of outside guests to a single dinner at Rundu in 1984. Following the move to Pomfret, such evenings became a regular event in the interest of fostering good relations between the military and the civilian population.

RELIGION

The Angolan members were almost equally divided into Roman Catholic and Protestant believers, and catering for both in the middle of the bush was never easy. But religion takes on a special meaning in a war zone, and every effort was made to accommodate the entire unit's needs.

As far back as Mpupa, Sergeant Jardim had functioned as a Catholic lay preacher, while Warrant Officer Mark Kanganjo, Sergeant Federico Dongua, Sergeant Duarte Correia and Rifleman Francisco da Cunha shared the duties of lay preachers for the interdenominational Protestants. Later, Staff Sergeant Armando Nkabinde, Sergeant João Appolinario and Lance Corporal Patricio Bento also performed these duties, and chaplains from Pretoria visited the base from time to time.

In September 1979, the Reverend Isaias de Almeida, who had come to know many of the members and their families while they were living in refugee camps around Rundu, was appointed the official unit chaplain. The Protestants held Sunday services in the community hall at Pica Pau, while the Catholics gathered in the school hall. White members held their own services in the mess or under the trees.

In 1982, Lieutenant Manie Taute became the first of several National Service chaplains to serve with the unit full time. In March 1985, Lieutenant Erns Endres was the first National Service chaplain to deploy operationally with the battalion, accompanying troops taking part in *Operation Forte*. In 1986 a Permanent Force chaplain based at Rundu, Sydney Middlemost, discovered that very few members of the unit were legally married, a factor that could have serious consequences for their next of kin once the unit was fully integrated into the SADF. He launched a campaign to legalise these unions, sometimes conducting up to ten ceremonies a day.

At a meeting in Pretoria in 1989, the Igreja Reformada, established by Chaplain Middlemost, became the first black congregation to be accepted as a full member of the Dutch Reformed Church's Northern Transvaal ring. On 4 March, the name was changed to Congregation Angolana and Chaplain Middlemost was appointed the first minister. He remained with the unit until disbandment, assisted in the last few years by Chaplain Diederik Venter. After moving to Pomfret, the Catholic members were ministered to by Father Karl-Erich Meindel from Morokeng.

SPORT

Throughout the SADF, active participation in sport was always encouraged, not only because of the obvious physical benefits, but as an exercise in mental discipline. Until the unit relocated to Pomfret, however, operational demands and lack of facilities offered scant opportunity for organised or competitive sport to be played. With troops deployed for up to nine months of the year, and with no coaches or sports officers, 32 Battalion's athletic recreation was largely confined to informal inter-company rivalry, and then only occasionally.

Soccer was by far the most popular sport, and the first time a team from the unit took part in an outside competition – the 1984 Cuca Tops tournament at Rundu – they emerged as victors. Running was second nature to the men from Buffalo and road races always drew good support, while volleyball was played purely for recreation. Only once could enough rugby players be mustered for a friendly game, against 201 Battalion from Omega Base.

Once settled at Pomfret, however, there was more than enough time for organised sport, played under the aegis of the Pomfret Defence Sports Club. A blazer badge was designed in 1992, and while the club colours were the same as those of all SADF sports teams, the buffalo head emblem ensured an individual identity.

The soccer team emerged as victors the first time they took part in the Northern Cape Command sports day in 1991, and held the title for three years running – the first team in the command to score a hat-trick.

In 1990, the unit's 11 best long-distance runners took part in the Comrades Marathon, ten of them finishing the race. Each year after that the number of participants increased, and they always performed well.

In 1991, and again in 1993, the volleyball team finished in the top three at the Northern Cape Command sports days, while the tug of war team did equally well.

While in the Operational Area, the unit never included more than six women in uniform, but at Pomfret there were enough women to form a netball team, which also acquitted itself well at the Northern Cape Command sports days.

But the biggest growth was seen in the rugby team, which not only found more than enough players at Pomfret, but benefited from coaching by the likes of legendary Springbok lock Frik du Preez, whose farm was in the district. As early as 1990 the combined 32 Battalion and community team won both the leagues in which they entered, and went on to become the Stellaland champions.

And for those who preferred a more sedate form of recreation there was bowls, with competitions soon becoming a regular feature of Saturday and Sunday afternoons.

6

The danger of Buffalo
MILITARY OPERATIONS 1976-1977

OPERATION BUDGIE – WEST OF THE CUITO RIVER

By the end of February 1976, all SADF forces had been withdrawn from Angola after *Operation Savannah*, leaving only the politically leaderless FNLA troops of Battle Group Bravo to keep the Cuando Cubango province from falling into FAPLA hands, under what official documents for the period January to October refer to as *Operation Budgie*.

When Jan Breytenbach returned from his leave in Pretoria, the only members qualified to serve in the leader group were sergeants Danny Roxo, Silva Sierro and Robbie Ribeiro. He sent Sierro and Ribeiro to Mpupa to start training the troops who had mustered there, while Roxo was despatched to the refugee camp at Calai to recruit all able-bodied FNLA supporters who were willing to fight.

Pockets of FNLA troops were scattered throughout the Cuando Cubango as far north as Vila Nova da Armada, where Zaire, a veteran of *Savannah*, had taken his men after being forced out of Cuito Cuanavale by FAPLA and running into a skirmish with UNITA. Other groups had gathered at Luenge, Mavinga, Baixa Longa, Cuancar and Savate, and in order to consolidate the available manpower, Breytenbach urgently requested additional leader group members from Pretoria. Among the first to arrive were Second Lieutenant Des Burman from Natal Command, Major Venter, Commandant Sybie van der Spuy and nine other members of 2 Reconnaissance Commando.

In order to stem FAPLA's advance, a company of trained men was deployed at Vila Nova da Armada under command of Roxo and Ribeiro, while Van der Spuy and Sergeant Mike Tippet took charge of forces commanded by Geraldo and Fatome at Savate. Soon afterwards, Warrant Officer Willy Ward was despatched

Angolan combat theatre and detailed area of 32 Battalion operations 1976 –1988

to Vila Nova da Armada to relieve Roxo, who went further north to Baixa Longa to assume command of the FNLA remnants there.

On 17 February, FAPLA captured Serpa Pinto and continued to advance southwards. Combat Group Piper, which was still holding Caiundo, was ordered to pull back to South West Africa immediately, but their route would take them through Savate. During the withdrawal, the Bravo Group members at Savate hid in the bush to maintain the secrecy surrounding *Operation Budgie*, and as soon as Piper had cleared the area, Willy Ward mined the airstrip and the north–south road to delay FAPLA's advance.

Sergeant Major Harry Botha also blew up the bridge across the Kavango River just north of Katwitwi after he and the Savate group, led by Van der Spuy, had crossed it to the south, leaving a small number of FNLA supporters – who had been given PPSh carbines after declining to join Bravo – to take their chances against the advancing FAPLA force.

Roxo had been left in command at Baixa Longo with strict instructions to set up defensive positions in the bush and not in the town itself. On a visit to the town in mid-March, Breytenbach was not pleased to find Roxo and his company comfortably installed in a group of buildings, and ordered them to withdraw immediately. Later that day, on arriving back at Rundu headquarters, Breytenbach was informed that Baixa Longo was under attack, and he naturally assumed the attack came from FAPLA. Sergeant Major Ward and some of his men were ordered to deploy between Baixa Longa and Vila Nova da Armada to act as a backstop in the event that Roxo had to retreat. They raced to the area in a Unimog, and while moving into position, were surprised to see Sergeant Sierro and some of his men emerging from the bush. They reported that Roxo's company had indeed been driven from Baixa Longa, and were now scattered throughout the bush.

Ward, sergeants Jan van der Merwe and Brian Walls and some of the black troops moved out in the Unimog to try to find Roxo and his men. As they crested a rise, they found themselves nose to nose with a 60-mm Panhard armoured car that had broken down in the middle of the track. Three white crewmen were huddled over the rear engine compartment.

Ward's group debussed without delay, taking cover in the bush, but Ward himself dashed straight towards the stranded vehicle, brandishing his rifle menacingly and ordering the trio – who had left their personal weapons in the armoured car while tinkering with the engine – to surrender.

On interrogation two turned out to be French and the third Portuguese. They said they were the advance patrol for a UNITA force that had just attacked Baixa Longa and was now making for Vila Nova da Armada. Ward ordered one of the prisoners to contact the main force and tell them that they were surrounded and should come forward to surrender. Astonishingly, they did – 70 UNITA troops and 13 French mercenaries in all, who reluctantly threw their weapons in a pile at the sergeant major's feet. There was a tricky moment when one of the Frenchmen challenged the claim that they were surrounded, but on Ward's command the handful of black troops – the only ones for miles around – showed themselves and put on a sufficiently impressive show of bravado to convince the prisoners that they had fallen into the hands of a far superior force.

The booty from this audacious confrontation included the Panhard armoured car, five Land Rovers mounted with 12,7-mm machine guns or 106-mm anti-tank guns, several Unimogs and other vehicles, 82-mm mortars, machine guns, Entac anti-tank guided missile systems, RPG 7 rocket launchers, four SA 7 ground-to-air missiles, AK47, G3 and R1 rifles, and UNITA leader Jonas Savimbi's personal Citroën, which was loaded on a truck and promptly destroyed by Ward before his prisoners were taken to Vila Nova da Armada.

It soon became clear that Savimbi, who had been driven out of Cago Coutinho by FAPLA, had reneged on the agreement that his troops and those of Bravo would not engage one another, and had tried to gain some ground by advancing southwards via Baixa Longa to Vila Nova da Armada.

Ward and his men proceeded to Baixa Longa, while the prisoners were sent downstream to Mpupa by boat, where many of them immediately signed on with Bravo Group, including Major Fonseca dos Santos, the UNITA commander, and Amilcar Queiroz, who went on to become a well-known SADF reconnaissance operator.

With FAPLA advancing in full force from Cuito Cuanavale, defensive positions were set up some nine kilometres north of Baixa Longa, with Ward and a small number of his troops manning an RPG 7, a B10 anti-tank gun and a machine-gun nest close to a destroyed bridge, while Sergeant van der Merwe and another group set up an 82-mm mortar position further back. Ward heard vehicles approaching across the river, but could hardly believe his eyes when two tanks, four BRDM armoured cars and a truck packed with infantrymen suddenly hove into view on the high ground beyond the bridge. He immediately knocked out the lead tank with three RPG 7 rockets, but the second tank withdrew and took up a hull-down position about 1 000 m away, behind the high ground, and began to hammer Ward's position with high explosive shells.

One of his troops emptied a machine-gun belt into the back of the truck, killing dozens of Cubans, but the amphibious BRDMs moved through the river and into position for a flanking attack. The second tank hit the recently captured UNITA Suzuki jeep Ward was using, and he and his men began running back to the mortar position, where Van der Merwe was already blasting away at the BRDMs. A lucky shot put a mortar shell into the open hatch of one of the BRDMs, which exploded.

Ward ordered the withdrawal of all the mortars except one, and as the rest of the group pulled back, he and a lone black soldier mounted a rearguard action with the remaining tube. When it became too dangerous for them to stay any longer, they tried to manhandle the mortar tube onto the back of a Land Rover, but a shell exploded between them, severing one of the troop's hands. Ward grabbed the wounded man and ran for the Land Rover. The starter motor turned but the engine refused to start. With the remaining BRDMs closing in, Ward slung the bleeding troop over his shoulders and ran the four kilometres back to Baixa Longa, dodging heavy fire all the way from the armoured cars, the tank and mortars.

Hasty preparations were made at Baixa Longa to take on the vehicles expected to be in pursuit, but they never arrived. The men concluded that FAPLA must have thought them part of a much larger force, and abandoned the hunt.

Breytenbach decided there was no profit to be gained from further defence of towns, and ordered Ward to delay FAPLA's advance by laying ambushes and mines. On 24 March, 101 Task Force ordered Bravo Group to withdraw to Pica Pau, and Ward received fresh orders. He was to delay FAPLA long enough to allow the withdrawal of all the Bravo forces by mining the route between Baixa Longa and Vila Nova da Armada, booby-trapping the barracks at Vila Nova da Armada, and mining the airfield and the road to Rito, the next town downstream. It was a splendid plan, and before long reports were received of tanks and various other vehicles being blown up between Baixa Longa and Vila Nova da Armada.

In mid-June, three months after all the Bravo Group personnel and their families had vacated the area west of the Cuito River, Commandant Philip du Preez, liaison officer between UNITA and the FNLA in 1 Military Area, insisted that Bravo make contact with the UNITA groups floating around aimlessly between Baixa Longa and Cuito Cuanavale. Alpha Company, commanded by Major Fourie of Walvis Bay Commando, moved north, bypassing a now deserted Mpupa before turning west at Rito to avoid the heavily mined floodplain and the road to Vila Nova da Armada. They followed the tracks of FAPLA's tanks to Baixa Longa and once tried to make contact with UNITA, but this sparked a firefight, started by Bravo Group. The problem was that the former FNLA troops still saw UNITA as the enemy, and the forced alliance between the two groups was never truly successful. A second attempt to make contact also failed, and eventually the newly arrived Lieutenant Mike Malone, who spoke fluent Portuguese, was sent ahead as an emissary.

With the rest of the company following at some distance, Malone drove until he reached a UNITA roadblock, manned by Epelanga, the local commander, who told Malone that UNITA was desperate to make friendly contact, and would Bravo Group 'please stop shooting'.

The next few days became an exercise in human bridge building, until eventually the black Bravo soldiers accepted that they would henceforth have to live with UNITA, whether they liked it or not.

Malone brought Epelanga and a UNITA commander, Johnny Katala, to Rito, where they met with Breytenbach and Du Preez and concluded an uneasy truce, which it was hoped would see future operations in the Cuando Cubango province conducted by an alliance of Bravo and UNITA.

The first nine months of 1976 passed in a blur of continuous action by the veteran troops and intensive training of the rookies, who needed to be deployed as soon as possible. Shortly after the meeting with Epelanga, Major Fourie decided it was time to 'rev' the FAPLA garrison at Cuito Cuanavale. With as many troops as a Unimog could carry he made his way to the north undetected, set up mortars on the outskirts of the town and launched a barrage against the transport park, which contained a fleet of tanks, BRDMs, BTRs and trucks. Just for good measure, the mortarists lobbed shells at a group of MiG 17 fighters parked on the airfield as well.

FAPLA counter-attacked immediately, and the Bravo patrol suddenly found themselves engaging full mechanised brigades. They exited the area in haste, but not before one of the black sergeants was killed. As the vehicle sped back to Baixa Longa, MiG 17s dogged them from the sky, firing both rockets and machine guns at the Unimog. Fortunately, the pilots were poor marksmen, and the group made it back safely. Bravo and UNITA forces immediately set up defensive positions, and Major Charlie Hochapfel, called in to replace Fourie, who had broken his ankle during the flight from Cuito, arrived just as a concerted air attack began.

As the MiGs dived and strafed the town – without hitting a single strategic target – an Antonov appeared overhead, and huge bombs began rolling down its open rear loading ramp. Simultaneously, FAPLA's ground forces opened up with artillery and the dreaded 122-mm rocket launchers, but every shell fell short of the target. At the height of the battle, orders came from 101 Task Force for Bravo Group to break off the contact with FAPLA, and they slowly began to retreat to Vila Nova da Armada where the UNITA contingent stayed, while the Bravo troops made their way back to Pica Pau.

Not long after this incident, Breytenbach sent a company under command of Major Swannie Swanepoel back into the Cuando Cubango, this time to Chimbueta, about 40 km south of Caiundo. Their orders were to observe FAPLA movement through patrols and to institute delaying tactics at the first sign of FAPLA resuming its push to the south. Unexpectedly, members of the local population informed Swanepoel that they were being constantly harassed by SWAPO elements from a large camp east of the river. It was an unusual position for a SWAPO base, far removed from the protection of FAPLA and situated between two rivers, but

SWAPO still being Bravo Group's primary target, Breytenbach authorised an attack on the base. Under cover of darkness the troops crossed the Kavango River in makorros provided by the local population, and attacked at dawn. The company commander claimed 90 kills, but the body count had to be substantiated by captured weapons, and soon afterwards a stack of G3 rifles was deposited outside Bravo Group's headquarters in Rundu. On investigation, however, it emerged that the camp had not been occupied by SWAPO at all, but by a UNITA group under command of Dr Jorge Valentim, and that the perfidious local population had drawn an unwitting Bravo Group into yet another armed confrontation with their new-found allies.

With a FAPLA push from Caiundo expected within days, Swanepoel was sent to Savate, where a group of FNLA supporters under command of Chuangari had moved from Cuangar for no apparent reason. Lieutenant Willie Greef took command of the company at Chimbueta, with orders to send a patrol to Caiundo and assess FAPLA's situation before moving to Savate. The reconnaissance patrol returned in record time to report that the enemy force consisted of some 20 tanks, a large number of BRDMs, BTRs, trucks and artillery pieces, and even had four helicopters on the airstrip. While Greef was still debriefing the patrol, the first FAPLA tank fitted with mine rollers on the front moved past their hiding place in the bush.

Greef hastily gathered his men, loaded all the heavy equipment onto the company's single Unimog, and led the way to Savate on foot, staying just ahead of the FAPLA column. Swanepoel, meanwhile, sent the FNLA troops at Savate – and their camp followers – to hide in the bush on the western side of the town. He and Greef had agreed to rendezvous in the town itself, so Swanepoel and five men returned to one of the houses to wait, unfortunately leaving both his radio and the radio operator with the group in the bush.

Hearing a vehicle approach, Swanepoel assumed it was Greef's Unimog, but on looking through a window he saw a T34 tank moving slowly down the street, followed by infantry on foot. He and his men quietly crept out of the house and into the nearest dense bush, from where they watched the FAPLA force conduct a textbook sweep of the town. From his hidden vantage point to the west, the radio operator observed the same operation, and took it upon himself to report to the operations room at Rundu that Swanepoel had been captured. It was simply beyond his comprehension that anyone could have escaped the thorough sweep.

Breytenbach, while reluctant to accept that Swanepoel had failed to evade capture, ordered the radio operator to lead the rest of the group back to the cutline on foot without delay. For Swanepoel and the five men with him, what had turned into their longest day finally ended as darkness fell, when they managed to slip out of town and cross the river to the east bank. For the next few days they stayed one step ahead of the FAPLA force, gathering vital intelligence about its strength and composition, but without a radio were unable to pass on the information until reunited with Greef and his men at Katwitwi.

When Greef's group had arrived at the cutline, FAPLA was close on their heels. They took up position on high ground overlooking the cutline at Katwitwi, which was to their north. In front of them was a full FAPLA brigade, heavily staffed with Cuban soldiers. Shortly afterwards, Greef observed a clash between a routine SADF patrol and the FAPLA force, and reported to Colonel Breytenbach by radio that he believed some South African troops might have been taken prisoner. Breytenbach immediately ordered Greef to withdraw five kilometres south before moving east to Nkurenkuru.

By October, FAPLA had succeeded in occupying most of Angola and had pushed Bravo Group back across the border into South West Africa.

OPERATION BUDGIE – EAST OF THE CUITO RIVER
With pockets of FNLA troops still ranging the area around Mavinga and Luenge, sergeants Roxo, Sierro and Ribeiro were despatched on 3 April to bring these leaderless groups under control and patrol the terrain as far north as Mavinga.

By 15 April they received their first supplies from Rundu, along with Lieutenant PP Joubert, who deployed Ribeiro at Luenge with 34 black troops, 15 women and eight children; Roxo and Sierro 40 km north of Luenge at the two bridges that cross the Lutungando River, with five white Portuguese and 82 black troops, 15 women and nine children; a white Portuguese and 24 black troops at the Cupemba bridge 30 km north of Roxo's position; another white Portuguese with 24 troops at the Matunyo bridge 20 km to the north; and a group of 17 black troops and one white Portuguese to patrol downstream of the Matunyo River.

After the first re-supply run, all the women and children were taken to Pica Pau by road.

By early June, Second Lieutenant Peter Mills relieved Joubert, and in conjunction with Roxo's men, his company cleared Mavinga of all FAPLA forces. Leaving Roxo in command at Mavinga, Mills moved his company north towards Cunjamba, which appeared so peaceful that the troops allowed their guard to drop. Mills did send patrols into the town and across the river, and they reported seeing fresh tracks made by heavy vehicles, but the local residents were unable to shed any light on the situation.

The next morning, Mills and nine troops drove down to the river in a Unimog to perform their ablutions, and ran headlong into a FAPLA force that included armour, BTRs and BRDMs. The lieutenant's Unimog was destroyed, and he and the nine troops with him were cut off from the rest of the company. Hearing the gunfire, the main body of the company concluded that Mills and his companions

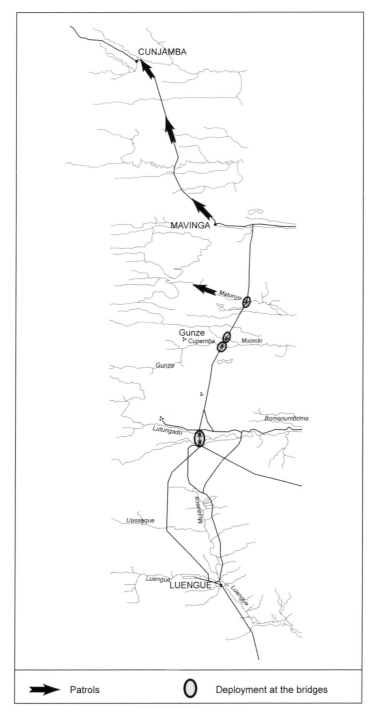

Patrols   Deployment at the bridges

Operations west of the Quito River with deployments and patrols as far north as Cunjamba

must have been either killed or captured. The next in command, a black NCO, decided that the company would fight it out, but they found themselves surrounded almost immediately by an overwhelming FAPLA force.

Back in the operations room at Rundu, Breytenbach was following the course of the battle on the radio, but with Cunjamba being 320 km inside Angola, he was unable to send the air support the situation demanded. In desperation he ordered the sergeant who had taken charge to forget about Mills and the other missing men, and to try to break through the lines and head for Mavinga. Although they had to abandon two Unimogs in the process, the company did manage to reach Mavinga, from where Roxo and his men set off for Cunjamba to assist Mills and his companions.

Roxo reported in due course that the missing men appeared somehow to have escaped from the battle zone, but soon afterwards intercepted radio traffic indicated that Mills had indeed been captured, and was on the way to Luanda in an aircraft, presumably for a show trial.

But Breytenbach was not ready to give up on the lieutenant just yet, and decided to maintain silence about his disappearance for three days. His instincts were validated when Roxo reported just two days later that Mills and most of his companions had reached Mavinga after walking 60 km from Cunjamba, and were unscathed, though Bravo Group had lost three men in the battle. Following this incident, Lieutenant Barry Roper relieved Mills.

Roxo stayed on at Luenge, continuing to send out regular patrols, but it soon became clear that a single company could not possibly halt FAPLA's aggressive advance. On 17 August, FAPLA was just 15 km from Luenge, moving along both the Mavinga road and the Cubango River to the south. Captain B Vorster, who had relieved Roper just a fortnight earlier, had no idea that FAPLA had deployed a strong force south of Luenge along the road to Coutado do Mucusso, and was waiting to ambush any Bravo Group element.

At 05h00 on 19 August, a convoy of six Unimogs and one Bosvark – a Unimog loaded with sandbags to deflect landmine explosions – set off from Luenge to the south. The orders were that the Bosvark should be the lead vehicle, followed at a ten-minute interval by three of the Unimogs, and a few minutes later, by Unimogs 4, 5 and 6. Vorster, Lieutenant Hough, nine troops and Queiroz were in the last vehicle.

Due to the poor state of the road, the first four Unimogs closed up quickly, and for some inexplicable reason the Bosvark fell back into second position in the convoy, while a Unimog commanded by Sergeant Ribeiro's younger brother, a corporal universally known as 'Little Robbie', took the lead. Then another Unimog moved up, placing the Bosvark even further back.

At about 07h30, the convoy drove into a massive FAPLA ambush. The lead Unimog took a direct frontal hit from an RPG 7, and simultaneously a mine exploded under the vehicle while heavy rifle and machine-gun fire broke out from the left side of the road. With a chana on the right-hand side offering no cover, the troops were forced to take their chances in the open as they fled towards the rear on foot. One of the first to make it back to Luenge was Nqueji Yau Samuel.

Paulo Dondo was in the second Unimog, about 30 m behind the first. When the attack began, the vehicle stopped immediately and the occupants wasted no time heading for Luenge. Clesio José da Sivera was on Unimog No. 4, directly behind the Bosvark. As he debussed, he saw the Bosvark, which was loaded with explosives, explode in a ball of flame.

Mario Costa and Dessonga Andrea were on Unimog No. 6 with Captain Vorster, approximately two kilometres behind the first vehicle. When the ambush began, Vorster ordered that his vehicle and the fifth Unimog be driven into the bush and camouflaged. As the enemy fire intensified, Vorster was no longer sure he and the men with him would be safe from detection, and, not wanting to wait around and find out, Costa and Andrea took to the road, linking up at Luenge with Nqueji Yau Samuel, Dondo and Da Sivera. The five decided to move south until they reached Pica Pau, but somewhere along the way Andrea became separated from the rest of the group. He carried on alone, but near Dirico was taken prisoner by FAPLA and admitted to the local hospital. He admitted to his captors that he was from Pica Pau and was serving in the SA Army. At the hospital he was shown six badly wounded soldiers, whom he recognised as comrades who had been caught in the ambush. Through a window he was also shown the wreckage of two Unimogs and a Bosvark, covered in blood. The local FAPLA commander assured him that the vehicles were those that had been ambushed.

On 30 August, Andrea managed to escape from the hospital and make his way to Pica Pau. Other survivors of the ambush had been arriving at intervals, but on 2 September, 12 members of the party remained unaccounted for, including Corporal Ribeiro.

Breytenbach decided enough time had passed, and ordered Captain Vorster and his company to return to the scene of the attack and search for the missing men. They had to follow the route from Pica Pau to Mucusso, cross the border and move to Dirico, and had orders to blow up the bridge across the Cuito River before it could be taken by the FAPLA force rapidly advancing south along the western bank of the river.

Sergeants Roxo, Sierro and Ribeiro went ahead, travelling in a mine-resistant Unimog known as a Wolf, to blow the bridge. The rest of the convoy followed about 20 minutes behind. Near Macunde, on the northern bank of the Okavango River, the Wolf detonated an anti-tank mine, heavily boosted with extra explosives. The vehicle tipped sideways before crashing down with brutal force.

Sergeant Sierro's skull was crushed like an eggshell, but he was still alive.

Sergeant Roxo had suffered mortal internal injuries, and was pinned under the full weight of the vehicle. The survivors made a desperate attempt to lift the vehicle and pull him free, but it was too heavy.

They dragged the unconscious Sergeant Sierro into the shade, and Sergeant Ribeiro left the uninjured team members to protect the others. He had not been able to call for assistance because the radio was destroyed, so he ran back down the road until he reached the oncoming convoy. He told Vorster what had happened, and was totally astonished when, instead of proceeding to the scene of the accident to render assistance to the dying men, the captain ordered the column to turn around and return to Pica Pau to summon help!

Breytenbach was not at Pica Pau, but further up the Kavango River on a mission, but he was immediately contacted by Major Hochapfel, whom he authorised to lay on a helicopter and casevac the injured men at all cost. One might have thought a disastrous day could not possibly get worse, but in the time it took for Hochapfel to get airborne, an Antonov had appeared over the accident scene and the crew had rolled one bomb after another out of the rear door. Amazingly, none of them hit the vehicle, but because of the Antonov's presence, the helicopter pilot refused to fly across the river to land as close as possible to the Wolf. Instead, he put the chopper down some distance south of the river and remained there, even after the Antonov had left the area, forcing Hochapfel and the survivors to struggle through two or three kilometres of swamp and reeds, after crossing the river several times in a makorro carrying the dead and wounded. Danny Roxo, a legend in life, was already dead by the time Hochapfel reached him. Whether he could have survived his terrible wounds if help had come sooner will never be known, but there can be no doubt that he was a good man, a fine and fearless warrior, who did not deserve to die that way – and certainly not as a result of asinine decisions made by comrades-in-arms to err on the side of caution instead of rendering whatever aid they could.

Silva Sierro had clung to life throughout the lengthy evacuation, surviving even the river crossing and the trudge through the swamps. It was the final stretch, over a bumpy field in the back of a Land Rover that had meanwhile arrived from Pica Pau, that finished him off, and he was pronounced dead on arrival at the waiting helicopter. Charlie Hochapfel was so disgusted, as a measure of his contempt he ordered the pilot to return to base empty. The wounded, none of them critically injured, and the bodies of sergeants Roxo and Sierro were taken back to Pica Pau by road.

The four wounded were evacuated to Rundu the next day in a Land Rover driven by Sergeant Ribeiro, the last surviving Portuguese reconnaissance operator. A young white conscript, on his way home after his tour of duty, rode with them in the front passenger seat.

When Ribeiro saw a convoy of ten-ton trucks from 16 Maintenance Unit approaching from the front, he hugged the left-hand shoulder of the dirt road, driving with extra caution as the dust swirled and visibility dropped to almost zero. The driver of the second truck in the convoy evidently felt less constrained to drive safely, or perhaps he found the dusty conditions inconvenient. Whatever the reason, he pulled out to overtake the lead truck in the convoy and collided head-on with Ribeiro's Land Rover, flattening the vehicle and killing all six men aboard.

Robbie Ribeiro and four of those men had survived the Wolf explosion, but just 24 hours later they, too, were dead, victims of a stupid mistake by a selfish driver. The loss of the three Portuguese sergeants and the other men cast a pall over Bravo Group for a long time, for they were exceptional men, outstanding soldiers, and none of them should have died as the result of careless disregard by their own comrades.

RECONNAISSANCE PATROLS TO THE NORTH

When Bravo launched operations north of the border in the area between beacons 26 and 38, intelligence reports indicated no enemy presence east of the Cubango River, and patrols thus focused on the western region where small groups of hard-core FNLA fighters were still waging their own battle. This was also the area most vulnerable to infiltration by the MPLA and SWAPO.

Lieutenant Peter Rose led the first patrol from Pica Pau to a point 30 km north-west of Dima, reporting on 3 March 1976 that no enemy presence had been detected. He did, however, find a group of 40 FNLA troops at Mavinga and another 74 at Luenge.

Around the same time, four Bravo Group members under command of Sergeant NG Clark of 2 Reconnaissance Commando were sent to Caiundo to carry out several tasks. They not only had to establish whether there was an enemy presence anywhere in proximity to the town, but also had to make certain contingency plans with a view to future possible action. The cable of the pontoon used to cross the river was to be cut, unless this would prevent it from being rejoined for use by own forces at a later stage. They also had to damage a large pontoon still under construction, with the same proviso, and mine the road to Pereira D'Eca.

Travelling in a civilian Land Rover, they were to drive from Katwitwi to Savate and up the Tandaue chana before turning west. However, it was the rainy season and the chana was a mire of mud, making progress slow and difficult. Clark was granted permission to return to the road, but warned to proceed with caution, as a protective element of FAPLA was known to be at Linguele, 20 km south of Caiundo. The patrol waited until nightfall, and on reaching what they calculated was a point close to Linguele, hid their vehicle in the bush. With each man carrying rations for three days, weapons and mines, they proceeded on foot, covering 18 km from 03h00 to 05h00, when they found a suitable position to lay up for the day. It was 13 April and they were within five kilometres of Caiundo.

That night they moved stealthily into the town, and while his men took up position on the high ground near the airfield, Clark scouted the river bank. It was raining hard and a dense fog hung over the water, limiting his visibility, and he was unable to locate either the pontoon mooring or the craft reportedly under construction. Clark aborted the mission and rejoined his men at the airfield, where they spent the night in a tree, moving about 20 paces into the surrounding low, dense bush at first light. From this vantage point they observed groups of FAPLA soldiers walking between the airfield and the town throughout the day. Only later did they realise that their hiding place was less than 50 m from a guard assembly point!

At 15h00 the men heard voices – which they were sure were those of Cubans – coming from the south end of the runway. Suddenly, one of the Bravo troops coughed. The FAPLA guards fell silent, and within moments two of them passed by very close to where the men were hiding, and stopped to peer into the bush. Seeing nothing, they moved on and resumed their routine.

The Bravo patrol waited until 21h20 before moving out in single file, but as they made their way from the airfield, they were challenged by two black FAPLA troops. One member of the patrol, Luis, muttered some assurance as he and the others nonchalantly went on their way, acting as though they, too, were FAPLA, with every right to be there. As a precaution, the patrol steered clear of the road until they were sure they were not being followed, and covered the distance to their hidden Land Rover in record time. By 08h00 they were well clear of the Caiundo area and able to make radio contact with their headquarters at Rundu. On the way back, they mined the road to Pereira D'Eca as planned.

OPERATION TAMBOTIE

For the first few months of 1976, operations were conducted on an area defence/patrol system, with only verbal orders being issued. On 28 April, Colonel Breytenbach issued the first formal order for deployment – Operational Order No. 1, aimed at preventing FAPLA from occupying Mpupa and the area south to Calai.

Intelligence had indicated that a SWAPO and FAPLA agent known as February was holed up at Tuni, while a second agent was reported to be at Xamavera. On the night of 29 April, Corporal Evans was to take four members of 1 Reconnaissance Commando, 16 Bravo Group members and a section of engineers commanded by Staff Sergeant Charlie Spiller, and capture both agents for interrogation. At the same time a combat team led by Commandant Sybie van der Spuy, and consisting of Alpha Company, two sections of Bravo Company, the Sabre troop and a group of 60-mm mortarists, were to reconnoitre the size of the enemy force at Mpupa, locate and destroy them. They had until first light on 3 May to carry out this mission.

The abduction team left Rundu at 21h00, travelling in three Unimogs and carrying two inflatable boats, with an informer on the payroll of Chief of Staff Intelligence (CSI) as their guide. They followed the Kavango River for a distance before stopping to change into enemy uniforms and be briefed in detail about the mission by Evans, who spoke only broken Portuguese. Whether this caused the informer to become confused is not known, but the first point at which they offloaded the inflatable craft at 00h30 was the wrong one. Loading both boats onto one of the Unimogs, they set off again, reaching the correct launching point at 03h00. The engineers prepared the boats, and by 04h00, with Evans, Corporal Louis Klopper, the informer and eight Bravo troops in one boat, corporals Jacobs, Fourie and the rest of the Bravo troops in the other, they crossed the river, fighting a strong current and landing the boats some 300 m apart. They regrouped and set off on foot for the hut where the informer had indicated February and one other person would be. But, on surrounding and entering the hut, they found only one man, who was taken back to the boats by five Bravo Group members while the rest of the party moved to another village nearby, where the informer now believed their quarry would be. On entering the house the informer pointed out, three men were found, one of whom lunged at the intruders with a spear. He was shot and his two companions taken back to the boats. The plan to capture the agent at Xamavera was abandoned when information indicated that he had left the area a few days before.

While the engineers returned to Rundu with the boats, the rest of the group waited at a predetermined point to rendezvous with Van der Spuy's combat team. They left Pica Pau at first light on 30 April, crossing the border at Mucusso and first making sure that there were no radios in the town that could be used to report their presence. They followed the Kavango River to Dirico, where they secured the bridge and crossed the river at 14h00.

Reaching Tuni at 16h00, the team left two sections of Bravo Company under Evans to set up a stopper group on the road to Calai, while the main force moved on to Mpupa. By last light, they were within 15 km of Bravo Group's old stomping ground.

Earlier radio intercepts had indicated that the town was occupied by FAPLA, but a night reconnaissance patrol showed it to be deserted. The next morning the combat team moved into Mpupa, securing it and sending out day patrols in the immediate vicinity.

Back at the Evans roadblock, three men sneaking around the maize fields in a suspicious manner had been apprehended. They first claimed to be from the Kavango and said that they had only been trying to steal some food. Later they changed their story, claiming they had come to visit their sister in the area. In due course, it was established that one of the three was related to the headman at Tuni, a notorious MPLA supporter.

At 19h00 on 1 May, the combat and reconnaissance teams linked up and returned to Pica Pau, where they could report that FAPLA had not advanced as far south as Mpupa after all.

OPERATIONS IN THE CUNENE PROVINCE

The Cuando Cubango province was always a priority for Bravo Group, as until late 1976 it was the only area of Angola not under FAPLA control. After *Operation Savannah*, the objective was to keep the region free of FAPLA for as long as possible. However, once incorporated into the SADF, Bravo's primary task was to act against SWAPO, and their first official deployment in this role began on 10 May, when Major General Constand Viljoen, General Officer Commanding 101 Task Force, authorised *Operation Cobra*, designed to achieve domination of the area north of the South West Africa border between Beacon 28 and the 16°30' cutline, by locating and destroying SWAPO bases.

Three Bravo Group companies under command of Commandant van der Spuy were given additional firepower in the form of Unimogs on which were mounted a double-barrel, water-cooled Browning, and 106-mm anti-tank guns or mortars, all sporting pro-FAPLA slogans and graffiti.

The team left Pica Pau in great secrecy and took a roundabout route, heading north to Chana Hangadima after crossing into Angola, then turning south, as though they were a FAPLA group moving down from the north. But the ruse was detected, and the SWAPO bases near Hangadima, reached on 15 May, had been hastily evacuated. Two nights later, while laagered south of Hangadima, Van der Spuy's group came under attack from a large SWAPO force, but succeeded in driving them off with a spectacular display of firepower. Whenever possible, SWAPO carried their dead and wounded from the battlefield, and as a rule it was impossible to estimate the number of casualties they had suffered. But an early morning sweep of the area turned up enough pools of blood, blood-soaked bandages and items of clothing to indicate that they must have taken heavy losses.

The rest of Van der Spuy's journey southwards produced no contact with the enemy at all, and the group returned to Pica Pau on 10 June, exactly one month after their departure. This was the last time a Reconnaissance Commando operator led an operation against SWAPO, as all future missions were commanded by

National Servicemen or Permanent Force members transferred to 32 Battalion to form the leader group.

OPERATION SEILJAG 1

The next deployment against SWAPO by the officially renamed 32 Battalion was in November 1976, and involved 'special operations' companies under command of Omauni base, as well as companies deployed in Owamboland and acting under command of a battalion headquarters in that area. Troops involved in special operations wore a wide variety of uniforms, while those active in Owamboland wore conventional SADF 'browns'. The code-name *Seiljag* (sailboat) covered a series of 'normal' operations.

From the beginning of November, platoon commanders were allocated specific areas of responsibility to patrol, seek and destroy SWAPO guerrillas between beacons 25 and 34. Deployment was for a minimum period of three months, sometimes longer.

A platoon, loaded with enough rations and ammunition to last a fortnight, would be dropped off by road in the Yati Strip at the southern end of their designated area. Once the vehicles left, they would move as far as possible away from the drop zone, carefully obliterating their tracks as they went. At a position of their choice they would establish a supply cache, burying the bulk of their food and extra ammunition before booby-trapping the site with anti-personnel mines, which they would carefully plot. It was an inviolate rule that those who laid the mines also had to lift them when returning to the cache. As an added precaution, caches were normally used only once for re-supply before another location was chosen.

The first shots in *Seiljag 1* were fired on the evening of 26 November, when the platoon spotted a group of SWAPO at a waterhole on the edge of Chana Onaimbungu, three kilometres south of the border. The platoon shook out into an extended line and got to within 50 m of the waterhole before opening fire. The enemy fled in a westerly direction.

Just 40 minutes later another platoon, deployed north-west of the waterhole, killed six SWAPO who walked straight into their temporary base. The platoon commanders concluded that this was the same group that had fled the waterhole.

In mid-December, Colonel Breytenbach's brother Cloete, a photographer at the *Sunday Times* in Johannesburg, expressed a wish to visit the Operational Area to write a feature on the Border War. Even though the very existence of 32 Battalion was still classified top secret, Breytenbach agreed, on condition that neither the unit's name nor the fact that it was operating inside Angola was published.

On 23 December, the brothers left Omauni in a convoy under command of Corporal Tony Viera, who was to re-supply troops deployed in western

Owamboland and Angola. The Bosvark and five Unimogs followed the route to Ohikik, and at Beacon 35 a tracker spotted the spoor of bare feet and a dog entering Owamboland. Viera backtracked on the spoor two kilometres into Angola, as far as Chana Lupale, where his men took up position in the bush while he went ahead to assess the situation. It wasn't long before he returned with the news that he had sighted seven SWAPO in conversation with some of the local residents under a lone tree north of a village some 200 m away.

The platoon formed an extended line in the bush fringing the chana and leopard-crawled to within 70 m of the target before rising up and opening fire. The element of surprise was total, and only one of the SWAPO guerrillas survived to run away. The *Sunday Times* duly published Cloete Breytenbach's exclusive report, with photographs, of an anti-SWAPO operation by 'our boys on the border'.

On Christmas Day, a group of 25 SWAPO crossed into Owamboland at Beacon 25 and attacked a 32 Battalion platoon deployed a kilometre south of the border. After a heavy firefight, with no casualties to 32, the enemy fled back across the border.

January 1977 produced no tangible results of fleeting contacts with small groups of SWAPO, but on 19 February, troops deployed at Beacon 34 followed enemy tracks leading into Angola. Breytenbach, who was visiting the tactical headquarters to take his leave of the troops before returning to Pretoria for a staff officer's course, decided to lead two platoons in pursuit. At 19h30, in bright moonlight, they set out for Chana Namuhango, 14 km inside Angola, where they spotted seven SWAPO at the waterholes. Two were killed and at least one wounded before the guerrillas ran, leaving behind five RPG 7 rockets, six 60-mm mortar bombs and various other pieces of equipment. One member of Breytenbach's platoons was shot in the leg, and died the next day.

On 22 February, while patrolling from north of Chana Henombe, a platoon stumbled on a well-camouflaged SWAPO base two kilometres south-east of the chana. An estimated 100 SWAPO were entrenched in the base when the platoon walked smack into the middle of it, almost immediately coming under fire from small arms, mortars and RPG 7s. After a firefight lasting nearly ten minutes, which caused no casualties on either side, the guerrillas abandoned their trenches and scattered into the bush.

On 1 March, the platoon led by Lieutenant Gert Keulder found signs of enemy activity around Chana Mamuandi. As they moved north around the chana, the platoon came face to face with a group of five SWAPO. Keulder's men opened fire first, and the enemy fled. Eight days later, Keulder and his men located a SWAPO base in the Nutalala area, and destroyed it without meeting any real resistance. However, during their withdrawal, which started at 15h35, the platoon came under attack from a 300-strong SWAPO force. Despite the fact that they far outnumbered the 32 platoon, the guerrillas engaged them for only five minutes before melting into the bush, leaving five of their dead behind. Unfortunately, 32 paid a high price for their kills, as Lieutenant Keulder was fatally wounded during the skirmish.

Whether it was because word of 32's prowess on the battlefield had spread, or simply because they had little heart for sustained combat, SWAPO's tactics during this phase of the conflict amounted to little more than hit-and-run contacts. Even when they far outnumbered their opponents, it was customary for them to pour on the heat for a brief period, then disappear into the bush. This was the pattern even when they were defending well-prepared bases, such as the one found by Lieutenant Des Burman's platoon on a patrol along the Huavala River north of Beacon 31. SWAPO answered an attack with small arms, machine guns and RPG 7s for about ten minutes before fleeing to the north-west. The base was found to have a 1,2-m deep trench system stretching over some 150 m, with covered bunkers big enough for two men to sleep in at a time. Interrogation of a group of women who stayed behind when the guerrillas fled, revealed that the base had been set up some three months before, and that the SWAPO soldiers spent their days tending the maize fields, returning to the base at night.

The end of March marked the end of *Seiljag 1*, when the companies deployed originally were relieved by fresh troops.

PSEUDO-OPERATIONS

Towards the end of 1976, Colonel Breytenbach began experimenting with pseudo-operations as a more effective way of gleaning intelligence about SWAPO movements. The local population in much of the Operational Area was openly anti-SADF and of no help at all in keeping tabs on SWAPO, and the only way to obtain information was to infiltrate the movement's ranks.

A group of 30 troops from 32 Battalion, mostly from the Kuanyama tribe that straddled the border of South West Africa and Angola, were sent to Dodge City for training as SWAPO cadres. Captain Gert Brits, the intelligence officer, Second Lieutenant Des Burman and three black instructors who had previously been trained as guerrillas spent 90 days turning the group into operators who could pass themselves off as committed SWAPO fighters in any circumstances.

Their first mission was to make contact with a SWAPO group residing in the Opepela area, south-west of Nkongo base. On 4 January 1977, ten of the pseudo-operators were routed to Omauni for a final briefing and to be kitted out with SWAPO equipment.

About eight kilometres from Opepela, the operators changed into their SWAPO uniforms and set off into the bush. At 22h00 on 9 January they entered a village, where the local population professed to be terrified, maintaining that these were the first SWAPO to appear in the area for some considerable time. Over the next four days the operators visited all the waterholes in the area, making contact with more members of the local population, who now seemed to accept them. Then they moved on to the village of Petrus at Omutwewomunhu, where they were given food and warned that the direct route to the south offered no water at all.

Eight days after setting out the operators contacted their controllers by radio to report that they had made contact with the SWAPO group at Opepela, and expected to meet with them shortly. Breytenbach, waiting at Ondangwa with a reaction force, was informed accordingly and issued instructions that the pseudo-operators should not go to the meeting place, as once the location was known he would despatch a fireforce to attack the real SWAPO group.

Before the meeting could be set up, however, 101 Task Force received a signal from Army headquarters ordering that the operation be scrubbed immediately, as it had not been authorised in advance. The bureaucrats won the day, and 32 Battalion's first foray into the spy game was abandoned.

OPERATION BUCKSAW

Operational Order No. 21, issued by 101 Task Force on 28 March 1977, required 32 Battalion to pinpoint enemy bases or groups on the Angolan side of the border between beacons 26 and 38 as part of *Operation Bucksaw*.

However, for the first time 32 Battalion was ordered not to attack the enemy, merely to report to Tactical Headquarters on what they found. Assault forces would then be transported in Puma helicopters to launch the attacks, while 32 continued to patrol the area in search of targets.

Five platoons from 32 were already deployed in the area under command of second lieutenants Burman and Kriel, and sergeants S Hearn, Blue Kelly and R Oosthuizen.

The reaction force, waiting at Eenhana, consisted of 60 members of 1 Parachute Battalion, with a company from 8 SA Infantry Battalion held in reserve. Two Super Frelon and three Puma helicopters were available to airlift the troops, two Alouette gunships would provide support, and two Cessnas would be used as airborne command and control centres.

On 30 March the 32 platoons began patrolling the designated area, which stretched six kilometres into Angola. They found numerous tracks, but it was not until 6 April that they made contact with SWAPO. The platoons led by Kriel and Kelly were attacked while lying in ambush after they had been spotted by two individuals on a donkey the night before. The platoon leaders knew reports of their presence would prompt an attack, and deliberately remained in position to wait.

At 11h00, a group of about 100 SWAPO initiated a 30-minute firefight before fleeing in a northerly direction when the helicopter gunships arrived to offer air support. SWAPO suffered two dead, while 32 lost one man and another was wounded. The deserted SWAPO base was found about a kilometre to the north, complete with a trench system.

The patrolling platoons now concentrated on the chanas between beacons 34 and 36, and on the night of 9 April an attack on Sergeant Blue Kelly's temporary base was repulsed. In a follow-up operation the next day, the platoon found 50 trenches each large enough to accommodate between two and four people about 1,5 km to the north. It was clear that SWAPO was applying the same tactics throughout the area: preparing fallback positions in advance and attacking the patrols, then making for the trenches from where they could launch a second assault in the event that 32 immediately launched a follow-up. When the tactics failed to lure the patrols into the ambushes, SWAPO simply abandoned their positions and moved on. At the base found by Kelly's men, the spoor of 40 men could be seen heading west, possibly to Chana Golf.

On 12 April, Kriel's platoon located three deserted enemy bases along the edge of Chana Mamuandi. Five nights later they set up a temporary base three kilometres east of the chana, and the next day found the tracks of at least ten men about a kilometre to the south. They followed the spoor in a southerly direction, and then for about six kilometres to the west. Some 500 m east of Chana Mamuandi, the patrol and an enemy group spotted one another at virtually the same instant and immediately began to exchange fire. Kriel took one of the first hits, in the throat, and another ten men were also wounded, leaving command in the hands of the platoon sergeant, who decided to break off the contact due to the number of casualties taken. The wounded were carried to the border, from where they were casevaced.

By this time the paratroopers from the reaction force had also been deployed in the area, but it was soon apparent that the strategy envisaged would not be effective against the tactics employed by the enemy. On 19 April, the 32 Battalion platoons were redeployed to provide saturation coverage of the area. Two platoons were assigned to the area two kilometres north of Beacon 27, and another two, with what remained of Kriel's platoon, were sent two kilometres north of Beacon 29 in the vicinity of Chana Tofima. The two eastern platoons deployed along the Odilla River.

On 3 May, after an inexplicable lull in enemy activity, a Cessna sent to conduct an aerial reconnaissance of the area around Tofima spotted trenches on the western side of the chana and vehicle tracks leading north. Sergeant Hearn's platoon was sent from east of Chana Oanga to carry out ground reconnaissance on this newly located base.

North-west of Tofima, they picked up vehicle tracks running both to and from the north. The base was still under construction, a clear sign that SWAPO was intent on establishing a presence north of Beacon 29, but were being hindered by the 32 patrols. It was later learned that all the recent attacks had been launched by the group involved in building the base.

Patrols between beacons 26 and 28 continued until 21 May, when all the 32 forces drew back to Omauni, no further signs of enemy activity having been found. However, it was strongly suspected that SWAPO had pulled back to a large base somewhere between 20 and 30 km inside Angola.

Bucksaw was the first operation that 32 Battalion conducted in conjunction with the SA Army. In his debriefing report, Major Sedge Dunning, Air Staff Officer for the operation, made the following observation: 'It seems the battle tactics of 32 Battalion and those of 8 SAI and the Parachute Battalion differ markedly. The standard of clandestine operations conducted by 32 Battalion and those of the other two units cannot be compared. The Parachute Battalion soldiers showed no confidence in their capabilities, as became obvious to their platoon commander, Lieutenant Blaauw, when they informed him that they were astonished at the amount of equipment and ammunition carried by 32 Battalion soldiers, adding that they would have suffered enormous casualties if required to act against SWAPO in Angola, as they had no idea of the enemy's capabilities.'

Though no one has ever said so, and it is unlikely they would do so now, that report might very well have planted the seed that germinated in 32 Battalion consistently finding itself in the front line for the duration of the Angolan conflict.

OPERATION SEILJAG 2

Operation Bucksaw was followed almost immediately by deployment of a company south of the Angolan border, with Alpha, Delta and Foxtrot companies finding themselves north of the border yet again on 17 May.

At 18h00 on 27 May, Second Lieutenant H Rademeyer's platoon from Alpha Company noted a huge pile of food about 400 m from their position east of Chana Buabuena, along with three SWAPO cadres, one carrying a PPSh carbine, one an axe and the third a Seminof rifle. The platoon opened fire, killing the man with the Seminof, while the other two escaped.

The platoon destroyed the food cache, but walked into an ambush while withdrawing. The enemy broke contact after about a minute, leaving two of their dead behind. The platoon swept the area, finding discarded AK47 ammunition and an enemy base large enough for 150 men, west of the chana, which appeared to have been evacuated a day before.

On 6 June, Corporal FH le Roux of the protection platoon at Omauni was sent with nine vehicles, one mechanic and a medical orderly to drop off two additional platoons at Beacon 29 and re-supply those deployed in the Yati Strip.

They drove along 'Oom Willie se pad' (Uncle Willie's road), which linked

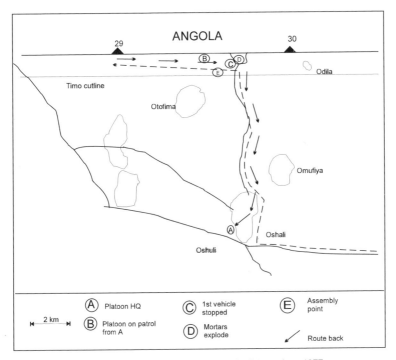

SWAPO ambush of Corporal le Roux's platoon, June 1977

military bases from Nkongo in the east to Etale in the west, before turning north to the cutline at Chana Oshali. In the Yati the convoy veered west, and the two platoons were dropped off just south of Beacon 29 on the morning of 7 June. Le Roux then backtracked on the same route, stopping about nine kilometres down the road to check his map. Suddenly, his driver noticed three SWAPO, armed with machine guns, to the left of the vehicle. Le Roux and his crew immediately debussed and opened fire on the trio. Almost at once the vehicles at the rear of the convoy came under fire as well, and pulled out of the line one by one to move up to the front. As they approached, Le Roux signalled to them not to stop, but to drive through the ambush at maximum speed. Up to that point, enemy fire had come only from the north, the left-hand side of the convoy.

With all the vehicles now under fire, the drivers debussed and moved into position closer to Le Roux. The 14 men had barely begun to return fire when a new attack came from the east. The corporal realised they had been caught in an L-shaped ambush, and they now found themselves under fire from 82-mm mortars aimed at predetermined targets too close to the vehicles for comfort. Le Roux ordered the drivers to return to their vehicles and get the hell out of there to the south. About a kilometre from the ambush they turned west, heading for a point two kilometres away where a platoon was known to be patrolling.

117

As the drivers took off, Le Roux noticed that one vehicle was not moving. He jumped into the driver's seat and, as he turned south, saw the wounded driver lying next to the road. He stopped to pick up the wounded man, then followed the rest of the convoy at speed. Reunited with his men, Le Roux was told by one of the drivers that as they returned to their vehicles, they saw SWAPO men and some women looting food from some of the Unimogs. After firing a few shots at the looters, they fled north, leaving the food behind.

The platoon patrolling the area advanced towards the contact point and promptly came under fire themselves. Only then did Le Roux notice that two of his vehicles had remained behind, smack in the middle of the ambush. In the face of an attack by a full platoon, SWAPO fled fairly quickly, and the two damaged vehicles were recovered. The convoy regrouped and proceeded to platoon head-quarters six kilometres to the south, returning to Omauni the next day.

Unfortunately, while waiting for the convoy to arrive, two 32 patrols became involved in a skirmish with one another. A platoon deployed in the Omundaungilo area was under command of the company headquarters at Elundu, while another, operating directly north of the area in the Yati, was under command of Omauni. The commander of the platoon in the Yati sent a section to the cutline to wait for Le Roux's convoy and guide them to the temporary base. Unbeknown to them, the patrol from Elundu was following the Timo Line, and had reached a position about 100 m south when the platoon in the Yati noticed a flock of birds taking sudden flight. A convoy had been ambushed in almost exactly the same area a few weeks before, and the section leader sent two scouts to investigate.

Just a few metres south of the Timo Line, they heard noise coming from what turned out to be the Elundu patrol taking a break. Without carrying out visual confirmation, and without any command to do so, the scouts opened fire in the general direction of the sounds. The men from Elundu returned fire immediately, and it was only when their commander began shouting commands in Portuguese that the two scouts realised they had attacked their own forces. Fortunately, casualties were light, with only one of the scouts being wounded. After this, how-ever, the two platoon commanders made regular radio contact with one another.

From the beginning of July, there was one of the sudden lulls in enemy activity that the troops had come to recognise as the calm before a storm. For three weeks not a sign of enemy movement was detected by any of the platoons. Then, on 24 July, Second Lieutenant H Fourie took a patrol out of the Yati Strip to Chana Oanga, where SWAPO had set up a temporary base. Assuming that the guerrillas were still in the area and had spotted his patrol, Fourie bombarded the base with 30 60-mm mortar bombs, firing another ten in the direction of the most likely escape route before withdrawing from the area. Unfortunately, Fourie and his platoon fell into a predictable routine while on patrol, and this did not escape the enemy's unseen but not unseeing eyes. On 28 July, the platoon found itself on the receiving end of a heavy 82-mm bombardment, and was lucky not to sustain any casualties. On the same day, Corporal Eloff's patrol was moving south to the Yati when they walked into a well-laid ambush north of Chana Oanga. An estimated 17 SWAPO were waiting in an L-formation along a dirt track, but, as usual, after a brief exchange of fire, they scattered both north and south. Follow-up operations over four kilometres revealed marks indicating that SWAPO were dragging either two dead or wounded soldiers with them.

Lieutenant Burman had concentrated his platoon's efforts around Chana Namixi, and was determined to gain domination of the area. At 12h05 on 28 July, the platoon went to replenish their water supplies in the chana, but Burman felt it prudent to first lay an ambush south-east of the waterholes, just in case the enemy was overcome by thirst at the same time. While lying in wait they saw some members of the local population, and after a while a group of herdboys arrived, driving scrawny cattle before them. After a brief conversation with one of the adults, one of the herdboys left.

Shortly afterwards, three SWAPO guerrillas appeared from the north and made themselves comfortable under a shady tree directly opposite Burman's ambush. A few minutes later, another six SWAPO, all toting machine guns, made their appearance too. Burman waited until all nine were at the waterhole before opening fire, but what he had not allowed for was the presence of more SWAPO in the bush to the north. They returned fire with machine guns, RPG 7 rockets and AK47s, deliberately firing the rockets into the trees under which Burman and his men had taken cover, thus effectively achieving an airburst, which resulted in several men being showered with shrapnel that lodged in their heads and upper bodies.

Rifleman Fernando, the 30 Browning machine-gunner, poured one long burst of fire after another at the enemy position, while Rifleman Gabriel dropped high-explosive 60-mm mortar shells on the SWAPO group with devastating accuracy.

Burman had difficulty restraining his troops from rushing headlong into a premature frontal attack, but as soon as the SWAPO fire began to abate, the platoon moved forward in short dashes, covering one another as they went. The enemy turned and ran, hotly pursued for 200 m before the men from 32 turned back to make sure the area was clear. Seven SWAPO bodies were found, and their weapons and ammunition duly collected for future use. One of Burman's men had been seriously wounded and required evacuation. It was strict SADF policy at the time that no helicopters were to cross the border under any circumstances, but on this occasion, after a great deal of pressure had been applied by the right people in the right places, an exception was made and a helicopter was sent from Eenhana to pick up the wounded man and the captured equipment.

The platoon stayed in their ambush position, and at 14h00 a sentry reported that SWAPO cadres were approaching. About five minutes later an enemy patrol walking in a semicircle formation appeared. Thirty minutes later the firefight was still raging, with SWAPO using 82-mm mortars in addition to small arms. Burman's platoon began to run out of ammunition and were forced to use some of the weapons captured during the earlier contact.

About a kilometre to the south, a platoon under the command of Corporal Pieters heard the gunfire and immediately moved to the aid of their comrades. Approaching from the south they launched their attack on the enemy's eastern flank, and thanks to the arrival of the reinforcements the enemy force eventually fled.

What made this contact different from previous encounters was the standard of leadership and control shown by the enemy. At the debriefing, just about everyone involved in the firefight confirmed seeing two white men directing the attack from the centre of the semicircle.

Eight members of 32 were wounded, but having flouted the standing regulations once that day already, there was no way Omauni could persuade Eenhana to send helicopters to evacuate them, so the wounded men were bodily carried back to the Yati Strip, the group arriving towards evening.

From August, the area around Namixi was swarming with SWAPO, groups of up to 200 being reported on the move, and on the 19th, platoons led by lieutenants Burman and Van der Westhuizen laid an ambush at Chana Bau. At 15h30, a herd of cattle driven by a boy aged about ten appeared, along with ten SWAPO. The troops misjudged their position, opening fire before the guerrillas were in the kill zone, and only the herdboy was killed. Six members of the platoon were wounded by RPG 7 shrapnel when SWAPO returned fire. The platoons withdrew to the south and set up a temporary base in the Yati Strip.

At 10h00 the next day, their temporary position came under bombardment from 82-mm mortars and 75-mm and 82-mm recoilless guns. The bombs fell short, but the reaction force was summoned from Eenhana, Major Dave Mentz arriving with an 81-mm mortar group. With an Alouette acting as aerial observer, the mortarists were right on the mark, and as the battle died down the Alouette reported the enemy moving north in vehicles, taking their hardware with them.

Seiljag 2 ended on 9 September, when the deployed troops were relieved by fresh companies from Buffalo Base.

OPERATION SEILJAG 3
This offensive differed from its predecessors in that all the 32 companies were deployed in Owamboland, and spent the first seven days attacking designated targets in the 'shallow' area between four and nine kilometres inside Angola.

A tactical headquarters was set up at Elundu, and on 11 September platoons crossed the border to Chana Hangadima. Finding no enemy, they returned to the Yati Strip towards evening and began preparing to attack a base at Chana Henombe. On reaching the base, they estimated that it had been abandoned some three weeks earlier. On the way back to the Yati, the platoons conducted a sweep through Chana Bau, but again no sign of the enemy was found.

A third search-and-destroy mission south and east of Chana Tofima produced very different results. Six platoons crossed the border on foot at 02h00 on 13 September, and began a sweep to the south just after first light. Both flanks made contact with SWAPO three kilometres south-east of the chana, and a ten-minute firefight broke out. As the estimated 200 SWAPO fled to the north, the platoons pursued them, walking into an ambush four kilometres east of the chana. This contact lasted about 20 minutes, and because the platoons were conserving ammunition, they did not pursue the enemy any further. A sweep of the area turned up seven dead guerrillas, as well as a large number of weapons and documents. Seven members of the platoon took shrapnel wounds and one was hit by an AK47 round.

After limited success in the 'shallow' area, normal patrols resumed between beacons 29 and 31. On 22 September, platoons led by Captain Pieter Botes and Second Lieutenant H Louw picked up enemy spoor moving to the south at Chana Hangadima. The lead scout reported sentries on the run and hearing enemy movement to the south. Moving in an extended line, the two platoons approached to within 30 m of the enemy before opening fire with small arms, RPG 7s, 60-mm mortars and 7,62-mm GPMG machine guns. A fierce firefight ended with the enemy abandoning their 1,2-m deep trenches, but Botes immediately despatched Louw's platoon to follow them. A second contact was made some 500 m into the bush, lasting about three minutes before the enemy 'bombshelled'.

A sweep of the area showed that SWAPO had been in a favourable position, with a 150-m trench system. The only problem was, their defences were directed towards an attack from the south, and 32 had come in from the north, throwing the well-prepared plan into disarray. Five dead SWAPO were found, all aged about 18 and wearing brand new mustard-coloured uniforms. Three AK47 rifles, a 60-mm mortar, two VZ52 light machine guns, four RPG 7 rockets, three RGD 5 hand grenades and a large quantity of food were confiscated.

That night a temporary base 600 m south of Beacon 28, where the platoons of Second Lieutenant R Griessel and Sergeant S Gericke had laid up, came under attack by a large group of enemy using RPG 7s as well as 82-mm mortars, and either a 75-mm or 82-mm recoilless gun firing from inside Angola. The bombardment was brief but heavy.

Meanwhile, the platoon led by Botes had moved towards Chana Chinota, and at 04h00 on 25 September, during an attack on their temporary base, the sound of an enemy helicopter was heard for the first time, to the north, for about

20 minutes. The SWAPO assault came in three waves, the first lasting 30 minutes and the other two about five minutes each. A sweep of the area at first light revealed 78 shallow foxholes and four 82-mm mortar positions to the north, while seven LMG nests were found 200 m south of the temporary base, covering both the western and eastern flanks. Had the platoon moved southwards during the battle, as SWAPO had clearly expected them to do, they would have run straight into the machine guns.

Low on ammunition, Botes took the platoon back to the Yati for replenishment, but the next day they returned to Chana Chinota in search of their attackers. During a night patrol on 27 September, the platoon found them, exchanging fire briefly before going into hot pursuit of the enemy for four kilometres before they melted into the night.

At Chana Namixi, patrols led by Second Lieutenant Griessel and Lieutenant Daan de la Rey ambushed seven SWAPO on their way to the waterholes, killing two and wounding another. For the first time, an AK47 with a folding butt was captured.

In the first week of October, all the companies were recalled to Buffalo to prepare for a combined operation with Special Forces. It would be the biggest offensive since *Operation Savannah*.

OPERATION KROPDUIF

Six months earlier, during *Operation Bucksaw*, it had been determined that there was a major SWAPO base some six kilometres north-west of Chana Golf. Aerial reconnaissance photographs of the base had been taken, and documents captured at Tofima during *Seiljag 3* referred to a SWAPO regimental headquarters at Ohaipete, or Eheke. Interrogation of prisoners had confirmed that this was the main SWAPO base, which was given the SADF code-name Target 21.

Operation Kropduif (pouter pigeon) would take place in two phases, with attacks on Chana Tofima and Chana Nutalala before 24 October, to be followed by a combined 32 Battalion and Special Forces assault on Eheke. On 21 October, 12 rifle platoons and an 81-mm mortar group were transported from Omauni to Chana Nunda, between beacons 27 and 28. A tactical headquarters was set up at Elundu under command of Commandant Gert Nel, OC 32 Battalion, and Commandant J Kriel of the SAAF, who would be in charge of the helicopters used during the operation.

By 17h00 on 22 October, Corporal FH le Roux's mortar group and Second Lieutenant PSC Myburg's protection platoon were in position south of the border. At 05h15 the next day, five platoons under command of Major Eddie Viljoen crossed into Angola, attacking the SWAPO base at Chana Tofima 45 minutes later from the east. The enemy fled north-west towards Mamuandi, and while in pursuit the platoons came across two deserted bases, capturing a large number of RPG 7 rockets in one. They also found drag marks and blood along the trail, indicating that SWAPO had taken casualties at Chana Tofima.

On 24 October, the tactical headquarters moved to Eenhana under command of Major General Ian Gleeson, Officer Commanding 101 Task Force, and two days later, at 20h00, all 12 rifle platoons and the mortar group began moving north to Chana Namuidi under Major Viljoen's command. In the early hours of 27 October, the mortarists and a protection platoon were in position 800 m north of the chana, from where they were to provide fire support during 32's attack on Chana Golf. At first light, six platoons moved in from the east for the assault, the remaining five platoons held in reserve two kilometres north of Namuidi. Somehow the attack group misjudged their distance from the target, reaching it only at 08h30, but it was empty in any event and appeared to have been vacated at least a week before. Vehicle tracks and footprints indicated that the enemy had moved further north, and Viljoen's group was ordered to join the reserve force at Namuidi.

On the way they heard the sound of small-arms fire, RPG 7 rockets and mortars coming from the position of the reserves, which had been attacked by a group of about 30 SWAPO, and suffered one fatality during a ten-minute firefight. By the time the main force reached the reserves, it was 14h10 and the battle was over, but a Puma helicopter sent in to pick up the body of the dead man drew 82-mm mortar fire from the direction of Eheke, indicating that the main target was still occupied by the enemy.

At 16h15 on 27 October, tactical headquarters issued the go-ahead for Special Forces to attack Eheke 1, and for 32 Battalion to attack Eheke 2. But at 04h10 on 28 October, SWAPO launched a pre-emptive strike against the 32 positions with 122-mm rockets and 82-mm recoilless guns, followed by a simultaneous infantry assault from the north-east and north-west, and an RPG 7 barrage from the south-east. In addition to heavy small-arms fire, 60-mm white phosphorous mortar bombs rained down on the 32 men. In the face of a counter-attack SWAPO withdrew briefly, but almost immediately initiated another bombardment with 82-mm mortars and recoilless guns. One member of 32 was killed, and seven wounded by shrapnel.

Tactical headquarters ordered the rifle companies to bombard Eheke 2 as soon as the Special Forces were ready to attack Eheke 1. At 15h10 the bombardment began, and ten minutes later nine platoons started advancing on the target in attack formation, while Pumas flew in to evacuate the dead and wounded and replenish the dangerously low water supply.

Approximately 1,5 km west of the chana, the platoons found a large group of huts containing food and water, which had most likely served as a rest or transit facility. From there, all tracks led to Eheke.

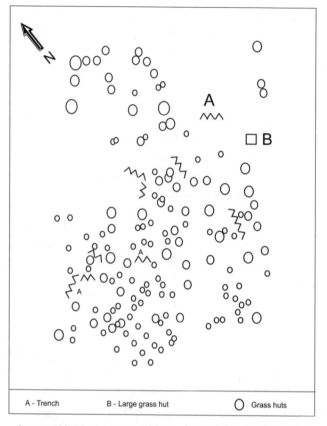

A - Trench   B - Large grass hut   ◯ Grass huts

Layout of Eheke 2 base attacked by 32 Battalion, October 1977

Special Forces attacked Eheke 1 at 16h30, but lost seven men – including Sergeant Vingers Kruger – in a heavy battle. The base 32 was supposed to attack on the southern side turned out to consist of nothing more than a few huts and shelters, with no sign of enemy presence. In rapidly fading light it was impossible for them to carry out further reconnaissance to the south-east, and the platoons joined up with the Special Forces group just before dark, at which point tactical headquarters ordered the immediate withdrawal of all forces back to Owamboland. They began moving south at 21h45 and crossed the border at 06h45 on 29 October.

In his debriefing report on the operation, Commandant Nel recommended that 32 Battalion be equipped with larger calibre support weapons, such as the 140-mm G2 artillery pieces. He also urged that Eheke be attacked again before the end of the year, and that Mulembo and Anime should be attacked in 1978, as these had been identified as the most important SWAPO bases in the area.

7

To fight ... to fight

MILITARY OPERATIONS 1978-1979

AS THE CALENDAR rolled over to 1978, South Africa's politicians and military high command already knew what 32 Battalion was about to find out. Extension of compulsory National Service from 12 months to two years as of January 1978 was one of the first signs that operations against SWAPO – even the still top secret confrontations with FAPLA and its surrogate foreign forces – were merely the dress rehearsal for a full decade of war that would culminate in the heaviest conventional fighting in southern Africa's history in 1988.

On 25 October 1977, Major General Wally Black had informed the decision-makers in Pretoria that at least 300 SWAPO insurgents had penetrated the Operational Area, and that on average 100 contacts were taking place each month between South African security forces and small groups of SWAPO. Just two days after this briefing, another 80 SWAPO insurgents slipped into Owamboland, and over the next several months the intensity of terrorist incidents escalated dramatically, with the murder of prominent tribal headmen becoming the order of the day.

In December 1977, a decision that would ultimately touch the lives of virtually every South African was taken at the scenic coastal resort of Oubos, near Port Elizabeth, where Prime Minister BJ Vorster had his holiday home. Vorster himself was not wildly enthusiastic about the strategy proposed by his security ministers and the SADF's most senior generals, but he allowed himself to be persuaded that in order to counter the growing threat to stability in South West Africa – and stem the rising tide of internal unrest following the 1976 student uprising in South Africa – a programme of pre-emptive strikes and cross-border raids into neighbouring states would have to be launched. He insisted, however, that such operations would have to be authorised at the highest level, namely by him.

It was a watershed decision that would shape both the face of war and the psyche of an entire generation on the African subcontinent.

For 32, the year began badly enough as it was. On 4 January, while clearing the anti-personnel mines protecting one of Charlie Company's food caches in the Yati Strip, Sergeant Eloff accidentally stepped on one of the mines, losing the toes on one foot and sustaining serious burns.

OPERATION SEILJAG 4

The start of the year found Charlie Company deployed between beacons 26 and 29, with all patrols confined to Owamboland. Explicit orders had been issued that no one was to cross into Angola without prior authorisation. It didn't take long for SWAPO to figure out that hot pursuit operations had become a thing of the past, and they adapted their tactics accordingly, attacking temporary bases situated closest to the border, then immediately withdrawing into Angola.

The first such incident took place at 10h50 on New Year's Day, when a Charlie Company platoon's temporary base west of Chana Onhunda, some 800 m south of the border, was attacked briefly from inside Angola, with a 12,7-mm DSHK machine gun being used in support for the first time.

One week later, a temporary base west of Chana Omelepapa came under mortar attack at 01h05. On 9 January, while replenishing their water supply at a chana six kilometres south of Beacon 28, the platoon was ambushed by a group of 90 SWAPO who had infiltrated during the night. Fortunately the guerrillas opened fire prematurely, and in the face of a counter-attack fled north-east and back into Angola.

With a pattern now beginning to emerge, it was obvious that 32 would have to go on the offensive if the platoons were not to become sitting ducks for SWAPO attacks. Staff Sergeant Blue Kelly's third platoon was authorised to go across the border and reconnoitre the area around Chana Eongue, four kilometres west of Beacon 26.

They slipped into Angola on the night of 14 January and set up an observation post on the eastern edge of the chana, just 400 m across the border. At 09h30 the next day, two enemy passed Kelly's position heading south and entered South West Africa. The observation post was manned for the entire day, and Kelly also sent out small reconnaissance patrols in the immediate vicinity, which discovered a perfectly laid ambush some 200 m to the east at a road junction not marked on the map. Big enough for 50 men, 150 m long and facing south, the position had almost certainly been prepared in anticipation of a follow-up after a SWAPO attack.

Kelly's men occupied the ambush site until late that afternoon, then moved about 400 m north after laying a mechanical ambush of Claymore mines linked with Cordex to TM 57 anti-tank mines.

After an uneventful night, Kelly returned to the observation post. Around noon, a heavy downpour wiped out any tracks the platoon might have missed, and Kelly was confident that the enemy would have no inkling of their presence. On the afternoon of 16 January he moved across the northern edge of the chana to a point 2,5 km north of the border, and spent the night there. An early morning sweep of the immediate surroundings showed tracks two to three days old at a point 200 m north of the observation post. At 09h50 the mechanical ambush detonated, but Kelly waited until afternoon to inspect the damage. He estimated that SWAPO must have suffered at least two dead and two wounded before moving north-east. Kelly set up another three mechanical ambushes in the same area and moved 800 m to the north.

On the evening of 18 January, a patrol sent to fetch water from the chana to the north spotted 12 SWAPO walking away from the waterhole, and opened fire on them. The rest of the platoon began lobbing 60-mm mortars in the general direction of the gunfire, and while pursuing the enemy in bright moonlight for about a kilometre, one dead body was found in the bush. The platoon remained at the observation post until 12h00 the next day, when they returned to their base.

Analysis of the intelligence gleaned indicated that SWAPO was using the area between beacons 27 and 28 as an infiltration route. The six platoons from Charlie Company withdrew from the area to Elundu, with orders to locate any SWAPO up to five kilometres north of the cutline between the two beacons.

On 26 January, six platoons and an 81-mm mortar group under command of Major Eddie Viljoen were taken by road from Elundu to a point north of Chana Oshipala. At 06h15 the next day, five platoons moved north to Chana Hacaonde while the sixth, along with the mortar group, took up a support position four kilometres south of the chana.

Tracks of what was probably a reconnaissance group of 30, walking two abreast in single file about 20 m apart and moving from east to west were picked up, but a thorough search of the chana proved fruitless. The platoons moved due north to Chana Namixe, which was also quiet, although the spoor of what appeared to be another reconnaissance patrol, this time consisting of only five people, was found a kilometre to the east. The platoons followed the customary routes to chanas at Bau, Hangadima and Oanga without finding any signs of the enemy before returning to Elundu.

The conclusion reached was that SWAPO had moved their bases deeper into Angola, possibly as far as 12 km from the border. Aerial reconnaissance confirmed that around Henombe, Chinota, Mamuandi, Candombe and Cuanhama, crops were in the fields and a fairly large local population group was spotted.

Major Viljoen recommended that operations be launched against all these chanas, but quite suddenly all signs of enemy activity ceased, and for the next three months not a single SWAPO sighting was reported. By the middle of April, Alpha and Bravo companies were ordered back to Elundu to join forces with another three companies for *Operation Reindeer*, the first official cross-border raid since *Savannah*.

Following *Reindeer*, 32 resumed deployment of companies between beacons 26 and 30, but from July to December the area was unusually quiet. Bravo Company alone made contact, first in the form of a minor skirmish between the third platoon, led by Second Lieutenant JHF Fourie, and four SWAPO trying to cross into South West Africa in September, and again on 12 September, when Second Lieutenant AL Opperman and the second platoon walked into an ambush 200 m south of the border on the edge of Chana Omelepapa.

SWAPO had set up a PKM machine gun at one point of the 38-man ambush, and waited until half of the platoon was in the kill zone before opening fire. Opperman died just eight metres from the machine-gun position, and two of his men were wounded before the enemy pulled back into Angola.

But despite the long intervals between action during 1978, the statistics for *Seiljag 4* confirmed what the generals and cabinet ministers had known when the year began: the nature of the Border War had undergone a sea change, and it would consume ever more men, money and machines in future. In exchange for 23 SWAPO killed during 1978, eight members of 32 Battalion had given their lives. It was not one of their better years.

OPERATION REINDEER

On 22 April 1978, a group of SWAPO hijacked a bus travelling between Oshakati and Ruacana and drove the 73 passengers aboard across the border into Angola. Three days later, the South African government formally accepted proposals for a negotiated settlement to the problem of South West Africa, and three days after that a group of 100 SWAPO engaged security forces in western Owamboland before making for the safety of Angola.

What neither the international community nor SWAPO realised was that even as South Africa was agreeing to seek a political solution and withdraw its forces, it was planning the first major attack inside Angola since *Operation Savannah*.

According to official records, *Operation Reindeer* was the first time since December 1975 that the SADF engaged the forces of another country on foreign soil. This, of course, is neither historically accurate nor true, since 32 Battalion had been fighting against FAPLA and its Cuban surrogates inside Angola since 1976, albeit on a limited and non-conventional scale.

Reindeer was to be a three-phase operation, starting with an airborne attack by 44 Parachute Brigade, led by Colonel Jan Breytenbach, on Target Alpha, or Cassinga – SWAPO's main training and logistical base 250 km inside Angola, heavily defended with an elaborate trench system, artillery and anti-aircraft guns, known as Moscow. Battle Group Juliet, commanded by Commandant Frank Bestbier, would launch ground attacks in the western sector around Chetaquera on Target Bravo, SWAPO's headquarters – called Vietnam – the Mahama transit camp to the south; the logistical base known as Windhoek; and four smaller bases – Chatua, Dombondala 1 and 2 and Haimona.

In the third and final phase, 32 Battalion would attack 17 suspected SWAPO bases in the eastern sector between beacons 26 and 30, operating up to 30 km inside Angola. The battalion's mission was spelled out in Operational Order No. 4/78, issued on 26 April. Major Eddie Viljoen would command five 32 Battalion companies, one medium artillery troop of 140-mm guns and an 81-mm mortar platoon. No offensive air support would be available.

During the planning stage, it was found that very little or no information was available on the bases earmarked for attack by 32, and a decision was made to focus on the 'shallow' targets rather than going for deep penetration into unknown territory.

Alpha, Bravo, Charlie, Delta and Echo companies linked up with the artillery troop at Elundu, but the gunners only arrived at a late stage in the preparations, leaving very little time for coordinated drills. It wasn't long before the realisation set in that Phase 3 of the operation had been accorded less priority during the planning stage than the attacks on targets Alpha and Bravo, a deficiency that would prove critical as *Reindeer* progressed.

The airborne assault – the largest operational parachute drop since World War II – and Battle Group Juliet's offensive began on 4 May, but it was not until 6 May that 32 Battalion was authorised to initiate Phase 3. The plan was to systematically destroy one base after another in the following sequence: Minquita (or H, Hotel being the name used by 32 for this chana), Namuidi, Omelepapa, Henombe, Target 3 (a chana three kilometres north-west of Henombe), Onalumona, Ohaipeto, Target 6, Jaano, Mamuandi, Chinota, Hangadima, Bau (the closest base, just three kilometres from the border), Namixi, Candombe, Canhama and Tecole.

During the night of 5 May, Viljoen's force moved from Elundu to Chana Nunda, and by 04h00 on 6 May the artillery was in position just south of the border. At 04h15, Alpha, Bravo and Delta companies crossed the cutline, leaving Charlie as protection for the artillery and Echo in reserve at the tactical headquarters at Elundu.

At 08h00, contact was made with SWAPO at Chana Minquita. After firing mortars at the 32 platoons, the enemy hightailed it north-east to Chana Namuidi. Viljoen's men immediately pushed north, forming up 500 m south of Chana Namuidi, with one company deployed on each side of the road from Minquita.

Artillery support was called in, directed by an officer in a spotter aircraft piloted by João Martins, a former Angolan flying for the SAAF. Orders from the ground

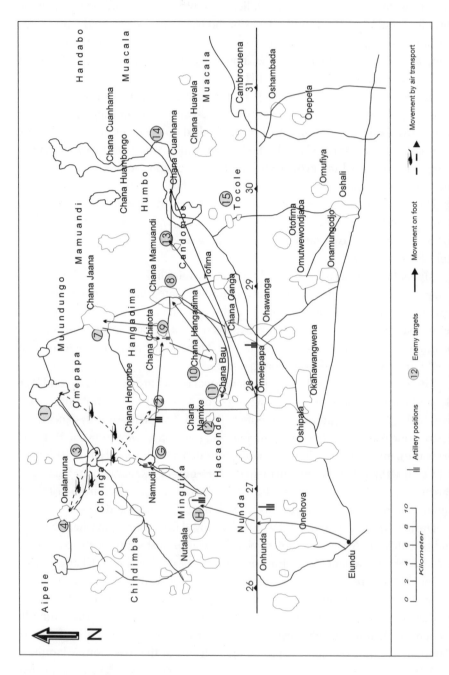

Operation Reindeer: third-phase movement and attacks by 32 Battalion

were for a single gun to be fired to 'shoot in' or find the range. The first shell exploded some 500 m short of the base. The correction was communicated, but instead of waiting for a second single shell to be fired to confirm that it was on target, the airborne controller issued the order: 'Troop bombardment, five shots fire for effect.'

The first shell hit the mark, but the two rounds fired by each of the other three guns either exploded while still in the air, or hit the ground some six metres in front of the 32 troops. The bombardment was halted immediately, but the damage had already been done. Sergeant CJ Theron was killed, sergeants Ron Gregory and Blue Kelly suffered serious shrapnel wounds, and another 16 troops were less seriously wounded.

With that number of casualties, any attempt to attack the base would have been disastrous, and Viljoen withdrew his men three kilometres south to regroup and evacuate the wounded. The bitter fruit of late and inadequate planning for Phase 3 of *Reindeer* was plucked when it took two hours for the casevac helicopters to arrive. No one had thought to inform the SAAF that their services would be required during Phase 3, and the time lapse afforded SWAPO the ideal opportunity to evacuate their base and head for Chana Omelepapa.

That night, Viljoen's force remained in position three kilometres south of Chana Minquita. The next morning the artillery and Charlie Company moved up to join them, and were in position by noon. Predictably, when the three assault companies entered the base, they found it deserted. By 18h00 the facilities had been destroyed, and the companies formed a laager north of the chana for the night. The artillery, meanwhile, moved to a new position at Chana Namuidi.

At 20h00, the overnight base was attacked with 14 122-mm rockets fired from the direction of Onalumona. Fortunately there were no casualties, but the bombardment confirmed that the enemy was still in the vicinity.

A change of strategy was clearly needed, however, and the SAAF was called in to airlift the troops to the next target in Puma and Super Frelon helicopters.

This gave 32 a much needed advantage, and by noon on 8 May, Chana Omelepapa had been cleared and the SWAPO base destroyed. By 12h30, Target 3 had suffered the same fate, followed in quick succession by Onalumona (16h00), Henombe (17h00) and Ohaipeto (18h00). By 19h00, all the companies involved were back at Chana Namuidi.

Throughout the day the same tactics had been applied – the targets being bombarded by the artillery or mortars before the ground troops moved in by helicopter or on foot. After this, however, the helicopters returned to base, and the rest of the operation was carried out according to the original plan.

By 11h00 on 9 May the artillery was in position at Chana Henombe to fire on the remaining targets, and by 13h00 Chana Chinota was secured. By 16h00 the base at Chana Jaano had been destroyed and the force moved back to Chinota, where they set up a defensive position for the night.

At 10h00 on 10 May, officially the last day of the operation, the base at Chana Hangadima was attacked. While this assault was in progress, Charlie Company was sent back to the cutline to secure the area at Chana Omelepapa, to which the artillery would pull back. At 14h00, the base at Mamuandi was destroyed, followed by Chana Bau. When no enemy presence was found at Candombe and Canhama, Alpha Company was sent back to the border, leaving Bravo and Delta to destroy the base at Namixe, which was accomplished by 18h00. The last target on the list, Tecole, was attacked at 09h00 on 11 May, after which the two companies moved south, rejoining Charlie and Alpha companies and the artillery troop south of the border by 10h00.

An official inquiry into the death of Sergeant Theron showed that the guns used during the operation had been standing at Grootfontein since *Savannah*, and due to lack of routine maintenance, seals had perished, rendering them wholly inaccurate. In the hasty preparation for *Reindeer* the guns had not been calibrated, thus presenting a far greater danger to their own forces than to any enemy.

RECONNAISSANCE PATROLS
By early March 1979, 32 Battalion's reconnaissance wing was ready for deployment, the junior leaders drawn from the School of Infantry having completed the rigorous training that began in November 1978. None of them had any operational experience as yet, but the teams they would lead had plenty, having been with the unit since early 1976.

The concept of recce teams being attached to specific units was entirely new, and the battalion's operational commanders wasted no time testing their mettle. Initial deployments were under command of Staff Sergeant Blue Kelly, head of the recce wing, and took place north of Elundu. The first recce wing mission outside 32's traditional theatre of operations saw a group of 19, commanded by Sergeant Ron Gregory, detached to 52 Battalion for deployment in the area between beacons 6 and 12. They arrived on 7 May, and were immediately despatched to establish whether SWAPO had a presence in the area north of Beacon 6 as far as Naulila. They crossed the border that same night, moving north/north-east for 12 km, and then due east for another three kilometres before sleeping from 02h30 to 05h30. At 09h40, the team encountered two SWAPO crossing their path about 50 m ahead. When the guerrillas spotted the patrol they ran, but the recce group opened fire and killed one of them. On turning south, the patrol observed four more SWAPO climbing over a village fence at Chana Chamobe and again opened fire, but the guerrillas disappeared into a lush grain field.

About a kilometre south of this village, a temporary base and defensive position were set up. At 11h55, Corporal Piet Nortje, manning LMG No. 1, and his counterpart manning LMG No. 2, each spotted guerrillas moving towards them. The man in Nortje's sights was armed with a PKB machine gun and wearing the typical mustard-coloured SWAPO uniform. He appeared to be following the tracks to the temporary base, and when spotted was only five metres from the perimeter.

The second intruder, sporting a green SWAPO beret, spotted the 32 force when he was about 20 m from the base, and dived for cover. Right on cue, the rest of the SWAPO group opened fire in an arc from west to east, sparking a seven-minute firefight that included three PKB machine guns and two RPG 7s, to which 32 replied with light machine-gun and 60-mm mortar fire.

The initial enemy fire was low and accurate, wounding riflemen J Breio and C Santana, while RPG 7 rockets exploding in a tree wounded second lieutenants Stef Naude and Willy Botha. Corporal Nortje killed the guerrilla who had been creeping up on LMG No. 1, as well as one of his comrades, who tried to recover the PKB.

As soon as the tempo of the enemy fire abated, 32 ceased firing, and Sergeant Gregory began attending to the wounded while Mahanene base was contacted by radio with a request for air support, the patrol having been told in advance that two Impalas would be on standby.

But SWAPO had not withdrawn, and within minutes launched a second attack from the west, again firing RPG 7s, machine guns and AK47s for some three minutes.

Again the firing stopped, but as the 32 men began cutting wood for stretcher poles, their temporary base came under fire from RPG 7s and small arms for the third time. The request for air support was repeated at 12h27.

Unsure where the enemy now was, the group moved 500 m south to secure a landing zone for the casevac helicopters, but it was not until 14h30, two hours after the second call for air support had gone out, that two Impala strike aircraft appeared overhead. The ground troops made radio contact with the pilots before marking their own position with coloured smoke, and the aircraft strafed an area about 300 m in front of the smoke. On the ground, loud shouts and agonised groans in Kuanyama could be heard coming from the bush north-west of the landing zone.

A few minutes later, a Puma and an Alouette gunship flew in, the Puma landing to pick up the wounded and excess equipment, and drop off fresh ammunition. As the Puma lifted off, the Alouette pinpointed targets for the still airborne Impalas in the surrounding bush and villages. Another Puma flew in at 14h45 and airlifted the remaining troops to Mahanene, from where they made their way to Ogongo.

This uncharacteristically aggressive attack by SWAPO could have been because they mistook the 32 group for UNITA, which was known to be active in the area. Although it caused the recce wing to cut short their mission, it did confirm a significant SWAPO presence north of Beacon 6.

The fledgling recce wing's next operation was carried out in conjunction with two platoons from 4 SA Infantry, north of Beacon 12. The patrol leader, Major Willie 'Owambo' Snyders, defined the objective as 'seek and destroy SWAPO'. The two recce teams were to act as advance scouts.

They crossed into Angola at 05h00 on 12 May, stopping for a break seven kilometres north of the border at 07h30 – and promptly heard the sound of SWAPO singing approximately 800 m away. Snyders requested that the standby force be deployed in stopper group positions to the north, but was informed they would only be available an hour later. The patrol moved about six kilometres west and spent the rest of the day and that night in an old and deserted SWAPO base.

The next morning they returned to their previous position, only to find that the base from which the singing had been heard was empty. The platoon followed tracks leading from the base, and at 12h00 Major Snyders spotted two guerrillas and opened fire on them, but they got away. Later in the day another deserted enemy base was found before the patrol turned south for about five kilometres and spent the night. The next morning, while moving west, a 103-mm rifle grenade was fired at a man seen running away from a hut, but he, too, escaped.

Proceeding in a north-westerly direction, the patrol encountered a group of people in a chana at 12h50. A weapon was spotted in their midst and the patrol opened fire, killing a FAPLA soldier who was found to be carrying an MPLA membership card and a Mauser Model 98 rifle. A woman and child who were wounded were evacuated to Oshakati for medical treatment.

After covering another four kilometres the patrol stopped for the night, and moved back over the border the next morning. On 21 May the recce wing returned to Buffalo Base, having gained valuable experience in the field.

Commandant Chris Serfontein, commander of 52 Battalion, made no bones about his opinion of the recce teams, however. He was singularly unimpressed, quite possibly because, like many others, he had made the mistake of comparing 32's recce wing with the Army's Special Forces. While the two groups certainly shared specific skills and abilities, there were clear-cut distinctions between their application and deployment. The men themselves understood this, and shared a mutual respect for their similar yet divergent roles, but outsiders never quite grasped the differences.

Happily, Serfontein's troops would work side by side with members of 32's recce wing again in later years, and the outcome caused him to completely revise his initial assessment.

8

We want fire!

MILITARY OPERATIONS 1980-1982

THE ERA OF the Falcon – Commandant Deon Ferreira – found 32 Battalion involved in a series of major operations that frequently included other SADF elements, ranging from the Air Force and paratroopers to artillery and Special Forces. In May 1978, *Operation Reindeer* had dealt SWAPO a mortal blow, with 856 guerrillas confirmed dead and another 200 taken prisoner (the SADF casualties were four dead and 11 wounded), to say nothing of disrupting its supply and logistical lines.

But the operation had also caused a major international uproar, with the SADF accused of butchering women and children in what SWAPO claimed were nothing but refugee camps. As Colonel Jan Breytenbach ironically remarked: 'Those were the best armed and best trained refugees *I'd* ever encountered.'

During 1979, Ferreira's first year in command of 32 Battalion, the eyes of the world were firmly fixed on the conflict raging throughout southern Africa, but this did not prevent 32 from engaging the enemy whenever and wherever possible. With the help of their sponsors in Moscow, FAPLA and SWAPO wasted little time reasserting their position, and by October 1979, despite continuous clandestine action by the SADF's Special Forces to destroy strategic targets on the supply routes to the south, FAPLA had established a stronghold at Caiundo.

In neighbouring Rhodesia, politics swiftly overtook military action as the preferred solution, and by December 1979 the controversial Lancaster House Agreement had been signed, guaranteeing a one-man, one-vote election within months. In Pretoria, the securocrats led by PW Botha and his Minister of Defence, General Magnus Malan, were coming to terms with the fact that once Rhodesia became independent under the leadership of ZANU-PF leader Robert Mugabe, the full focus of international attention would turn to South West Africa, the final bulwark between a communist-dominated subcontinent and South Africa itself. They had no intention of surrendering the military option, and even as Rhodesians prepared to go to the polls on 27 February 1980, southern Angola was the scene of an ongoing offensive designed to inflict maximum casualties on SWAPO.

OPERATION DRIEHOEK

When radio intercepts indicated that SWAPO was stockpiling supplies for a possible attack on Eenhana or Elundu, it became necessary to disrupt the so-called Far Eastern Front. Measured against the frequency of contact with the enemy, *Operation Driehoek* (triangle) was one of the most intense involving 32 Battalion. Clashes with small groups of SWAPO occurred on a daily basis, and there were also occasional confrontations with larger groups.

While troops from Elundu were involved in *Operation Hammer*, sweeping an area north of the base and two kilometres into Angola, 32 Battalion was assigned to the area north of Beacon 21. Under command of Ferreira, Echo and Foxtrot companies, as well as two reconnaissance teams with the call signs WR and ZG, entered Angola on 4 February 1980, with Echo deploying over a ten-kilometre area east of Chiede, Foxtrot covering a similar sized area to the south, and the two recce teams airlifted by helicopter 14 km to the north-east.

The recce teams were barely out of the Puma before exchanging fire with two SWAPO. The helicopter pilot reported fresh vehicle tracks north of the drop zone, and the recce team immediately set up an ambush. The next day, it was the turn of Echo Company's first and fourth platoons, which killed two guerrillas while patrolling ten kilometres north-east of Namacunde.

On 6 February, the platoons found an empty base at Chana Nacondo and destroyed a stash of food. That evening, they spotted SWAPO guerrillas in a kraal to the north and opened fire, but the presence of civilians hampered the action and the cadres fled, leaving one dead body behind. At just about the same time, the two reconnaissance teams were in a lay-up close to the road 12 km north-east of Chiede, when a Land Rover driven by a white man passed by. As the recces moved closer to the road, five SWAPO appeared. A short firefight left three of them dead. Ninety minutes later, the Land Rover drove into the ambush the recces had laid. The driver was killed instantly when an RPG 7 rocket, fired head-on, turned the vehicle into an inferno. The co-driver escaped and ran into the bush, where his body was found later that night.

On the afternoon of 7 February, Foxtrot Company's first platoon was attacked by approximately 40 SWAPO, and had to call for gunship support. At 19h00, Echo Company's second platoon went to replenish their water supply at Chana Euxe, only to find that a group of SWAPO had the same idea. Thirst cost one guerrilla his life, while his comrades escaped.

On the morning of 8 February, the reconnaissance teams heard explosions from the area 16 km north-east of Chiede, where they had set an automatic ambush with anti-personnel mines the day before. On investigating, they found two dead SWAPO. At 14h00, Echo Company's platoon returned to the waterhole, exchanged fire with a 25-strong SWAPO patrol guarding the chana, and killed one guerrilla.

At 08h45 the next day, a four-man recce team and a group of SWAPO ran into one another on the road from Chiede to the east. Realising they were greatly outnumbered, the recces called in the gunships, and SWAPO lost three men. At 13h45, recce team WR was in a lay-up 18 km north of Chiede when they realised there was enemy movement around their position. The gunships were called in again, but could find no targets. When Lieutenant Willem Ratte led his men to investigate, however, they encountered a group of 40 SWAPO, and between the gunships and the four men on the ground, 13 SWAPO were killed and three captured. Rifleman J Antonio was wounded and evacuated, and the prisoners were transported to the tactical headquarters.

Under interrogation they disclosed that SWAPO's 150-strong detachment headquarters was at Onesheshe, 16 km north of Chiede. The captives had moved south from their platoon base at Cadueia with orders to attack any targets they found. Based on this information, reinforcements from Echo Company were sent to the contact area and an additional Puma helicopter was placed on standby at Eenhana to airlift more troops, if needed. By sundown nothing had happened, and the recce teams in the field were sent to Chiede to locate the enemy base. From the next day, patrols were carried out in company rather than platoon strength. Echo Company found the tracks of a 75-mm recoilless gun leading south from Chana Hengue, and at 08h30 on 11 February, Foxtrot Company's third platoon made contact with a group of 40 SWAPO 12 km south-east of Chiede. Two helicopter gunships provided air support, and SWAPO lost two men before splitting into smaller groups and fleeing to the north.

Two days later the companies were moved six kilometres south of Chiede in preparation for an attack on a possible base at Chitumbo. The road from Chiede to Namacunde and Ongiva was mined, and the 81-mm mortar group was ordered to move from Elundu to Eenhana by 15 February. Companies in the field, due to have been relieved on 13 February, were ordered to remain in position for at least another ten days.

The plan was that Impalas would attack the suspected base on 18 February before the assault force was airlifted in by helicopter. However, the operation was cancelled 24 hours before the scheduled launch due to the fact that the target had not been positively identified. The reconnaissance teams set up a rearguard while the companies withdrew back to the border, killing one member of a five-man

SWAPO team in an ambush. During the journey to the south, a number of young men were seen moving around the area – an unusual occurrence, as most men their age had long since left to join SWAPO – but because they were unarmed, they were not confronted. By 22 February, fresh troops were in the field, and 55 SWAPO cadres had died during the 18-day operation.

OPERATION MAKALANI

On 20 February, Sector 10 headquarters issued Operational Order 2/80, authorising 52 Battalion and 32 Battalion to conduct an operation to clear the area north of Beacon 6 to Beacon 13 of SWAPO. From his tactical headquarters at Ogongo, Ferreira would command six platoons from 32's Bravo, Echo and Golf companies, consisting of 171 men; three companies from 52 Battalion totalling 277 men; two groups from 1 Parachute Battalion; and mine-laying and mine-locating teams from 25 Field Squadron.

It was to be a seek-and-destroy operation, with 52 Battalion sweeping north from the border to an imaginary line called Bravo, moving east to west through Nepolo. The six platoons of 32 Battalion would sweep south from positions 45 km north of Cuamato to the Bravo line. In the second phase, 52 Battalion had to establish dominance of the area between the border and Bravo, while 32 Battalion conducted an east-west sweep to another imaginary line, Alpha.

The 32 platoons arrived at Ondangwa on 22 February, and three days later were transported to Ombalantu in Buffel armoured personnel carriers. At 07h45 on 26 February, they were airlifted in Puma helicopters to positions 45 km inside Angola.

The companies from 52 Battalion first saw action on 1 March, when they captured one of six SWAPO guerrillas after a contact at Caco, about 20 km north of the border. Under interrogation, the captive admitted he was a member of a forward reconnaissance patrol, due to link up with a larger group armed with 82-mm mortars and a B10 recoilless gun, prior to attacking the bases at Mahanene and Okalongo. He also led his captors to a cache, about ten kilometres away, of 21 anti-tank mines and mortars.

On 3 March, 32's platoons were about ten kilometres inside Angola when a member of the local population provided information about a SWAPO base west of the Cunene River, a kilometre from Calueque. Since this was well outside the area they had been assigned to patrol, they did not follow up. At 10h45, Golf Company's second platoon was following the tracks of ten SWAPO seven kilometres east of Naulila, when they found a large underground cache containing 17 bags of maize meal. After the platoon sergeant had prodded the bags to check for anti-personnel mines, Rifleman M Yenga made to remove one. It was booby-trapped after all, and an APPMISR anti-personnel jump mine detonated, killing Yenga and wounding riflemen M Bocolo and M Carlos, as well as Corporal B Dixisi.

At 08h05 on 5 March, Bravo Company's first platoon spotted five SWAPO about 12 km south of Naulila. As they opened fire, the platoon came under attack from a group of buildings 400 m away. With two enemy confirmed dead, the first and second platoons joined forces and swept through the buildings, but SWAPO had already moved on. The platoons continued moving south, arriving at Beacon 3 around last light, then returned to Ruacana. This marked the end of *Makalani*, but no sooner were the troops back in their base than orders for *Makalani II* were issued. This time, the area between beacons 8 and 12 was to be patrolled as far as Cuamato and Dombondola. Echo Company was brought in from Elundu to boost the ranks of 32 to nine platoons.

Bravo and Golf companies crossed the border by last light on 7 March, with two platoons each crossing at beacons 10, 11 and 12, moving north for five kilometres and assuming ambush positions for the night.

The next day, Ferreira informed Sector 10 headquarters that although a large area had already been covered, no enemy presence was found, and he believed SWAPO had moved further north. Echo Company arrived at Ondangwa later that day, and by the evening of 9 March, Bravo Company's first and third companies were deployed seven kilometres north of Beacon 10. The second platoon, along with Golf Company's first platoon, was 12 km north of Beacon 11, and Golf Company's second and third platoons were eight kilometres north of Beacon 13.

At 07h30 the next morning, Bravo Company's first and third platoons made contact with SWAPO for the first time in the area. Guards spotted a large group of enemy passing close to their temporary base, and the platoons immediately formed an extended line and began to advance. After a brief but intense firefight, two enemy dead were found, and the platoon captured two 82-mm mortars and 40 bombs, AK47 rifles and a Draganov sniper rifle – a source of particular concern, as only SWAPO specialist groups on a specific mission were known to carry this weapon.

At noon on 11 March, Bravo Company's first and third platoons were lying in ambush at a chana 15 km north of Beacon 9, when a group of SWAPO appeared about 300 m away, moving from north to south. The platoons opened fire, killing one man. He was found to be carrying a Tokarev pistol and documents indicating that he was a commander in SWAPO's naval force. Echo Company moved into the area around Dombondola that day and began sweeping the area. At 19h00, a member of the local population steered the company's third platoon to a SWAPO temporary base. A sentry spotted them at about 75 m and was shot as he ran to warn his ten comrades, who fled at the first sound of gunfire. Twice during the night, at 00h12 and again at 04h00, the platoon's temporary base came under 60-mm mortar fire, but the bombs fell about 100 m short during both attacks. That night, three Echo Company platoons in the area heard three vehicles moving from north to south, stopping for about 30 minutes and then returning to the north, indicating that troops and equipment had been offloaded for a possible attack on Mahanene base. Around lunch-time the next day, air reconnaissance confirmed fresh vehicle tracks between the chanas, and some two hours later the third platoon also found human and donkey tracks, another familiar omen of an impending attack.

Bravo Company's second platoon was sent to Oncuaoncua, about 14 km west of Dombondola, to try to find the attack force and lay ambushes. The other platoons took up ambush positions on the roads between beacons 7 and 12. Echo Company's first platoon came upon a group of SWAPO doing their laundry in a shona north-east of Dombondola, wounded one and captured another. That evening, the second platoon made contact with a 50-strong group of SWAPO in the same general area. A 45-minute confrontation, including air support from the helicopter gunships, left six enemy dead and platoon commander Second Lieutenant MJ van Staden wounded in the stomach.

Interrogation of the captured guerrilla revealed that SWAPO had a base for about 60 men west/south-west of Chetaquera. Despite informing headquarters at Oshakati that the exact position of the base was unknown, and that there was no certainty that it was occupied, Ferreira was ordered to attack. A detailed plan, including the use of gunships and Pumas to airlift the ground troops, reserve forces at Ombalantu and air support from four Impalas, was approved by Brigadier Witkop Badenhorst, Officer Commanding Sector 10, and swung into action at 08h15 on 13 March, but neither a base nor any enemy were found.

Two days later, an Echo Company platoon returned to the scene of the earlier contact at Dombondola, and found a SWAPO guerilla's body that had been missed during the post-contact sweep. At 18h50, while following the spoor of four enemy, the platoon spotted their quarry and opened fire with 60-mm mortars. Unfortunately, due to wet charges, one of the bombs fell horribly short, exploding among the platoon's own members and wounding Second Lieutenant AW Kruger, riflemen RE Evaristo and P Frans, and Corporal CC da Trinidade. The corporal died of his wounds in the hospital at Grootfontein.

With three lieutenants wounded or in hospital for routine medical treatment and a corporal dead, the platoons were thrown into a leadership crisis, and combined forces to overcome the problem.

At 07h00 on 18 March, while patrolling the area south of Cuamato, members of Golf Company's second and third platoons were talking to members of the local population when eight SWAPO strolled into sight. Both sides opened fire simultaneously, but the SWAPO cadres swiftly scattered to the south and west, hotly pursued by members of the platoon. By 09h00 the Alouette gunships were aloft, coming under fire from RPG 7 rockets and small arms four kilometres east of Cuamato. Two 7,62-mm rounds hit one of the helicopters.

At 09h30, Impalas were placed on standby at Ondangwa when the gunships again drew fire, this time from buildings in the town. The Alouette crews opened fire with their 20-mm guns on a group of up to 30 SWAPO running for the safety of a house with a red roof, and noted that two wounded soldiers were being dragged towards the house. The gunships poured 20-mm fire into the building through the roof, and reported spotting radio masts in the backyard, a sure sign that it was being used as some type of headquarters. At 10h00, two Impalas bombarded the target, and at 11h35 two Pumas dropped off troops to sweep the town. SWAPO was long gone, leaving behind one dead, the blood trails of several wounded, food and clothing, and a series of shallow trenches.

By 17h00 on 20 March, three platoons were back at Ombalantu, followed 24 hours later by the rest. One Echo Company platoon was flown to Chetaquera to launch *Operation Makalani III*, and spent the next five days searching for the SWAPO group that had escaped. Despite reports from the local population that three separate SWAPO groups were still in the area, and that one had visited their village to obtain food, nothing but tracks were found before the platoon was relieved on 25 March by a company from 1 Parachute Battalion.

OPERATION LOODVOET

This operation was the first in which 32's deployment area stretched 50 km into Angola, giving Alpha, Charlie and Foxtrot companies a vast tract of land to patrol on foot.

Eenhana served as tactical headquarters, and four Alouette gunships, three Puma helicopters and a Super Frelon were placed on standby at the base. A platoon from 37 Battalion was attached to Foxtrot Company for field evaluation. *Loodvoet* (lead foot) required 32 Battalion to locate and attack the enemy, while members of 1 Parachute Battalion were airlifted in to set up stopper groups and prevent the usual flight into the bush.

Phase 1 covered the area between beacons 26 and 30, Phase 2 entailed patrols south and east of Chana Matuanjamba, and Phase 3 would take patrols ten kilometres south of the Timo Line, then west from beacons 32 to 36.

On the night of 25 March, Alpha Company moved eight kilometres into Angola. The next morning, the third platoon set off on patrol towards Chana Cuanhama under command of Second Lieutenant DA Still, Corporal H Labitzke and Corporal CP Wessels. Around 11h15, Still and 13 men made contact with three SWAPO on their way to the waterhole, killing two with 60-mm mortars. The patrol then moved west to Chana Mamuandi and linked up with Charlie

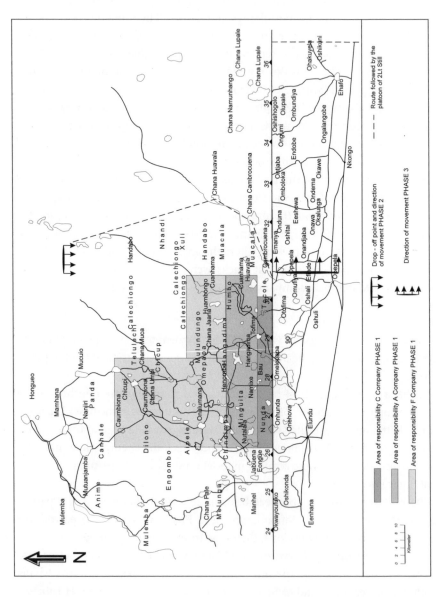

Operation Loodvoet

Company's third platoon. During the day, Wessels had to be casevaced to Eenhana for treatment of malaria – a necessary step, but one with enormous potential to jeopardise the entire operation due to the helicopter's presence.

Intelligence had indicated that SWAPO's Far Eastern detachment was operating from a base at Chana Namaudi, but Still's platoon found no sign of enemy presence there, despite spending the whole of 1 April in stopper group positions on the edge of the chana, while Charlie Company's second and third platoons swept down from the north. At Chana Onalumona, the only signs of SWAPO activity were at least a week old. For the next ten days the companies swept their entire area of responsibility, but apart from killing one suspected guerrilla in civilian clothes when he approached a temporary base on the night of 7 April, reported no enemy presence. The third phase of the operation produced equally disappointing results. Tracks were found and followed, ambushes laid and abandoned, but Alpha Company's only contact was on 16 April east of Ongalongabe, when two enemy escaped by shedding their boots and pulling on civilian shoes before riding off on a bicycle commandeered from a group of local inhabitants. Charlie Company killed two enemy in a contact at Chana Tofima soon after entering Angola on 29 March, and by 25 April both companies were back at Buffalo.

Foxtrot Company had better hunting. Their patrols centred on the most northerly area around Chana Henombe and Chana Caumbonia, and after the first platoon's commander was evacuated with malaria, the men joined forces with the second platoon, placing 51 troops under command of Second Lieutenant S O'Reilly.

As they prepared to leave their temporary base at Chana Umbi on the morning of 30 March, a group of 30 SWAPO was spotted approaching in extended line. A heavy five-minute firefight ensued, during which riflemen L Isequias, M Gomes and R Samba were wounded. As the enemy fled, O'Reilly called in the gunships and led the second platoon in hot pursuit through the dense bush. Moving in an L-shaped formation, they opened fire on a group of ten SWAPO sitting under a tree. The enemy fled, and as the platoon pursued them, a barrage of 82-mm mortar fire came out of nowhere, lightly wounding Corporal D Estima, Lance Corporal D Kapato and riflemen D Zua, P Ndima, F Braca and A José. Platoon sergeant BZ Gericke was seriously wounded when a mortar bomb detonated just a metre in front of him, and he later died. After the casualties had been evacuated by helicopter, the platoon swept the area, finding a two-night-old sleeping place for 90 people and a rudimentary headquarters, along with several mortar positions. Morale was low as a result of the casualties, but the platoon continued to Chana Mutuanjamba and linked up with Alpha and Charlie companies for a sweep before returning to Buffalo.

All nine platoon commanders reported having reached the same conclusions during *Operation Loodvoet*: SWAPO's bases were further north than had been estimated, perhaps as far as 60 km inside Angola. Due to the number of hastily evacuated positions found, they also raised concerns about the security of radio communications on patrol.

OPERATION FERREIRA

It is a measure of both the man and the success achieved while he was Officer Commanding 32 Battalion that a military operation was named after Commandant Deon Ferreira, respected as much by his own troops as he was feared by those of SWAPO and FAPLA.

On the night of 30 April, five platoons from Delta and Golf companies were driven from Etale to Beacon 19 and each allocated a four-kilometre deep strip inside Angola to patrol in an easterly direction. During a five-week operation, every village or kraal in an area stretching 20 km into Angola was to be visited and the local residents – a constant source of food and shelter for SWAPO – persuaded to relocate. The platoons had strict orders to stay well clear of FAPLA forces concentrated at Santa Clara and Namacunde, unless attacked.

As early as 2 May, members of the local population confirmed that SWAPO cadres regularly made use of their villages for night stops, and that a group of Cubans were running a serious campaign to win their hearts and minds, even to the extent of providing transport to the nearest shops! Dire warnings were issued to all inhabitants that 'fireworks' could start at any time, and that they would be well advised to move out of the area to avoid being caught in the crossfire.

It was quite clear that SWAPO and its foreign allies held sway over the entire region, but on 3 May the platoons learned that FAPLA, too, came and went at will. At 12h40, just 12 km north of Beacon 19, two FAPLA troops walked right into a temporary base set up by Delta Company's second platoon next to a village. One of the intruders was killed, the other wounded before he escaped.

Ten minutes later, the same platoon killed a SWAPO cadre in an ambush two kilometres from the village. That night, while setting up a fresh ambush along a footpath, the platoon's third contact in less than seven hours netted two more SWAPO. Clearly, the area in which *Operation Ferreira* was to be executed was swarming with enemy from all camps.

On 5 May, while flying over a chana 14 km north of Beacon 20 on a re-supply run, the crew of an Alouette gunship spotted ten SWAPO cadres at a waterhole. They opened fire, and the Puma they were escorting immediately turned back to Eenhana to pick up a reaction force from 1 Parachute Battalion. In the ensuing fracas, five SWAPO were killed and a large amount of equipment and ammunition captured. Rifleman Visagie was lightly wounded in the thigh.

As word of the various contacts spread, the local population began heeding the earlier warnings, most of them moving closer to the town of Chiede. By 7 May the area was unnaturally quiet, and the platoons realised that SWAPO had also moved to Chiede. An attack on the town was inevitable, and was scheduled for first light the next day. But at 19h35 the assault was postponed to 12 May, and strict orders were issued that when it did take place, it was to be confined to the SWAPO camp on the southern rim of the town. FAPLA, concentrated in the centre of Chiede, was not to be engaged.

Over the next few days normal patrols resumed, and one of the platoons learned from the local population that Cubans had begun moving civilians to Chiede in the hope that a large concentration of non-combatants around the town might spare it from attack.

However, by 06h40 on 12 May, three platoons from Delta Company were in position, and at 07h00 four gunships were directly over the target and opened fire with their 20-mm guns. The helicopters left Eenhana without a command ship or the assigned Bosbok light aircraft, as both were unserviceable. The ground troops – who had deployed in the wrong area and took 30 minutes to move to the correct position – met minimal resistance, and on sweeping through the town found it deserted, except for three SWAPO guerrillas who were taken prisoner, and a civilian woman and a small child who had been hit by crossfire and were evacuated to Oshakati for treatment. At the SWAPO base, 28 dead bodies were counted. The prisoners revealed that the radio station believed to have been in Chiede, was actually situated at Namacunde.

After being re-supplied, the platoons laid ambushes eight kilometres south of Chiede and resumed normal patrols, but it was not until 16 May that contact was again made with the enemy. The platoon patrolling seven kilometres north-west of Beacon 22 had been following the tracks of a group of 20 since 11h00, and walked into a well-laid ambush at 18h00. Two members of the platoon were wounded, one – Corporal Danie Vrey – seriously. Five days later, Delta Company's first and second platoons attacked about 50 SWAPO in a temporary base near Chana Hengue, nine kilometres north of Beacon 22. The enemy fled, leaving behind two dead and three wounded. One platoon member was hit in the arm. For the first time, a VHF (very high frequency) radio was recovered among the SWAPO equipment.

By 23 May, *Operation Ferreira* was over, and a small corner of Angola had been cleared – at least for the moment – of SWAPO's support base, the local population.

Routes taken to Savate. Inset: Position of Savate

N

20 km

Route travelled by 32 Bn

UNITA advance to the north

Small villages

TANDAUE

SAVATE

CAPASSO

KATWITWI

CAUNGAR

NKURUNKURU

MPUNGU

OMAUNI

18°00 CUTLINE

Rio Cubango

Chana dos Elphantos

Dala

Jamba
Camara
Candingo
Pande

38

40

42

44

ANGOLA

SWA

OPERATION TIRO-A-TIRO (SAVATE)

'Savimbi denied the allegations by Belmundo and
Edwards. Of the Englishman's claim that two UNITA
soldiers had stood by to claim Savate in UNITA's name
after 32 Battalion's attack, he said: "It is too beautiful to
be true, because if we wanted to take over a town after
the South Africans have attacked it we are not going to
send just two people."'
Jonas Savimbi: A Key to Africa – Fred Bridgland, 1986

By early 1980, FAPLA occupied all the small towns along the Kavango River as far
north as Caiundo. Until the end of 1979, UNITA had applied a scorched earth
policy against all towns and territory captured from FAPLA, but in line with a
political decision by the organisation's leaders, it then became customary for
UNITA to occupy and defend former FAPLA strongholds.

On 14 April, UNITA took Cuangar after driving a 900-strong FAPLA force
out. This was the first major town captured by Savimbi's forces, and the taking of
Cuangar marked the beginning of a new phase in UNITA's war, aimed at securing
the entire southern region of Angola.

As part of the plan, Savimbi asked the South African authorities to authorise
the attack and destruction of Savate, a major FAPLA base 75 km inside Angola on
the Cubango River, by 32 Battalion. Ferreira was provisionally ordered to plan an
attack, based on UNITA intelligence that an under-strength battalion held the
base. Savate was also home to FAPLA's brigade headquarters, and two more
battalions were deployed upstream at Caiundo.

Ferreira's assault force would consist of three rifle companies (one to be held
in reserve), a mortar platoon and 32's reconnaissance teams acting as stopper
groups. The element of surprise was crucial to success, so no air support could be
relied on. Pumas would be on standby at Rundu to evacuate casualties, and a
Bosbok spotter aircraft would be available if needed.

By 15 May the assault group and mortar platoon were at Omauni, preparing
for an attack on what they were told was a SWAPO base deep inside Angola.
The 270 men from the rifle companies, the six recce teams and the mortarists
would be taken in by road on ten-ton trucks and four Buffel armoured personnel
carriers, while three Kwêvoël cargo trucks would carry ammunition, rations
and other equipment. Ferreira's headquarters element was small, but included an
intelligence officer.

Also attached to the column was one Francisco Lopes, better known as
'Senhor Lobbs', a UNITA agent working for the SADF's Chief of Staff Intelligence.

He had claimed to know the Savate area intimately, and would guide the assault force to the base.

Ferreira's battle plan was simple. Armed with both high explosive and white phosphorous bombs, the mortar platoon would bombard the base with four 81-mm mortars set up four kilometres to the south. Alpha and Foxtrot companies would attack from the west, pushing the enemy towards the river and leaving them with nowhere else to go but north. Two platoons from Charlie Company under command of Lieutenant Sam Heap would attack the vehicle park north of the airfield, two kilometres outside the town, where reconnaissance photographs had shown no troops were deployed. The attack would thus concentrate on the trench system surrounding Savate. Heap's third platoon would be held in reserve.

On the night of 17/18 May, despite not yet having received final authorisation for the attack, Ferreira sent Lieutenant Willem Ratte's reconnaissance team to Savate to confirm the information gleaned from the photographs and UNITA intelligence. Senhor Lobbs and another UNITA guide accompanied Ratte's team from Omauni to a point supposedly north-west of Savate, assuring them that if they walked due east, they would reach the Cubango River, where they could assemble their Klepper kayaks and row downstream to the target area. It should take no more than six hours to cover the distance to the water, according to Senhor Lobbs.

After the recce team was dropped off at 23h15, Senhor Lobbs returned to Omauni, leaving only the other UNITA guide with Ratte. By daybreak the river was nowhere in sight, and the team laid up for the day, finally reaching the water – after considerably more than a six-hour walk – on the night of 18 May. A seven-kilometre kayak trip lay ahead, but it was obvious from the start that the territory was completely unfamiliar to the UNITA guide. After several hours the team reached a small town on the west bank of the river, and laid up for the day. The guide fell strangely silent as Ratte informed him that they would enter the town after dark to confirm FAPLA's presence and deployment, but it was not until he and three members of the team stepped ashore, finding the entire settlement deserted, with not even a chicken in sight, that the guide apparently realised what had happened.

Instead of being dropped off north-west of Savate, Senhor Lobbs had led the teams to a point *south*-west of the target. The unsuspecting recces had then rowed approximately nine kilometres downstream, arriving at the long-abandoned town of Pande, some 20 km south of Savate.

But the attack was scheduled for 21 May, and ground reconnaissance was vital, so at 23h00 on 19 May the teams slipped their kayaks back into the water and spent the entire night rowing upstream, negotiating a dangerous stretch of rapids into the bargain, finally reaching the outskirts of Savate just before first light. While laid up on the east bank, they constantly heard vehicle movement to the north, confirming that both the town and the base were still occupied.

At just about the time the recces were moving into their daylight 'hide', the main assault force set off from Omauni, again under the guidance of Senhor Lobbs. They followed the same route as the recce teams, but would debus at a crossroads some distance east of Savate and proceed on foot. By the time Ratte managed to contact the column and suggest a 24-hour delay in order to ensure that detailed reconnaissance could be done, it was too late. The assault force had already travelled so far north that any unscheduled layover could lead to detection. The entire battle plan was based on the assault force debussing long before last light on 20 May.

As soon as darkness fell, Ratte, Sergeant Piet van Eeden and Corporal C Paulo slipped into Savate to pinpoint the enemy's troop deployments, defences and mortar positions. UNITA's intelligence about an extensive trench system around the town proved accurate, but far from an under-strength battalion, Ratte found a force well in excess of battalion strength. He also identified a strong deployment of troops north of the airfield, and instead of an unmanned vehicle park, he discovered a 14,5-mm anti-aircraft gun position.

Ratte was unable to reach the assault force by radio to convey this fresh intelligence, so he and Van Eeden moved to pre-arranged positions to await the arrival of the troops. First light on 21 May came and went with no sign of the assault force, and the recce teams withdrew to the east bank of the river and set up observation posts from which they could direct the mortar fire.

Senhor Lobbs had struck again. When the column had not reached the crossroads by 18h00 on 19 May, and found themselves facing an open chana instead, Ferreira realised that his 'guide' had led them no less than 16 km north-west of Savate, to Chana dos Elephantos. The road to Savate was nowhere in sight, and Ferreira had no choice but to laager at the chana overnight and for the next day, unable to communicate with his recce teams by radio.

At 20h00 on 20 May, the column began backtracking on its own route. Due west of Savate, the force turned east – relying on a compass rather than Senhor Lobbs – and found the road, which turned out not to be an intersection after all, 15 km from the town. The troops would cover the last eight kilometres to the town on foot, while the vehicles were to wait ten kilometres away and move up once the mortar bombardment began.

Each troop was given an 81-mm mortar bomb to carry over the last stretch to the assembly point. From there, the mortar crews themselves would have to move the tubes and some 200 bombs to the launch position.

At 02h00 on 21 May, the force began moving towards Savate in single file, with

Charlie and another company on the left shoulder of the road, the third company, headquarters, the recce teams and the mortar platoon on the right.

It was dark moon and the bush was dense, making for slow progress. The troops had to hold on to one another to avoid getting lost, and about six kilometres out of Savate it became impossible to proceed. Ferreira ordered the column to wait until first light, when visibility would improve. The original timetable for the attack had already been abandoned, and a further setback occurred when the column leaders ran into a FAPLA vehicle patrol just seven kilometres from Savate. At least five FAPLA troops escaped, and Ferreira realised that they would raise the alarm at the base, costing him the element of surprise.

He immediately stepped up the pace of the advance, and by 09h00 the mortars were in position, the ten three-man recce teams in stopper groups to the north. Only then could Ratte inform Ferreira that he and his men had found a somewhat different situation to the one on which the battle plan was based.

The mortars opened fire immediately, drawing a heavy counter-bombardment as the rifle companies, armed with assault rifles, machine guns and 60-mm mortars, advanced towards the trenches, trying to dodge the bombs exploding around and among them. At the airfield, two platoons from Charlie Company unsuspectingly took on a full FAPLA air defence company, using the 14,5-mm gun in a ground role. The first salvo killed three Charlie troops and seriously wounded four more.

At the main base, FAPLA was pouring everything it had at the rifle companies, pinning them down. Ferreira's command group was one of those unable to advance, and his intelligence officer was shot and killed just two metres from his side. One of the companies managed to break through into the trenches, where they were forced to fight hand to hand.

At the airfield, Heap's platoons had taken more casualties and he sought permission to retreat. Orders went out for the platoons to break off engagement and report to the main assault force as reserves. The vehicles, meanwhile, had moved up as planned, but while the dead and wounded were being loaded into them prior to being airlifted to Rundu, enemy forces moved between the convoy and the assault force, cutting the vehicles off and forcing the crews to enter the battle as well.

By noon the enemy fire began to abate, but they remained in position in the trenches. From their observation post on the river bank, Ratte's recce team reported a large group of enemy moving on foot along the road to the north, some carrying 122-mm single tube rocket launchers. FAPLA had apparently decided to move the rocket launchers to their effective firing range of six kilometres. What they did not know, however, was that stopper groups were waiting, and when these opened fire, chaos erupted within the FAPLA ranks. Radio intercepts showed that the brigade commander was arranging an organised withdrawal to the north even as

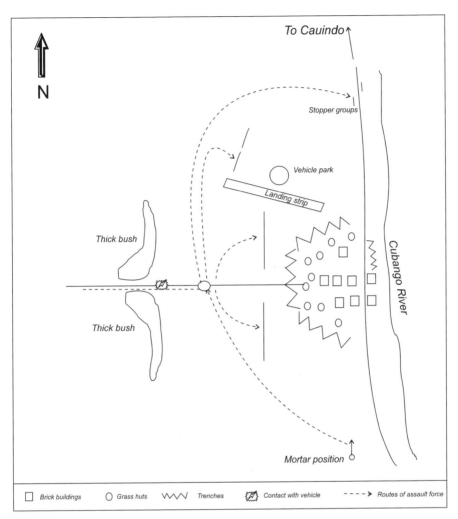

Layout of Savate and positions of assault force

the first gunfire was heard from that direction, and he apparently decided it was wise to proceed with this plan. As the first convoy of 29 vehicles loaded with troops was reported to be leaving the base, Ferreira ordered the Bosbok spotter aircraft, with his second-in-command Major Eddie Viljoen aboard, to fly in from Omauni and report on the enemy withdrawal from the air.

One of the companies sent through an urgent radio message to report Captain Charl Muller, 32's operations officer who was acting as company commander, missing. Ferreira's first thought was that he had been captured by the FAPLA column escaping to the north, and he ordered the four Buffels under command of Staff Sergeant Ron Gregory forward. The reserve company piled into the vehicles, and with Ferreira in the lead Buffel, Sam Heap in the second, Lieutenant Tony Nienaber in the third and Lieutenant Jim Ross in the fourth, the chase was on. The Buffels, each mounted with a 7,62-mm Browning machine gun, caught up with the escaping column while it was engaged in a heavy battle with the stopper groups, and opened fire on the vehicles from the rear. From the Bosbok, Viljoen was able to steer the Buffels straight towards the enemy, now running all over the floodplain like mad dogs. Those who tried to escape across the Cubango River either drowned or were taken by crocodiles. While this melee was in progress, Ferreira received a radio signal informing him that Captain Muller's body had been found lying face down in one of the trenches. He had been shot in the head.

Although the stopper groups and the Buffels were unable to halt the flight of the FAPLA column, they did ensure that 12 vehicles and a large number of dead travelled no further north.

Back at the base, close combat had become the order of the day in the trenches, shacks and buildings. It was now evident that the entire FAPLA command structure had collapsed, and by 14h00, mopping up could start. A nominal roll-call among the assault force accounted for 13 dead and 22 wounded, with one corporal and one troop missing. An immediate search was launched, but by last light there was still no sign of the two men, and the assault force pulled back four kilometres to the south-west for the night.

By this time the SA Army Chief, Lieutenant General Constand Viljoen, had arrived at Rundu to launch a top-level inquiry into the day's events. Despite the fact that CSI coordinator Colonel Fred Oelschig had flown to the battlefront in one of the casevac helicopters and spent most of the day there, it appeared that the signals sent via CSI channels authorising the attack should never have gone to 32 Battalion. Authorisation had been granted for UNITA to attack Savate, with 32 only assisting with mortar fire support and stopper groups.

By 09h00 on 22 May, with two men still unaccounted for despite another search, Ferreira's force had orders to start moving back to Omauni. A small UNITA advance party had arrived by that time to claim victory and to hold the captured base. About 30 km from the base, however, Rundu ordered the column to locate the two missing men at all cost. Charlie Company was sent back to Savate with orders to find them even if this meant travelling all the way to Caiundo. The UNITA garrison that had moved in assisted in the search, and the bodies of both men were found in dense bush, though how they came to be in a position well outside the assault area remains a mystery.

In the aftermath of the battle, it was established that FAPLA had grouped a full brigade at Savate three weeks before in anticipation of a possible UNITA advance from the south. UNITA was acutely aware that this was the position, but deliberately failed to inform 32 Battalion, knowing that the authorities would never agree to sending 32 up against an entire brigade. Captured documents showed that at the time of the attack, Savate held at least 1 060 heavily armed troops – a far cry from the 300 estimated by UNITA.

Yet, even with all the odds against them, 32 won the day, capturing tons of ammunition and equipment. All in all 19 Fifa trucks, two Star fuel tankers, a complete and well-equipped Star mobile workshop and a Land Rover were driven back to Omauni. A Russian-made motorcycle with sidecar promptly became the official transport of 32 Battalion's Regimental Sergeant Major at Buffalo. Another 24 vehicles, including a mobile bridge, were destroyed before 32 left Savate.

But the toll in human terms was terrible. Of the more than 150 men who died while fighting with 32 Battalion, 15 were killed at Savate, where the battalion took its heaviest casualties in four years of almost constant action. Those who died are Captain C de J Muller (operations officer), Captain A Erasmus (intelligence officer), second lieutenants TC Patrick and P van der Walt, Sergeant SD Braz, Corporal EC Engelbrecht, lance corporals J Kaumba and AJ Falcus, and riflemen R Alberto, B Albino, A Caliango, M Augusto, C Marcellino, A Livingue and J Matamba.

Radio intercepts later indicated that 558 FAPLA had been killed, with dozens, perhaps hundreds more wounded or reported missing. By 24 May, all participating forces were back at Buffalo.

OPERATION SCEPTIC

On 30 May, orders were issued for Sector 10 to destroy SWAPO's command, control and logistical structures by capturing the QFL complex at Chifufua, as well as bases at Mulola and Chitumbo. No MPLA/FAPLA targets were to be included in what would be the biggest mechanised infantry assault by South African forces since World War II. Three of 32 Battalion's companies were withdrawn from ongoing operations to take part in *Sceptic*, launched on 10 June 1980. From 24 May, the following forces began to gather:

- Battle Group 61: 61 Mechanised Battalion; one company from 1 Parachute Battalion; one mechanised company from 1 SA Infantry Battalion; and two sections of engineers from 25 Field Squadron, under command of Commandant Dippies Dippenaar. They would attack QFL and Ionde.
- Battle Group 10: two companies from 1 Parachute Battalion; one Eland 90 armoured car squadron from 61 Mechanised Battalion; one section of engineers from 25 Field Squadron; and one 81-mm mortar group from Army headquarters, under command of Commandant Chris Serfontein. Their target was Mulola.
- Battle Group 53: 32 Battalion's Bravo Company; two armoured car troops; one 81-mm mortar group from Army headquarters; and two sections of engineers

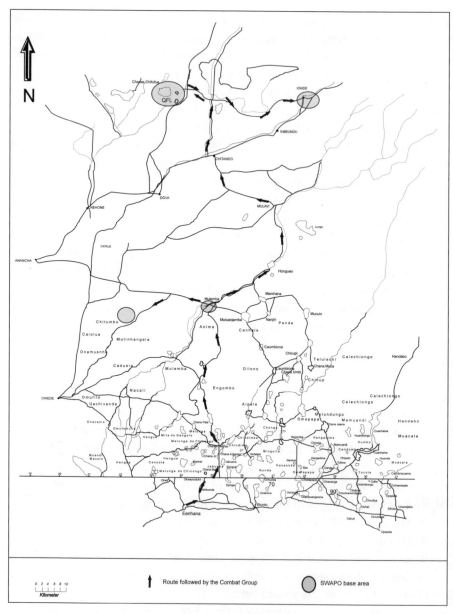

Operation Sceptic

from 25 Field Squadron, commanded by Commandant Jorrie Jordaan. They would secure the route and attack Chitumbo.

- 54 Battalion: 32's Delta and Echo companies; one company from 1 Parachute Battalion; one 81-mm mortar platoon from 32; and two sections of engineers from 25 Field Squadron, led by Commandant Anton van Graan. They would carry out area operations from north of Beacon 24 to Beacon 36 up to Mulemba, proceeding to Okatale Kongwe in order to secure the area for the main force.

For a week before the attack, 54 Battalion swept the area around Mulemba, destroying a large cache of equipment at Chana Nanjiri and making contact with a group of 100 SWAPO on 4 June, when Corporal M van Wyk was killed and Rifleman J João, also of Delta Company, wounded in the stomach. Afterwards João could not be found, even though the search for him continued until 14h00 on 5 June. The next day the company found another large ammunition cache 15 km south of Mulemba, including mortars and RPG 7 rockets.

At 10h30 on 7 June, 16 Mirages bombarded THTC (Tobias Hanyeko Training Centre), SWAPO's main training base near Lubango, and immediately afterwards 12 Mirages and four Buccaneers bombed QFL. While very little air defence was

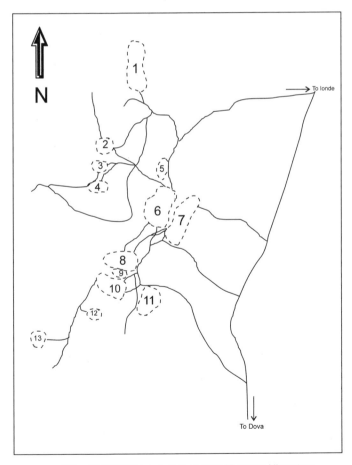

QFL - 13 SWAPO bases spread over 45 square kilometres

155

encountered at QFL, where two SWAPO were killed and one wounded, two Mirages were damaged – possibly by SAMs – at THTC, and had to return to base.

By 9 June, 54 Battalion had secured both the route from Beacon 25 via Jofima–Mulemba to Okatale Kongwe, and a staging area for the attack. The other three battle groups left Eenhana for Mulemba at 02h00 on 10 June.

At 08h00, 18 Mirages, each carrying eight 250-kg bombs, struck QFL again. Simultaneously, four Buccaneers each dropped eight 450-kg bombs on Mulola. This time, QFL offered heavy air defence from SA 7 missiles and 23-mm guns before the air strike knocked out four of them. Impala aircraft patrolled the road between QFL and Mulola when stopper groups could not be deployed, due to delayed delivery of helicopter fuel to the staging area. The Impalas also attacked Ondova.

While Battle Group 10 prepared to attack Mulola, and Battle Group 53 made ready to engage a group of SWAPO moving east to Chitumbo, Battle Group 61 moved through Mulavi and attacked QFL at 13h15. The enemy was eating lunch, but quickly recovered from their surprise and launched a heavy counter-attack. Sustained anti-aircraft fire not only hampered the use of helicopters but was also directed at the ground troops, and Battle Group 10 was ordered to join forces with Battle Group 61. The attack was extremely difficult, as the target sprawled over 45 square kilometres, containing 13 small bases, and at 17h30 the assault force was ordered to withdraw due to failing light. The next morning QFL was deserted, but because of the size of the area and the number of concealed trenches, mopping up was a slow process. By nightfall, battle groups 61 and 10 had cleared only about 10 per cent of the terrain, and Battle Group 10's attack on Mulola was postponed until 14 June. On 12 June, radio intercepts revealed that the SWAPO commander at Mulola had been ordered to evacuate the area. Despite stopper groups being deployed early the next morning north, south and west of Mulola, the camp was deserted when Battle Group 10 got there. An enormous amount of equipment was destroyed or taken back to Oshakati. Documents found in the abandoned bases confirmed that there were other SWAPO camps in the area, and the operation was extended. But the enemy had fled, and bases at Chitumbo, Mongua, Cuamato and Mupa were all empty. On 29 June, FAPLA entered the fray, engaging Battle Group 10 as it was withdrawing back to South West Africa. An air strike was called in and FAPLA broke contact, but just for good measure the aircraft attacked Menongue as well, leaving 90 FAPLA dead. By 1 July the withdrawal was complete, with *Operation Sceptic* having accounted for the deaths of 380 enemy, against the loss of 17 own forces.

OPERATION VASTRAP

In July 1980, radio intercepts showed that SWAPO's North-Western Front head-quarters, previously north of the Xangongo–Mongua road, had moved south to the vicinity of Cuamato, probably with a view to infiltrating between beacons 7 and 14. Unlike the Far Eastern Front, this area was teeming with FAPLA, with known deployments at Namacunde, Ongiva, Mongua, Xangongo, Cuamato, Naulila and Calueque, and there was no way of telling whether tracks had been made by SWAPO or FAPLA patrols.

On 28 July 1980, a group of 30 FAPLA troops was spotted about 400 m from a temporary base 12 km south-west of Cuamato. The platoon opened fire with 60-mm mortars and the group withdrew, but a follow-up operation had to be aborted when the platoon was ordered by tactical headquarters to stay at least three kilometres from Cuamato.

Having established that FAPLA's bases were all in or close to towns, the platoon began to find increasing proof of SWAPO's presence. An attempt to destroy a bunker crammed with food by lobbing three M26 hand grenades into it failed, and the platoon commander decided that a shrapnel mine in the roof would do the job. Corporal DM Grobler, the platoon sergeant, entered the bunker to plant the mine, while Corporal MC Coetzee stood in the door. The bunker was booby-trapped, and the explosion killed both Grobler and Coetzee, while second lieutenants AG Slabber and J Smith, and corporals HJ Botha, PF Brink and AJ Vlok, all sustained shrapnel wounds to the upper and lower legs.

By August it was clear that both SWAPO and FAPLA were aware of the SADF patrols, and SWAPO began moving in larger than usual groups, sometimes up to 50, but their bases could not be located.

On 13 August, shortly before being relieved by Delta Company and a reconnaissance team, the platoons from Charlie Company followed the spoor of 40 people over difficult terrain for five hours. At 17h30 the commander called for gunship support, and as the helicopters hovered into view the enemy was spotted about 300 m ahead. Just before last light the enemy disengaged, leaving behind 21 dead and a large amount of equipment.

On 5 September, Lance Corporal E Sophia was killed by friendly fire. During a brief contact the platoon commander had lost his pistol, and when some of the troops returned later to look for it, they walked straight into one of their own stopper groups, which did not recognise them and opened fire.

On 10 September the recce team began operating independently of the company in a bid to find the elusive SWAPO headquarters. Five days later, the team tracked a single SWAPO member from a food cache in a deserted village 20 km south-east of Cuamato to a small base housing another ten guerrillas. The gunships were called in as the seven-man recce team attacked on the ground, killing two of the enemy. Meanwhile, a member of the local population told Delta Company's first platoon that a group of SWAPO troops were drinking beer in a village south-west of Cuamato. On investigating, the platoon saw three guerrillas changing out of their SWAPO uniforms into civilian clothes and opened fire, killing all three. The rest of the group, hiding behind baobab trees, found themselves on the receiving end of the gunships' firepower, and during a fierce 40-minute encounter, the remaining 20 SWAPO were killed.

This was Delta Company's last major contact with the enemy before being relieved on 16 October, by which time the North-Western Front headquarters had still not been found. It was beginning to look increasingly as though the main SWAPO base must be in Cuamato, under FAPLA protection.

By mid-January 1981 there had been no further contact between any of the patrols and SWAPO, and Ferreira was ordered to take personal command of further deployment – and find the SWAPO headquarters.

In order to do so he would need more resources, consisting of 32 Battalion's Alpha and Bravo companies and an 81-mm mortar group, one company each from 1 Parachute Battalion and 201 Battalion, two reconnaissance teams from each of Special Forces, 201 Battalion and 44 Parachute Brigade. Ferreira also wanted adequate air support, and although only two gunships were initially allocated to him, six Puma helicopters, six gunships, a command and control Alouette, two Bosbok reconnaissance aircraft and four Impala strike aircraft on standby at Ondangwa were later made available.

By 14h00 on 15 January all the ground troops were in position, and the parabats were driven to Cuamato to secure the town, which was reportedly deserted, with the nearest FAPLA contingent 16 km north-west on the road to Xangongo. While deploying, the company made contact with two members of the local militia, the ODP, killing one and capturing the other. At 17h30, while moving north to lay ambushes, one platoon encountered 15 SWAPO and called in the gunships. The pilots spotted an active enemy base from the air, and a platoon from 32's Alpha Company was airlifted to attack it. They drew heavy fire, and three platoons of parabats and four gunships had to be called in to provide support, but the anti-aircraft and ground fire was so heavy that none of them could get closer to the base.

The waiting Impalas were scrambled at Ondangwa and flew over the base five times, knocking out the anti-aircraft guns and destroying three vehicles. As the firing died down the gunships withdrew, low on fuel, and at 21h00 the parabats returned to tactical headquarters, leaving one platoon from Alpha Company as the nightwatch. Two enemy captured during the night confirmed that the base was occupied by 150 FAPLA troops, and the next morning heavy anti-aircraft fire was again directed at the helicopter gunships. At 08h20, two Impalas struck again, firing rockets and their 30-mm guns with little success. At 08h47, a second air strike was called in, and this time the Impalas dropped napalm while the helicopter gunships circled the base. At 08h55 Bravo Company was airlifted in for a ground

Angolan opposition leaders (from left) Daniel
Chipenda, Jonas Savimbi, Holden Roberto

Colonel Jan Breytenbach,
founder of 32 Battalion

Sergeants Danny Roxo, Silva Sierro, Brian Walls, Jan van der Merwe and Robbie Ribeiro at Vila Nova
da Armada, March 1976, with captured 106-mm recoilless anti-tank gun mounted on a Land Rover

The entrance to Buffalo Base, with guardroom (left) and reinforced sentry posts (right)

Buffalo Base December 1978 – the old company line with the 15 × 15 tents

A patrol displaying their firepower during a patrol break.
Note the .303 Browning machine gun carried by members on foot patrols

Operation Seiljag – a foot patrol patrolling 'Oom Willie se Pad' south of Beacon 21

32 Battalion's colour, with battle distinctions (top left), and banners for the various companies

Operation Seiljag – Corporal Tony Viera and his platoon members with
captured equipment after a contact at Chana Lupale

A 32 Battalion soldier in action

The grim reality of Angola's civil war

Lieutenant Mike Geldenhuys (back left) and sergeant Gawie Venter (front right) with a patrol from Golf Company deep behind enemy lines, masquerading as UNITA troops

Fast-rope training from a Puma helicopter

Crossing the crocodile-infested Kavango River with full kit

Prime Minister PW Botha presents Lance Corporal Feliciano Costa with the Honoris Crux (silver) – the first time South Africa's highest medal for bravery was presented in the Operational Area

Operation Protea – Commandant Ferreira, Officer Commanding
Battle Group 40 and 32 Battalion at his forward headquarters

Francisco Lopes, or 'Senhor
Lobbs' – a Military Intelligence
agent and UNITA guide with
no sense of direction!

Self-sufficiency was second nature to 32 members.
Here, a dead enemy is stripped of equipment for own use

Operation Askari – one of the captured 23-mm anti-aircraft guns
deployed on a hill overlooking the town of Tetchamutete

Members of 32's reconnaissance wing inspect a Russian T54/55 tank
bogged down outside Tetchamutete

Patrolling the Angolan bush

A foot patrol tracking enemy movements

Captured enemy weapons after Operation Protea

Operation Modular – Bravo Company and the MRL troop ready to leave Buffalo Base for Mavinga

Operation Modular – devastation on the Lomba River after bombardment by the MRLs and G5s on 21 Brigade positions

The headquarters at
Buffalo Base, 1987

Remembering those
who fell at Savate

Sergeant Majors Piet Slade, Piet Nortje and Pep van Zyl at the opening of the Shuva Club

Arial view of Pomfret

The end of an era – erasing
the unit's name at Buffalo
Base headquarters

Part of the tent town at Pomfret, 1989

The officer commanding, second-in-command and regimental sergeant major
with colour ensigns and escorts after receiving the national colours, 1990

32 Battalion columns march through the streets of Kempton Park
during the freedom of the city parade, 21 September 1991

Sergeant Segunda at the Tree of Honour

The beer tankards of the 11 officers who died fighting with 32

Pomfret cemetery. The crosses are the same as the ones at Buffalo Base

attack, and by 11h30, with 70 FAPLA dead, the base finally fell quiet. Two of 32's men were wounded in the attack.

On 17 January gunships located a base nine kilometres south of Cuamato, drawing anti-aircraft fire before returning to the tactical headquarters. This time the Impalas succeeded in destroying the 23-mm guns, and by noon 32's Alpha and Bravo companies, along with 201 Battalion's Charlie Company, were in position to attack on the ground.

Fifteen minutes later, as the Impalas came in for a second strike, Ferreira was ordered to halt the engagement immediately and withdraw with his entire force to Ombalantu, avoiding any contact with FAPLA on the way. By 18h00, all troops were south of the cutline.

Early the next morning a detailed planning session was held at Sector 10 headquarters in Oshakati, at which Ferreira was ordered, in no uncertain terms, to refrain from any confrontation with FAPLA and to confine the interrupted operation to locating and acting against SWAPO. By 12h30 the assault force was back in Angola. While flying to the tactical headquarters, the helicopter gunships drew fire at Damaguera, 18 km south of Xangongo. Sector 10 authorised Ferreira to send two platoons to the area to investigate but not engage the enemy, which turned out to be FAPLA.

On the evening of 19 January, two Special Forces teams deployed to try to locate the SWAPO base. The team designated call sign MB entered Angola at Beacon 4, proceeding on foot to four kilometres south of the Cunene River. At 03h00 on 21 January the team crossed the river about two kilometres upstream from the Calueque Dam wall. Time was of the essence, and team leader Captain Bourne decided that the quickest way to glean intelligence was to question local residents. As it happened, the first habitation he approached was occupied by a white Portuguese farmer, who not only confirmed that no SWAPO presence had been seen in the area and that all bases surrounding Calueque were those of FAPLA, but pleaded with the officer to help him and his family of nine escape from Angola, where their lives had become unbearable. Shortly before first light on 21 January, call sign MB and the refugees crossed the river and laid up in a sparse line of trees on the south bank. Bourne requested a pick-up by Puma, but due to the impending attack on a SWAPO base south of Donguena this could not be done until several hours later.

The second Special Forces team, call sign MJ, had infiltrated the area east of Donguena on 19 January. The town itself was deserted, but the team was struck by the fact that the windows in all the buildings had been bricked up, except for narrow, head-high firing slits. West of the Humbe–Calueque road, they detained two members of the local population who confirmed that there was a SWAPO base near the FAPLA outpost at Oshahenda, eight kilometres south of Donguena.

Armed with this intelligence, Ferreira deployed his forces, moving the tactical headquarters 20 km south-east of Cuamato, sending Alpha Company 20 km north of the town and despatching 201 Battalion's Charlie Company ten kilometres east of Naulila. In the event of an attack, 32's Bravo Company would be the main assault force, and remained in reserve at Ombalantu.

Shortly afterwards, platoons from Alpha Company heard vehicle movement, and an observation post near the Xangongo–Cuamato road reported three Ural trucks on the move. Two were loaded with troops, but a tarpaulin hid the cargo on the third.

The gunships were called in, but had to turn back in haste when seven SA 7 anti-aircraft missiles were launched from the convoy. The Impalas were next, firing both rockets and their 30-mm guns at the trucks. After the air strike, however, it was found that the vehicles had all escaped, and two platoons from Bravo Company were airlifted in as reinforcements. But when a signal from Sector 10 headquarters reiterated that ground troops were not to engage FAPLA, both platoons were withdrawn.

At 08h45 on 21 January, six 14-man teams from 32 Battalion were airlifted by Puma to within 1,5 km of the suspected SWAPO base at Donguena, only to find that it was actually two kilometres further south, and empty when they got there. Furthermore, evidence in the 32 trenches and elsewhere within the base indicated that it had been occupied by FAPLA. A young boy, wandering around, was questioned, and he claimed that the SWAPO base was yet another kilometre to the south-west.

The information proved accurate, but the camp had obviously been hastily evacuated, with plates of food still on the tables. After redeploying his forces yet again, Ferreira moved the tactical headquarters back to Ombalantu and handed over command of the operation to Commandant James Hills. On 23 February, SWAPO staged hit-and-run raids on the bases at Okalongo and Mahanene. But despite continued patrols and sweeps of the area and a few minor contacts, the location of the SWAPO base in the vicinity of the Calueque Dam was still a mystery when *Operation Vastrap* (stand firm) was called off on 16 March.

OPERATION BUTTERFLY

On 2 September 1980, Ferreira received orders to prepare 32 Battalion for action on the North-Eastern Front. Three of the rifle companies were already operationally deployed, but interrogation of a SWAPO captive had indicated that the North-Eastern Front headquarters, under command of Mbulunganga, was probably deployed along the dry river bed north-east of Mulemba, or at Chana Omehemba. The prisoner also claimed that the North-Eastern Front reserve, 100-strong under command of Davy, was at Chana Nanjiri, that George's detachment was in the

Ohaipeto area, Shikuma Kamati's at Huanbongo, Kelola's at Chana Nalama and Kafindeko's at Onalumona.

Supported by the SAAF, 32 was to attack and destroy the North-Eastern Front headquarters, then pick off the detachments one by one. Ferreira had at his disposal Alpha, Charlie and Foxtrot companies, one reconnaissance team, an 81-mm mortar group, an assault pioneer section, six helicopter gunships, nine Pumas, a Bosbok spotter aircraft and four Impalas.

Because the operation would employ new tactics, the companies were re-organised during preparation at Eenhana. Alpha, commanded by Lieutenant Tony Nienaber, was divided into three platoons of 28 men each – 14 to a Puma – and designated the main assault force. Charlie Company, under Lieutenant Sam Heap, was similarly divided, but would provide stopper groups, along with some elements of Foxtrot Company, while the rest were held in reserve. A 28-man platoon from Foxtrot Company, commanded by Lieutenant Rental, would form stopper groups north of Chana Mucuio, while the second platoon, under Lieutenant Jerry Green, would remain at Eenhana as a mobile reserve. The third platoon, commanded by Second Lieutenant Olivier, the mortar group under Second Lieutenant Roodt and the assault pioneer section would establish a helicopter administrative area at Chana Umbi.

By 09h00 on 10 September all the forces were in position, but the first two bases on the target list had already been evacuated. The next day, no sign could be found of the detachments reported to be at Ohaipeto and Onalumona. On the morning of 12 September, after two platoons from Alpha Company had been airlifted east of Chana Huabonga, the gunship crews spotted movement to the north and pinned the enemy down as the ground troops moved in.

After initially fighting back hard with mortars and RPG 7s, the 80-strong group in the base found the gunships too intimidating, and fled to the north-west. With Alpha in hot pursuit, a running battle took place over the next three hours and four kilometres, but as soon as the gunships withdrew to refuel, the enemy split into small groups and took off in all directions. Back at the base, 27 SWAPO bodies were found and one cadre was taken prisoner. Rifleman FJ Shipo of Alpha Company was the only SADF casualty, sustaining a leg wound.

The exercise proved the merit of Ferreira's new strategy of moving troops in quickly by helicopter, and initiated a series of operations under the code-name *Butterfly*. One of the most valuable lessons learned at Chana Huabonga was that the gunships needed to be on target for at least 60 minutes before having to with-draw and refuel, and Elundu was thus chosen as the launch pad for the next assault. Flying time to and from the target was a mere 28 minutes for the Pumas, which meant that in the space of an hour, 168 troops could be placed on the ground by just three helicopters.

Area covered by *Operation Butterfly*

After three potential targets from Chana Onalumona to Chana Huambongo turned up empty on 12 February, Ferreira was authorised to attack the suspected North-Eastern Front headquarters at Mulemba with 140 troops. By 11h00 the next day, the assault force was champing at the bit in the staging area four kilometres south-east of the target, but the helicopters had been delayed due to technical problems.

While waiting, one of Foxtrot Company's platoons had a run-in with eight SWAPO cadres dressed in civilian clothes. Neither side suffered any casualties, but before running away the guerrillas discarded a brand new PKM machine gun, an RPG 7 launcher with four rockets and a backpack containing four AK47 magazines. It later transpired that this had been the rearguard of one group of 30 and another of 40 guerrillas passing south of the contact area.

The helicopters finally arrived at 12h25, but when the troops got there Mulemba was a ghost town. They moved to Ediva Lomwandi next, and from the air the gunship crews reported seeing cooking fires and bags of maize meal. At 13h05, Golf Company's third platoon swiftly overran the base, killing 13 SWAPO and capturing one. All other bases visited that day bore signs of hasty evacuation within the past 12 hours, and it was clear to the troops that SWAPO had some kind of early warning system that allowed them to abandon their bases just hours before they were attacked.

OPERATION ZULU

On 4 January 1981, 32 Battalion's Alpha, Bravo and Charlie companies joined forces with a company from 1 Parachute Battalion to seek and destroy SWAPO's Northern Front headquarters, believed to lie west of Ongiva. The parabats deployed south-east of Mongua in anticipation of SWAPO evacuating their bases and moving towards Ongiva, where they could be shielded by FAPLA. The 32 companies would be waiting for them along the most likely route.

The very next day, a SWAPO base 13 km west of Ongiva was attacked from the air and on the ground. Puma helicopters flying in advance stopper groups had to withdraw from the area due to heavy anti-aircraft fire, while radio problems forced two gunships called in for support to turn back to Eenhana. Nevertheless, two platoons from Bravo Company were successfully airlifted to the target area before an Impala air strike with 68-mm rockets silenced the 14,5-mm anti-aircraft guns. An hour later two more Bravo platoons were flown in, and they attacked the base while the gunships offered air support. As expected, SWAPO began withdrawing to the west, but no stopper groups could be inserted due to an operational restriction on air traffic within ten kilometres of Ongiva. Mopping-up operations confirmed that this had been SWAPO's regional headquarters, and that at least 400 cadres must have been in the base at the time of the assault. The base was spread over an area of 5 000 square metres, with all defences directed towards the east, but the attack had come from the south-west. The bodies of 30 guerrillas were found in the base. A large quantity of documents, three anti-aircraft guns with nine crates of ammunition, a 60-mm mortar and 34 AK47 rifles were taken back to Eenhana.

On 6 January, Bravo Company's second platoon made contact with 30 SWAPO at a waterhole two kilometres east of Omupande, a known FAPLA stronghold. Later that day, a five-minute mortar bombardment was launched against the same platoon from the direction of Omupande, followed an hour later by a second, and another hour afterwards by a third attack, despite the fact that the platoon had moved position.

By 16 February, despite almost daily contact with small groups of SWAPO, no more large concentrations had been found, and it appeared that the enemy had withdrawn from the area. However, intelligence indicated that detachments on the Northern Front had been ordered to infiltrate into South West Africa between beacons 20 and 21, possibly carrying with them the deadly 122-mm rocket launchers.

On 17 February, one company each from 1 SA Infantry and 8 SA Infantry were deployed as stopper groups, three kilometres apart, east of the Santa Clara–Namacunde road. Two platoons from 32 Battalion were assigned to patrol the area north of Chiede, with another two operating further west, but no SWAPO were found during the seven-day operation.

OPERATION HOUTPAAL

On 14 April, Ferreira was ordered to attack SWAPO's North-Western Front headquarters, situated near Chana Mundejavala, about six kilometres north-east of Cuamato. Radio intercepts had identified the location, and as with several other operations, *Houtpaal* (wooden pole) would be a joint effort between 32 Battalion and the parabats. Colonel Jan Breytenbach, founder of both 32 Battalion and 44 Parachute Brigade, would lead a Sabre team from the parabats. The Air Force and engineers from 25 Field Squadron would provide support.

The target was huge, spread over an estimated 880 000 square metres, and believed to house a force between 150 and 200 strong. Operational Order 12/81 stipulated that physical reconnaissance was to be done prior to attack, and a team led by Lieutenant Willem Ratte confirmed a large number of foxholes east of the base and three anti-aircraft guns on the western side, facing a chana.

On 15 April, Echo Company crossed the border on foot just west of Beacon 13 and began moving north. At 13h08 contact was made with a group of 40 SWAPO at a waterhole. One enemy was killed and the others fled north, causing concern that they would raise the alarm about the presence of SADF personnel.

Breytenbach's Sabre team entered Angola shortly before last light the next day. The vehicles were all mounted with heavy-calibre machine guns, and their task was to take out the anti-aircraft guns in the event that the air strike failed to do so.

Unfortunately, Breytenbach's team got lost on their way to link up with Echo Company and had to fire flares to determine their position – within ten kilometres of the base, and cause for even greater concern that the entire operation could be compromised.

By first light on 17 April, all the elements were in position to launch the ground attack immediately after the scheduled air strike. At 06h20, however, a heavy 122-mm and 82-mm barrage, lasting about ten minutes, was launched towards the east from inside the base. The ground troops were puzzled, as none of their forces were deployed in that area. The air strike began at 07h45, but the Impalas missed the anti-aircraft guns, which had to be taken out by the helicopter gunships. One Alouette was hit, but made it back to the assembly area safely.

Meanwhile, four Pumas dropped a string of parabats into three stopper group positions a kilometre north, and by 08h13 Echo Company's troops were in the centre of the base, which was deserted except for a few individual SWAPO soldiers. It then became clear that the early morning bombardment had been a ploy to delay the attack in order to allow the main SWAPO force to complete its withdrawal.

By 11h50 the base had been destroyed, but because of the likelihood of running into FAPLA forces, Ferreira was refused permission to pursue the enemy to Cuamato. Ferreira's report on the attack was critical of the air strike, pointing out that only one 250-kg bomb dropped by the six Impalas actually fell within the base, and that the gunships had started their run so far east of the base that they missed all signs of the withdrawal.

The South African forces were still strictly prohibited from striking against FAPLA, but the MPLA's army was clearly not operating under similar restrictions. On the morning of 20 April, Charlie Company's temporary base south of Cuamato was bombarded by FAPLA with 122-mm rockets. Permission for a follow-up operation was again denied, and at 16h00 a patrol from Charlie Company again made contact with FAPLA, exchanging fire with ten troops seven kilometres south-west of Cuamato. After a brief firefight, FAPLA withdrew and the patrol moved east to avoid any further contact, but soon found themselves under heavy 82-mm mortar fire. The gunships were called in for support, and two SA 7 anti-aircraft missiles, in turn, targeted them. SWAPO's new strategy was to run to FAPLA for protection, and FAPLA was apparently more than happy to deploy patrols of up to 50 men to harass the South African forces. But the orders to avoid contact with FAPLA remained in place, and 32 was left with no option but to withdraw from the area on 21 April, having achieved little beyond forcing SWAPO to move its regional headquarters yet again.

OPERATION DOMINO

On the Western Front, action against SWAPO intensified from the beginning of 1981, with regular ambushes and destruction of road links between specific towns. On the night of 26/27 May, a combined operation involving 32 Battalion, 44 Parachute Brigade and Special Forces was conducted to set up vehicle ambushes on the road between Xangongo and Lubango and destroy stormwater drains on the road from Xangongo to Ongiva.

An 18-man reconnaissance team led by Lieutenant Ratte was responsible for the ambushes, consisting of three TM 46 mines on the road surface, connected to one another with Cordex for detonation by the team leader. The first victim was a Star truck, which flew through the air and came to rest among the trees at the side of the road, where it was set alight with a white phosphorous grenade later that night. At 04h45, the driver of the next vehicle spotted the burning Star, but it was too late, and the recce team opened fire with small arms and an RPG 7 rocket launcher. The truck was loaded with fuel drums and exploded almost at once, killing all three SWAPO inside.

Ten kilometres north of Chiemba, the Special Forces team took out a single vehicle with an RPG 7 rocket just after 19h00. Meanwhile, one of two Sabre teams from 44 Parachute Brigade under command of Colonel Breytenbach spent the night rigging a culvert 30 km north-east of Ongiva with explosives, which left a four-metre wide gap in the road when detonated at 04h50.

The second Sabre team surprised a group of six SWAPO manning an obser-vation post 12 km south-east of Cuamato, killing three and capturing two bicycles before moving on to their actual target, a culvert on the road between Xangongo and Mongua, which was blown up at 07h00.

OPERATION CARNATION

Launched on 20 June, this operation continued until the start of *Operation Protea* in August, and was designed to destroy all SWAPO's logistical routes and bases in the area north of beacons 12 to 19, as far north as Cuvelai. It was later extended to cover the area east to Beacon 28.

The brunt of the operation was borne by 32 Battalion and 44 Parachute Brigade, but from time to time elements from 6 and 3 SA Infantry, 101, 201 and 701 Battalions, 1 SA Coloured Corps and 5 Reconnaissance Regiment were drawn in.

The first base found had been evacuated the day before, but an attack on the next resulted in one SWAPO being killed. Acting on information from a member of the local population, Bravo Company's first platoon attacked a base six kilometres east of Omupanda on the morning of 22 June, killing two more SWAPO. That night, another two died when a Star truck was ambushed on the road between Mongua and Ongiva.

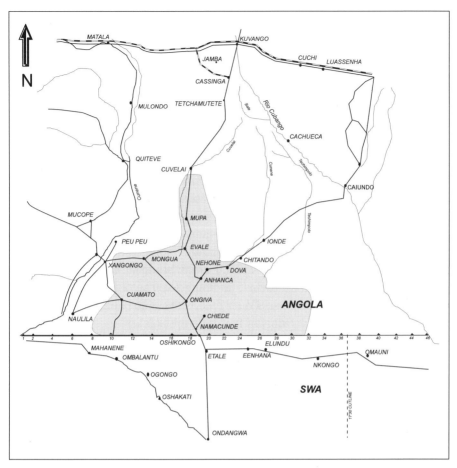

Operation Carnation

The pattern for the operation was set: SWAPO would move from one base to another every three to five days to avoid detection by patrolling gunships, establishing food and arms caches throughout the area, which would be found by the ground forces and destroyed.

On 1 July, Ferreira despatched Golf Company to Chana Pale, where they found and attacked a base, killing 17 and capturing three SWAPO. Four days later, a SWAPO patrol was surprised just east of Anhanca and three more enemy died.

But the main prize – finding the Northern Front headquarters – continued to elude the patrols. Each time they moved against what appeared to be the correct location, they found it abandoned, sometimes just hours earlier. On 7 July, Foxtrot Company killed seven SWAPO south-east of Dova, and the gunships spotted a base big enough to house 200 men. Foxtrot immediately moved to the base, found two enemy and shot them. Any other inhabitants had already left.

Foxtrot Company moved on to Mupa and occupied the town after killing one more SWAPO.

At 14h15 the next day, the gunships located another base, eight kilometres north-east of Chana Umbi. Alpha Company was airlifted in by Puma to investigate, made contact and killed two enemy. When the helicopters drew 14,5-mm and SA 7 fire, they withdrew, and the Impalas were called in for an air strike. It took two hours for them to appear over the target, and by the time the ground troops moved in the enemy had withdrawn, taking their anti-aircraft guns with them, but leaving one SA 7 system behind.

On 11 July, acting on information from a source inside Angola, Alpha Company successfully attacked the Northern Front logistical base two kilometres north-east of Ongiva, killing four enemy and capturing a huge amount of equipment. For the first time, complete 82-mm B10 recoilless guns and 122-mm single tube rocket launchers with sights, operating instructions and tool kits were recovered.

The hunt was also on for the Central Front headquarters, and on 10 July, Foxtrot Company uncovered a cache containing 4 000 kg of canned food. On 13 July, Golf Company attacked Joel's Point, a SWAPO maintenance base, killing two guards and destroying two drums of fuel, an empty tanker, and a large quantity of vehicle parts and spares.

By this time, food and arms caches were being uncovered on an almost daily basis, but the enemy was staying well away from the patrols. The area of operations had shifted from west to north-east of Ongiva, and on 17 July, Ferreira, who had to prepare for another major operation, was relieved by Major Manie van Rensburg. On 22 July, Alpha Company made contact with a group of SWAPO 25 km west of Anhanca, killing 16 and capturing four. Under interrogation, the prisoners revealed that they had been waiting for vehicles to pick them up and move them further north after all detachments had been ordered to evacuate the area, and take as much equipment with them as they could.

The cat and mouse game continued. SWAPO was obviously keeping the South African troop movements under close surveillance, managing to stay one step ahead of the patrols and avoiding carefully laid ambushes while moving steadily towards the FAPLA concentrations at Mongua and Ongiva, as a captured FAPLA officer confirmed early in August.

The situation took on a totally different hue on 7 August, however, when FAPLA emerged from the shadows to face the SA forces head on. The first confrontation was with members of 5 Reconnaissance Regiment, deployed 20 km west of Ongiva on the road to Cuamato. Two enemy vehicles were shot out, and later that night, when FAPLA returned to recover their dead, they ran into an ambush which took out three BTR 60 armoured cars and resulted in further fatalities, including one member of 5 Recce.

Next, FAPLA ordered all ODP members to report to Namacunde with their rifles, and members of the local population reported a FAPLA presence at Dova. On 15 August, Bravo Company's fourth platoon made contact with SWAPO south of Chiede, killing seven, and one of Charlie Company's platoons found a temporary base housing 20 men, who hastily withdrew. After every contact, the SWAPO cadres made for the nearest FAPLA deployment, confident in the knowledge that the South African forces were under orders not to attack the MPLA's regular army.

OPERATION KONYN/PROTEA

Operation Protea's objective was to gain military control of central Angola and halt FAPLA's continued logistical support for SWAPO. From 24 August to 6 September, Brigadier Witkop Badenhorst would command four task forces – Alpha, Bravo, Charlie and Mamba – consisting of mechanised, motorised, counter-insurgency and artillery elements, and involving some 4 000 SADF members all told.

The four battle groups of Task Force Alpha, commanded by Colonel Joep Joubert, would launch the main attacks on Xangongo and Ongiva. Support would be provided by Eland 90 armoured cars, 120-mm artillery, 127-mm multiple rocket launchers and 120-mm mortars. In one of the biggest air operations during the SWA/Angolan conflict, the Air Force would make available 138 aircraft, including 35 Mirage jet fighters, 18 Impalas, four Buccaneers, six Canberra bombers, 23 Alouette, 16 Puma and two Super Frelon helicopters, and a small fleet of transport and light aircraft.

Protea would once again see 32 Battalion in the front lines, the natural position of a unit that had more than earned its spurs in six years of hard and continuous conflict. Ferreira would command Battle Group 40, with his own second-in-command, Major Eddie Viljoen, as his combat 2IC. Captain Tony Nienaber would command Alpha Company, Captain Jan Hougaard would lead Golf Company and Lieutenant Jim Ross would take Charlie Company into battle.

Battle Group 60, commanded by Commandant James Hills, would consist of 32's Bravo, Delta, Echo and Foxtrot companies, as well as a mortar platoon.

On 21 August, *Operation Konyn* (rabbit) – precursor of *Protea* – swung into action with the movement of the various battle groups to Oshikongo. Two days later, at 11h00, the air strike was launched with Cahama being hit by two Canberras, each armed with four 450-kg bombs and 18 weighing 250 kg apiece, eight Mirage F-1CZs and two Buccaneers carrying 30 missiles each. Seven minutes later two Canberras with the same payloads, two Buccaneers and 16 Mirage F1s armed with Mk 82 bombs attacked the radar installations at Chibemba, drawing heavy flak from SA 7s. At 16h00, five Canberras bombed Cahama again, and five hours

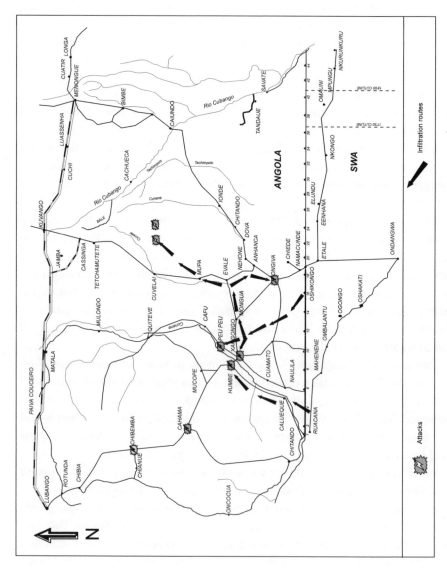

Primary targets Operation Protea

Attacks

Infiltration routes

later the Buccaneers bombed a complex north-east of the town, which it was later learned had been the transport depot.

With Special Forces teams in position to monitor overnight enemy movement on the road between Cahama and Xangongo, *Protea* began with Task Force Alpha crossing into Angola from 03h00 on 24 August. Battle Group 10 was in the vanguard, moving from Ruacana towards Calueque, then north along the west bank of the Cunene River. At 03h30, battle groups 20, 30 and 40 crossed the border at Beacon 16 and began moving north. By 08h00, the column came to a standstill 12 km north-east of Cuamato when one of the ten-ton trucks detonated an anti-personnel mine. Extremely difficult terrain, and the fact that the Buffel armoured personnel carriers could not move as fast as the Ratel armoured cars, had put the advance behind schedule, but by 10h30 the force halted ten kilometres east of Xangongo to await the scheduled air attack.

At 11h05, eight Impalas swooped over Peu Peu and Humbe to knock out the anti-aircraft guns. Ten minutes later, the artillery launched a 20-minute barrage with the 140-mm G2 guns and the 127-mm MRLs. In a well-coordinated operation, this was followed immediately by another air assault, this time from the Buccaneers on Peu Peu. At 12h39, the ground troops began moving towards their designated targets. Battle Group 10 was to attack Humbe, while Battle Group 20 assaulted the southern part of Xangongo, and Battle Group 40 concentrated on the central and northern sections of the town. Battle Group 30 headed for Peu Peu.

Ferreira's group attacked central Xangongo at 12h50, Alpha Company (Combat Team 41) operating from the north-east and Golf Company (Combat Team 42) from the south-east. Simultaneously, Battle Group 20 attacked the airfield and southern section of the town. Initially, Battle Group 40 met with little resistance, but ten minutes into the attack they were pinned down close to the fort by anti-aircraft guns firing in the ground role and heavy 122-mm artillery. Four Mirages and eight Impalas, Buccaneers and Canberras answered Ferreira's call for air support against the anti-aircraft guns and MRLs, as well as the main headquarters.

By 15h00, Battle Group 10 had taken Humbe. Battle Group 20 was still fighting its way through the southern section of Xangongo, while Battle Group 40 was clearing the fort in the town centre. At 18h00, Battle Group 10 had secured the area west of the bridge at Xangongo, and Battle Group 20 had captured the southern part of the town, destroying four T34 tanks and capturing a large number of vehicles, ammunition and other equipment.

Commandant Chris Serfontein's Battle Group 30 took Peu Peu, but could not conduct a proper sweep of the town before dark and reported that there was still an enemy presence to the west. They had also destroyed two T34s and captured valuable equipment before occupying the medical and communications centres.

The attack on central Xangongo, 24 August 1981

Kraal   ■ Buildings   Tar road   Gravel road

Combat Team 41

Combat Team 41

Combat Team 41

CombatTteam 41

Combat Team 41

Combat Team 41

CombatTteam 41

Battle Group 20

Combat Team 42

Combat Team 42

Combat Team 42

Assembly area

D - Day 11h00

D - Day 11h30

D - Day 11h30

Cunene

N

After sweeping central Xangongo, Battle Group 40 joined forces at the bridge with Battle Group 10, a mechanised company led by Commandant Roland de Vries. Under command of Commandant Dippies Dippenaar, Battle Group 20 had taken the airfield and the southern section of the town, destroying four more T34 tanks in the process.

The next day was spent mopping up and sweeping the area, with more than 100 enemy bodies found at Xangongo and five prisoners taken. At Peu Peu, Battle Group 30 confiscated more than 200 tons of equipment, 120 000 litres of diesel fuel and 90 000 litres of petrol – enough to fill the tanks of all the motorised group's vehicles!

Meanwhile, Task Force Bravo, commanded by Colonel Vos Benade and assigned to conduct counter-insurgency operations, had begun moving to its designated assembly area. On the way, one company from Battle Group 50, a motorised unit with four companies and a mortar platoon under command of Commandant Frans Botes, made contact with a combined SWAPO/FAPLA patrol 20 km south-west of Xangongo, killing one. Ten members of the company were wounded. Delta Company, led by Lieutenant Thinus van Staden, was to link up with Battle Group 60 east of Mongua, and on arrival was immediately despatched to monitor the northern road between Ongiva and Anhanca. Battle Group 60 was conducting reconnaissance in the Nehone and Evale area.

On 25 August, Battle Group 10 sent a patrol along the road towards Cahama, making contact with a combined SWAPO/FAPLA convoy on the way to Xangongo. Three BTR 60 armoured cars were destroyed and two BM 21 multiple rocket launchers captured.

The reserve task force, Mamba, consisting of two parachute companies, was despatched to Mongua when enemy presence was reported there. They overran the town, but the gunships drew heavy anti-aircraft fire. One of the helicopters was shot down and all the crew members killed.

Battle Group 50 moved on to Nehone after securing Mupa, where two platoons and four gunships were used to attack a SWAPO listening post, killing two enemy before the rest fled, leaving their radio behind. Two companies from Battle Group 60 secured Evale, and Delta Company remained in ambush position along the Ongiva–Nehone road while the rest of the group moved to Dova. That night, a light aircraft dropped leaflets over Ongiva warning residents that a South African attack was imminent and that they should evacuate the town.

On 26 August, radio intercepts picked up messages from Lubango urging FAPLA's 11th Brigade and SWAPO to defend Ongiva. Should this prove impossible, FAPLA's commander was ordered to destroy all classified documents, kill all prisoners in the town jail, retain only those radios that were essential for communication and destroy the rest, hide all the money that could be removed from the bank, destroy the airfield and plant as many landmines as possible.

FAPLA's 21st Brigade at Cahama was ordered to launch an offensive to recover two BM 21 vehicles lost the day before, but the commanding officer refused to do so. SWAPO was ordered to go around the assault force and attack from the rear. During an early morning contact with a FAPLA convoy 35 km south-east of Cahama, Battle Group 50 destroyed three BTR armoured cars, four GAZ trucks and the 23-mm anti-aircraft guns mounted on them before coming under 122-mm artillery bombardment from Cahama.

Battle Group 20 found their next target, a SWAPO base 18 km north-west of Cuamato, abandoned, but they captured six GAZ trucks and two complete 82-mm mortars. Battle Group 40 began moving towards Evale to form part of Task Force Bravo for the remainder of the operation. Battle Group 50 established a headquarters at Dova from which reconnaissance patrols were sent out 30 km north and east of Nehone, and Battle Group 60 set up a headquarters at Mupa.

Parabats were dropped west and 15 km south of Tetchamutete to secure the area and monitor enemy movement. Five Special Forces teams parachuted into an area 20 km north of Cuvelai to cut off any enemy reinforcements. The Air Force again bombed Cahama and Chibembe, dropping 48 450-kg and 42 250-kg bombs on the two targets.

On 27 August, FAPLA engineers from Quihita and Lubango began fortifying defensive positions and rebuilding the radar installations at Chibemba and Cahama, as well as repairing the bridge at Xangongo. A 500-strong SWAPO battalion with 32 BTR 60 armoured cars under command of FAPLA's 21st Brigade took up defensive positions around Cahama, and messages were sent from Ongiva to Lubango reporting that the town was surrounded by South African forces, and that both air and artillery support were needed. By gaining control of the access routes, the South Africans had made certain such support would not materialise.

The assault on Ongiva started with a rocket, bomb and gun attack by 14 Mirages, one of which was hit just above the tail fin by an SA 7 missile, but the pilot made it back to Ondangwa safely. An artillery barrage followed before the ground troops of Battle Group 20 went in from the north-east. Despite heavy resistance, FAPLA's headquarters had been taken by 10h00, but at the airfield, despite the reserve force being inserted, the battle raged on until four Impalas were called in to provide air support. At 11h50, someone realised that the slow advance of the ground troops was due to heavy fire from anti-aircraft guns, directed from a radar station on top of a water tower. Once the artillery took this out, the airfield fell. By this time six T34 tanks had been shot out at the airfield.

In the town itself resistance was exceptionally heavy, particularly from the enemy tanks, and the reserves had to be brought in once again, along with a combat team from Battle Group 10. At nightfall, Battle Group 30 pulled back, resuming the assault at first light on 28 August. At 11h00, a convoy of vehicles tried to escape to the north, running straight into the ambush prepared by Battle Group 60 on the road to Anhanca. It was an historic confrontation, with four Russian advisers killed and 32's Delta Company becoming the first SADF unit to capture a Russian combatant in Angola – Warrant Officer Nikolai Petretsov, caught while guarding the dead body of his wife.

Battle Group 20 had moved on to Santa Clara, capturing 30 tons of food and 20 tons of medical supplies at Namacunde. At 09h40, the Mirages attacked Mupa, and by 12h08 Ongiva was secure, though surrounded by enemy minefields and booby-trapped trenches, bunkers and buildings. Investigation showed that the FAPLA tanks had been of little use as they were dug in and had restricted trajectories, and they were all facing south. The battle had been launched from the north.

While moving to Mupa, one company from Battle Group 60 made contact with the rearguard of a 50-strong SWAPO force, killing 20 and capturing 20 122-mm rockets. On 29 August, FAPLA reported that the refugees from Xangongo had reached Cavungo, 18 km south of Cahama, and a SWAPO company was sent to Ediva to assist FAPLA. Battle Team 10, still at Xangongo, began making preparations to withdraw, while Battle Group 20 set about sweeping the road for mines between Ongiva and Santa Clara, in anticipation of the South African forces returning south. Battle Group 30 moved 35 km north-west of Mongua to collect captured equipment, and donate food and clothing from the caches to the local population.

Battle Group 40 took up stopper positions around a base 70 km north-east of Mupa, while Battle Group 60 attacked it, killing 20 and capturing two SWAPO. The next day, battle groups 10 and 20 began loading the captured equipment, weaponry and vehicles for transport back to Oshakati, while Battle Group 40 swept through the target area 70 km north-east of Mupa, but found no enemy. Battle groups 50 and 60 launched an area sweep north-west of Embundu and north of Mupa, killing 22 SWAPO and capturing three 30 km north of the town.

On 31 August, elements of 44 Parachute Brigade deployed 23 km west of Xangongo to provide withdrawal cover for Battle Group 10. At 16h00 UNITA forces appeared and took control of Xangongo, and the parabats could withdraw. Battle Group 20 found another huge depot containing 400 000 litres of fuel on the outskirts of Ongiva. All the vehicles filled their tanks before the rest of the fuel was destroyed. Battle Group 30 joined Task Force Bravo at Anhanca, and at 16h50 Battle Group 60 made contact with SWAPO 45 km north-west of Embundu, killing 15.

Battle Group 40 began an area operation from north of Mupa to the south; Battle Group 50, commanded by Commandant Frans Botes, did the same 20 km north-east of Nehone, and Battle Group 60 followed suit north-west of Embundu.

At 17h37 on 1 September, all elements of Battle Group 10 crossed back into

South West Africa at Santa Clara, followed over the next five days by all other forces. On 2 September, Battle Group 60 made contact with SWAPO 30 km north-west of Embundu, killing two and capturing one. Battle groups 40 and 50 slowly began making their way south.

SWAPO's command, control and support structures on the North-Eastern Front had been either effectively disrupted or destroyed, and vast quantities of equipment confiscated or rendered inactive. Vehicles taken back to Oshakati included nine T34 and four PT76 amphibious tanks, 165 cargo trucks, 13 mobile workshops, fuel tankers, armoured cars, ambulances, trailers and generators. In addition to 250 tons of ammunition and 18 000 small arms, the enemy also lost 46 anti-aircraft guns, 94 SA 7 anti-aircraft missiles, 43 field guns and two multiple rocket launchers.

The cost in human terms was 438 FAPLA/SWAPO killed, including the four Russians, and 46 captured. The South African forces lost 14 men, and 61 were wounded.

OPERATION DAHLIA

On 2 October, Bravo, Charlie and Delta companies, along with the 81-mm mortar group and a reconnaissance team, were deployed on the Western Front in order to prevent SWAPO from regrouping. Since *Protea* the area had been quiet, and the authorities wanted to keep it that way. On 13 October, Charlie Company captured an ODP member, who claimed that all SWAPO and FAPLA forces had withdrawn to the north. On the same day Delta Company shot a man wearing civilian clothes, but who was carrying a VZ 57 rifle, a SWAPO membership card and a letter from Soviet defence headquarters in Leningrad. There was no further contact before the operation ended on 3 November.

OPERATION HANDSAK

From 12 October 1981 to 30 May 1982, a series of operations took place under the umbrella of *Handsak* (handbag), with companies being deployed for five weeks at a stretch. The first deployment covered the area east of Cahama as far north as Techipa and Peu Peu, but no major bases or large concentrations of SWAPO were located, only occasional groups of three to five men. By mid-October, intelligence sources reported a large SWAPO base for 300 men west of the bridge and south of the river at Cahama. The town was occupied by a strong combined force of FAPLA, Russians and Cubans, and it had become impossible to conduct aerial reconnaissance because of the anti-aircraft guns.

On 26 October an assault force was airlifted to the area. The lead helicopter drew heavy fire and had to make an emergency landing eight kilometres from the target after one of the troops on board was wounded.

The rest of the assault force approached the target on foot, and came under fire from FAPLA as they reached the river. During a brief firefight, they killed 11 enemy before continuing eastwards, drawing sporadic heavy fire along the way. About three kilometres from the target they detained a Portuguese man, who confirmed that there was a base occupied by Cuban and Russian troops near the bridge, but no SWAPO presence.

The commander decided to return to the scene of the earlier confrontation, where a number of vehicles had been parked under camouflage. By the time they got there, the intermittent exchanges with FAPLA had accounted for 30 enemy dead. The troops destroyed 12 GAZ trucks loaded with clothing and ammunition, one Land Cruiser and one Land Rover, as well as a few ramshackle buildings used as stores, before returning to base. The next day, they were redeployed in the same area.

On 18 November, while patrolling the road north of Techipa, the platoon led by Second Lieutenant LJ van Rensburg and Sergeant GL van Niekerk found and followed vehicle tracks to a point where they moved into the bush about six kilometres north of the town. As Van Rensburg was taking a closer look at the tracks, some of his troops signalled that the enemy was moving in behind the platoon. They immediately formed an extended line and Van Rensburg called in the gunships, but they were about 25 minutes away.

At the same time the enemy – on slightly higher ground and with better cover – also moved into attack formation. For several minutes the two forces held their positions about 200 m apart, each waiting for the other to open fire. Van Rensburg was playing for time and waiting for the gunships to arrive, but the enemy blinked first and the firefight began. Bombarded with 60-mm mortars, however, the enemy soon withdrew, splitting into groups of three to five men, making it impossible to pursue them effectively.

From the middle of November the movement of SWAPO and/or FAPLA in the area around Techipa escalated, and it was not unusual for FAPLA convoys to be escorted by up to 100 soldiers. Shortly after 05h00 on 4 December, 20 GAZ trucks, loaded with food, clothing and ammunition and protected by 150 FAPLA troops, drove into the killing ground of an ambush laid by Alpha Company's second and third platoons nine kilometres north-east of Peu Peu. Their arrival coincided perfectly with the appearance of helicopter gunships called in as soon as the vehicle movement was detected, but the ground troops had not realised that 14,5-mm anti-aircraft guns were mounted on three of the trucks. While two of the guns repeatedly fired at the helicopters, the third was directed at the troops on the ground, forcing them to retreat out of range. The first vehicles that had been shot out blocked the road, and the rest of the convoy had nowhere to go.

By 10h00, the enemy's 82-mm mortars had opened up and it was time to bring in the reinforcements. Golf Company and an 81-mm mortar group joined the battle at 13h00, followed 20 minutes later by two Impalas. By 16h00, mopping up could start, with 13 GAZ trucks destroyed and another four captured. The enemy had long since disappeared into the bush, taking any dead and wounded with them.

On 20 December, two platoons from Delta Company laid an ambush along the Cahama–Xangongo road after hearing vehicle movement. Two helicopter gunships arrived at just about the same moment that a BRDM armoured vehicle drove into view, followed at 500 m by a BTR 60 armoured personnel carrier on which a 14,5-mm gun was mounted. About 80 FAPLA soldiers were walking ahead and alongside the vehicles. During a 45-minute air and ground attack, 50 enemy were killed and two captured. Both vehicles were destroyed.

On 1 February 1982, two companies from 201 Battalion and an Eland armoured car squadron were attached to 32, along with fresh orders: set up ambushes on all roads to Xangongo to prevent FAPLA from reoccupying the town. Secondary orders: to locate SWAPO in the area between beacons 11 and 14 as far north as Cuamato. For this operation, two companies from 201 Battalion and an Eland armoured car squadron would boost 32's ranks.

On 23 February, Golf Company's second platoon located and attacked a SWAPO base seven kilometres east of Techipa, killing 11. By now, both SWAPO and FAPLA had obviously realised that the forces operating in the western sector of Angola were not UNITA, but their most dreaded enemies, 32 Battalion, and they were keeping movement in the region to a minimum. It was nearly a month before the next report of SWAPO presence was received, when an elderly civilian offered to lead Golf Company's second platoon to a group of SWAPO who had raped his wife. One of the five guerrillas resting under a tree was killed, while his companions escaped into the bush.

At 01h00 on 23 March, Echo Company's second platoon was attacked in their temporary base 30 km south-east of Cahama. During a ten-minute firefight, some members of the platoon took it on themselves to 'bombshell', and by 07h00 nine of them were still unaccounted for. Fearing they might have been captured, the rest of the platoon moved from one emergency point to another looking for the lost men, who were all located by 16h45.

On 9 April, Ferreira took personal command of the ongoing operation, deploying 583 members of the rifle companies and 48 members of the recce wing to seek and destroy SWAPO detachments in the western sector. But SWAPO remained a hidden enemy, and by the middle of June the entire force was withdrawn.

OPERATION DAISY

Information gathered during *Protea* indicated that SWAPO's main command, control and logistical headquarters were situated in the Bambi and Chetaquera area. Their destruction would see the deepest penetration into Angola of any South

African forces since *Operation Savannah* in 1975. It would fall to 32 Battalion to protect the tactical headquarters and supply routes for the main mechanised force, with recce teams led by Captain Willem Ratte being instrumental in locating SWAPO positions. The assault force would be led by 61 Mechanised Battalion and include elements from 201 Battalion, 1 Parachute Battalion and 5 Reconnaissance Regiment.

The first task for 32 was to reconnoitre Ionde and establish whether there was any enemy presence in the town. On 2 November, one of the recce teams made brief contact with a small group of SWAPO four kilometres north-west of Embundu, killing one. Two hours later another recce team also ran into a group of SWAPO, killing eight and capturing four, who not only confirmed a huge concentration of guerrillas at Bambi, but disclosed the exact location of the base between Cassinga and Tetchamutete.

After 61 Mechanised Battalion's 4 November attack on Bambi, followed on the radio by Echo Company at Ionde, one of 32's recce teams captured the SWAPO detachment commander's clerk at Chana Cacula, 25 km north-west of Chitando. Under interrogation, he revealed that SWAPO scouts had been monitoring the movements of the South African forces around the clock, which explained why every base found had been evacuated shortly before. On 8 November a raid on yet another empty base produced items never before found in the tons of equipment abandoned by SWAPO when they fled their bases: gas masks for protection in the event of chemical attack. A new threat had been added to the hazards of combat in Angola.

Later that day, as forces that had taken part in *Daisy* made their way back south, two Buffel armoured personnel carriers detonated landmines near Mupa, four hours and 14 km apart. By 18 November, the operation was officially over.

OPERATION OLYFHOUT

For the first time in many years, patrols were introduced in the Olukula area, 11 km south of Beacon 36, in January 1982. Largely thanks to Project Spiderweb, the area had been quiet for some time, and perhaps the platoon from 8 SA Infantry had grown complacent, as an attack by SWAPO on 27 January, which left three South Africans dead, took them totally by surprise.

Intelligence officers were convinced that the attack was the work of SWAPO's Far East detachment, which had infiltrated from north of Beacon 36. Both UNITA and air reconnaissance confirmed a plentiful supply of water at Chana Chanadenge, 30 km north of the beacon, and UNITA also reported a possible SWAPO base close by, with another 45 km south of Ionde.

On 17 February, 32 Battalion's entire reconnaissance wing, divided into eight teams, set off from Omauni in a vehicle convoy, carrying both diesel and aviation fuel in anticipation of an attack, to try to locate the bases. Five days later, an early morning patrol made contact with a small group of SWAPO near Ionde, killing one and wounding another. For the next ten days of *Olyfhout* (olive wood), no further enemy presence was detected, and the morning of 27 February found the convoy at Chana Mocapo awaiting re-supply.

In accordance with standard operating procedure, the vehicles were drawn into a laager and camouflaged, with Captain Willem Ratte's command vehicle in the centre. Sergeant Phil Smit, leader of Team 8, flew out on one of the re-supply helicopters to be with his wife, who was due to have a baby. The rest of the group remained in position to wait for nightfall, but at 18h00 two Impala strike aircraft passed overhead on patrol – not an unusual sight in the area, except that some of the ground troops noted afterwards that they seemed to be in attack mode.

They were – but even as the flight leader opened fire on the laager with his 30-mm gun, Sergeant Mark Craig could not comprehend what was going on, recording afterwards: 'My first thought was that this isn't happening, but the screams of the injured and the roaring after-burners of the jets as they pulled up told me I was in serious trouble.'

There was smoke and fire everywhere. Captain Ratte's command vehicle took the brunt of the attack, but all around drums of fuel were exploding and being thrown high into the air. No one on the ground could communicate with the aircraft, but fortunately the second pilot had already realised that the attack was a mistake, and did not launch his rockets. The damage, however, was done. Rifleman S Haefeni took a 30-mm round in the chest, and 17 men were wounded. One of the drivers, a National Serviceman, was badly burned but survived. The Bushman tracker was seriously injured by shrapnel. As team medic Corporal Robert Clifford worked on the wounded, Captain Ratte emerged from the inferno in the centre of the circle. There was blood on his face, his eyeglasses were shattered and he seemed disoriented, but refused medical treatment until all the other injured had been attended to.

Drums were still exploding, showering the men with burning fuel, and a column of thick black smoke reached high into the sky. The two Puma helicopters that had brought supplies earlier returned to evacuate the wounded. Ratte refused to climb aboard until one of the pilots, who outranked him, ordered him to do so. Lieutenants Jim Savory and Charlie Loxton and Sergeant Craig directed the clean-up operation. Days later the damaged vehicles were still smouldering, but the group, their numbers severely depleted and sitting ducks for any SWAPO in the area, was refused permission to withdraw from the area and told to wait until recovery vehicles arrived. After SWAPO tracks were found close to the scene, Craig requested explosives to blow up what was left of the vehicles, but this, too, was denied. No SADF equipment was to be left behind in Angola, the military authorities ordered.

Foxtrot Company and the recovery team ran into problems of their own on the way to the scene. SWAPO had accurately assessed the situation and laid numerous landmines on the route the rescue team would have to take, causing damage to several vehicles.

Ten days after being attacked by their own aircraft, the group exited Angola. An official inquiry showed that while the recce team's position had been plotted on the map in the Air Force operations room, the two Impala pilots had not been aware of their deployment, and had assumed the vehicles belonged to the enemy.

OPERATION SUPER

From February 1982, SWAPO activity was detected in the normally quiet western sector of Angola, north of Kaokoland. First indications of this came when intercepts of the enemy military radio network picked up a report of aircraft in the vicinity of Point Zero, flying from Shinonya to Uuyona. SADF authorities were puzzled. No air traffic could be matched to the times or locations mentioned in the report – until someone at Oshakati realised that SWAPO operatives used the phonetic pronunciation of place names, and that Uuyona was actually Iona.

Documents captured during *Operation Sceptic* in June 1980 confirmed this, and the flight in question was thought most likely to have been one by the International Red Cross from Lubango via Baios Dos Tigres along the Cunene River to Ruacana and then to Ongiva. The aircraft had obviously been spotted by SWAPO troops on the ground.

Two days later, a sub-unit with headquarters in the vicinity of Cahama was ordered to meet SWAPO's chief of staff from Lubango at Iona on 22 February, and a confidential source reported to the SADF that PLAN's defence secretary, Peter Nanyemba, was taking a personal interest in Point Zero, thereby confirming that it was of strategic importance.

From 21 February to 1 March, nine cargo trucks made the trip from Cahama to Iona via Otchinjou and Oncucua, returning to Lubango on 4 March. On the same day a SWAPO radio message reported 'Area cleared of all,' indicating that a mission had been completed. At Sector 10 headquarters there was grave concern that SWAPO was establishing a presence in Kaokoland and Damaraland, but the information from the radio intercepts was vague, and it was decided to deploy a ten-man team from 5 Reconnaissance Regiment to investigate the situation.

At 18h00 on 9 March they began moving to a point 20 km east of Iona. A tactical headquarters under command of Captain Jan Hougaard was set up at Marienfluss, where 36 members of 32 Battalion, two Puma helicopters and two Alouette gunships were placed on standby as a reaction force.

On the way to Iona the recces mined the road from Moçâmedes, and at 03h00 on 10 March the first of six vehicles in a convoy moving south detonated

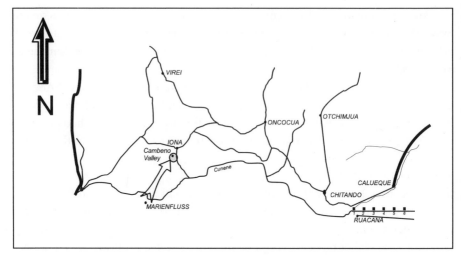

Area map showing Iona, Cambeno Valley and Marienfluss

a mine. Tactical headquarters requested an air strike against the stranded vehicles, but bad weather prevented the Impalas from taking off. Three of the vehicles turned around and drove back to the north, while the remaining two continued southwards.

The next day the recces reported that Iona was empty, though they found numerous vehicle and human tracks leading to the south. They captured three SWAPO moving towards their lay-up south of Iona, and shortly afterwards another 17 SWAPO appeared. When they were about 800 m from the lay-up, the recces called in the gunships and a 12-man reaction force. Contact was made at 14h00, with 14 enemy killed and six captured. Under interrogation at Marienfluss, the prisoners disclosed that some 200 SWAPO were at a base ten kilometres south of Iona in the Cambena Valley.

Planning began immediately for an attack at noon on 12 March. Hougaard would command the ground troops – 45 members of Delta Company, three 12-man stopper groups and a 12-man mortar group armed with two 81-mm mortars. Four Alouette gunships would be under command of Major Neil Ellis, and five Pumas would be commanded by Major Polla Kruger. A reserve force of 36 men would wait at Marienfluss.

At the appointed time the four Alouettes and four of the Pumas took off on schedule. However, heavy rain reduced visibility over the mountains to almost zero, and the assault force had to return to Marienfluss until 07h30 the next day. While Delta Company and the stopper and mortar groups deployed, the gunships pinpointed the base from the air. The target area was relatively contained and the dry thorn trees offered little cover. The gunships poured one burst of 20-mm fire after another into the base, sending the enemy scattering directly towards the stopper groups, but not before four SA 7 missiles had been launched against the helicopters. For the ground troops it was heavy going. The terrain was etched by a profusion of hollows, rocky outcrops and cliff faces, and after the group led by Second Lieutenant PJS Nel (known to his comrades as Nella) made first contact, the troops found themselves constantly under fire. As heat and thirst began to take their toll as well, the ground force – outnumbered four to one – began to lose cohesion, but at noon headquarters denied Captain Hougaard's request for an Impala strike with napalm.

The gunships rendered outstanding air support, but only the infantrymen could penetrate the cracks and crevices where the enemy instinctively took cover from the 20-mm guns. Nel's stopper group was dropped in a ravine, and immediately made contact with a group of between 50 and 100 SWAPO just metres away from the landing zone. Another stopper group, commanded by Sergeant Peter Williams, also came under fire as soon as their feet hit the ground. Major Ellis ordered the gunship piloted by Captain Angelo Maranta to support the Williams group from the air while he himself circled the base, both coordinating the attack and offering support to Nel's group.

Nel and his nine men fought their way along the ravine for three hours before he called a halt and made radio contact with Hougaard, who was on a hill about 200 m away. Almost at once, the men on the left flank engaged the enemy again. Nel ordered the rest of the group to attack, but before they could do so the right flank also came under fire. Nel gave the order to advance, and he and two of his men charged the enemy. He was shot and killed, and Sergeant Victor Dracula assumed command.

With five enemy to the left and 12 on their right flank, the stopper group was firmly pinned down. Dracula wanted to call in gunship support, but realised that Nel had been carrying the only radio, now lying with his body some 40 m away and directly in the line of fire. He and Rifleman Bernardo Domingos tried twice, under murderous fire, to reach Nel's body and retrieve the radio, but were forced to retreat. Their third attempt succeeded, and both the dead officer's body and the vital radio were recovered.

As the day wore on the battle showed no sign of abating. First Sergeant PT Steward, then Corporal J João were killed. The mortar group offering support from the top of a hill had to engage in close combat to avoid being overrun, and by 15h00, when the last shots rang out over the valley, most of 32's men had run out of ammunition and been fighting for some time with enemy weapons taken off the dead. After seven hours of hard and unrelenting battle they were both physically and mentally exhausted, and fervently hoped SWAPO would not launch a counter-attack from the north that night.

While Hougaard flew to tactical headquarters at Marienfluss to report back to Oshakati, Lieutenant du Plessis regrouped the troops and arranged security patrols. The night passed fairly uneventfully, except for a few stray SWAPO stumbling into the temporary base. The next day, 24 men were flown in as reinforcements and to assist with mopping up. One guerrilla was killed and another captured when they were found hiding inside what was left of the base. Captured documents confirmed that Cambeno had been occupied by 200 members of a mechanised SWAPO unit at Lubango, and that their task had been to establish supply caches in advance of the Kaokoveld becoming SWAPO's latest battleground. Interrogation of the prisoners revealed that the guerrillas at Cambeno were all from the July 1981 intake, while a group of 50 longer-serving SWAPO was stationed to the south, closer to the Cunene River. According to one captive, another group of 200 from Lubango was due to join them. A boat large enough to carry 18 men was also mentioned, probably for crossing the Cunene.

Among the equipment captured or destroyed in the base were seven RPG 7 launchers and 1 005 rockets; 648 SKS rifle grenades; 8 000 TM57 and 1 152 TMA3 anti-tank mines; 1 587 F1 and 22 crates of RG3 hand grenades; 463 anti-personnel mines; four SA 7 missiles; 1 143 60-mm and 309 82-mm mortar bombs; 76 AK47 rifles and 20 160 rounds of ammunition; 27 B10 anti-tank recoilless gun rockets; and 37 kg of TNT.

The troops also found 5 750 kg of maize meal, 54 boxes of soup and 4 000 cans of meat. An additional 1 000 kg of food was destroyed.

The human cost of wrecking SWAPO's plans to open up Kaokoland was 197 enemy dead and seven captured. Three SADF members were killed and five wounded.

It was only after the base had been cleared that the operation was named *Super*. Two days after the battle in the valley, Hougaard was given a new mission: clear the area south of Iona and locate SWAPO over a three-week period. Specific tasks were to seek and destroy the 50-man base south of Iona and find the boat reported by prisoners taken at Cambeno.

Delta Company provided 126 men under command of Lieutenant du Plessis for the operation, along with the 12-man mortar group, two helicopter gunships, two Pumas, a Bosbok light aircraft for reconnaissance and a Dakota for re-supply.

Despite an intensive sweep of the area, neither boat nor SWAPO could be found, and when the troops finally returned to Buffalo they were given a hero's welcome. *Super* had been the battalion's biggest and most successful battle to date, but the men were more than happy to share credit for the victory with the gunships commanded by Major Ellis.

As soon as the dust settled, senior officers emerged from their air-conditioned offices with the media in tow to bask in the glory of those who braved both inhospitable terrain and enemy fire to win the day. For the first time in the unit's history, an officer – Captain Hougaard – received the personal congratulations of the South African Prime Minister, PW Botha.

OPERATION BOOMSLANG

At 18h00 on 13 May, while deployed during *Operation Handsak*, tactical head-quarters at Cuamato was ordered to prepare a company and two reconnaissance teams for an airborne assault on a SWAPO force occupying the town of Oncocua. The orders were based on intelligence intercepts of radio messages, so Ferreira requested permission to first send recce teams out to confirm SWAPO's presence. Permission was refused on the grounds that valuable time would be lost, since intelligence believed evacuation of the base was imminent.

On 14 May, *Boomslang* (tree snake) swung into action when two Puma heli-copters airlifted a company of men 20 km north-west of the target. At 11h00 the next day, two eight-man offensive recce teams were flown to positions 13 km north of Cuamato to set up ambushes on the road to the north.

Forty-five minutes later, all 25 members of the assault group were flown by Puma to a point south-west of the town. The second Puma could not be used due to technical problems. At 12h30, with the gunships overhead, the assault began. The town was deserted, and a patrol sent north-west for five kilometres found no sign of SWAPO. During a sweep through the town an old school building was found, its walls plastered with FAPLA propaganda posters. At an abandoned hospital there were clear signs that the front door had been booby-trapped. A bunker bomb was used to gain entry, and a large amount of medical supplies was destroyed by the blast.

On 16 May, 15 troops were flown 14 km north-west of the town where the gunships had picked up vehicle tracks, but nothing else was found. By 10h30 the force was on its way back to Ruacana.

Over the entire two-day period the only people encountered were six members of the Ovihimba tribe living in a small kraal two kilometres outside Cuamato. They reported that FAPLA had evacuated the town at least a year before, and said the vehicle tracks belonged to an ODP patrol that visited once a month. The group said there was no SWAPO presence in the area at all. So much for the 'hot' intelligence.

THE SPIDERWEB PROJECT

For some reason the area known as far-eastern Owamboland (between the 17°30' and 18°00' cutline) was seldom or never patrolled, and by early 1981 the Kavango and the white farming region of the Mangeti were regarded as 'clean', except during the annual infiltration of SWAPO through the Nkongo area, some 60 km west of Omauni.

By February 1981, however, SWAPO had realised that they could cut the length of this route by half if they established a firm base in the Kavango. However, the inhabitants were overwhelmingly pro-SADF, and to keep them that way Captain Willem Ratte, head of 32's reconnaissance wing, suggested establishing 'strong points' throughout the sparsely populated area from which the local population could patrol, monitor and report on SWAPO infiltration.

The people of Kavango welcomed the proposal, but it found no immediate favour with the military authorities, and by May, SWAPO was moving through the area unchecked. When headmen were murdered at Ohikik and Oshatotwa, others feared they would be next, and on 29 October Ratte urgently sought authority from the Officer Commanding Sector 20 to implement Project Spiderweb, pointing out that unless action was taken without delay, 'the local population will lose all faith in the security forces and the entire area might as well just be handed to SWAPO. To do nothing is tantamount to asking farmers in the Grootfontein area to lay down their arms and leave the safety of their families entirely in the hands of the occasional patrols that drop in for a cup of coffee.'

The initial phase of the plan would establish a strong point at Ohikik, to which the families of the two murdered headmen would move. Until members of the local population had been armed and trained to defend themselves against SWAPO, they were to be protected by a minimum of ten troops from 32 Battalion, who would be in radio contact with Omauni on a 24-hour basis. Ratte also proposed that one of the women at the strong point be trained in nursing by the doctor at Omauni, and that in due course a small clinic be set up at Ohikik.

Success for what amounted to the ultimate 'hearts and minds' project would depend on the involvement of various government departments, which would have to provide support in the fields of agriculture, health and education.

Something in Ratte's urgent request must have struck the right chord, and in November implementation of the first phase was authorised by Colonel Gert Nel. Ratte moved a section of troops from Omauni under command of Staff Sergeant Ron Gregory to Ohikik, and set about forming a quick reaction force from the administrative and support staff at the base. By the end of December, families from Onghwiya, Oshatotwa and various shonas in a 25-km radius had moved to the strong point. The only headman who did not relocate was Chief Silas, whose kraal was guarded by some 20 'home guard' members paid by the Owamboland authorities.

Gregory began training the men and older boys to defend the settlement and patrol the surrounding area, and by February 1982 the community numbered 60 souls, of whom 22 were armed with R1 rifles. The doctor and chaplain from 32 visited Ohikik regularly, and Staff Sergeant Theuns Eloff set up a rudimentary woodwork factory where local residents were trained to fashion a variety of

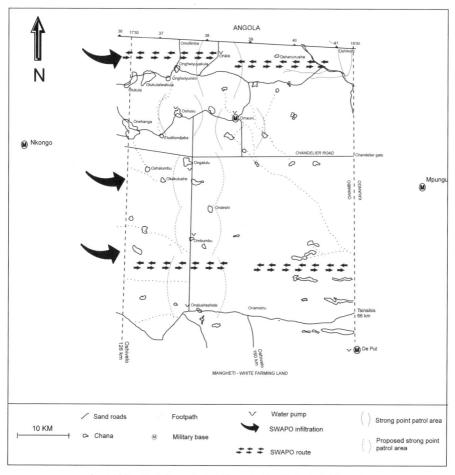

Area of Far East Owamboland targeted by Project Spiderweb

decorative articles and utensils from the teak that abounds in the region. Once a month, maize meal and tobacco were distributed to the community, and when Ratte found an abandoned prefabricated building at Olukula, he dismantled and moved it to Omauni, where it was set up just outside the main gate to serve as a school. The children from Ohikik walked 20 km every day to attend classes offered by Private Coenie Brits, a clerk at the base.

By the end of May, Ohikik was running just as planned – whereas south of the Chandelier Road, SWAPO infiltration of the Kavango had actually increased. Early in June Chief Silas was murdered, and his guards withdrew to Nkongo. A year later authorisation was granted to set up strong points at Ongalulu, Ombumbo and Omamishu, but attempts to establish these settlements became bogged down in bureaucracy, and Ohikik remained the only success story.

When Omauni was handed over to the newly formed South West Africa Special Forces, Ratte's plan was scuppered by the new commanding officer, and he was transferred out of the area soon afterwards. By the middle of 1986, SWAPO was again roaming the Kavango freely, and the traditional infiltration route through Ohikik was back in business.

9

My funeral will
be on patrol

MILITARY OPERATIONS 1983-1985

HAVING SUFFERED SEVERAL major setbacks and disruptions to their command, control and logistical structures during 1982, SWAPO became more reliant than ever on FAPLA for both facilities and protection. It was now common knowledge in the theatre of conflict that South African politicians had declared Angola's regular forces royal game, and that their installations were strictly off-limits as targets. In the western sector SWAPO became an invisible enemy, neither their movements nor their bases detectable by routine patrols.

OPERATION FAKKEL

On 11 January 1983, Sergeant Dave van der Merwe and the four members of his reconnaissance team were flown by helicopter to a point 20 km east of the Virulundo mountain, 65 km south of Varai. It took them four days to hike to the top of the mountain, which offered visibility of up to 30 km to the north. *Fakkel* (torch) required the team to man a 24-hour observation post for the next four weeks, but as early as the second day they noted explosions to the north.

After this, regular blasts, personnel and vehicle movements were observed in the same area, and by 8 February intelligence officers had enough information to plot a possible SWAPO base in a 100-square-kilometre grid some nine kilometres north of the mountain. Ground reconnaissance was needed to pinpoint the location, and between 12 and 24 February, Captain Willem Ratte sent five teams of four men each, led by sergeants KD Clark and Kevin Sydow, lieutenants Nick de la Casa and Peter Waugh, and Sergeant Major Phill Kearns, to find the base.

On 26 February a large base – the first set up by SWAPO in the area – was detected eight kilometres north-east of the mountain near the Rolundo River. Having obtained this information, however, 32 Battalion was never ordered to attack the base.

OPERATION KWARTEL

At the end of March, two recce teams under leadership of sergeants Peter Williams and Harry Roelofse traversed the area west of the 17°30' cutline on foot, to identify local population settlements with a view to possible relocation as part of Project Spiderweb. At the same time, *Kwartel* (quail) required them to monitor any SWAPO movement in the Nkongo area.

At Groot Omemba they found a small group of Bushmen who were willing to move to Ohikik, provided they could count on a regular food supply. Other Bushman clans found by the recce teams were less eager, however, especially those living closest to Kuanyama villages. The Kuanyama were not only hostile towards the SADF, they openly opposed the concept of protected settlements – hardly surprising, since they were known to support SWAPO and formed a vital link in the guerrillas' logistical chain. Obtaining useful information from the Kuanyama about SWAPO movements was impossible, despite the infiltration of the SADF's Bushman interpreter, Lazarus, until the recce teams abducted a 12-year-old boy from Groot Omemba. During the six days he spent with them, he proved a mine of information. By the time the boy was told he could go home, he didn't want to leave, having meanwhile been given a pair of army boots and his own sleeping bag, but eventually he was persuaded to return to his family.

The recces confirmed an infiltration route used by SWAPO and that a group of 30 had established themselves in the dense bush near Capaco, 12 km north of Efufe. Two days of tracking showed that this was a particularly wily group that would, for example, wait until cattle appeared on the path between Groot Omemba and Engawa, then walk ahead of the animals to ensure that their tracks were obliterated. Several times, three to five members of this group were spotted at waterholes, but the recce teams refrained from making contact so as not to alert the larger force to their presence.

On 4 April another SWAPO group, also numbering about 30, was located in the Ipanda area. The next day the teams returned to Omauni, and the information they had gathered was passed on to headquarters, along with recommendations that a thorough reconnaissance of the area be carried out in order to introduce a long-term plan to win the hearts and minds of the local population.

OPERATION SNOEK

By early 1983 the South African forces had established unrestricted mobility in central Angola for at least 100 km on either side of the road from Cuvelai–Ongiva to Santa Clara. Ongiva became the general operational base, and 32 Battalion's operations were controlled from a tactical headquarters there.

On 24 February, while deployed north of Mupa, Foxtrot Company ran into a minor skirmish with a group of SWAPO, and all patrols were alerted to the possibility that some kind of build-up was in progress. On 6 March, Foxtrot Company's temporary base was attacked and one SWAPO killed. That evening, the first platoon also made contact with a group of SWAPO west of Mupa.

After these incidents, Bravo Company was deployed in the area of Bambi Post and Mulola, 40 km north-east of Cuvelai. Two days later they, too, made contact – but although enemy tracks were being picked up on a daily basis, no large concentration of SWAPO could be found.

On 12 March, Second Lieutenant Swart's platoon killed four of the five SWAPO they had been tracking for about five kilometres, and the next day a platoon led by Lieutenant Bosch and Corporal JP Botha found vehicle tracks leading into the bush from the road between Cuvelai and Bambi. Ordered by Captain Tom Barron from tactical headquarters to follow the tracks, the platoon found that about three kilometres to the east the vehicle had returned to the road, a clear indication that something had either been picked up or offloaded on the way.

About 500 m further the platoon found a bag of maize meal, and shortly afterwards a SWAPO groundsheet. The platoon immediately moved from box formation to extended line, and was about ten metres from the perimeter of a SWAPO base when the enemy opened fire with small arms and 82-mm mortars. The platoon responded with 60-mm mortars and 40-mm grenade launchers, and after about ten minutes SWAPO withdrew, leaving ten of their dead behind in the base and another three on the outskirts. Low on ammunition the platoon left the area, and the next day a platoon from Charlie Company was sent to investigate whether or not SWAPO had returned.

While moving through the base, they heard someone call out. They found a wounded SWAPO, who had been overlooked the day before, in a trench. He was evacuated to Ongiva for medical treatment and interrogation.

At 19h10 on 3 April, Alpha Company's first and fourth platoons were moving to lay an ambush on the road four kilometres north-east of Vinte Sete when they saw six SWAPO ahead. Before a single shot was fired, the enemy ran – only to turn and open fire from a more favourable position, pinning the platoon down for a good 15 minutes before withdrawing under cover of an 82-mm mortar bombardment. The third platoon, some distance behind the others, had moved up to assist, but despite the reinforcements Sergeant A Mande and Rifleman JD Kativa were killed, and 11 members of Alpha Company wounded, including the two platoon commanders, second lieutenants A du Plessis and GW Roos. Darkness had already fallen and only the wounded were evacuated that night.

At 10h30 the next day, while the entire Alpha Company was waiting for helicopters to pick up the bodies of the two dead men, a guard saw a group of SWAPO approaching. In the ensuing firefight, seven SWAPO were killed and another 13 members of Alpha wounded, including company commander Lieutenant BG Olivier and platoon commander Second Lieutenant M Lourens. Inspection of the battle ground showed it had been pounded by 80 mortar bombs.

OPERATION DOLFYN

On 25 April, Alpha, Echo and Golf companies, five of 32's reconnaissance teams, a mortar group from the State President's Guard and an engineer element were deployed in the Calolola area. A company from 44 Parachute Brigade was placed on standby. Radio intercepts had indicated a possible SWAPO base 20 km north of Cuvelai. If close reconnaissance confirmed this, it would be attacked on 5 May.

On 3 May, one of the reconnaissance teams set up an observation post on the Camene hill, and at 17h30 another team, scouting the area east of the hill, reported hearing voices and what sounded like people stacking ammunition crates. Similar sounds were picked up the next day, and at 11h30 the team on the hill made contact with nine SWAPO, who more than likely had also hiked up the slopes with the intention of establishing an observation post. One was wounded and captured, while the other eight escaped. The recce team dragged the wounded man to the crest of the hill, where he not only confirmed that a base existed north of the Camene River, but pointed out the direction. It was the same position from which the noise had previously been heard.

The ground commander immediately relayed this information to Oshakati and suggested an attack no later than 16h00, since the captive's companions would probably reach the base by 15h00 and raise the alarm. At 14h45 Echo and Golf companies were moved into the area to prepare for the attack, and at 15h30 the recce team closest to the base reported a vehicle leaving and heading east. As expected the evacuation had begun, and time was of the essence. Deployment of stopper groups was influenced by the fact that the Air Force had strict orders not to enter the airspace east of the hill. At 16h00 the Officer Commanding Sector 10 halted the advance because the helicopter gunships were not yet ready to take off. Permission was denied for the ground troops to attack without air support. The advance resumed at 16h25, with the ground force drawing heavy fire from three 14,5-mm anti-aircraft guns. The first three gunships joined the battle at 17h55, one immediately being hit by anti-aircraft fire, forcing it to land. It was well after last light before the three 14,5-mm guns were knocked out and the enemy withdrew.

At first light on 5 May the assault force moved in to clean up the base and bury the dead before moving on to Bambi. Their patrol was cut short when a member of the State President's Guard, the 23rd man in a single file, stepped on an anti-personnel mine that all 22 men ahead of him had miraculously managed to miss. Knowing that SWAPO would investigate the explosion the patrol set up an ambush, killing four of the guerrillas who had indeed come to examine the source of the blast.

On 19 June, Bravo Company's first platoon made contact with a group of SWAPO guarding an ammunition cache 20 km east of Mupa. When the enemy fled, the patrol destroyed 120 82-mm mortar bombs, 40 anti-personnel rifle grenades and 25 anti-aircraft magazines containing 23-mm shells.

From 21 to 30 June, all the deployed companies made minor contacts, but the next major confrontation was not until 1 July. Alpha Company's third platoon was waiting to be joined at a temporary base between Dova and Nehone by the first platoon, and when guards saw a group of men in uniform approaching, they assumed the platoon had arrived. Even when the newcomers opened fire, those in the base thought it was a mistake, and instead of returning fire took to the bush to prevent friendly fire casualties.

But the intruders were a group of 50 SWAPO, and because the platoon members had taken only their personal weapons with them, an effective counter-attack was impossible. Sergeant GH du Randt and Rifleman E Cassera were killed, and Second Lieutenant GW Roos, Corporal PG Grobler and two troops wounded. SWAPO looted all the equipment in the base, including 26 bigpacks and groundsheets, 25 sleeping bags, 144 water bottles, an A72 radio and the B22 VHF radio, the only means of making contact with company or tactical headquarters. Lieutenant Gert Kruger's platoon was despatched from Ionde to rescue the plundered patrol.

On 3 July, SWAPO attacked Alpha Company's second platoon 20 km north of Dova, where one guerrilla was killed. On 5 July, the same platoon killed another SWAPO on the road between Dova and Nehone. The next month of *Dolfyn* (dolphin) saw almost daily contact between 32 and SWAPO, until all companies returned to tactical headquarters on 3 August.

OPERATION ASKARI

By early 1983 it was evident that the success achieved by *Operation Protea* in expelling SWAPO from the Xangongo and Ongiva areas had been eroded, and that the guerrillas were back, sheltering under the aegis of the FAPLA brigade at Cuvelai. Despite sustained action against SWAPO, this garrison also frustrated efforts by the South African forces to exercise the same measure of control as they had further south. But the ban on engaging FAPLA remained in force.

When SWAPO first began infiltrating into South West Africa, they used a route from Jamba through Cassinga and then to Cuvelai. In November 1983, South African forces were finally given the green light to attack and occupy Cuvelai, while at the same time launching a diversionary attack on Cahama and Caiundo. Four mechanised battle groups of 500 men each would act against SWAPO as far north as Cuvelai, while 32 Battalion was assigned to Cassinga, 250 km to the north. The operation would be known as *Askari*.

From 26 November, three of 32's reconnaissance teams moved into the target area and began liaising with the UNITA forces deployed around Chipolo. A helicopter administrative area – or HAA – was established ten kilometres south of the Bale River, and by 8 December access routes and possible enemy positions had been identified east of Cassinga.

While 32's assault force was moving towards the HAA, a radio message from Oshakati warned that one company should be placed on standby for possible action against the FAPLA base at Caiundo. On 14 December, a mini-HAA was established south of the Bale River about 50 km east of Tetchamutete, bringing the reconnaissance groups within reach of the helicopters.

At 02h18 on 17 December, a base halfway between the Bale and Cubango rivers was attacked with 81-mm mortars, but there was no answering fire. The next day, however, Lieutenant Peter Williams and his eight-man recce team made contact close to the base with enemy who withdrew before the gunships arrived. One wounded enemy was captured, but later died from his injuries. Williams reported that another base to the north was also abandoned, but that there were signs of a fair amount of vehicle activity. The rest of the recce teams were sent in on Buffel mine-resistant personnel carriers as support, in light of indications that there were numerous enemy bases all over the area.

At this point SWAPO almost certainly thought the foreign troops were from UNITA, and on 19 December they sent a strong force up against the eight-man recce team. The helicopter gunships and two rifle companies were rushed to the area, and four SWAPO died in the counter-attack. In their base, four SA 7 missile systems were captured, along with a pile of documents indicating that a base known as Vienna was the Shield Battalion's headquarters. Before long the entire region around Cassinga was a battle zone, with contact on a regular basis. On 20 December at 07h30, three enemy were killed and one prisoner taken. He confirmed that the base attacked the day before was called Berlin, and that the rest of his company was patrolling along the Bale River. Two 32 companies were despatched to the area without delay, making contact with the enemy as they stepped off the helicopter and killing four. Various caches of food, ammunition and clothing were found, and on 22 December four more enemy were killed in a contact that started at 18h30. Three platoon members were evacuated with shrapnel wounds.

As the patrols moved closer to Cassinga and Tetchamutete, contact was also made with FAPLA forces. At 06h35 on 23 December, one of six FAPLA soldiers

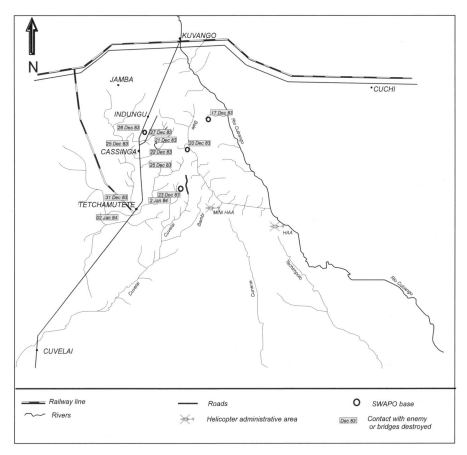

Operation Askari. Note the number of rivers in the area

was killed and another captured. He revealed that the South African forces could expect to encounter some 150 FAPLA soldiers, 82-mm mortars and four 23-mm anti-aircraft guns at Tetchamutete when they deployed just four hours later.

The Christmas Eve attack on Cassinga by one company and one reconnaissance team was a cakewalk, but three captured ODP members confirmed the deployments at Tetchamutete. Colonel Eddie Viljoen, by now Officer Commanding 32 Battalion, sent one of the ODP men to the town with a letter advising FAPLA to withdraw.

Patrols around Cassinga were introduced immediately, and Christmas Day opened with a bang when five of the enemy fled north from a contact at 06h00, leaving behind their 82-mm mortar bombs and RPG 7 rockets. Any lingering thoughts of a peaceful holiday were shattered when one of the recce teams made contact with 20 enemy at 07h50, killing six and taking one prisoner. Two members of the recce team were wounded and evacuated. According to the captive, this was an engineer element from Jamba, making their way to Cuvelai. When he also confirmed several enemy bases north of Cassinga, two companies and two recce teams moved to the area to launch attacks at first light.

The ground troops were indeed ready for battle at 06h00 on 26 December, but the four helicopter gunships got lost and overflew the target. However, the pilots spotted another enemy base from the air and opened fire on it with their 20-mm guns before 30 troops in Buffels were sent in on the ground. Four enemy died and one was captured. The driver of a Land Cruiser was killed trying to break out of the base to the north and the vehicle destroyed. Large quantities of weapons, clothing, mines, food and fuel were found in the base, which the prisoner confirmed was home to the Red Square Battalion, whose task it was to protect SWAPO's central headquarters. He also disclosed that seven companies of the Specialised Unit were at Indungu preparing to infiltrate South West Africa.

The base that had offered the original target was empty, but contained large amounts of food, mines, clothing and documents, and had served as Moscow Battalion's logistical camp. Two more logistical bases were also found in the area and cleared.

On 27 December the reconnaissance team demolished a home-made bridge over a stream on a well-used vehicle route to prevent any reinforcements arriving from the north. Later that day, unfortunately, a Puma helicopter crashed while airlifting troops, killing one and injuring another nine.

On 31 December the reconnaissance group demolished the train bridge at a crossing about nine kilometres east of Tetchamutete, and observation posts were set up on the mountains surrounding the town in order to determine the exact enemy positions.

On 2 January 1984, 81-mm mortars were launched to probe possible enemy positions, but provoked no response. The recce team and one rifle company were sent to the area south of Tetchamutete to demolish the bridge on a secondary road, lay ambushes and assume positions on the high ground. What they did not realise was that one of their ambushes was right inside an enemy position! At 01h00 on 3 January, a patrol found the mechanical mines on the road. While still puzzling over their presence, the team leader detonated the charges, and a heavy firefight broke out. At first light, a search of the area revealed four 23-mm anti-aircraft guns, seven vehicles, ammunition, food and other equipment.

Colonel Viljoen concluded that this must have been the main defensive position and decided to occupy Tetchamutete. By 12h30 on 4 January, four of 32's companies, the 81-mm mortar group and the reconnaissance teams were in control of the town and the surrounding high ground. The captured 23-mm guns had a 360-degree fire arc from the top of one of the mountains, and the tactical headquarters was set up on a platform inside an old mine building.

Colonel Viljoen, finding himself suddenly and unexpectedly in possession of an entire town, signalled headquarters to inform Brigadier Joep Joubert of his good fortune. Reliable sources recall the conversation going something like this.

VILJOEN: 'Juliet, Juliet, this is Echo Victor. We have taken Tetchamutete, over.'

JOUBERT (after a lengthy silence): 'Echo Victor this is Juliet Juliet. Now who the hell told you to take Tetchamutete?'

There was another long silence, then Joubert continued: 'But now that you're there, you had better stay there, over.'

At 04h00 on 5 January, the gun crew on the mountain saw vehicle lights approaching from Cuvelai, which was under attack by South African forces. At 05h30 the vehicles were about 1,5 km away, and the newest occupiers of Tetchamutete opened fire with 81-mm mortars and the anti-aircraft guns. It looked and sounded like something out of *Star Wars* as burst after burst and bomb after bomb thundered through the darkness. It was as if fire was running down the mountain and stars were falling out of the sky. The bombardment was frightening, and then, suddenly, there was silence. Not a sound from the target area and only a shout of 'cease fire' to the town's defenders. Then the high-pitched revs of an engine screamed into the night and on the shouted order 'Fire!' the deadly pyrotechnical display began again. Once or twice more the mysterious engine was revved to screaming pitch, only to be silenced by another bombardment. Finally, there was nothing more to break the deathly silence.

At first light and in gentle rain a company moved down the road, and was understandably shocked to find that they were looking down the barrel of a genuine Russian tank. The mystery vehicle had been the vanguard of the Cuvelai garrison, a single T54/55, with infantry support walking ahead to scout for possible ambushes. When the night exploded all around them, the tank crew panicked, drove off the road, flattened a hut and drove straight through a kraal, ending up in a little swamp. After the recent heavy rains the sodden ground proved too much even for the tank tracks, and having provoked another fierce bombardment each time they tried to drive out of the bog, the crew finally decided their best bet was to abandon the vehicle and get away on foot.

Six of the guards left to protect the vehicle were killed and another five captured. The rest fled – but without realising that the forces in control of Tetchamutete were South Africans. The only troops at the entrance to the town were from Angolan tribes and spoke Portuguese. Armed with AK47s and wearing camouflage fatigues, they were easily mistaken for some of FAPLA's own, and it soon became almost routine for FAPLA troops to advance on the control points with their arms raised in greeting.

Two early arrivals were a FAPLA lieutenant and a sergeant, who immediately began to pour out their hearts to the checkpoint guards about their depressing experience in Cuvelai. The guards listened but made no attempt to hide their mirth, so much so that the lieutenant eventually demanded to see their commander.

Still carrying their arms, the two were escorted to Colonel Viljoen's headquarters, where they complained bitterly about the way the guards had laughed at them. Sergeant Major Koos Kruger, whose Portuguese was impeccable, was acting as interpreter and urged the men to sit down. Refreshments were brought, and in a relaxed atmosphere they relayed to Viljoen the woeful tale of Cuvelai. It had been nothing less than a life-and-death battle, with 'the Boers' throwing artillery, aircraft and armoured cars at them without letting up. They were so glad, said the lieutenant, to be safe and back with their own people.

Both Viljoen and Kruger were obviously white men underneath their long and matted beards, and curiosity led the FAPLA lieutenant to ask them about themselves.

'Are you Cubans?'

'No', said Kruger, 'guess again.'

'Russians, perhaps?'

'Sorry, no, wrong again.'

'Well then,' said the lieutenant, having run out of options, 'you must be from East Germany?'

'No!' yelled Kruger, pushing his face into the startled lieutenant's. 'We aren't Cubans, or Russians, or East Germans – we are Boers!'

The FAPLA lieutenant and sergeant were visibly stunned, and could only watch helplessly as Kruger grabbed their weapons. The pair cursed and blamed each other for their misfortune all the way to Oshakati, and Viljoen and Kruger dined out on their delightful encounter for months.

That evening at 18h15, the observation post opened fire on vehicles approaching from the north with mortars and anti-aircraft guns. When they pulled off the road, air support was called in, but due to poor visibility the Impala strike at 19h30 missed the mark.

From 6 to 20 January, the HAA was moved from Chipolo to Tetchamutete, and the town's defences were reinforced by deployment of a combat team from 61 Mechanised Infantry Battalion. The 32 reconnaissance teams continued to monitor activity in the Cassinga area and harass the enemy west of the Cuvelai River. Following a heavy bombardment of BM 21 rockets, they moved to Cuvelai on 12 January. When all other South African forces withdrew from Angola, 32 Battalion stayed behind, as usual, acting against SWAPO stragglers in the bush around Cassinga and Tetchamutete. On 20 January, all the companies moved back to the tactical headquarters at Ionde.

The white leader group for *Askari* was made up of former 32 members who volunteered for the task, the National Servicemen serving with the battalion having been demobilised early in December. During the operation, 32 Battalion killed 48 SWAPO and captured five, along with 22 FAPLA soldiers. On the South African side, the casualty figures were four dead and 23 wounded.

OPERATION OPSAAL

According to official records *Askari* ended on 20 January, but in fact 32 Battalion's contingent, referred to as Task Force EV, stayed in the area east of Tetchamutete to continue operating against SWAPO, and *Opsaal* (saddle up) was actually the third phase of *Askari*.

On 21 January, three companies were stationed at Colonel Viljoen's tactical headquarters seven kilometres north-east of Tetchamutete. Two companies found themselves 27 km south-east of Cassinga, while another company, one platoon and elements of the reconnaissance group were deployed around Tetchamutete.

On 23 January the anti-tank platoon was patrolling four kilometres south-west of Tetchamutete with their 106-mm and Milan Unimogs, when one of the Milan vehicles detonated a mine, killing one soldier and injuring another five. The casualties were caused by the fact that the vehicle was overloaded, the men not only filling the two rear seats fitted with safety harnesses, but standing upright and unprotected.

Bravo and Foxtrot companies were sent to patrol the area to the south, and on 22 February Bravo was ten kilometres north-west of Mupa, while Foxtrot was deployed 36 km west of Ionde, where a tactical headquarters had been set up to control patrols in the Mupa area. Companies operating as far south as Cuvelai were under command of Viljoen's tactical headquarters near Tetchamutete.

On 23 January, Charlie Company engaged a group of SWAPO building a bunker 15 km east of Cassinga. In the absence of air support against SWAPO's mortars and recoilless guns, the platoon was forced to break contact and withdraw fairly quickly, one member suffering serious wounds. On the same day, engineers operating with a company ten kilometres south-west of Cuvelai located a minefield and lifted 46 TM 57 anti-tank mines.

On 27 January, while probing towards Cuvelai to determine if the enemy had reoccupied the town, Alpha Company came upon a GAZ truck loaded with 23-mm ammunition, probably abandoned by the task force responsible for clearing the town during *Operation Askari*. The truck was driven to Ionde and the cargo used to replenish 32's ammunition supplies. The next day, Charlie Company tracked and made contact with a group of 40 SWAPO eight kilometres east of Cassinga. The firefight left two members of the platoon wounded. Meanwhile, the force deployed east of Cassinga began moving south, deploying 23-mm guns and two 81-mm mortars 27 km south-east of Cassinga, and one company ten kilometres south-west of Cuvelai. Another minefield was cleared, and nine PMD 6 and four

TM 57 mines were lifted before all companies were ordered to withdraw from the Cuvelai and Cassinga area in terms of political negotiations that were under way. Bravo, Foxtrot and Golf companies, under control of the tactical headquarters at Ionde, continued to patrol the area, making contact with small groups of SWAPO around Dova and Mupa.

On 19 March a member of the local population handed a SWAPO prisoner over to Golf Company ten kilometres north-west of Dova, and a day later, with agreement reached on the Joint Monitoring Commission (JMC), orders were issued for the tactical headquarters at Ionde to be vacated and for all troops to return to Buffalo Base.

OPERATION SCRELA

On 19 February, 101 Battalion arrived at Cuvelai to establish the first Joint Monitoring Commission headquarters from which South African and Angolan forces would conduct combined anti-SWAPO operations. Because of their fluency in Portuguese and intimate knowledge of the terrain, 32 Battalion's members would play a leading role in the JMC patrols from February to June.

On 3 March the inaugural joint patrols moved into the field, a group of 120 assigned to sweep the area from Cassinga to the south, while another group of 100 – including 32's Foxtrot Company – was despatched to monitor routes in the Cuvelai area traditionally used by SWAPO. Despite assurances by SWAPO that all its members had been withdrawn from areas under the JMC's jurisdiction, the first skirmishes took place within 24 hours.

At 09h04 on 4 March, a combined Foxtrot–FAPLA platoon ambushed two members of SWAPO on horseback who had ridden past their temporary base six kilometres north of Nehone. One was killed while the other leapt from his mount and fled. During a follow-up operation, another seven SWAPO were encountered three kilometres away, and one was taken prisoner. He revealed that groups of up to ten were roaming the area to monitor the JMC patrol movements and identify safe infiltration routes for larger groups of SWAPO headed for South West Africa. This early indication that FAPLA was unable or unwilling to exercise control over SWAPO seriously eroded the already fragile trust on which the success of the JMC was based. At 11h45 on 12 March, the situation deteriorated even further when members of Golf Company were attacked with 82-mm and 60-mm mortars, RPG 7 rockets and small arms while searching a deserted SWAPO base 60 km north-east of Cuvelai. The FAPLA contingent of the patrol ran away, leaving Golf to deal with SWAPO. Shrapnel wounded Lieutenant Fred Turner and a troop, and one dead SWAPO was found about a kilometre from the contact area.

A series of high-level meetings followed, and on 20 March SWAPO evacuated all bases in the Bambi area. The JMC headquarters was moved to Mupa two days later, but FAPLA immediately presented another obstacle to the success of the exercise, refusing to take part in routine patrols and providing personnel only to investigate specific incidents. The status quo was maintained until early April, when 32 Battalion's members were withdrawn in what was ostensibly a normal relieve-and-replace operation. In fact, the battalion was about to launch one of its most successful covert operations to date, designed to show conclusively that SWAPO had not, after all, evacuated its bases around Bambi.

OPERATION FORTE

'This is my guerrilla battalion.'

General Constand Viljoen, chief of the SA Defence
Force, following the victory at Savate, May 1980

With the JMC in full swing around Cuvelai and regular deployments of 32 Battalion, it became increasingly evident that SWAPO was capitalising on the agreement negotiated by the politicians by infiltrating the so-called 'free zone'. In the absence of a mechanism to control 'free-zone' activity, the South African authorities took clandestine steps to determine whether SWAPO was re-establishing itself in areas controlled by FAPLA. For political reasons, troops from 32 Battalion would masquerade as members of UNITA under the banner of 154 Battalion.

Major Jan Hougaard, second-in-command of 32, and Commandant Johan Schutte of Military Intelligence were responsible for obtaining all the equipment and arms needed for the operation. From depots controlled by the Chief of Staff Intelligence in Pretoria, they drew everything from civilian T-shirts to Russian-made RPD machine guns. In addition to uniforms and boots of the type favoured by UNITA, brand new *velskoene* – shoes made from soft rawhide and popularly known as *vellies* – were shipped to the Operational Area along with AK47 rifles, RPG 7 rocket launchers, and Mercedes Benz and Samil 100 trucks.

The top secret nature of the planned operation ruled out provision of standard SADF ration packs, as well as any food item bearing a South African label. Hougaard and Schutte were given the task of developing alternatives, and came up with an innovative design for all ration pack items to be packed in unmarked plastic tubes, like polony. Even pre-cooked maize meal porridge was packed this way.

With all planning and preparation taking place at Battalion Headquarters at Rundu, the soldiers earmarked for participation in the operation had no idea what they were in for. Only a handful of people knew what *Operation Forte* would entail, and extremely tight security was in force during the run-up to deployment, with most vehicles and the bulk of equipment being hidden in the CSI stores at the far end of Rundu military base.

On 1 September, Echo Company, commanded by Lieutenant Neil Walker; Foxtrot, under command of Captain Buttons Heyns; Golf Company, led by Captain Fred Turner; and Support Company elements under the command of Sergeant Major Mike Rogers, were ferried from Buffalo Base to Rundu, where a convoy of special vehicles was lined up under tarpaulins and cargo nets. Colonel Eddie Viljoen, Officer Commanding 32 Battalion, and Sergeant Major Faan Joubert, the RSM, led the convoy east towards Omauni. No briefing was given to the troops, who assumed they were being taken to Elundu for a normal deployment. After spending the night at the old Nepara base, the convoy moved out early on 2 September towards Mpungu, halting at the 18°00' north-south cutline to await delivery of vehicle spares, which arrived by helicopter some two hours later, along with Major Jan van der Vyver, the logistics officer. In keeping with the high security of the operation, Van der Vyver had shaved off his moustache and smeared 'black is beautiful' camouflage cream over all areas of his body not hidden by the civilian clothes he wore.

With the spare parts in hand, the convoy turned north along the cutline instead of continuing west to Omauni. The route had not been used for several months, and some of the two-wheel drive Mercedes Benz trucks got stuck in the thick sand, causing delays in the timetable.

Just before crossing into Angola, Viljoen called the command group from the first two vehicles together. Warrant Officer Piet Nortje – the author – was assigned to the lead vehicle to navigate the 25-km stretch of uncharted territory that lay ahead. It was to be 'bundu-bashing' in the full sense of the term, with neither roads nor landmarks to guide him. At the point of departure, Viljoen told the command group: 'We are UNITA now. We have to start thinking and acting like UNITA, and since they have no sense of time, the watchword is koesasa' – a word taken from Fanagalo, the lingua franca of South Africa's gold mines, which means 'tomorrow is another day'.

For the rest of the day the convoy travelled north-east, halting shortly before sunset about 20 km north of Katwitwi on the road to Savate. That night, Viljoen disclosed the true nature of the operation to the leader group for the first time. After the briefing, an uncomfortable silence hung over the camp as each man came to terms with his own thoughts and feelings about the task that lay ahead.

At first light the next day, Sergeant Major Nortje and four armed escorts took the lead vehicle, a Buffel, to a UNITA base some 15 km south to pick up a guide. But, instead of being allowed to enter the base, the group was detained by heavily armed UNITA guards whose suspicions were aroused by the fact that they had approached from the north. No amount of explanation convinced the guards that these were, indeed, the visitors the base commander was expecting, and it took

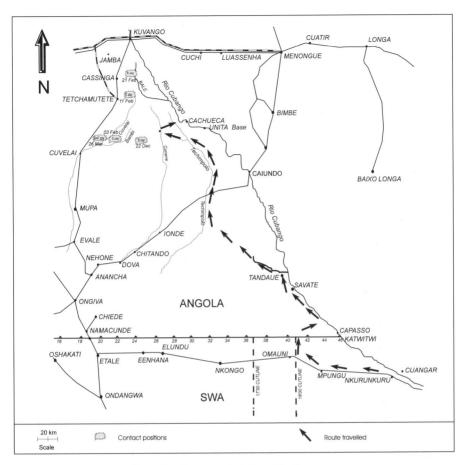

Operation Forte – route followed to Cachueca

more than 30 minutes and the threat of reporting their conduct to Dr Savimbi himself before an officer was called.

The well-dressed man in UNITA's traditional green uniform and carrying a walking stick introduced himself as Colonel Severino, commander of the UNITA base further north. After another hour of interrogation, particularly about how the convoy had managed to pass through UNITA territory undetected, Colonel Severino's GAZ truck, driven by a youngster who looked about nine years old, set off for the north with the Buffel in tow.

It immediately became apparent that the GAZ driver knew only two things about driving: how to find second gear and how to floor the accelerator! It had taken the Buffel some 90 minutes to travel to the base that morning, but the return trip was covered in 20, the vehicles speeding along the sandy track at 65 km/h at one point! Welcome to the land of UNITA, Nortje thought wryly.

On reaching the main body of the convoy, Severino and Viljoen exchanged the usual pleasantries before the GAZ led the way north along the Cubango River. After passing Savate, where 32 Battalion had scored a major victory in 1980, the reasonably good road ran out, making way for two barely visible tracks in the sand leading to the Tandaue River. By evening the convoy had arrived at a site selected by UNITA in advance, a well-established complex of four large grass structures and a few smaller huts, at least a kilometre from the nearest water. As the sun slipped below the horizon, Viljoen briefed the entire group about the operation, and the troops learned for the first time what was expected of them.

Early the next morning Van der Vyver began issuing new uniforms and arms to the group, and by 16h00 three companies of 32 Battalion had been transformed into a component of UNITA. Over the next few days the men familiarised themselves with their equipment, especially the KY 500 communication system, for which all the data commands were in Portuguese. At 18h00 on 7 September, the main force set off for what Severino promised was a well-prepared base 90 km to the north near the Techimpolo River. On arrival at 04h00, the base was bathed in bright moonlight and indeed appeared extremely hospitable, but Viljoen issued orders that instead of offloading the trucks, the men should simply rest until first light.

Daylight brought an explanation for Viljoen's strange orders. UNITA's regional headquarters lay directly east of the base on the banks of the Cubango River, and the base allocated to 32 Battalion would serve as a perfect buffer between UNITA and FAPLA brigades deployed to the west around Tetchamutete and Cassinga. Ignoring Severino's objections, Viljoen selected another site for his base, further east and close to the Cubango River at Cachueca. Two days later, the first companies were ready for deployment, Echo and Foxtrot being despatched to the Cunene and Chipolo rivers to gather information and to try to locate any enemy presence.

Over the next three months, 53 patrols traversed the area west of the base, gathering conclusive evidence that SWAPO was re-establishing itself around Cassinga and Tetchamutete, right under the noses of the JMC patrols. On 19 October, Foxtrot Company made contact with a group of SWAPO 30 km east of Cassinga and south of the Bale River. The six enemies fled after being bombarded with 60-mm mortars and 40-mm M79 grenades.

At 09h30 on 3 November, Foxtrot Company made contact with a FAPLA patrol in the Bambi area, taking Ernesto Sidjeme prisoner. He confirmed that SWAPO cadres were moving through Tetchamutete to assembly points just north of the South West Africa border, and the information was duly relayed to the JMC.

By the end of November, the base sported an underground operations room and a kitchen complete with clay oven for baking bread. The troops had also begun to construct their own sleeping quarters in the form of grass huts. The first re-supply run from the logistics base at Tandaue was led by Sergeant Chris Myburgh, and took three nights to complete. Because of the threat of detection by FAPLA aircraft, all vehicles travelled only after dark. The polony-style ration packs had proved a major problem in the Angolan heat, as on reaching a certain temperature they simply exploded, covering the contents of backpacks in a messy goo. Before the first re-supply run, a message was sent to Tandaue requesting dry rations, but when Myburgh arrived back at the base, it was without any maize meal, tinned meat or flour. He was promptly sent back the very next night, returning six days later with the correct food items.

One morning in November, without prior warning, Colonel Viljoen summoned the leader group and informed them that the time had come to be circumcised, and he would be the first to go under the knife. To the great amusement of everyone, Lieutenant Piet Coetzee, a Special Forces doctor assigned to the unit, carried out the first circumcision on a South African soldier almost 200 km inside enemy territory, on a rudimentary operating table inside a guerrilla base!

While Viljoen's decision was primarily made on hygienic grounds – it was not unusual for troops to spend up to four weeks in conditions that precluded bathing – it is not impossible that the tedium of the daily routine might have played a role. Obviously, the procedures were carried out on a strictly voluntary basis, but several troops availed themselves of the opportunity, leading Sergeant Major Mike Rogers to suggest that the name of the military operation be changed from *Forte* to *Foreskin*. When news of the surgical campaign reached the logistical base at Tandaue, Sergeant Thinus Ferreira volunteered to escort the next supply convoy, since he, too, wanted to be circumcised. The poor man travelled for three nights to reach the base, only to learn when examined by the doctor that he had been circumcised as a baby! One good thing about his otherwise wasted trip was that he brought with him 500 kg of flour, and fresh-baked bread was soon a regular item on the camp menu.

From 3 October to 10 November, Golf Company was deployed to patrol an area eight kilometres on either side of the Cubango River, as far north as Malova, some 70 km from the base. But although intelligence reports indicated that SWAPO groups were moving south, the patrols found no signs of enemy presence. Captain Herman Mulder, the intelligence officer, concluded that Bambi Post, destroyed during *Operation Askari*, might be in use once more, since all tracks seemed to lead in that direction.

The weight of UNITA's traditional backpacks began to exact a toll on the men, and several had to be casevaced with back and shoulder injuries. An average patrol carried food and water for up to 14 days in addition to full first-line ammunition and, in some cases, 81-mm mortar bombs. Eventually permission was granted for the familiar green 32 Battalion backpacks to be carried instead.

The troops deployed at the outset of the operation were relieved in mid-November, and by 25 November, Bravo Company, commanded by Lieutenant Richard Olsen, Charlie Company, under command of Captain Frank Krenenburg, and Delta Company, led by Lieutenant AM Prodgers, began patrolling to the west, finding signs of large groups of both SWAPO and FAPLA on several occasions.

At 16h00 on 22 December, Bravo Company made contact with 150 FAPLA soldiers about 45 km west of the headquarters base. Led by two SWAPO guides, the FAPLA company was moving in single file when Bravo opened fire, sparking no less than three attempts to launch an effective counter-attack before a two-hour battle erupted. One FAPLA member was shot in the tree from which he had been directing 82-mm mortar fire. It was a particularly aggressive attack against what FAPLA evidently thought was a UNITA base that they could easily overrun. Shortly before withdrawing, someone in the enemy ranks must have realised their mistake and shouted that this was no UNITA force, but 32 Battalion. They immediately withdrew, abandoning two 82-mm mortars and various small arms, as well as the bodies of 13 dead, including a FAPLA sergeant. Radio intercepts later confirmed that the toll was actually 15 dead, 11 wounded and one captured. Several members of Bravo Company noted during the battle that the FAPLA company was carrying an Angolan flag of the type used to identify JMC patrols.

There was no logical reason for an enemy patrol of this strength to be in the area, unless an attack was planned on UNITA's regional headquarters. If Viljoen had not rejected the site originally allocated to his group as a base, 32 would have found itself directly in the path of the attackers.

By the end of January 1985 the headquarters base was well equipped, with a hospital bunker and strong defences, including two 81-mm mortars, two Russian-made 14,5-mm anti-aircraft guns, an 82-mm B10 recoilless gun and a Chinese-made 75-mm recoilless gun deployed in well-prepared bunkers. An airstrip formerly used by Portuguese farmers was discovered four kilometres north-west of the base, which would prove of great strategic value after being swept for mines. Routine patrols found signs of increased enemy movement directly east of Tetchamutete and the Cuvelai road, and SWAPO activity was reported almost daily.

Relations with the neighbouring UNITA base improved dramatically after Colonel Severino stepped on an anti-personnel mine and was killed. His replacement, Colonel Jaul, was a friendly man, and before long instructors from the covert unit began training his men in the basic principles of warfare.

Locating the reactivated Bambi Post remained a priority, and at 12h45 on 3 February, while patrolling in the vicinity of the Cuvelai and Bambi rivers 80 km west of the main base, a platoon from Echo Company heard the sound of trees being chopped. As they moved closer to investigate, the platoon came under fire before seven men jumped into a URAL truck and sped out of the area. Since SWAPO did not use vehicles in this area, the platoon assumed that this was a FAPLA detachment, probably cutting wood to fortify their bunkers at Tetchamutete.

The company moved five kilometres to the east and set up a temporary base, which was attacked with four 122-mm rockets at 16h00. Fortunately, none of the rockets was on target.

On 11 February, Charlie Company had far worse luck when a routine patrol near the Bale River went horribly wrong. An over-eager company commander ignored warnings from headquarters about a possible SWAPO concentration in the area and decided to take a short cut, leading his men straight into a well-prepared SWAPO base. Initially taken by surprise, the enemy quickly regrouped and opened fire with everything they had.

Over the next 25 minutes, the company took heavy casualties, especially during an 82-mm mortar barrage. One of the first to fall was a British citizen, Lieutenant Dave Light, who was shot below the left eye. SWAPO cadres tried to capture his body, but succeeded only in removing his wristwatch and cutting an A72 radio free from his webbing before being driven off by his comrades.

Lieutenant HG van Wyk, the doctor attached to the company, and medical orderlies lost no time attending to the wounded, but the doctor's debriefing report made grim reading: in addition to Light, six members of the company were killed: riflemen P Kahete (severe shrapnel wounds); A de Almeida (gunshot penetrating both lungs); P José (multiple shrapnel wounds); K Kalonga and JC Chihamba (multiple shrapnel wounds to head and torso) and Lance Corporal JA Sachilombo (multiple shrapnel wounds including abdomen, with protruding gut). According to Van Wyk's report: 'Seven persons were killed immediately on making contact and in the ensuing 15 minutes. Most of the patients sustained serious wounds and therapy was initiated. Of the seven patients four had wounds caused by 82-mm mortar bombs, two were shot by AK47 rifle and had severe injuries caused by direct hits with a rifle grenade. The patients all sustained multiple wounds of the abdomen, chest and head. One patient with multiple wounds and a large injury committed suicide.'

After dark, while the casualties were being moved to a temporary emergency base, another three wounded men – riflemen J Fernando, M Joaquim and M Chipoya – died from massive chest wounds, and during the night another rifleman, MA Kinguelke, also succumbed to his wounds.

At first light on 12 February, the doctor reassessed the condition of the wounded, changing field dressings where necessary and administering painkillers and antibiotics. By this time, according to his report, 'there was a serious shortage of bandages, plaster, intravenous fluids and painkillers. The wounded were separated from one another to minimise casualties in the event of another bombardment.'

At 10h00, Rifleman M Muema died from shrapnel wounds. Shortly afterwards, two enemy approaching the temporary base were shot and killed, a third taken prisoner.

Bravo Company had already been despatched from headquarters to go to the assistance of Charlie Company, but the terrain was so inhospitable that their vehicles could get no closer than six kilometres to the emergency base. At 17h30, the gruelling trek through dense bush with able-bodied men carrying the 19 wounded on home-made stretchers and the bodies of the 12 dead, began. It was early on the morning of 13 February that they reached the vehicles waiting at the source of the Bale River, and 13h00 before the convoy arrived back at the headquarters base.

Just before last light, vehicles carrying the casualties set off for the nearby airstrip to wait for a Dakota summoned from Rundu. Colonel Viljoen took the precaution of having a mine-resistant vehicle check the landing strip for mines first, and it was just as well he did, as halfway through the assignment the vehicle detonated an anti-personnel mine. With the aircraft due to land within five minutes, the UNITA liaison officer, Captain Epelanga, was instructed to cancel the flight. However, several attempts to contact the pilot failed to draw a response, and at the appointed time the diesel fuel torches lining the runway were set alight and the Dakota landed uneventfully. Within six minutes it was airborne once again with all the dead and wounded 'UNITA' soldiers on board.

Under interrogation, the SWAPO captive revealed that he was the commander of a group making its way to the Eastern Area Headquarters, and had mistaken Charlie Company's temporary base for SWAPO's 8th Battalion re-supply camp, which was actually about 600 m further north – and into which Charlie Company had stumbled with catastrophic results. Radio intercepts confirmed that there had been 100 SWAPO soldiers in the base and that 15 had been killed.

As routine patrols continued, increasing signs of an enemy build-up became apparent. Just as it had in the past, SWAPO was once again using the area east of Cassinga along the Bale River as an assembly point, the JMC notwithstanding. Echo Company was assigned to the 'hot' zone, and at 10h00 on 21 February a patrol on the way to lay an ambush 30 km east of Cassinga found the tracks of six men north of their temporary base. Soon afterwards, the group of six was spotted approaching the base from the east, and 16 members of the company were sent out to intercept the enemy. When bombs from a heavy and accurate mortar bombardment began falling inside the base, the company prepared to withdraw to the south to regroup. Before they could do so, however, the main enemy force, numbering about 70, surrounded the base to the west, east and south, systematically moving in and forcing Echo Company to retreat to the north. During the furious firefight that followed, the enemy captured all Echo Company's equipment, including the commander's KY 500 and B22 radio code cards, as well as an area map indicating all bases and patrol routes. Lance Corporal L Dumba was killed, and Rifleman B Paulo wounded and captured by the enemy.

After this contact it became more difficult than ever to make re-supply runs with vehicles, and, at Staff Sergeant Ron Gregory's suggestion, the unit began to use donkeys captured from SWAPO patrols to transport food and equipment. Apart from solving the problem, the system caused great confusion in SWAPO's ranks, as they were unable to distinguish between their own and the unit's supply lines.

As the area became more active, reinforcements in the form of 140 men from Alpha and Foxtrot companies were shipped in with the specific task of locating Bambi. On the evening of 23 March this group crossed the Cuvelai River and moved approximately three kilometres west before turning south. Approaching their temporary base the next day, they found two sets of tracks no more than 12 hours old, leading north. Intelligence had indicated that Bambi lay west of the river, and given the freshness of the tracks the company was confident that it could not be too far.

The group split in two, with a reconnaissance team commanded by Corporal Louis Lombard acting as scouts for Foxtrot, and Major Mike Bastin's reconnaissance team leading the way for Alpha. Moving south-east Foxtrot found more tracks, and heard both voices and the sound of pots and pans. Lombard noted the position. The next morning Foxtrot and Alpha joined forces once again, headquarters was informed that Bambi had been found, and an attack was authorised for 15h00 on 26 March. With a 55-strong stopper group in position north of the base, the assault force of 85 men began their advance. Major Bastin saw the first hut some 75 m from the base, and at 30 m gave the order to attack when a SWAPO guerrilla began walking straight towards the assault line.

During ten minutes of heavy small-arms fire in pouring rain, Rifleman Andre sustained a shrapnel wound in one knee, while seven SWAPO and two FAPLA soldiers, including a lieutenant, were killed. Several weapons and a large amount of clothing were captured, and substantial food supplies destroyed.

Patrols in the area continued until 29 April, but destruction of the base put an end to SWAPO's freedom of movement to the south. On 15 April the South African government announced that its forces had withdrawn from the JMC as the result of repeated violations of the agreement, and the JMC ceased to exist on 25 May.

During 32 Battalion's withdrawal, Golf Company, commanded by Captain Fred Turner, was diverted from Cachueca to Sequendiva, 180 km to the west, to escort some 500 UNITA dependants through FAPLA-controlled territory. The operation took several days, mainly on foot, and was carried out without incident. Soldiers at the UNITA base were delighted at the safe arrival of their wives and children, along with herds of goats and other livestock, donkeys and dogs, and all elements of 32 Battalion's covert group returned to Buffalo Base without SWAPO or FAPLA knowing they had been deployed at Cachueca in the first place.

OPERATION BOLSON

Throughout 1984, SWAPO's infiltration of the eastern and southern Kavango was cause for concern at the headquarters of the South West African Territorial Force (SWATF), as no proof could be found that traditional routes through far-eastern Owamboland were being used.

Military Intelligence informers in Botswana reported that SWAPO was using a transit camp in the Rekonga area to enter South West Africa via Zambia, and on 4 August, 32 Battalion was ordered to investigate these claims. Colonel Viljoen decided that this was a task for the reconnaissance teams, with operational planning being done at Nova de Marco, 32's training base, by Major Daan van der Merwe and Captain Peter Waugh. Captain Werner Sott, the unit's staff officer operations, and Captain Herman Mulder, the intelligence officer, assisted them.

With very little information at their disposal and only one 1:250 000 scale map of the area available, planning was a challenge, but after five days of brainstorming the officers came up with a plan to use four reconnaissance teams to cover the area of interest. Lieutenant Leon Myburgh's team would operate up to 16 km south-west of Rekonga, while Waugh's team was assigned to the area seven kilometres south-east. Corporal H Labitzke's team was to set up an observation post in the Mahango game reserve to monitor the Botswana Defence Force (BDF) border post at Mahango, while Lieutenant M Devenish's team would form a reserve and reaction force.

With Labitzke's team already in place, the other three teams, all wearing civilian clothes, were transported in two Buffels to Mukwe via Bagani, then south to the Botswana/SWA border and ten kilometres east to the infiltration point on 7 September. The empty vehicles moved approximately one kilometre north of the border to be on hand in the event of an emergency.

Labitzke's team had reported no BDF patrols along the border since 3 September, so crossing into Botswana presented no difficulty, but the lack of maps dictated strict adherence to compass bearings. Myburgh's team entered Botswana at 22h00 and walked south for five kilometres before sleeping for three hours. For the next two days and nights they combed their designated area, but found no sign of SWAPO before returning to Buffalo on 10 September.

Waugh's team had equally little success, and during debriefing the recce team leaders suggested that air reconnaissance should be carried out before any further operations were launched in the Rekonga area. Early in November, however, informers again reported a SWAPO presence, and 32 was again required to carry out reconnaissance, this time extending to Ngaratja, eight kilometres east of Rekonga.

This time only one team would be used, led by Waugh, who insisted that Military Intelligence supply a guide. They crossed into Botswana at 21h00 on 28 November, and two days later learned from members of the local population that a group of four armed SWAPO had been seen at a waterhole on 24 November. Two of the men then moved east towards Shakawe, while the other two headed north to the Kavango. On 1 December, villagers at Ngaratja reported that a SWAPO member from Dovesra had visited the area on 20 November seeking recruits, and claimed that they had seen four SWAPO women and one man in a temporary base to the west between 16 and 26 October. Once again, Waugh's team returned to Buffalo without finding evidence of SWAPO's presence, and the operation ended with the conclusion that SWAPO might be using the area between Rekonga and Ngaratja as a transit camp, were most likely recruiting in the Mbukushu tribal area north of the Kavango/Botswana border, and that there was possible collusion between SWAPO and the BDF.

OPERATION CALUTZ

During implementation of the Joint Monitoring Commission, various covert operations were carried out behind enemy lines to determine whether SWAPO was continuing to build up its forces. At the same time, secret negotiations were taking place between the SADF and UNITA to ensure that the moment the South African security forces withdrew from Angola, UNITA would occupy areas formerly under their control. But the South Africans, only too aware of both UNITA's capabilities and shortcomings, knew it would be necessary to monitor Savimbi's forces and guide them in the execution of their tasks. Operational Order No. 1/85 thus authorised 32 Battalion to attach a liaison team to UNITA's area headquarters 40 km north-east of Ionde from 26 May 1985 until further notice.

Ten members of the reconnaissance wing set off from Rundu to join the 49th Semi-Regular Battalion, with instructions to monitor UNITA's activity, offer motivation and guidance on target selection, and coordinate logistical support. They arrived at the headquarters on 29 May and immediately established that UNITA's troop deployment was concentrated around the main base, with patrols going out to Nehone and Dova without specific objectives or strategies for locating and attacking SWAPO. The liaison team tried everything possible to encourage UNITA to operate according to a plan, but by the end of June it was obvious that the exercise was pointless, since the senior UNITA commanders were simply not prepared to take advice from a lowly major and his team. Regular clashes occurred between UNITA and SWAPO, and by the middle of July, when the liaison team returned to Rundu, SWAPO had driven UNITA completely out of the Dova and Nehone areas.

OPERATION EGRET

On 16 July, 32 Battalion received orders to deploy in the Nehone area to monitor UNITA's actions and determine the extent of SWAPO infiltration. UNITA forces were slowly but surely withdrawing to the east, and there were fears that SWAPO would once again be able to establish a Forward Command Post (FCP) in the area, presenting a serious threat to farms across the border.

On 27 July, two reconnaissance teams of eight men each and a four-man liaison team left Rundu for Katwitwi. Mindful of the UNITA commander's earlier stubborn refusal to heed the advice of a less senior officer, the group was commanded by 32's second-in-command, Commandant Jan Hougaard. The reconnaissance teams were led by sergeants Mac da Trinidade and AF Mendes. Since South Africa had officially declared that it had no forces deployed in Angola, the group went in as UNITA members, drawing on the uniforms, weapons and equipment first used during *Operation Forte*.

On 29 July the group reached the main UNITA base 30 km north-east of Ionde and presented themselves to Colonel Jaul, before moving west to UNITA's battalion headquarters 15 km north-west of Dova, where they learned that UNITA had already ceased to patrol the surrounding area. Harsh words were exchanged before UNITA assigned a company to travel with the reconnaissance teams to a point four kilometres north of Nehone, where they set up a headquarters on 5 August.

For the next ten days one of the teams monitored the area north of the Evale–Nehone road as far west as Acuittela, while the second made its way to the Mulola River 20 km north of Nehone and then to the Chanangala River, seven kilometres to the west, to gather information on the Gengo area. During the same period UNITA sent reconnaissance groups to Catale, 50 km to the south-east, as usual choosing an area some distance from any possible enemy concentration.

Sergeant da Trinidade's team found and followed enemy tracks leading to the north-east just six kilometres from Nehone, and soon afterwards spotted a group of SWAPO cutting grass and poles in the bush. The team also confirmed a SWAPO base close to the Gengo River 14 km north-east of Nehone, and were told by members of the local population that a SWAPO vehicle from the base fetched water from the wells outside Nehone on a daily basis.

On 10 August the team led by Sergeant Mendes established that the wells west of Nehone were dry, and while waiting to see if SWAPO visited the town after dark, heard five shots fired to the east. Forty minutes later another five shots were fired, this time only about 800 m away, and 20 minutes later Mendes saw a group of between 30 and 50 SWAPO, armed only with AK47 rifles, walking in extended line north of the team's hiding place and firing speculative shots into the bush. The team split up and withdrew three kilometres to the south, sure they had not been spotted.

That night, the team saw several illuminating flares fired from the direction of Nehone, and the next morning they moved back to their headquarters.

Having located the SWAPO base, plans were put into effect to attack it. From 29 August, 32 Battalion was to inflict maximum casualties on the SWAPO concentration north of Nehone using three rifle companies, the two reconnaissance teams already in the area, an 81-mm mortar group, machine-gun section, assault pioneer section and six reaction force teams from 101 Battalion. The Air Force would provide an airborne observation team, and five medical officers would be attached to the force.

Meanwhile, UNITA reported more SWAPO bases at Chana Kukuve and at the Mutala River east of Cassinga, as well as a possible logistical base at Chana Viunde. Sergeant da Trinidade's team confirmed that SWAPO troops and supplies were being moved in seven URAL trucks to Chana Viunde.

While the political implications of the assault plan were being pondered, the operation was delayed. When no authority had been granted by 8 September, the reconnaissance teams withdrew back to Rundu. A week later, when 12 40-man reaction teams from 101 Battalion swept through the area, the bases had all been evacuated, and the only SWAPO found were small groups from the FCP. On 17 September, after killing 15 SWAPO in all, the troops returned to South West Africa.

OPERATION WALLPAPER

The MPLA had done everything possible since taking power in 1975 to destroy UNITA both politically and militarily, but Savimbi's force continued to extend its sphere of influence over large tracts of Angola, albeit mainly in the rural areas. In mid-1985, FAPLA was ordered to launch a massive simultaneous operation in the Moxico and Cuando Cubango provinces, both traditional UNITA strongholds. *Operation Second Congress* was a two-pronged operation designed to regain control of the Cazombo block and recapture Mavinga by 2 September, after which two FAPLA brigades would attack UNITA's headquarters at Jamba. Before the offensive even began, it was identified as a serious threat to the South African position.

Both FAPLA and FAPA (the Angolan air force) already had a strong deployment in the two regions, but for the attack on Moxico Province, the 3rd military region, six brigades were allocated to the FCP at Lubango. Luena would be used as the base for the fighter planes, while Luacano would serve as the helicopter administration area. In mid-September, Saurimo airfield was upgraded and prepared as an alternative to Luena, and by the end of September FAPA had deployed 14 MiG 21s, six MiG 23s, six MI 25s, ten MI 8/17s, six Alouette III helicopters and an AN 26 to Luena.

In the 6th military region of Cuando Cubango, seven brigades – 7, 8, 13, 16, 25 BRIM and 82 BRIL – were allocated to the FCP at Cuito Cuanavale. The BRIM forces were primarily used and equipped for conventional mobile operations, and included SA anti-aircraft missiles, medium tanks and heavy artillery guns. The BRIL forces were customarily used for counter-guerrilla operations, and consisted of infantry without heavy artillery or anti-aircraft guns. Most of the BRIL and BRIM brigades deployed in the offensive were under-strength in terms of personnel and equipment.

There were only two air bases in south-east Angola, namely Menongue and Cuito Cuanavale. Menongue was used for fighter operations, and Cuito Cuanavale for helicopter-borne assaults. As with the 3rd military region, the existing FAPA forces at Menongue were strengthened, and helicopters were deployed on a permanent basis at Cuito Cuanavale for the first time. By September, Menongue was home to eight each MiG 21s and 23s, four SU 22s, five MI 25s and six each MI 8/17s, Alouettes and AN 26s. At Cuito Cuanavale there were two MI 8s and two MI 25s, as well as four MI 17s.

Preparations for the offensive were visible long before it was launched in the 3rd military region in late July and in the 6th region in August. The airfield at Cuito Cuanavale was lengthened and resurfaced, and upgraded from a mere landing strip to an airfield capable of handling fighter jets. As early as January a radar installation had become operational at Cuito, covering all but the most south-eastern tip of Angola. Air defence at Menongue was boosted by the deployment of SA 3 anti-aircraft missiles, the runway aprons were extended and a new control tower built. From May, transport flights to both Cuito and Menongue increased notably from an average of 2,8 per day in May to 13,4 by late August.

Seven Russian advisers were attached to each brigade to direct FAPLA operations at the front, but they also became actively involved in planning and controlling the entire operation, and participated in operational flying for the first time in Angola.

As the build-up continued, the South African government became more and more concerned, especially about the situation in the 6th military region, because if FAPLA succeeded in taking Mavinga, they would cut off and isolate UNITA at Jamba, leaving the entire eastern border with South West Africa open for SWAPO to infiltrate the Kavango and Caprivi. For this reason, 32 Battalion was placed on standby to render assistance to UNITA if needed.

The offensive was launched from Luacano on 29 July by a total of five brigades. FAPLA forces advanced along two axes; the first group, consisting of 14, 21 and

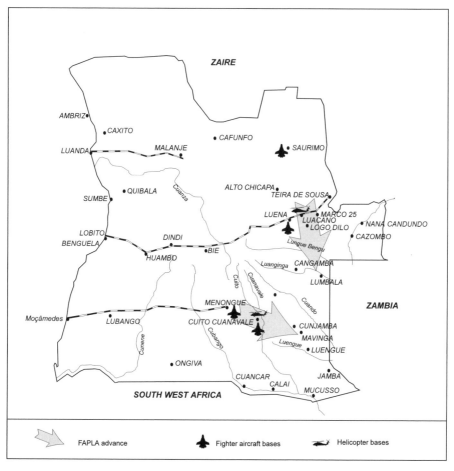

FAPLA's push southwards in the 3rd and 6th military regions

67 brigades, moved to Muccussuege, Marco 25, Mupila, Nana Candundo and Cazombo, which they reached on 19 September. The second group, 63 Brigade and a battalion from 18 Brigade advanced to Logo Dilolo, Chiesso and Cazombo, linking up with the first group on 30 October.

To assist UNITA in countering this advance, the South African forces launched *Operation Magneto*, in terms of which a troop of multiple rocket launchers with crew, an SA 9 anti-aircraft missile team, Special Forces, artillery advisers and medical personnel were attached to UNITA.

Due to the advance along two axes, the use of outflanking manoeuvres, the general aggressiveness of the advances on both fronts and the effective use of armour, UNITA was unable to counter the attack, and Cazombo fell to FAPLA on 19 September. UNITA retreated south to Lumbala, and at least a third of

215

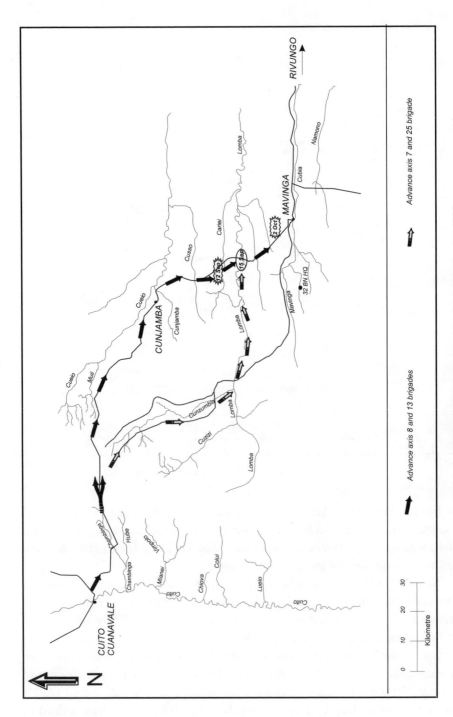

Advance of the FAPLA brigades and the final assault point, 1985

its force was pulled back to the Mavinga front. A massive operation by the SA Air Force saw at least 1 000 UNITA troops airlifted over three nights in C130 transport aircraft.

On 15 August, four brigades began to advance on Mavinga from Cuito Cuanavale, with 8 and 13 brigades moving via Cunjamba, and 7 and 25 brigades moving between the Cunzumbia and Cuzizi rivers along the southern banks of the Lomba River.

On 7 September the Chief of the SA Army ordered the General Officer Commanding SWATF to counter the threat against Mavinga in conjunction with UNITA, and 32 Battalion entered the fray under cover once more. They were to wear UNITA uniforms, but were allowed to use their R4 rifles. The two SA 9 teams previously deployed in the 3rd military region were to be placed under 32's command, and, if requested, they were also to be given control of the two MRLs.

The battalion had expected the call, and at 19h00 three rifle companies, an 81-mm mortar group, machine-gun section, assault pioneer section, three reconnaissance teams and the headquarters commanded by Colonel Viljoen were airlifted from Omega to Mavinga. The force totalled 30 white and 390 black soldiers armed with first-line ammunition and rations for seven days. The echelon commanded by Commandant Hougaard left Buffalo for Mavinga by road two hours before the troops became airborne. That night, Savimbi himself briefed Colonel Viljoen and the liaison officer from Chief of Staff Intelligence about the situation around Mavinga.

UNITA had deployed 2 400 men in all, with 250 specifically assigned to defend Mavinga. The enemy force was a mere 50 km north-west of the strategic town, and after reporting this to headquarters at Rundu, 61 Mechanised Infantry Battalion was placed on standby for possible deployment.

The next day the rifle companies were deployed 500 m north of the airfield, and the two MRLs arrived. Viljoen set up his headquarters 28 km east of Mavinga, and after moving to new positions the battalion was ready to engage the enemy by 11 September.

In the early hours of the next morning, FAPLA's advancing 8 and 13 brigades stopped for re-supply 25 km west of the Cunjamba–Mavinga road along the Lomba River, and 32 swung into action with the MRLs. The barrage began with the first ripple at 03h00, followed by another at 05h00, and the last of the day at 07h00. The Angolan air force immediately began searching for the artillery from the sky, while the ground forces continued their advance. This bombardment, however, did not stop the advance of the two brigades. On 15 September, FAPLA's four brigades joined forces south of the Lomba River about 30 km north-west of Mavinga. It was now brutally clear that UNITA would not be able to stop the advance.

Colonel Viljoen sent one of his reconnaissance teams to the airfield at Cuito Cuanavale to report on aircraft movement, and learned that the enemy brigades were now being re-supplied by helicopter. He and Colonel Dick Lord, the Air Force coordinator, worked out a plan to shoot down the helicopters, mainly MI 17s and 25s. The moment the helicopters took off from Cuito Cuanavale airfield, the reconnaissance team reported to the headquarters at Rundu, from where Impala fighter aircraft were sent to intercept and destroy the helicopters in flight. The absence of supplies took the desired toll on FAPLA morale.

After losing four MI 17 and six MI 25 helicopters, FAPLA began using Alouettes to re-supply the brigades, and by 2 October they were a mere ten kilometres from Mavinga. But they had suffered heavy losses of aircraft, vehicles and personnel, due in no small measure to the deadly accuracy with which 32 unleashed the MRLs. At this point, only genuine UNITA troops were taking on FAPLA in physical combat.

With the objective almost in sight, large numbers of FAPLA soldiers began going AWOL. Morale was already low, and it dipped even further when the Russian and Cuban advisers withdrew in an MI 25 helicopter. The shortage of manpower and equipment forced 27 and 7 brigades to band together, and the turning point of the battle came on 2 October, when they were attacked from the air by eight F-1AZ Mirage fighter aircraft, followed by a massive MRL bombardment. The advance was halted, and the UNITA observation post nearest to the 13th Brigade reported many vehicles on fire.

That night Viljoen and Savimbi again met for a planning session. Viljoen favoured a ground attack by 32 Battalion, while Savimbi seemed more concerned about the continued flow of logistical supplies to UNITA. The next night a heavy MRL bombardment was launched on the enemy positions, which were also attacked at 24h00 by three Impala aircraft armed with rockets. Soon afterwards FAPLA headquarters at Cuito Cuanavale sent a message to the brigades north of Mavinga to withdraw 30 km to the west. With FAPLA in full retreat, 32 Battalion began withdrawing on 4 October. The only fatality suffered by the unit was that of Major Jan van der Vyver, the logistics officer, who accidentally walked into the spinning propeller of a C130 aircraft while offloading supplies at the Mavinga airfield.

On 6 October, three of the four Alouette helicopters that were ferrying fuel to the FAPLA brigades were shot down by UNITA, and no further re-supply missions were undertaken by helicopter until the brigades reached the relative safety of Cuito Cuanavale. Mavinga had been saved, but, as in the past, UNITA had been unable to defend itself against FAPLA. Without the help of 32 Battalion the town would almost certainly have fallen. UNITA had, after all, lost the battle in the 3rd military region, and from the moment 32 became involved in the 6th military region, enemy losses rose dramatically.

The official FAPLA/FAPA losses for 1 August–31 October 1985 in both the 3rd and 6th military regions were as follows:

	3rd Region	6th Region	Total
FAPLA killed	737	1 589	2 326
Russians killed	1	2	3
FAPLA equipment			
T54/55 tanks	3	0	3
PT 76	0	1	1
BTR 60	0	17	17
BRDM 2	3	8	11
BM 21/14	1	16	17
23-mm anti-aircraft guns	0	6	6
14,5-mm anti-aircraft guns	0	3	3
FAPA (1)			
MI 8	1	0	1
MI 17	1	4	5
MI 25	1(1)	5(1)	6(2)
Alouette III	0	3	3
MiG 21	2(2)	1(1)	3(3)
MiG 23	2	0	2
AN 26	(1)	0	(1)
Pilots and crew killed			30+

Notes (1) Figures in brackets represent additional aircraft losses incurred for reasons other than South African, 32 Battalion or UNITA attack

10

We march without fear
MILITARY OPERATIONS 1985-1988

TWO MONTHS AFTER FAPLA's retreat from Mavinga, a fresh offensive bearing all the signs of a full-scale conventional battle was launched against UNITA in the 6th military region. This time, Savimbi's headquarters at Jamba was the target of a two-pronged assault from the Cazombo Front in the north and Cuito Cuanavale in the west. There was little doubt among the South African forces that UNITA would lose the fight, so when UNITA requested assistance, a Special Forces group under the command of Commandant H van Niekerk began harassing FAPLA's supply routes and bases between Menongue and Cuito Cuanavale. But by mid-December, it was clear that further involvement would be needed if UNITA was to survive the onslaught.

OPERATION JERRY

Operational Order No. 1/12/85 required 32 Battalion to inflict maximum damage on FAPLA personnel and equipment in the 3rd and 6th military regions through sustained MRL bombardment. The main targets were Cuito Cuanavale and the airstrip at Menongue, with specific instructions to attack the FAPLA force as soon as it began moving towards Jamba. Under no circumstances were the MRLs to fall into enemy hands.

Colonel Eddie Viljoen himself would command the MRL troop and Charlie Company at Menongue, while Captain Daan van der Merwe would direct the MRL troop and Golf Company at Cuito Cuanavale. It had been ten years since 32 Battalion's last deployment around Menongue during *Operation Savannah*, and aerial reconnaissance photographs were carefully studied in order to plan

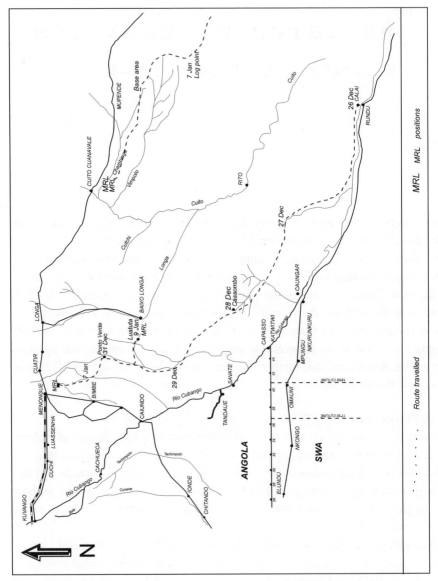

Operation Jerry

· · · · · · · Route travelled

MRL   MRL   positions

the bombardment. There would be two ripples: 96 rockets aimed at the radar installations, and another 96 at the airfield and surrounding base.

On 15 December, four MRLs were flown to Rundu from Air Force Base Waterkloof, and D-Day was set for 24 December. However, on 22 December Major Holtzhausen pointed out that he could not guarantee the accuracy of the bombardment, as his planning was based on maps dating back to 1972, and optimum effectiveness depended on the MRLs having an exact grid reference from the firing position. Colonel Viljoen immediately obtained authorisation for the use of SATNAV, the SADF's newest satellite navigation system, but it was so new that no one, not even the artillery crews who would operate the MRLs, had yet been trained to use it. Viljoen called SWATF headquarters again and was promised that an instructor from Armscor would be flown to Rundu immediately to provide the necessary instruction.

By the morning of 25 December there was no instructor in sight, and Viljoen was livid. Unable to get any information from SWATF headquarters, he telephoned Lieutenant General Jannie Geldenhuys, Chief of the Army, and explained the situation. By 11h00 a Citation jet with Armscor instructors on board had landed at Rundu, and by 15h00 the gun crews knew how the navigation system worked. That night a convoy of 32 vehicles began crossing into Angola over a specially built pontoon bridge just north of Rundu.

Under the guidance of UNITA's Captain Veneno, the column headed north, and despite being delayed at Cassombo while permission to proceed was obtained from Jamba, reached UNITA's base at Ponte Verde on 30 December. A UNITA company under command of Major Handa had been assigned to escort 32 Battalion to Menongue, but he was nowhere to be found, and another delay occurred. The time was used to train members of 32 to assist with the loading of the 127-mm rockets, a task they had never performed before, and to allow the leader group to familiarise itself with SATNAV. During this time one of the soldiers broke his hand, and Captain Herman Mulder, the intelligence officer, fell ill with a suspected kidney ailment. It was pouring with rain, and the Puma helicopter sent to casevac the two men hit a tree on landing and lost its tailpiece. The damaged helicopter was carefully camouflaged, and 24 hours later a team of Armscor technicians flew in to replace the tailpiece. Because of the covert nature of the operation, they were told the Puma had been evacuating UNITA casualties, and all the white members of the leader group had to hide in the bush while the black Portuguese soldiers assisted in the repair operation. By 23h50, the helicopter was back in the air.

Meanwhile Alpha Company, under command of Captain Fred Turner and accompanied by both a UNITA company and Captain van der Merwe, was heading for Cuito Cuanavale, picking up the MRLs that had been at Mavinga since *Operation*

Wallpaper on the way. By the night of 4 January, Turner's group was in position and Alpha Company was camped west of Mavinga, awaiting orders to advance. Permission finally came from Jamba on 3 January for Major Handa to escort 32 Battalion to Menongue, and Viljoen was able to finalise his plan of attack.

His force was divided into three groups: Mexico included Viljoen's command group, UNITA guides and liaison officers, the four MRLs and crews, a medical officer, four Samil 100 anti-mine vehicles carrying 100 rockets each, and Charlie Company.

Luengo, under command of Sergeant Dave du Toit, comprised the logistical element, recovery vehicle and mortar platoon, while the Verde group, commanded by Sergeant L Lindungu, would remain at Ponto Verde.

By the morning of 7 January, the Mexico and Luengo groups were 30 km south-west of Menongue when an urgent and personal message from Major General Georg Meiring, Officer Commanding SWATF, was relayed to them. Viljoen was to hold his position, as Special Forces had destroyed nine FAPLA vehicles in an ambush on the main road between Cuatir and Luassinga the day before, killing several FAPLA members and taking a prisoner, who was to be interrogated before the attack on Menongue proceeded.

At Cuito Cuanavale everything was going according to plan, and the first ripple of 96 rockets was fired at 24h00 on 8 January, followed at 02h35 by a second ripple, which drew a counter-bombardment of 13 D30 artillery shells, all of which missed the target.

Intercepted radio traffic to Menongue confirmed that significant damage had been done to the airfield at Cuito Cuanavale, that two Russians had been killed and that the attack had caused general chaos in FAPLA's ranks. After spending the day in a lay-up, the group moved 15 km south-east of Cuito Cuanavale at 17h30, and fired the third ripple at 19h25. The fourth ripple tore through the night air at midnight on 9 January, after which the group began moving back to Buffalo Base.

Informed that interrogation of the prisoner had failed to produce any new information, the Mexico group moved to within seven kilometres of their designated firing position on the night of 7 January. The vegetation was so dense that it took almost eight hours to cover just 12 km, and the lead Buffel became wedged between trees that had to be chopped down by soldiers with pangas. After that, Sergeant Major Piet Nortje guided the convoy through the bush on foot.

By 20h00 on 8 January the MRL was in position and loaded, but due to technical problems the first ripple was only fired at 22h30. Within minutes the enemy launched a counter-bombardment to the east, a clear sign that they had no idea where the MRL was positioned. The MRL was moved to a different position, but at 01h45 vehicle lights were spotted two kilometres to the east, and the group was ordered to withdraw from the area.

The Mexico group rendezvoused with the Verde group in pitch darkness and began moving south along the Cuito River. At 04h00 a heavy anti-aircraft bombardment was launched from Menongue, and what appeared to be four helicopters were spotted approaching the convoy at tree-top level from the rear.

Colonel Viljoen ordered all vehicles to take cover in the bush, but Sergeant Major Nortje's driver, Rifleman B Kassanga, became disoriented and turned left instead of right, heading straight for the open floodplain and the river beyond. The UNITA guide jumped off the vehicle as it sped along at about 40 km/h, and the more Nortje shouted at the driver to turn around and slow down, the more he panicked and accelerated. Later, the driver claimed he thought 'devagar', the word Nortje kept repeating, meant danger, and that he should drive as fast as possible! When the Buffel finally came to a stop, Nortje found himself lying on the spare wheel of the command vehicle. In all the dust and chaos, the driver had not even seen Viljoen's stationary Buffel before ploughing into the back of it at about 50 km/h.

Only after this breakneck ride did members of the group realise that what they had thought were helicopter lights were actually only tracers from an anti-aircraft gun, and they continued at a more modest pace to a lay-up on the banks of the Cuito River. The rockets were unloaded from the MRL, and plans were made to resume the attack on Menongue the following night.

By that time the area around the target was teeming with heavily armed FAPLA troops, even tank patrols. The Special Forces team leader planned to attack the FAPLA base called Odessa, near Bimbe, and requested a single ripple of 48 rockets on the target. Colonel Viljoen was not averse to the idea, but there were not enough rockets left to complete the assault on Menongue and assist Special Forces.

At noon on 9 January, UNITA headquarters reported a strong force with tank support at the source of the Pengo River, 20 km from the Mexico group's lay-up. Because the group was not equipped for the type of battle that would be required, Viljoen pulled back to Ponto Verde. On 12 January he sought authorisation to attack the FAPLA battalion at Baixa Longa, using the entire 32 contingent, as well as the Special Forces group and Major Handa's UNITA company.

Six groups, made up as follows, would carry out the attack:

- Dallas – 40 men and 16 vehicles (MRLs, logistical and Charlie Company vehicles).
- Verde – 20 men and ten vehicles.
- Carnation – 180 UNITA troops.
- Abrasion – Special Forces, 60 men and eight vehicles.
- 32 Battalion's recce group and UNITA elements.

UNITA would launch the attack, with Special Forces offering close support with 81-mm mortars, 106-mm anti-tank weapons and vehicle-mounted machine guns. The Dallas group would launch a softening-up bombardment of three MRL ripples.

The attack was authorised at 11h40 on 14 January, by which time the force was three kilometres from the selected firing position. At 16h00, when the group was due to move out, it was raining heavily, and the Carnation group appeared reluctant to proceed due to their concern about mines, enemy bunkers and a lack of evacuation plans for their expected casualties. But they agreed to leave with the rest of the group at 17h00.

The 32 Battalion recce team was already deployed eight kilometres north of Ponto Verde, and UNITA's 50-strong recce group was on the way to the Pengo River. By 21h00 the MRLs were in firing position, but there was no sign of the UNITA group. At 22h05 Viljoen ordered six rockets to be fired to give the local inhabitants a chance to move away from the FAPLA base. A full ripple followed at 22h10. Captain Veneno reported all rockets on target, and at 22h30, FAPLA reported to Cuito Cuanavale by radio: 'Situation very bad. First only six bombs, now a lot of bombs.'

There were even more 'bombs' when the second ripple was fired at 02h25, before the Dallas group moved 20 km south-west of Baixa Longa to wait for first light and the scheduled attack. At 05h00, however, the Special Forces commander aborted the attack in favour of firing his support weapons into the base from high ground to the west.

That night, the assault force began moving south and back to Rundu. The MRLs were flown back to Pretoria the next day.

ASSISTANCE TO UNITA

In December 1985, *Operation Wallpaper* put paid to FAPLA's conventional onslaught against UNITA for the moment, but from 1986 onwards the war between the Angolan forces and Savimbi's supporters would escalate dramatically. The focus of operations continued to be the area around Mavinga, now firmly in UNITA hands, with the headquarters at Jamba the ultimate objective. To this end, a constant stream of convoys began shipping massive amounts of equipment from Menongue to FAPLA's 13th Brigade at Cuito Cuanavale and to the 25th Brigade, firmly dug in across a wide front on the eastern bank of the Cuito River.

Taking into account lessons learned during 1985, the South African forces began planning a series of operations against FAPLA from February 1986, which would see 32 Battalion deployed around Cuito Cuanavale and Mavinga, and reconnaissance teams infiltrating as far north as Cago Coutinho in the Cazombo block.

OPERATION GOMMA

On 18 March, four of 32 Battalion's reconnaissance teams were despatched to reconnoitre the bridge at Cuito Cuanavale and the surrounding area, where FAPLA's 1st Brigade held sway. Twenty-one men under command of sergeants HJ Stander,

AF Mendes and G Scheepers, accompanied by a medical doctor, Lieutenant PG Diedericks, were to monitor both UNITA and FAPLA activity around Cago Coutinho, while Sergeant Harry Hollander and Corporal A Pinto would take a team of 12 and a second doctor, Lieutenant GHJ Verster, to the bridge.

Because of the 270-km distance between Cuito Cuanavale and Rundu, Captain LL du Plessis and five men were deployed at Mavinga as a signal relay team.

At 19h10 on 18 March the teams, their vehicles and enough supplies for 30 days were flown from Omega to Mavinga in a C160 transport. It took them eight days to reach UNITA's logistical base, with delays at every checkpoint along the way while permission was obtained from Jamba for the convoy to proceed to the battlefront. The actual reconnaissance operation was completed within six days, and the teams then returned to the relay station at Mavinga to await the launch of an artillery strike on the positions they had identified.

OPERATION SOUTHERN CROSS

On 13 May, 32 Battalion, supported by Western Air Command, Special Forces and UNITA, was ordered to capture Cuito Cuanavale by 23 July. A night attack that would include both air and artillery strikes was planned, but operational signal 947/4 July 1986 cancelled the assault in favour of an artillery bombardment with multiple rocket launchers and a battery of 155-mm G5 field guns. With 32 acting as escort and protection for the ordnance and crews, Cuito Cuanavale was heavily bombarded two nights running.

OPERATION ALPHA CENTAURI

When the bombardment of Cuito Cuanavale failed to achieve the desired outcome, the battle plan drawn up for *Operation Southern Cross* was revived, with UNITA's training base north-east of Dirico used to prepare an assault force consisting of four rifle companies from 32 Battalion, the mortar, anti-aircraft, anti-tank and assault pioneer platoons that made up the support company, a 120-mm mortar platoon from 61 Mechanised Battalion, Papa Battery MRL troop, a Ratel 90 anti-tank squadron, an Ystervark anti-aircraft platoon and 1 500 members of two UNITA battalions.

While the troops went through their battle drills using a specially constructed scale model of the defensive positions at Cuito Cuanavale, supplies were being shipped to Mavinga, and by 15 July the logistical depot was operational. A week later the G5 artillery arrived at Buffalo from 4 SA Infantry, and by 29 July four MRLs, two Ystervark systems and a BRDM SA 9 missile system had been flown to Mavinga.

Later that day, with everything in place for an attack both conceived by and tailor-made for 32 Battalion, the troops in training were dealt a major blow. Pretoria had decreed that UNITA was to carry out the assault on Cuito Cuanavale, with 32 providing support for the artillery only. The troops were bitterly disappointed. This would have been the biggest conventional operation in which they had ever taken part, and they had trained hard and well for the task. To be deprived of the opportunity on the eve of deployment was nothing short of devastating. As one of the sergeants put it: 'When that message came through, not a man in our ranks didn't curse and swear under his breath. We were thoroughly pissed off at the bloody politicians, sitting on their fat arses in their comfortable offices thousands of kilometres away, safe from any harm, and deciding that UNITA was to carry out one of the most important battles of the war. This was *our* plan, *our* fight, and now UNITA was going to execute it. We were *not* happy.'

But orders were orders, and as the highly professional soldiers they had become in a decade of sustained combat, 32 would do what was expected of them, no matter how little they liked the lesser role they had been assigned. By 4 August, Colonel Viljoen's tactical headquarters was in position 28 km east of Cuito Cuanavale at the Hube River, Bravo and Delta companies were deployed with the artillery 60 km east of the target, two platoons from Golf Company were 17 km east of Cuito, and another platoon was with the engineers building a pontoon bridge across the river seven kilometres south of the Cuito bridge. In addition, reconnaissance teams from 32 were monitoring enemy activity just four kilometres south-east of the town.

At 15h35, however, the attack was postponed for a week while everyone waited for Savimbi himself to arrive at the front and direct the operation. Colonel Koos 'Bom' Laubser would be in command of the artillery, and all the South African forces would fall under Colonel Viljoen's command. Colonel Jan Breytenbach would act as one of the UNITA advisers.

The plan was that a UNITA brigade would attack FAPLA's 25th Brigade east of the Cuito River, using artillery support to draw off any tanks from the 13th Brigade in the town, and capture the bridge. Twenty-four hours later, the second UNITA brigade would launch the main attack against the town, the airfield and defensive positions to the west from the south.

Predictably, UNITA was not ready at the appointed time, and it was only on 13 August that Viljoen's forward headquarters moved to high ground four kilometres south-east of the town. The G5s were deployed 30 km to the south-east along the Hube River, and the MRLs 14 km from the target. The artillery bombardment was scheduled to take place from 20h00 on 14 August to 01h00 on 15 August. By 14h00 on the 15th not a shot had yet been fired, and Viljoen informed headquarters at Rundu that unless UNITA launched the attack that night, he would withdraw all his forces. MiG 23 and SU 22 aircraft were patrolling the skies constantly in search of the artillery, and Viljoen made it clear that he could not guarantee the safety of his forces for much longer. At 16h40, Viljoen received an urgent message warning that a FAPLA reconnaissance aircraft with a Russian crew had been sent from Lubango to aid in the search, and the FCP was immediately moved to a new position four kilometres away.

The artillery bombardment did start that night, although later than planned. The UNITA brigade commanded by Brigadier Renato managed to take the town, but had to withdraw soon afterwards in the face of a heavy counter-attack and the failure of the second UNITA brigade to attack on schedule from the south. Thanks to the artillery, Cuito Cuanavale was ablaze with fires, and Savimbi decided that his troops should launch a daylight attack.

The skies overhead were buzzing with FAPLA aircraft, and one MiG had fired two rockets at an abandoned UNITA base about a kilometre east of Viljoen's headquarters by the time the Special Forces team moved in to destroy the bridge over the river. On 16 August radio intercepts and visual reports from Brigadier Renato, based on his brigade's brief occupation of Cuito Cuanavale, established that the artillery bombardment had rendered the airfield inoperative, and had destroyed three of the six radar installations, the fuel depot and the ammunition depot, which burned for three days. UNITA Stinger teams had shot down three MiG 23 aircraft, and nine PT76 tanks had been taken out, five by artillery and four by UNITA ground troops. On 17 August, 32 Battalion began withdrawing to Mavinga.

Thus ended UNITA's bid to take Cuito Cuanavale, which showed, not for the first time, that Savimbi's troops were simply not up to conventional warfare. They would have fared far better by expanding their capabilities as guerrilla fighters, as the South Africans had so often advised and recommended.

OPERATION FULLSTOP

With virtually the entire UNITA army concentrated around Cuito Cuanavale, a new FAPLA offensive from the north-east seemed likely. On 17 September, Major Peter Waugh's reconnaissance team, with two Unimogs and supplies for 60 days, was flown to Cago Coutinho to monitor both FAPLA and UNITA activity. They drove north on the tarred road to Lunge Bungu, and on 24 September made the shocking discovery that two full FAPLA brigades were deployed north and west of the town. Five days later they met with Savimbi at Cago Coutinho before settling in to monitor UNITA's actions against the brigades, which began moving southwards on 6 October.

A second reconnaissance team under Captain Leon Myburgh arrived on 11 October, and on 1 November FAPLA's advance was halted by UNITA north of Cago Coutinho.

OPERATION KAKEBEEN

On 18 December, 325 members of 32 Battalion and nine members of UNITA, an 81-mm mortar group, the anti-tank platoon and an anti-aircraft troop began deploying north-east of Cassinga with orders to disrupt SWAPO's preparations for the annual summer offensive.

On 30 December 1986 several explosions were heard north of the tactical headquarters. Patrols had already confirmed that there was no SWAPO presence in the immediate vicinity of Cassinga or Tetchamutete, and the unexplained blasts raised the possibility that SWAPO's 8th Battalion had moved into the Cassumbi base ten kilometres east of Cassinga. It was hoped that interrogation of a single SWAPO cadre captured on the same day by UNITA along the Cubango River would provide more information.

On 10 January 1987 more explosions were heard, and Second Lieutenant TT

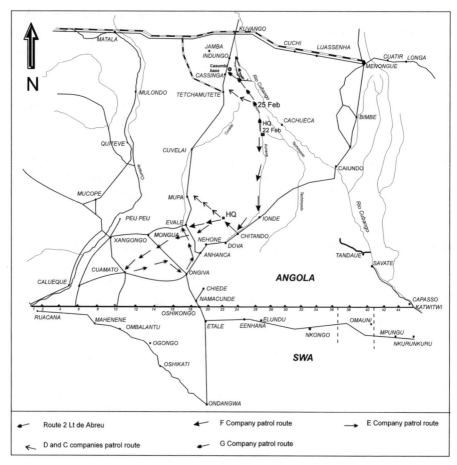

Operation Kakebeen

de Abreu and 36 members of Delta Company were sent 25 km east of Indungo to try to determine the source. Two days later the SWAPO captive was sent to Oshakati for interrogation, and Bravo Company began searching for the Cassumbi base.

Twenty days into *Operation Kakebeen* (jawbone) the SA Army Chief expressed concern over the lack of contact with the enemy, and requested a motivation for the operation to continue. On 24 January a SWAPO member captured in the Kavango confirmed the existence of a base west of Cassinga, as well as the position of Cassumbi. The General Officer Commanding SWATF immediately ordered 32 to locate the base near Cassinga. Meanwhile, Bravo Company's reconnaissance team found the Cassumbi base, and sought authorisation to attack at first light on 31 January. This was granted only after a furious exchange of telephone calls between SWATF headquarters and Sector 10, which began with SWATF demanding to know why the earlier order to locate the Cassinga base had not been carried out.

Lieutenant J Brand, the mortar group and one platoon from Delta Company prepared four 81-mm mortars with 115 high explosive and 44 white phosphorous bombs while the assault group moved into position. At 08h00 on 31 January, however, the reconnaissance team reported that the target was deserted, but that

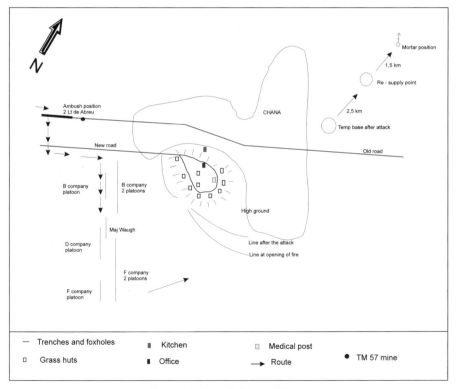

The attack on Cassumbi, February 1987

they had located a second base, which was a hive of activity. Major Peter Waugh decided to wait a day in order to confirm this information and review his plan of attack.

Communication with the mortar group had been lost, but Waugh decided to go ahead without their support. At 06h00 on 1 February, as the line advanced to attack, Bravo Company's left flank opened fire on a five-man enemy security patrol, immediately drawing 82-mm mortar and machine-gun fire. Brand's group was finally raised on the radio and began answering the mortar fire.

The attack killed five of the estimated 120 SWAPO in the base, but four members of 32 also died and another 11 were wounded. Large quantities of ammunition were destroyed and the huts in the base set alight. The main SWAPO force scattered to the Mucolo, Ngonto and Cassumbi areas, and on 3 February FAPLA sent a tank company, a ZU23 mobile platoon and a BM 21 to Cassumbi. Five days later, Charlie, Echo and Golf companies arrived to relieve the troops, who had been deployed for almost three months.

On 17 February, 32 was ordered to move to 101 Battalion's tactical headquarters at the Oimanha River for redeployment around Mupa, Evale, Anhanca and Nehone. A new tactical headquarters was set up seven kilometres north-west of Dova, and the patrols launched a concerted effort to flush out the enemy. At 14h15 on 5 March, Golf Company's four-man reconnaissance team briefly opened fire on 20 SWAPO 12 km north-east of Evale before withdrawing, as they were clearly outnumbered. On 11 March, in order to boost their cover as UNITA members, Charlie Company laid four mines on the road between Mongua and Ongiva, where Savimbi's men were known to operate.

Assigned to the area inside a 15-km radius of Evale, Golf Company made contact with the enemy at least once a day. At 11h50 on 12 March a patrol engaged a group of 40 in a heavy ten-minute firefight, which died down briefly before resuming for another five minutes, leaving Rifleman R Sikote dead and five others wounded. Another member was killed and four wounded, including Second Lieutenant D da Sousa, when his platoon made contact in the same area. It was clear that FAPLA troops from Evale were involved in these skirmishes, but as far as possible, 32 confined its actions to SWAPO and focused on locating the guerrilla positions. This approach was reinforced by a signal from SWATF on 17 March, emphasising that FAPLA was not to be confronted – a difficult order to obey, since after every contact the SWAPO groups made for Evale and the protection afforded by FAPLA.

On 21 March a platoon from Charlie Company was sent to confirm occupation of the base at Mupa. Entering from the south and sweeping north in an extended line, they made contact with 20 SWAPO hiding in trenches. The firefight broke off and resumed four times before the enemy fled north, leaving one dead.

Because of the SWATF orders no immediate follow-up was done, but the next day the company was given permission to proceed to Mupa. The town was deserted and Charlie Company was ordered to hold it until UNITA could take occupation, which happened two days later.

When a vehicle on a re-supply run detonated a landmine 25 km north-east of Evale, Charlie Company was ordered 30 km east to Mvongo to try to locate SWAPO's FCP. On 30 March, reconnaissance teams from Golf and Echo companies reported that only a handful of FAPLA troops were in Evale, and at 23h30 the next day Echo Company attacked the town from the south-west. Within 30 minutes the town was cleared, and by first light on 1 April it was occupied by UNITA, which now controlled 50 km of road between Mupa and Evale, thus cutting off any supplies from Cuvelai to Ongiva.

SWAPO moved east, and on 2 April Golf Company killed five members of a 40-strong group before the survivors fled south-west, straight into Echo Company, which killed another guerrilla.

On 12 April, 32 began withdrawing to Buffalo, wondering how long it would be before FAPLA recaptured the towns left in UNITA's hands.

OPERATION RADBRAAK

On 21 June, 291 men from Bravo, Delta and Foxtrot companies, the 81-mm mortar and 14,5-mm anti-aircraft platoons, two reconnaissance teams and 119 members of the support element, ranging from medical to logistics personnel, were deployed around Cafima, with Major Daan van der Merwe's tactical headquarters 100 km north of Beacon 37 on the Cubati River.

Patrols over the next six days turned up no sign of SWAPO, and at 23h00 on 28 June, Mupa was shelled with mortars in the hope of flushing out the enemy. It didn't work, and by 7 July, when Major Louis Scheepers relieved Van der Merwe, there was still no sign of SWAPO. Fresh bombardments of Mupa and Evale drew only cursory answering fire, and by 16 July *Radbraak* (mangle) ended with the companies starting to withdraw back to Buffalo. They had no idea that they were about to embark on the biggest conventional support ever offered to UNITA.

OPERATION MODULAR

Since early 1987 there had been clear signs that FAPLA was once again preparing for a major offensive against UNITA. The South Africans warned Savimbi about this, but he chose to ignore the danger for some months, despite evidence that FAPLA had strengthened its air defence system in the 3rd and 5th military regions in January.

By April, FAPLA was assembling its largest force to date at Cuito Cuanavale, bolstered by a steady supply of hardware from its communist sponsors, including enough T65 and T55 tanks and BMP 1 armoured cars to push the total number of these vehicles up to 500. Additional MiG 23 and SU 22 fighter planes, and MI 24/25/35 and MI 8/17 helicopters were also provided, putting the number available to FAPLA at more than 80 fighter planes and 123 helicopters.

On 1 May, UNITA having realised at last that FAPLA meant business, Savimbi's chief of staff, General Ben Ben, met with the SADF. He conceded that their south-east Angolan stronghold was in peril, and that South African involvement would be needed to stave off the expected onslaught. Liaison teams from Military Intelligence (MI) were deployed with UNITA from early June to monitor the situation, but a proposal that 32 Battalion should destroy the bridge over the river east of Cuito Cuanavale was turned down by Pretoria.

The SADF put forward three scenarios for assistance to UNITA:

- Clandestine support, including deployment of liaison teams and Special Forces teams to monitor FAPLA's forces, as well as one multiple rocket launcher troop protected by 32 Battalion and limited air support.
- As above, but with the additional deployment of 32 Battalion and 61 Mechanised Battalion to attack the FAPLA brigades as they advanced, but sparing the existing infrastructure and maintaining a 30-km distance from Cuito Cuanavale.
- In the event of Mavinga falling, carrying out harassment attacks on FAPLA, and using 32 Battalion and 61 Mechanised Battalion to retake the strategically important town.

With MI's liaison teams in place, a decision was made on 15 June to implement the first option and start preparing for the second. On 22 June *Operation Modular*, under command of Lieutenant General Kat Liebenberg, was authorised. It would unfold in four phases, starting with observation and harassment of FAPLA as it deployed and began to move, and ending with the advance being halted and the FAPLA force destroyed.

Colonel Jock Harris, Officer Commanding 32 Battalion, was appointed field commander, and the first decision was that the unit would not be directly involved in combat, but would provide protection for the MRLs and safeguard Mavinga from FAPLA attack.

FAPLA had begun its advance on 2 June and, unchecked by UNITA harassment, had reached the source of the Chambinga River by the end of July. Harris set up his headquarters south of the Lomba River where he, Colonel Mo Oelschig (liaison officer attached to UNITA) and Colonel Piet Muller from Rundu planned the operation. In mid-July, Commandant Robbie Hartslief, commander of 32's Support Group, was ordered to move the 32 Battalion contingent to Mavinga.

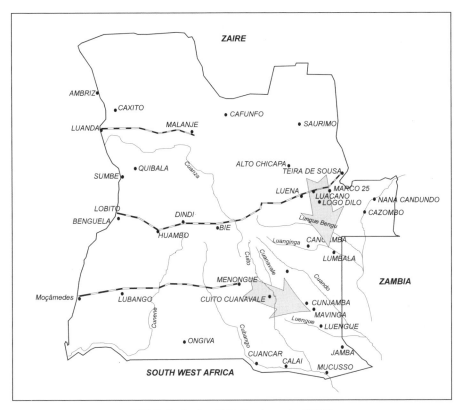

FAPLA's September 1987 offensive against UNITA

By the beginning of August, the situation in the field had undergone a dramatic change. From the two brigades originally detected in early March, the FAPLA force had grown to nine. Four brigades – 16, 21, 47 and 59 – plus two tactical groups with T55 tank battalions at their core, had been deployed east of the Cuito River. Four more brigades made up FAPLA's rearguard, with 8 Brigade protecting convoys between Menongue and Cuito Cuanavale, 13 Brigade assigned to defend Cuito Cuanavale, 25 Brigade to defend the logistical base at Tumpo and 66 Brigade protecting the bridge over the Chambinga River. 24 Brigade was held in reserve at Cuito Cuanavale.

Despite this, Harris was authorised to deploy only some elements of the proposed 32 Battalion and 61 Mechanised Battalion force, namely five rifle companies; two 20-mm Ystervark anti-aircraft troops; one MRL battery and one 120-mm mortar battery; a support company consisting of an 81-mm mortar platoon, a 14,5-mm anti-aircraft platoon, an anti-tank platoon armed with 106-mm recoilless guns and Milan missiles and an assault pioneer platoon; and three reconnaissance teams from 32. The original plan had included two anti-tank squadrons of Ratel 90

235

armoured cars and ZT3 missiles; two mechanised infantry companies; a platoon with 81-mm mortars mounted on Ratel Infantry Combat Vehicles; a motorised company of Casspirs from 101 Battalion; Special Forces reconnaissance teams; and a 155-mm G5 battery from 4 SA Infantry.

By early August, Commandant Hartslief was ready to mount the staged movement of troops and a convoy of more than 100 vehicles to Mavinga. On 10 August, Hartslief took one rifle company, the 106-mm recoilless gun anti-tank section, the 14,5-mm anti-aircraft platoon, the 20-mm anti-aircraft troop and the MRL battery around the Lomba River source to General Ben Ben's headquarters, then south of the Mianei River. The 120-mm mortar battery joined them there. Two days later, Harris moved his headquarters to the source of the Lomba River, leaving a protection element at the original headquarters south-east of Mavinga. UNITA was still trying to stop FAPLA's advance, but 47 and 59 Brigades had already reached the Chambinga River, and 16 and 21 brigades were 20 km west of the Cunzumbia River.

On 13 August, the first shots fired by South African forces during *Operation Modular* came from the 120-mm mortar battery at Samunguri and were directed at 47 and 49 brigades, temporarily halting the advance in the Catado woods.

The full threat posed by the FAPLA brigades now became apparent, and on 16 August deployment of the G5 battery and the anti-tank squadron was finally approved. The next day both Harris and Oelschig were ordered to join UNITA's General Demosthenes at his headquarters, from where they were to exercise further command of the operation. It was a strange decision, requiring Harris to command his forces from a great distance, but he duly handed temporary field command to Hartslief. On the same day, FAPLA began moving again, 47 and 59 brigades heading south towards the Lomba River, 16 and 21 brigades making for the source of the Cunzumbia River to the east. The advance resumed in broad daylight, sending a clear signal to the South African commanders that FAPLA's brigades were not the least bit intimidated by UNITA. This realisation caused Harris to be hastily recalled to take command of the ground forces once more.

At 23h59 on 19 August, the MRL battery fired a ripple of 96 rockets at the FAPLA forces still occupying the Catado woods. The projectiles missed the target by about 100 m, but alerted FAPLA to the fact that South African forces were involved, as UNITA had no MRLs. For the next five days a constant barrage of MRL fire was directed at the advancing brigades, and throughout this period the MRL battery and 32's small protection element made up the entire South African front line.

Harris moved his headquarters again, 12 km west of Mavinga, to await the arrival from Buffalo of 32's anti-tank squadron, Quebec Battery's logistical vehicles and eight G5s, flown in on C130 aircraft. At 18h30 on 26 August, in full view of

Major Pierre Franken, Papa Battery commander acting as the forward observer, 47 and 49 brigades settled in for the night on high ground near Mucobola. The next morning, MRL fire rained down on them from south of the Lomba River, 13 km away. For the first time the observers could monitor the results of the bombardment. One tank was set alight and 20 FAPLA soldiers killed. Another 96 were wounded, despite an ineffective BM 21 counter-bombardment. However, the advance was merely delayed, not halted, and by 28 August FAPLA was just three kilometres from the Lomba River source. The MRL and the two companies protecting it withdrew south of the river to avoid getting trapped.

During an urgent planning session at Rundu on 28 and 29 August, the earlier restrictions on deployment of 61 Mechanised Battalion were lifted. Authorisation was granted for deployment of two companies from 101 Battalion and for maximum air support to be used.

On 29 August the entire FAPLA force began advancing rapidly, covering 40 km in just two days. Tactical Group 1 and 47 Brigade moved west to the source of the Lomba River, 59 Brigade deployed six kilometres north of the Lomba–Cunzumbia confluence after crossing the Cuzizi River with the help of TMM bridging – Russian-made mechanical bridging mounted on a vehicle – and 21 Brigade moved from nine kilometres south-east of the Cunzumbia River source to the bridge over the Lomba, two kilometres east of the confluence. No one had anticipated such a rapid advance and, in particular, 21 had not been expected to cover the distance without encountering UNITA. The South African commanders realised that if FAPLA was to be stopped, it would be up to them to do so, as UNITA clearly lacked the capability.

The MRLs and 32's rifle companies moved 12 km south-east of the Lomba–Cuzizi confluence, then 20 km to the west to set up positions from which to engage 47 Brigade. The G5s were deployed 18 km south-east of the Lomba–Cunzumbia confluence. At 07h50 on 31 August, the MRLs fired full salvos of 127-mm rockets at 47 Brigade, pinning it down. At 21h00, the G5s lobbed 80 shells at 21 Brigade, stopping their advance.

Meanwhile, 32's anti-tank squadron and the 120-mm mortar battery moved to Hartslief's position five kilometres south-east of the Lomba–Cuzizi confluence. On 2 September, Commandant Bok Smit, Officer Commanding 61 Mechanised Battalion, joined Harris at his field headquarters to plan the next move, having despatched 55 Ratel ICVs and 62 logistical vehicles to Mavinga, where they set up a base 25 km south-west of the town on 7 September.

The reconnaissance team led by Sergeant Piet Fourie and a forward artillery observer had moved behind enemy lines on 2 September, and were in position to direct G5 fire. By 4 September, 32's other reconnaissance teams, under command of Sergeant Mac da Trinidade and Corporal Frenchie Gilbert, had located 47 and

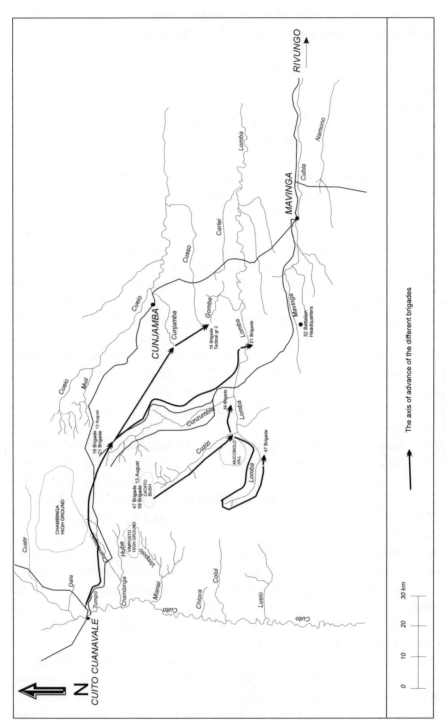

CUITO CUANAVALE

N

CHAMBINGA
HIGH GROUND

Cuatir

Dala

Tumpo

Chambinga

Mianei

Cuito

Chiova

Colui

Lueio

Cuito

Hube
VIMPOSTO
HIGH GROUND

Vimpoto

CUNJAMBA

Cueio

Muii

Cueio

16 Brigade 13 August
21 Brigade

47 Brigade 13 August
59 Brigade
CAIXTO
BUSH

Cunzumbia

Cuzizi

MUCOBOLO
HILL

Lomba

47 Brigade

59 Brigade

Lomba

Cunjamba

16 Brigade
Tactical gr 2

Gombe

Lomba

21 Brigade

Cueio

Cusso

Cariei

Lomba

Mavinga

32 Battalion
Headquarters

MAVINGA

Cubia

Namono

RIVUNGO

The axis of advance of the different brigades

FAPLA positions prior to battles of 13 September 1987

0   10   20   30 km

16 brigades and were monitoring their movements. On 6 September, Da Trinidade's team, attached to Commandant Les Rudman's liaison team, notched up 32's first contact with FAPLA during the operation.

As the FAPLA advance continued, headquarters realised that Harris lacked the experience needed to get the job done, and on 5 September, Colonel Deon Ferreira, former OC 32 Battalion, took command of the newly formed 20 Brigade and appointed Harris senior staff officer operations. With 20 Artillery Regiment for support, Ferreira divided the brigade into the following battle groups:

- Alpha (commanded by Commandant Smit and deployed 26 km south-east of Mavinga), consisting of one mechanised company in Ratel 20s; 32 Battalion's Golf Company, travelling in Buffels; an 81-mm mortar group with four mortars mounted on Ratels; and an anti-aircraft troop of six 20-mm Ystervark vehicles from 61 Mechanised Battalion.
- Bravo (commanded by Commandant Hartslief and deployed 11 km south/ south-east of the Lomba–Cunzumbia confluence), consisting of 32 Battalion's Foxtrot Company; one platoon from Bravo Company; the anti-tank squadron; the support company; and two motorised companies from 101 Battalion, travelling in Casspirs.
- Charlie (commanded by Major David Lotter), consisting of a mechanised company; anti-tank platoon; and 81-mm mortar group from 61 Mechanised Battalion.

The following forces made up 20 Artillery Regiment and could be detached to any battle group as required:

- Quebec Battery: 155-mm G5 guns protected by two platoons from 32 Battalion's Bravo Company; four Stinger anti-aircraft missile teams from UNITA; two SA 7 anti-aircraft missile teams; eight 14,5-mm anti-aircraft guns.
- Papa Battery: 127-mm multiple rocket launchers protected by 32 Battalion's Charlie Company; a 20-mm anti-aircraft troop; two Stinger anti-aircraft missile teams from UNITA; two SA 7 anti-aircraft missile teams.
- Sierra Battery: 120-mm mortars protected by one platoon from 32 Battalion.

On 9 September, following early morning reports from UNITA that FAPLA was trying to cross the Lomba–Gombe River 12 km east of Cunzumbia, Major Hannes Nortmann, 32 Battalion's anti-tank squadron commander, took his men and a company from 101 Battalion to assess the situation. A BTR 60 armoured car was taken out by a Ratel 90 while trying to ford the river, sparking a heavy counter-bombardment from FAPLA, which forced Nortmann to withdraw almost six kilometres in order to regroup.

The next day Nortmann returned to the Lomba River while 21 Brigade was trying to get across, and fired a rocket at FAPLA on the opposite bank. The enemy responded by sending three T55 tanks over the floodplain. Only one of Nortmann's ZT3 missile Ratels was serviceable, so the Ratel 90s opened fire on the tanks, but the range was too great and the tanks kept on coming. The first two missiles from the ZT3 system missed the lead tank, but the third stopped it in its tracks and the fourth caused the tank to burst into flames. The next missile fell short of the second tank, but the sixth scored a direct hit, and the seventh took out the third and last tank. By that time, MiGs were aloft and the Ratels withdrew to safety, having stopped 21 Brigade from crossing the Lomba.

On 13 September, 47 Brigade was halted by heavy artillery bombardment from both Quebec and Papa batteries, deployed four kilometres south of the Lomba–Cuzizi confluence. The same date saw 32's first casualties during *Modular* when a Ratel 90 was shot out after becoming bogged down in mud. Foxtrot Company commander Captain AD McCallum and troop commander Second Lieutenant JR Alves were killed, and Captain Piet van Zyl took command of the company.

By this time, Ferreira and other high-ranking SADF officers had realised that the only way to stop the FAPLA advance was to physically attack the columns, as the artillery bombardments succeeded only in slowing them down. On 16 September, 61 Mechanised Battalion attacked 47 Brigade, but achieved little success. During a top-level planning session at Mavinga on the same day, it was decided to divide the combat theatre into specific areas of responsibility for UNITA and the South African forces. The break in battle gave FAPLA a chance to re-supply, but by 19 September Battle Group Bravo had been ordered to act against 21 Brigade, while Alpha and Charlie would take on 47 Brigade, deployed 15 km south of the Lomba–Cunzumbia confluence.

On 21 September at 08h50, four Buccaneers launched a series of air strikes against 47 Brigade, followed by four Mirages at 13h00, and the four Buccaneers again at 17h50. Four days later a strike on 21 Brigade missed by some 200 m, but the continued artillery bombardment began to take its toll, inflicting heavy casualties and loss of equipment. On 28 September, FAPLA ordered 47 Brigade to cross the Lomba River and join forces with 59 Brigade. The combined force was then to move east across the Cunzumbia River to link up with 21 Brigade, but late that afternoon 21 was suddenly ordered to withdraw to the north-east.

That night, President PW Botha visited the South African headquarters at Mavinga, and after being thoroughly briefed about the situation he authorised a more offensive campaign to destroy the FAPLA brigades east of Cuito Cuanavale. On 30 September elements of FAPLA's 47 Brigade came under artillery fire as they prepared to link up with 59, and were forced to withdraw to their earlier positions. On 3 October Commandant Jan Hougaard, second-in-command of 32 Battalion, was called to Rundu to formulate plans for a small force to infiltrate the area west of the Cuito River and carry out stealth attacks along FAPLA's supply line between Menongue and Cuito Cuanavale.

On the same date, 61 Mechanised Battalion attacked 47 Brigade with air and artillery support, 32's Golf Company acting as the reserve force. At 05h20, 50 Ratels, driving three abreast, moved out for the assault. An hour later the column came under bombardment from D30 artillery firing from the direction of 47, 59 and 21 brigades. Shortly afterwards the MiGs were airborne and hunting the assault force, but 61 pressed on with the attack. When the battalion withdrew, Golf Company moved in to clear the target area and found the first SA 8 anti-aircraft system ever captured in the western hemisphere. The battle was decisive, with 47 Brigade destroyed, and on 5 October all other FAPLA brigades were ordered to withdraw to the north. The offensive had been stopped, but the operation was far from over.

By 10 October the remnants of 47 Brigade, as well as 16 and 21 and Tactical Group 2, had retreated to the source of the Cunzumbia River, and planning was under way for a South African-led operation to destroy FAPLA east of the Cuito River by 15 December. Under command of Major LL du Plessis, Task Force Delta was formed from the following elements of 32 Battalion: Foxtrot Company, travelling in Buffels; two 106-mm recoilless gun vehicles; two Unimog supply vehicles; four 81-mm mortars mounted on Unimogs; and two Milan vehicles. UNITA's 3rd Regular Battalion made up the rest of Delta.

Up to this time, 32 Battalion had been used chiefly to protect the artillery and supply convoys, causing enormous frustration among men who were some of the most experienced combat troops at the SADF's disposal. By the time Task Force Delta joined forces with UNITA's General Ben Ben on 8 October, all signs of resentment at the lesser role to which they had previously been limited had disappeared. Delta deployed five kilometres south-west of the Mianei River source and were ordered to hold the front until 20 October, when 4 SA Infantry, with tanks and more artillery, would arrive.

On 11 October, with FAPLA's MiGs patrolling the skies and launching sporadic attacks, two platoons and two reconnaissance teams infiltrated the northern sector to monitor FAPLA's 66 Brigade at the Chambinga bridge. Three days later the G5s pounded Cuito Cuanavale, and 59 Brigade was despatched to locate and destroy the guns. Task Force Delta shadowed the FAPLA brigade, but could not engage them because the terrain precluded use of their anti-tank weapons. Battle Group Alpha was then assigned to attack 59, and Delta moved to the high ground at Vimposto to prevent reinforcements from 16 or 66 Brigade getting through.

On 18 October, Task Force Delta was disbanded and some elements were incorporated into Battle Group Bravo. Captain Piet van Zyl and his company were to join 4 SAI when they arrived at the battlefront after a ten-day journey from Rundu. Meanwhile, Foxtrot Company was re-equipped and moved 70 km to the source of the Maquelengue River to await the arrival of battle groups Alpha and Charlie. Captains Jurg Human and Tai Theron, both platoon commanders from 32, joined Foxtrot, and the senior command structure also underwent some changes. Brigadier Fido Smit, commander of 7 SA Division, would be in overall command of the operation through a mini-divisional headquarters known as Task Force 10, but Colonel Ferreira remained in command of 20 Brigade.

On 30 October, 4 SAI arrived at Mavinga and was immediately assigned to form the core of Battle Group Charlie, which consisted of two mechanised companies in Ratel 20s, two motorised companies from 32 Battalion in Buffels, a squadron of 13 Olifant main battle tanks, a squadron of Ratel 90 armoured cars, a G5 battery and MRL troop, a 20-mm anti-aircraft troop and a mechanised support company.

By late October FAPLA began moving south again, and on 3 November Battle Group Charlie, 32 Battalion's Bravo, Delta and Golf companies, a company from 101 Battalion and 32's anti-tank platoon were deployed south of the Mianei River source to halt FAPLA's push against the artillery batteries. By 6 November plans were in place to attack 61 Brigade, which had been ordered to advance on Mavinga.

On 9 November, 32 Battalion had its first chance to engage FAPLA's 16 Brigade. Battle Group Charlie deployed 15 km north of the Chambinga source, and three G6 guns – the self-propelled version of the G5 – moved into position 15 km north-east of 16 Brigade. At 04h00, Battle Group Charlie began advancing on 16 Brigade, and at 05h36 the artillery launched a ten-minute barrage to soften the target. At 06h00, still four kilometres from the target, 32 Battalion's Delta Company debussed from their Ratels and proceeded on foot, forming a human screen 500 m ahead of the two mechanised companies. Behind them came the Ratel 90 anti-tank squadron, the Olifants, Ratel 20s and Ratels carrying ZT3 missile systems.

At 06h30, Mirage F-1AZ aircraft carried out a successful bombing raid on the target, and at 10h12 Bravo Company drew fire from small arms, machine guns and recoilless guns. They immediately reported FAPLA tanks to the front and right, and simultaneously UNITA reported more tanks to the left. Lieutenant W de Vos moved up and confirmed five T55 tanks in ambush position to the left. Bravo Company was struggling through dense bush in order to join the armoured car squadron, and one member of Delta Company was killed and another wounded by mortar fire. With the Olifant tanks closing in from the rear, 32 Battalion's rifle companies fought their way through the enemy trenches in what was the first combined tank and infantry battle involving South African forces since 1945.

With Bravo Company pinned down and drawing heavy FAPLA fire, and T55 tanks attacking their Ratels, Major A Retief called in the reserve Olifant squadron. In a tank-on-tank battle that began at 10h15, FAPLA damaged the track of one Olifant, but five T55s were knocked out and one captured. Soon afterwards, 32's men on the ground broke through to the main FAPLA trenches, but a heavy rocket attack by MiG aircraft from 11h10 allowed 16 Brigade to break away from the battle. By 14h30 their position had been taken, and FAPLA had lost 75 dead and four prisoners. FAPLA equipment destroyed included ten T54/55 tanks, a BM 21, a 76-mm gun, two 23-mm anti-aircraft guns and 11 supply trucks. Captured were one BM 21, one 76-mm gun, two 23-mm guns, 14 SA 7/SA 14 missile systems, a 14,5-mm anti-aircraft gun, one 82-mm mortar and 18 brand new Engesa trucks.

The South African/UNITA casualties were seven dead, nine wounded and one Ratel 20 shot out.

But most of 16 Brigade escaped back to the Chambinga and redeployed at two positions that became known as Target Alpha and Target Bravo. Another attack was planned for 11 November, but prior to this Battle Group Charlie was to carry out a diversionary attack on the combined 21/25 Brigade.

Battle groups Alpha and Charlie came under heavy air bombardment from FAPLA during the attack on 16 Brigade, and two members of 32's Delta Company – assigned to protect the tanks – were killed by enemy mortar fire. The rest of the company debussed from the tanks and moved 300 m forward, making contact with FAPLA at 10h05. A fire belt action, requiring all the Ratels to fire their 20-mm guns at the target simultaneously, had to be aborted when the infantry moved into the line of fire.

To the surprise of all concerned, 21/25 Brigade began withdrawing to the north on 13 November. Colonel Ferreira ordered the accelerated advance of Battle Group Charlie so that they could lay ambushes to prevent the retreating force from crossing the Vimpolo River. This area was well known to 32 Battalion, and during the night of 14/15 November, Captain van Zyl's company was to guide both tanks and infantry to a position two kilometres south-east of Sandumba. However, the battle group commander decided to deploy six kilometres south-east instead. Under cover of a heavy thunderstorm, 21/25 Brigade crossed the Vimpolo at the very point Van Zyl had indicated, before redeploying at the source of the Humbe River.

In what would be heavy clashes between Battle Group Charlie and the FAPLA brigades on 16 November, Foxtrot Company advanced on foot, using the armoured cars as a shield. A company from 4 SAI in Ratel 20s was ahead of the troops, the Olifant tanks to their right, protecting more infantry. Major Nortmann's anti-tank squadron brought up the rear, and a UNITA battalion was on the left flank.

BM 21 rockets were exploding between the tanks and armoured cars, and one troop was seriously wounded when an 82-mm mortar bomb exploded in a tree above his head. He had to be bodily carried to the rear of the column, as no ambulance could move up under the heavy barrage. Lieutenant de Vos was wounded in the shoulder by shrapnel, but carried on fighting. Two members of the platoon led by captains Human and Theron were killed by mortar fire, and the dead and wounded were loaded into an armoured car. To the left, 4 SAI was under such heavy fire that the Olifants had to offer support, knocking out four T55s and a BM 21 just 200 m in front of the advancing infantry, which was on the edge of the floodplain and managed to reach the trenches only late that afternoon.

By that time, FAPLA soldiers were running for their lives and were mowed down in droves as they tried to cross the floodplain. But enemy tanks had succeeded in moving around the assault force and were about to attack from the rear. The Olifants and anti-tank Ratels had to execute 180-degree turns in order to launch a counter-attack. Nortmann's anti-tank squadron, engaged in battle to the south, was virtually surrounded by tanks and Commandant Hartslief raced to his assistance.

Shortly before last light, with heavy fighting still in progress, Battle Group Charlie was ordered to break contact and move 12 km back in order to be re-supplied. Ammunition, in particular, was running low. Under cover of darkness, FAPLA moved around the source of the Hube River. The next day, Ferreira ordered a fresh attack by Battle Group Alpha, supported by 4 SAI's tanks and two companies from 32 Battalion. The assault was to be launched from north-east of the high ground between Chambinga and the Hube River source, but even before the first shots were fired, 21/25 Brigade began retreating to the bridge. Two hours before nightfall and three kilometres from the bridge, the assault force caught up with FAPLA, Nortmann's squadron taking out several tanks before the enemy managed to cross the bridge and slip away.

As SADF and UNITA generals debated their next move, the FAPLA brigades retreated to Tumpo to be re-equipped before 21 Brigade was sent north to protect the Cuatir River source. An unsuccessful attack on 26 November marked the end of *Operation Modular*.

OPERATION HOOPER

Although destruction of the FAPLA brigades remained a priority, political considerations forced a temporary hiatus in the military campaign, with strict orders that *Operation Hooper* was not to start before 10 December. FAPLA took advantage of the lull in fighting by setting up three defensive lines east of the Cuito River.

The first line saw 25 Brigade deployed north of the Chambinga bridge, with 59 Brigade further back and 21 Brigade south of the Cuatir River. The second line comprised Tactical Group 2 south-east of Tumpo and north of the Cuito and Chambinga rivers; 66 Brigade – strengthened by an additional 25 tanks –

around Tumpo; and 16 Brigade deployed at the Dala River. The third and last line consisted of 13 Brigade and a reinforced Cuban battalion as the defenders of Cuito Cuanavale; 13 Brigade's Alpha Company at Baixa Longa; and an FCP and motorised Cuban infantry regiment west of Cuito Cuanavale.

The first shots of *Hooper* came from an artillery bombardment of the logistical base at Tumpo and FAPLA's main base at Cuito Cuanavale. A campaign of harassment, launched on 16 December, formed an integral part of *Hooper*. Under command of Commandant Jan Hougaard, FAPLA's supply lines between Menongue and Cuito Cuanavale were continually attacked by 32's MRL battery, 81-mm mortar group, 106-mm anti-tank platoon, SA 7 anti-aircraft team and one rifle company, along with two sections of engineers and an electronic warfare team.

The first assault against Tumpo was a night attack, with 32 Battalion and UNITA moving in from the south and 61 Mechanised Battalion from the north. Commanded by Major Thinus van Staden, the 32 contingent consisted of Delta, Echo and Foxtrot companies, the anti-tank squadron, three tanks from 4 SA Infantry Battalion, a mechanised company, a 120-mm mortar troop and 1 400 men from UNITA's 3rd and 4th Regular Battalions.

On 23 February 1988 the rifle companies left their vehicles at Vimposto and marched towards the floodplain lining the Chambinga River, 45 km from FAPLA's front line. They crossed the floodplain in single file, 250 heavily laden men spread over two kilometres of knee-deep mud for 90 minutes. By the time the first troops reached the bush on the far side, the last man was just entering the morass. The troops waited in the tree line from 05h00 until nightfall on 24 February, then marched through the night to reach a position three kilometres south of 25 Brigade. At 03h00 they went into attack formation, the line extending over a front almost 1 000 m wide. It was dark moon, but as they neared the target the 120-mm mortars turned night into day with illuminating rounds, allowing Van Staden to confirm that his men were exactly where he wanted them, 600 m from the enemy line.

At daybreak the companies found themselves in an open chana from where they could clearly see Cuito Cuanavale, eight kilometres away. The troops became so excited that they began running forward, still in extended line, and as they rounded a hillock, they saw a FAPLA truck speeding away. A staff sergeant took it out with an RPG 7, and suddenly the troops found themselves in FAPLA's hastily evacuated trenches. The shot-out truck, a brand new BTR 60, and a large quantity of equipment were all that remained of the enemy's occupation. The troops were delighted at having taken a brigade position with a single RPG 7, but soon set up an all-round defence to await the arrival of 61 Mechanised Battalion, which had experienced some difficulty negotiating minefields along the way.

Just after 07h00, FAPLA launched an artillery bombardment, hopelessly off target at first, but as the D30 guns and BM 21 rocket launchers found their range, the troops had to take cover in the FAPLA trenches. Almost immediately, MiG 23s and SU 22s began dropping bombs from the air as well, and the three companies from 32 Battalion came under continuous bombardment for nine hours. The aircraft made no less than 56 passes to drop their ordnance, but fortunately the closest they came to the target was 100 m.

As 61 Mechanised Battalion approached the position, UNITA troops riding on the tanks opened fire on the men in the trenches. In accordance with standard drills, a 32 company commander threw yellow smoke grenades to denote friendly forces and UNITA ceased fire – but the smoke provided an accurate target indicator for FAPLA, which resumed firing. Tank and armoured car crews simply closed their hatches, but a number of UNITA troops were swept off the tanks by BM 21 rockets. Mercifully, only two 32 Battalion members were wounded during what military researchers have since estimated was a heavier and more intense air and ground bombardment than the devastating attack at Delville Wood in France during World War I.

On 26 February the rifle companies of 32 Battalion returned to their waiting vehicles at Vimposto and withdrew.

Meanwhile, Hougaard's harassment force had suffered the usual delays at UNITA checkpoints, and it was only on 9 January that the first MRL ripples were fired on an enemy convoy. After that, convoys of up to 170 vehicles at a time were bombarded nightly, with FAPLA MiGs taking to the air each day in search of the artillery.

On 2 February 1988 the force west of the Cuito River was relieved, with Commandant Hartslief assuming command of Major Nortmann's Ratel 20 squadron, a 20-mm anti-aircraft troop and three companies from 32 Battalion. On 13 February, Hartslief decided to 'rev' the main logistical assembly point at Menongue, and at 22h30 an MRL fired 96 rockets at the air base. Reconnaissance teams stationed just beyond the base perimeter provided the coordinates, and at 01h30 a second ripple was fired before the artillery withdrew to the Gimbe base area. By 07h00 two MiG 23s were aloft, firing their 30-mm guns at every position where ground troops could possibly take cover. Later, another six MiGs joined the hunt.

FAPLA sent a full brigade, including tanks and M46 field guns, to Gimbe, and on 3 March 32 Battalion was ordered to pull back to Buffalo. As a parting shot, a ripple of 96 rockets was fired at Baixa Longa on 5 March.

On 25 February another attack on Tumpo had been called off when 61 Mechanised Battalion, the tank squadron and UNITA's 3rd and 5th Regular Battalions, with a company from 32 in reserve, ran into extensive minefields. On 4 and 5 March, 61 Mechanised Battalion and 4 SA Infantry Battalion were relieved by 82 SA Brigade, made up of Citizen Force members. Companies from 32 held the front line while the newcomers found their feet.

An operational order issued on 5 March required 32 Battalion, working in concert with UNITA, to exercise dominance of the Anhanca–Lipanda area and prevent FAPLA from carrying out reconnaissance there. A company from 32 relieved 61 Mechanised Battalion in the former 59 Brigade positions, and began sweeping the area for mines and gathering intelligence about enemy deployments. On 8 March, FAPLA deployed a battalion north of Tumpo, and Colonel Paul Fouche assumed command and control of the South African forces. Two days later 32 Battalion deployed east of the FAPLA positions, and on 13 March *Operation Hooper* officially ended.

OPERATION PACKER

As *Hooper* moved seamlessly into *Packer*, a Citizen Force call-up injected both fresh troops and new life into the combined SADF–UNITA force intent on driving FAPLA from Cuito Cuanavale. With the exception of 32 Battalion and certain artillery units, a totally different army than the first two attempts would carry out the third assault on Tumpo. Commandant Gerrit Louw would lead the mission to 'drive the enemy out of Tumpo, hold and capture the terrain until last light on 23 March 1988 and allow field engineers, two companies of 32 Battalion, UNITA's 5th Regular Battalion and teams from 4 Reconnaissance Regiment to blow the bridge over the Cuito River'.

His primary assault force was made up of 13 Olifant main battle tanks with crews from Regiment President Steyn; Regiment Mooi River's Ratel 90 squadron; two mechanised infantry battalions from Regiment de la Rey and Regiment Great Karoo; a 120-mm mortar troop from 44 Parachute Brigade; a troop of MRLs from 19 Rocket Regiment; three companies from 32 Battalion; UNITA's 3rd, 4th and 5th Regular Battalions; and two of UNITA's semi-regular battalions.

The regular battalions would be deployed on the eastern bank of the Cuito River, with the semi-regular battalions on the opposite bank executing hit-and-run attacks. Two companies from 32 and elements from Regiment Great Karoo would stage a diversionary attack from the south-east, while the rest of the force prepared to attack from the north-east. The third company from 32 was deployed with UNITA's 4th Regular Battalion on the western slopes of the high ground at Chambinga to sweep for landmines. On 9 March, while engaged in this task, Captain Tai Theron stepped on an anti-personnel mine that blew off his right foot.

When Louw's assault force began moving at 04h00 on 23 March, 32 was waiting, six kilometres from FAPLA's 25 Brigade. The company used luminous markers to indicate the route for the main force to follow, but on the final approach to the target at 06h15, the force was trapped in a minefield. Three of the Olifants suffered such extensive damage that they had to be blown up. At 07h10 the enemy

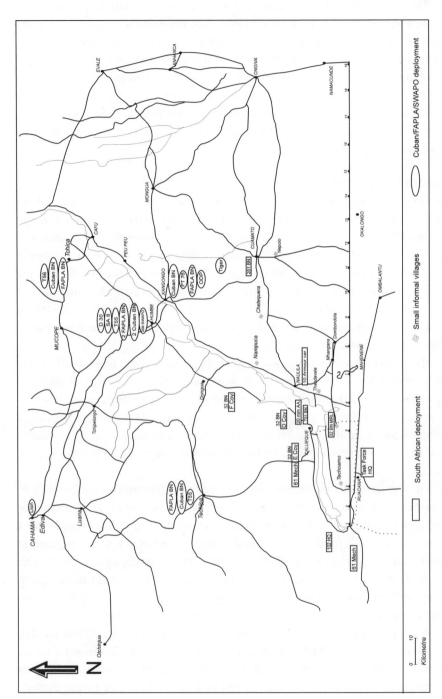

N

0   10
Kilometre

☐ South African deployment   ⬭ Cuban/FAPLA/SWAPO deployment

✤ Small informal villages

Operation Hilti: SADF, FAPLA/Cuban and SWAPO deployments on 13 June 1988

launched an artillery bombardment that prevented the assault force from reaching 25 Brigade, before being ordered to retreat to the assembly area.

What the fighting men did not know was that political negotiations regarding implementation of United Nations Resolution 435 had moved into top gear, and that South Africa had agreed to withdraw all its forces from Angola. On 30 April the SADF's last major campaign, *Operation Packer*, came to an end, with FAPLA still firmly ensconced at Cuito Cuanavale.

OPERATION HILTI/EXITE

Following *Packer*, 32 Battalion's focus shifted from the Cuando Cubango to the western sector, seat of SWAPO's central headquarters and familiar terrain to the men from Buffalo.

On 15 November 1987, Fidel Castro's 50th Division had arrived in Angola from Cuba, partly to assist with FAPLA's offensive in the 6th military region east of Cuito Cuanavale, but also to reinforce the defensive line in the 5th military region. Originally, this line stretched from Namibe to Kuvango, but in January 1988, 3 500 Cubans deployed south of the line. By May there were Cuban troops all the way from Namibe to Cassinga, and reports claimed that they were as far east as Ongiva. The air base at Cahama was upgraded, and the landing strip at Xangongo extended by 524 m to accommodate MiG 23 fighter jets.

The Cuban force in the 5th military region included six rifle regiments (1 500 – 2 000 men); a regiment of T62 and T55 tanks; an artillery regiment equipped with D30, BM 21 and BM 24 guns and rocket launchers; and an air defence regiment armed with SA 2, 3, 6, 8 and 13 missile systems, four ZSU 23-mm anti-aircraft guns and radar systems. Combined battalions of 200 Cubans and 250 SWAPO each, plus armour and artillery support, were based at Xangongo (Tiger), Cahama (Lion) and Mupa (Zebra). In addition, a group of 300 SWAPO was deployed at Techipa.

From 18 April, when a group of Cubans attacked elements of 101 Battalion conducting a routine anti-SWAPO operation south of Xangongo, it was clear that Castro's soldiers had every intention of making their presence felt. On 4 May they struck again, attacking 101 Battalion south of Humbe and taking Rifleman Johan Papenfus prisoner.

The proximity of the combined Cuban/SWAPO force to the South West Africa border was a source of grave concern, and on 12 May Commandant Jan Hougaard was called to Sector 10 headquarters at Oshakati to discuss ways of dealing with the situation. The senior officers present tabled a plan for 32 Battalion to attack the SWAPO force at Techipa immediately, but Hougaard persuaded them that reconnaissance was necessary first. This could be carried out while the battalion was moving to the area, thus causing no delay.

On 16 May, Hougaard and 32's intelligence officer, Captain Herman Mulder, set up a tactical headquarters at Ruacana from where two three-man reconnaissance teams could be sent into the field. Airlifted the next day by Alouette, the first team was assigned to the area south-east of Techipa around the Devangulu Mountains, while the second was deployed on the western bank of the Cunene River in the Henda Rotunda area, south of Xangongo.

Team 1 found the terrain heavy going, and when after three days they had still not sighted Techipa, had to be extracted due to lack of food and water. All they could report was that they had constantly heard large vehicles moving around. Team 2 picked up tank tracks almost immediately, and on just about every road. Their terrain offered almost no cover at all, and with Cubans patrolling the area around the clock they were lucky not to be spotted before being extracted three days later.

Team 1 was sent back to Techipa, this time by vehicle, approaching the town from the north. From his vantage point at the trenches surrounding the town, the team leader saw a large number of vehicles, including container carriers. The team also heard generators running on a 24-hour basis, and observed that Cubans were running the radar systems. A company from 201 Battalion deployed south of Cuamato had reported heavy vehicle movement, and Team 2 also confirmed that there was a Cuban outpost south-east of the crossroads between Cuamato and Chetaquera.

Clearly, with a substantial conventional force deployed around and within striking distance of Techipa, 32 Battalion could not attack alone. But the only comparable force still in the Operational Area was 61 Mechanised Battalion, which was regrouping after operations *Modular* and *Hooper*, and thus not available. It would be up to 32 after all to stem Cuban encroachment of southern Angola.

Delta, Echo and Foxtrot companies were airlifted to Ruacana for deployment, two companies moving to the area south of Techipa and the third operating south of Henda Rotunda to cover the eastern approach to Calueque. Each company had two 81-mm mortars and two 106-mm recoilless guns mounted on Unimogs for support. A combat team from 61 Mechanised Battalion was hastily scrambled to Calueque as a mobile reserve.

Reconnaissance Team 2 was sent south of Techipa on foot to mine the road from Otchinjau, and reported tank patrols leaving Techipa on a daily basis. Team 1 conducted reconnaissance on the Cuban outposts 15 km south-east and south-west of the town, after which Echo Company was ordered to raid the south-western post. However, Captain M Devenish decided against a full-on attack, preferring just to stir things up a little, then ambush the relief convoy from Techipa. Under cover of darkness, the 81-mm mortar was set up two kilometres from the outpost and the company laid the ambush a kilometre away.

While waiting for the mortar bombardment, the riflemen opened fire on five Cubans sweeping the road for mines. As Cuban infantrymen arrived on foot to investigate, Echo Company had just enough time to register the sound of vehicle engines starting before four BRDM 2 armoured cars came roaring out of the bush. The riflemen opened fire, killing the commander standing upright in the lead vehicle's turret. They then withdrew to replenish their ammunition. On returning to the ambush site they heard tanks starting up, and simultaneously the reconnaissance team warned that there was a second outpost manned by a company of Cubans, not previously detected and right next to the road.

The men of Echo Company ran all the way back to the mortar vehicles, which laid down covering fire that slowed down the Cubans in hot pursuit, and allowed 32's troops to reach the Unimogs just moments before the BRDMs appeared. One of the Unimogs was hit instantly by a 14,5-mm gun and burst into flames. Another got stuck in a hole, and in the rush to get clear of the area – and the Cuban firepower – a third Unimog ploughed into the stricken vehicle. As the first enemy tanks poked their barrels through the bush, Echo Company was ordered to abandon the vehicles, 'bombshell' and head for the pre-arranged emergency rendezvous point. By this time BM 21s had joined the party, and it took eight kilometres of sprinting through the bush before the command group could halt long enough to make radio contact with headquarters at Ruacana and report 12 troops missing. Then the tanks reappeared and the men started running again.

They ran for five hours before being able to make radio communication again at 14h00, and the Cubans only gave up their search and pursuit at 16h00. Echo Company was ordered to return to the contact area immediately to find the missing men. On the way they encountered a group of local women, who began banging their pots and pans together. A flare was fired, and within 30 minutes artillery fire rained down on the company. Four men went forward to scout the area but found nothing – the enemy had removed even the abandoned Unimogs.

At 09h00 the next day, five of the missing troops pitched up at Ruacana. By 16h00 the other seven had reported at Calueque. Any further thought of using 32 Battalion and 61 Mechanised Battalion to attack Techipa was shelved, and several platoons from 32 were sent to reconnoitre the area more intensively. Sergeant de Villiers and his platoon, monitoring the Humbe road, found yet another Cuban outpost 12 km from Techipa. Generators were heard, and close reconnaissance showed that this was an air defence post, including radar.

Colonel Mucho Delport, Officer Commanding 32 Battalion, was flown in to command a task force whose priority was to protect the water installations at Calueque, a vital component in the supply of water to the whole of Owamboland. Delport's Task Force Alpha comprised:

- 51 Battalion – one company each from 1 SWA Specialised Unit; 911 and 101 Battalion; and one 20-mm anti-aircraft troop from 61 Mechanised Battalion.
- 61 Mechanised Battalion Group – two combat teams consisting of infantry in Ratels; Ratel 90s and Olifant tanks; one company of parachutists; 32 Battalion's MRL troop; and an artillery troop from 51 Battalion, armed with 140-mm G2 guns.
- 32 Battalion – Delta, Echo and Foxtrot companies; the 20-mm anti-aircraft troop; one company from each of 701, 102 and 210 Battalion; a combat element from Sector 20; three intelligence teams; three 81-mm sections from 32; two reconnaissance teams from 32; a 120-mm mortar battery; a squadron of Eland armoured cars from Sector 20; and an artillery troop armed with 88-mm G1 guns.

On 13 June, Colonel Delport deployed one company from 61 Mechanised Battalion at Dongue, 25 km south-west of Xangongo and west of the Cunene River, with 32's Foxtrot Company 20 km to the south-west. At Calueque, Delta Company was 15 km to the north-west, Echo Company and another company from 61 were 20 km south-east, 32's MRL troop was to the south on the eastern side of the river, and the company from 701, along with the engineers, were deployed at the dam.

The headquarters of 61, 32 and the task force were at Ruacana, while one company from each of 102 and 61 battalions were 15 km north-west. The armoured car squadron was based at Naulila, and four reaction teams from 201 Battalion were deployed at Cuamato.

After the 88-mm troop lobbed 400 rounds at Ongiva from 03h30 on 13 June, radio intercepts confirmed that the bombardment had left the enemy in a 'very bad' situation. By 18 June, G5 and G2 batteries had been made available to 61 Mechanised Battalion, and for several days artillery fire rained down on the Cubans. On 24 June, South African forces guarding Cuamato repulsed a combined FAPLA/Cuban force from Xangongo. The reaction teams from 201 Battalion lost several vehicles during this clash, but prevented the Cubans from occupying the town.

Colonel Delport opted for a major artillery strike to stop the Cuban forces at Techipa from advancing any closer to the border. Platoons from 32 Battalion, each with a forward observer, infiltrated the target area to direct the fire, and Major Hannes Nortmann was ordered to report to Ruacana with his four ZT3 Ratels by noon on 26 June, after which he joined 61 Mechanised Battalion in ambush positions 30 km south of Techipa.

The artillery bombardment began at 20h00, the first salvo destroying the Cuban artillery command post and thus preventing a counter-bombardment.

Two hours later, the big guns withdrew to safety to avoid being spotted by enemy aircraft the next day.

East of Techipa a platoon from Delta Company, led by Lieutenant TT de Abreu, came under attack from enemy tanks, and waged a running battle with FAPLA infantry over a distance of 20 km before being able to break off the contact under cover of deadly accurate artillery fire.

On the morning of 27 June, 61 Mechanised Battalion and the ZT3 Ratels returned to their ambush positions and ran into a strong Cuban force, led by tanks. A fierce battle erupted, and by 10h40 even elements of 32, who were not equipped for a conventional fight, were involved. Yet again the artillery offered a chance for 32 to withdraw, but with MiG 23s overhead firing at anything that moved, the gunners, too, were ordered to break contact, and by 12h55 had crossed the Cunene River. By late afternoon the South African tanks had also crossed the river.

Inexplicably, the Cubans called off their advance after this battle and withdrew back to Techipa. At 13h55, however, four MiG 23s bombed the Calueque Dam, followed ten minutes later by another three aircraft. Both the bridge and water pipeline suffered serious damage, and ten members of 8 SA Infantry Battalion were killed during this raid.

For 32 Battalion, 27 June held a special significance, as it marked the end of more than 12 years of continuous combat. In terms of the final peace agreement that led to independence for Namibia, some members of 32 would be deployed at Beacon 1 as part of the second Joint Monitoring Commission. But for the indomitable Buffalo Soldiers, the war was over. For the next five years, however, the unit with an exceptional record of victory in combat would fight as never before for the right to survive. It would be 32's most important battle ever – and they would lose.

11

Fighting till the end
TOWNSHIP DUTY 1989-1992

THE FIRST WHISPERS of radical change in the lives of 32 Battalion's men and their families were heard in August 1988. As a fully fledged member of the SA Defence Force, the unit could neither escape the promised withdrawal of all South African security forces from what would soon become the independent state of Namibia, nor return to the war-ravaged homeland they had left 12 years before.

The concept of relocation to an alien environment was nothing new to 32 Battalion. The members had, after all, quit Angola to settle in the Caprivi, many first spending time in refugee camps along the way. But the proposed move to South Africa was an entirely different prospect, and would demand not only physical removal from the place that had been 'home' for more than a decade, but mental and cultural adjustments to an entirely new way of life. No more would wild elephants lumber through the company lines on the way to waterholes, or the fish eagle's cry be heard at sunset. No longer would soldiers give lusty voice to feelings of pride and bravado or softly croon songs of love and melancholy on the eve of battles from which they might not return. Never again would a troop sing 'I am going to die in Angola, with my rifle in my hand' and know that he more than likely would.

Dramatic and demanding as the change would be, 32 Battalion had proved repeatedly over the years that with the necessary guidance and right leadership, they were more than capable of adapting to the dictates of any circumstance, learning the skills of their trade so thoroughly that they retired undefeated from the battlefields of Angola.

The problem, however, was that their 'trade' was war – specifically irregular or guerrilla bush war. What they would face in South Africa were densely populated residential areas aflame with pre-democracy violence, and urban warfare of a category for which 32 Battalion was both untrained and, it must be said, unsuitable. Instead of military camps, the new enemy would hide in hostels. Cuban tank crews would make way for balaclava-clad men who threw innocent commuters from moving trains. Barricades of burning rubble would take the place of landmines, and entire families, including babes in arms, would be massacred in their own beds while they slept. And for the first time in their careers, battle-hardened soldiers would experience at first hand the ultimate horror of the 'necklace' – tyres placed around the neck of men and women first drenched in petrol, then set alight while bloodthirsty agitators watched them burn alive.

Their prowess in the field had long since earned 32 Battalion the name of 'Os Terriveis' – the terrible ones – among SWAPO, FAPLA and the surrogate communist forces who feared and faced them almost daily, but it would take the tumescent township unrest to vilify the SADF's 'finest fighting force since World War II' as mercenaries and murderers.

At least some of the backlash against 32 Battalion's deployment in unrest areas was due to public and media ignorance about the unit. Even within the South African security forces, the existence of the Buffalo Soldiers had been top secret until 1981, when deserter Trevor Edwards ensured that the army of former FNLA supporters made the front page of international newspapers. For at least the first five years, when 81 of 32's 146 combat fatalities occurred, not a single black member was publicly named, while the identity of white members killed in battle was never linked to the unit in which they had served. After the Edwards debacle, the SADF allowed a number of journalists to visit Buffalo and write about this truly unique group of soldiers in broad terms, but none were privy to the incalculable contribution made by 32 to the South African war effort.

Consequently, there was little understanding within the media about the role or operations of the only SADF unit besides Special Forces that maintained a constant presence in Angola from the end of 1975 to the signing of a peace treaty in 1988.

One might, however, have expected the SADF itself to appreciate the full implications of placing a group of men who had consciously been turned into a highly efficient killing machine, in the volatile civilian milieu of a country in transition. With little more than perfunctory retraining – and even less attention to the political and psychological ramifications – soldiers taught to measure success by their kill ratio were unleashed on ANC comrades and Zulu warriors whose hearts *and* minds rejected any semblance of apartheid authority, let alone black troops of foreign origin supporting the last vestiges of the white regime.

Within a year of being moved to the abandoned mining town of Pomfret in the Northern Cape, 400 men who had cut their combat teeth against FAPLA,

SWAPO, thousands of Cubans and hundreds of Russians, but were about to be deployed in some of Natal's hottest 'unrest' zones, were simply told by SADF Chief General Jannie Geldenhuys: 'You are here to play a different role than the one you are used to. You are going to have to adapt. Be firm but friendly, decisive but impartial, and above all, just.'

Small wonder that damning reports of action taken by 32 began surfacing almost immediately. Never before had the unit encountered traditional chiefs and headmen who controlled the vast areas they were expected to patrol. Never before had they been forced to ask permission of the local chief to establish a temporary base, or even to enter specific tracts of unmarked land. Never before had the former Angolans come up against the concept of illegal marches or gatherings, or been expected to arrest those who fired shots into the air or the walls of buildings during political rallies. Their only experience of taking prisoners was limited to enemy captives, using whatever physical force was required.

It was thus inevitable that criminal arrests – the traditional province of trained policemen rather than war veterans in any event – were made with more than acceptable force, and that the local population grew to fear the men of 32 as much as SWAPO and its supporters had done. Equally predictable was the media onslaught against the alleged brutality and human rights abuses that were reportedly 32's stock in trade. In July 1988, 32 Battalion was still actively involved in patrolling the Cunene province as part of the Joint Monitoring Commission. A year later, their base amid the lush vegetation of the Caprivi had been exchanged for the stark and barren Kalahari Desert, and one of the SADF's most secretive units was about to become a household name.

Three months before the move to Pomfret, the unit was reorganised into the original rifle companies, the Support Group elements returning to their mother units. The companies were divided into two operational groups under command respectively of majors Louis Scheepers and Flip le Roux, who reported directly to Colonel Mucho Delport, the commander-in-chief.

Operational Group 1 consisted of Delta, Echo and Foxtrot companies, commanded by lieutenants Villiers de Vos and Wouter de Vos, and Captain Wally Vrey. Bravo, Charlie and Golf companies, under command of captains Keith Evans, Jo Maree and William Schickerling, made up Operational Group 2.

OPERATION PEBBLE

In August 1989, Operational Group 2 was deployed to the Soutpansberg Military Area in the far northern Transvaal to patrol the border between South Africa and Zimbabwe. One company was based at Madimbo and another at Vhembe, while the third was attached to Group 13 at Phalaborwa.

Border patrols as such were nothing new to the battalion, but whereas their

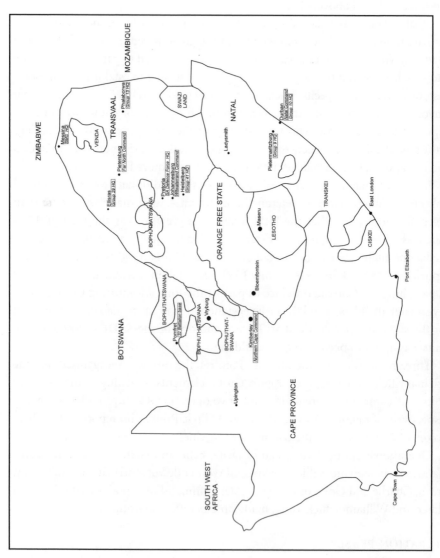

Pre-1994 South Africa, showing towns and areas relevant to 32 Battalion deployments from 1990

ZIMBABWE

MOZAMBIQUE

BOTSWANA

SOUTH WEST
AFRICA

TRANSVAAL

VENDA

Messina
Sida HQ

Phalaborwa
Group 13 HQ

SWAZI
LAND

NATAL

Durban
Natal Command
Group 10 HQ

Pietersburg
Far North Command

Ladysmith

Pietermaritzburg
Group 9 HQ

Ellisras
Group 24 HQ

Pretoria
SA Defence Force HQ
Johannesburg
Witwatersrand Command
Heidelberg
Group 41 HQ

East London

BOPHUTHATSWANA

ORANGE FREE STATE

Maseru

LESOTHO

TRANSKEI

CISKEI

Port Elizabeth

BOPHUTHATSWANA

Pomfret
32 Battalion base

Vryburg

BOPHUTHAT-
SWANA

Kimberley
Northern Cape Command

Bloemfontein

Upington

CAPE PROVINCE

Cape Town

task in South West Africa had been to pick up the spoor of SWAPO infiltrators, track and attack them, the quarry now was civilian illegal immigrants for the most part, and those who were found were to be apprehended and handed over to the police for repatriation.

The actual border also differed greatly from what the troops were used to. Across most of its considerable length, the border between South West Africa and Angola was little more than two faint dirt tracks, unfenced and unmarked. South Africa's northern border, on the other hand, was protected by a sturdy electrified fence along some stretches, an impenetrable sisal hedge along others, with wide and well-maintained roads on either side.

Occasionally, trained members of either MK (the African National Congress's armed wing) or APLA (military wing of the Pan Africanist Congress) would sneak across the border to carry out acts of urban terrorism against soft targets in the cities, or plant landmines on farm roads. In the middle of September, intelligence sources in Zimbabwe reported that a group of militants was planning to infiltrate South Africa east of Vhembe, where Echo Company was based.

The company commander, Lieutenant Wouter de Vos, sent Second Lieutenant Dirk van Straten's platoon to lay an ambush at the most likely crossing point, and in the early hours of 19 September the battalion notched up its first operational success inside South Africa, killing one guerrilla and wounding two more.

During the dry season it was not uncommon for local residents on both sides of the Limpopo River to walk across the sandy bed, regardless of the fact that the river's northern bank serves as an international boundary. As far as 32 was concerned, anyone in the riverbed was either trying to enter South Africa illegally, or was an enemy. On 22 November 1989, therefore, six members of the unit felt more than justified in apprehending Colin Bristow, a farmer from Sentinel Ranch in Zimbabwe, while he and his dog were hiking in the riverbed near Beit Bridge. Bristow was duly handed over to the South African Police at Messina, before being placed in the custody of Zimbabwe's Central Intelligence Organisation.

In late December a newspaper report appeared under the headline 'Border Snatch', in which Bristow claimed he had been abducted from his farm, shot at and assaulted. An investigation turned up no evidence to confirm his allegations, and in hindsight Bristow might well have been a pawn in the early stages of a well-organised propaganda war against 32 Battalion, since the ANC's opposition to the unit's presence and deployment in South Africa began around the same time.

At the beginning of December, Operational Group 1 had been withdrawn back to Pomfret and placed on standby as part of the larger Merlyn Force, which could be ordered to intervene if South West Africa was plunged into chaos in the run-up to independence. As it happened, the unit would never again be deployed in the neighbouring territory.

Early in January 1990 the group returned to the Soutpansberg military area, and once again patrolled the border in search of illegal immigrants.

OPERATION WINDMEUL

Towards the end of 1989, radical elements within the ANC launched a revolutionary onslaught against the so-called apartheid puppet states – the self-governing territories of Lebowa, Gazankulu, KwaZulu, Kwangane, Qwa-Qwa and KwaNdebele. None of them had their own military force, but various black units within the SADF had been undergoing training for some time in preparation for assuming this role when the remaining 'bantustans' elected to follow the example of the four existing independent homelands of Transkei, Venda, Bophuthatswana and Ciskei. When unrest broke out, the South African Army was mandated to operate independently of the police in acting against the agitators, and Echo Company was deployed under command of Group 13 in the Bushbuckridge and Acornhoek area of the Eastern Transvaal.

From a headquarters in the old stadium at Thulemahase, one of Gazankulu's most populous townships, they spent two months conducting *Windmeul* (windmill) – high visibility patrols as far south as Mkhuhlu. At the end of February, 113 Battalion took over these duties and 32 Battalion was sent to Natal.

THE SEVEN DAY WAR

Even before President FW de Klerk's historic speech on 2 February 1990, which unbanned organisations such as the ANC and PAC and instantly turned apartheid's enemies into partners in search of a peaceful solution to the escalating violence, Natal and KwaZulu were steeped in a vicious internecine war. The rivalry between the ANC and Chief Mangosuthu Buthelezi's Inkatha Freedom Party (IFP) was both bloody and out of control, and thousands would die in the battles and tit-for-tat massacres that marked the ongoing conflict over control of communities and geographical areas. Political intolerance – a euphemism for what was, in reality, a low-intensity war – reached its peak in the weeks following Nelson Mandela's release from prison after 27 years.

South Africa poured security forces into the province to deal with the violence, but more than 2 000 troops and hundreds of policemen were unable to stop the killing. By the end of March, Group 9's area of responsibility around Pietermaritzburg was swarming with traditional white SADF infantry battalions, as well as the Zulu battalion, 121.

Residents of the Edendale and Lower Vulindlela valleys south of Pietermaritzburg openly supported the pro-ANC United Democratic Front (UDF) and Congress of South African Trade Unions (Cosatu), while those of Upper Vulindlela tended to be more traditional and had thrown their political weight behind Inkatha. As the violence spread, UDF supporters frequently threw stones or fired gunshots at commuters from Upper Vulindlela, who had to pass through Edendale in order to reach Pietermaritzburg.

From 25 to 31 March, thousands of armed men invaded the Vulindlela and Edendale valleys. By the end of that bloody week, at least 200 people were dead, hundreds of houses had been looted and burned down, and up to 20 000 people had fled in terror from communities such as Ashdown, Caluza, Mpumuza, Gezubuso, KwaShange and KwaMnyandu.

A senior Inkatha official's warning sparked the Seven Day War, which he issued during a rally at Durban's King's Park Stadium on Sunday, 25 March – if buses travelling through Edendale were stoned again, action would be taken against the culprits. That very afternoon, buses ferrying supporters home from the rally were attacked, with numerous passengers injured, vehicles damaged and at least three people killed by the roadside.

Throughout the next day, when no buses ran from Vulindlela to Pietermaritz-burg, waves of armed men swept down from the hills, striking terror into the hearts of thousands as they went on the attack with pangas, assegais and guns. Unarmed community leaders tried to intervene before they, too, were forced to flee for their lives. On Tuesday, 27 March the violence intensified as groups of up to 2 500 Inkatha supporters swept down into the Edendale valley from Sweetwaters and Mpumuza, armed with both traditional Zulu weapons and firearms. That night, UDF supporters struck back against residents of Payiphini and Mpumuta, killing one person and setting 19 houses alight.

On Day 3 of the 'war', following a meeting between Inkatha officials and the police at Elandskop, a member of the riot squad took a group of special consta-bles to Gezubuso and instructed them to follow a large group of armed men on foot to KwaShange. Shortly afterwards, violence broke out in the eSigodini valley, leaving 35 people dead, 150 huts in flames and hundreds of people from Gezubuso, KwaShange and KwaMnyandu running for their lives.

At KwaShange, 15 people were killed, numerous houses destroyed and cattle driven into the veld by what eyewitnesses reported were special constables and armed Inkatha supporters. Members of the riot squad did nothing to halt the violence, after reportedly being warned by an Inkatha official not to interfere.

After a member of the Democratic Party and a journalist from the *Natal Witness* flew over the Vulindlela and Edendale valleys in a chartered light aircraft, the reporter wrote: 'By mid-morning the sight that confronted us was a war zone. Scores of houses were burning and the sky was filled with smoke from thatched roofs. We witnessed large groups of men and boys moving through the area. There were a number of dead, or what seemed to be dead, bodies lying on some of the roads and paths … Over Vulisaka and KwaShange and KwaMnyandu there was devastation and mayhem.'

Thursday, 29 March saw no let-up in the attacks, and late that night Khokhwane was targeted. The situation began to quieten down from the next day, and by Sunday, 31 March, when a large group of Inkatha supporters gathered at the homes of two prominent chiefs in the area, only sporadic incidents were reported.

Victims, eyewitnesses and peace monitors all alleged police complicity in the attacks, claiming that ANC supporters were shot at without provocation and that policemen had not only transported Inkatha militants to the affected areas, but had stood idly by while people were attacked and houses set alight. Special constables were singled out as actively participating in the violence on the side of Inkatha.

In 1995, Father Tim Smith, a missionary at Elandskop, described the devastating consequences of the 'Seven Day War' as follows: 'Drive out to Edendale past Esigodini up the hills to KwaMnyandu, KwaShange and Gezubuso. There, in a band of land about four kilometres wide, you will see the effects of destruction of that week of March 1990. Houses and shops burned to the ground, schools abandoned, weeds growing in fields and up through the insides of dwellings where a few years ago, thousands and thousands of people lived.'

In the immediate aftermath, politicians of all persuasions clamoured for the government to act against the perpetrators of the wholesale violence in Natal, but even as Buthelezi was demanding the withdrawal of all black troops from the hot spots on the grounds that they had sided with the ANC against Inkatha, Nelson Mandela was urging De Klerk to expand the SADF's role in combating the violence.

OPERATION EARDRUM

The 'Seven Day War' resulted in thousands of troops being sent to Group 9's area of responsibility from 1 April, when the first of 11 infantry companies was deployed in Natal. Probably the only black troops with no tribal or political affiliation to the warring factions were the men of 32 Battalion, and a decision was made to move the companies patrolling the Soutpansberg and Gazankulu to the Natal Midlands.

On 22 April, the 400 members of Operational Battalion 1, under command of Commandant Flip le Roux, were airlifted from Pomfret to the air force base at Durban. On the runway they were met by SADF chief General Jannie Geldenhuys, who delivered his stirring message about the need for the troops to be friendly, firm and fair. After a brief period of induction, the battalion moved into the heart of the unrest area. Almost as soon as they arrived, local ANC and UDF representatives were whipping the media into a frenzy over the deployment of 'foreign mercenaries' to combat urban unrest. Ironically, as the effect of their presence

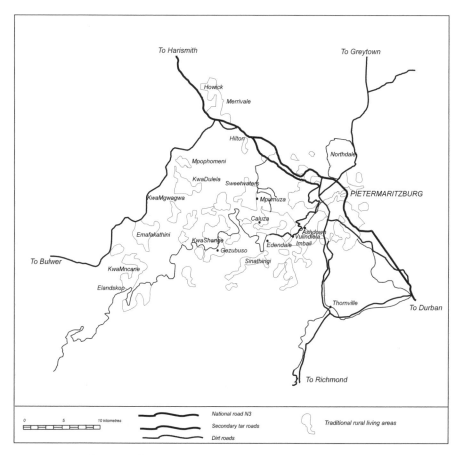

Operation Eardrum – area to the south-west of Pietermaritzburg

began to show and the violence diminished, the same politicians demanded that 32 stay on in certain areas, as they were clearly neutral and meted out the same treatment to members of both warring factions.

By the end of June the death toll from 'political violence' in the Edendale valley had dropped from 96 to 13 per month, while arson was down to an average of 12 incidents a month. When peace monitors visited the area, Major William Schickerling, a company commander, was able to stand on a mountain overlooking the valley and point out a large tract of land which had been a no-go area in April, but was now routinely crossed by IFP and ANC members alike, without incident.

OPERATION FIREFLY

From 29 April to 4 May, a series of attacks against Inkatha supporters turned the previously peaceful Enhlalakahle township near Greytown into a hot spot.

Homes were petrol-bombed, the mayor's shop was looted, and schools closed and pupils ordered not to return until Inkatha had moved out of the area. The commander of Group 9 realised that the violence could quickly escalate to the same level that had paralysed townships near Pietermaritzburg, and 32 Battalion's reconnaissance wing, led by Commandant GM Jacobs, was sent to Greytown on 5 May to assist the police in stabilising the area.

Jacobs proposed that two offensive teams of 12 troops and two SAP members each should patrol the township around the clock, while three teams of three men each manned observation posts to identify the most dangerous areas and report any suspicious activity to the patrols. It didn't take long for 15 young agitators to be identified and singled out for surveillance. Echo Company assisted in manning a roadblock and searching all vehicles entering or leaving the township for weapons, and by 24 May life in the township was back to normal. On 14 June, Mr JW Grabe, town clerk of Enhlalakale, sent a letter of thanks to 32 Battalion in which he made special mention of the 'unbiased and good behaviour' of the troops.

OPERATION PIKADEL
In September 1990 both Operational Battalions were moved from Pietermaritzburg to Heidelberg, south-east of Johannesburg, for deployment in Group 41's area of responsibility. *Pikadel*, which covered the entire region served by the Witwatersrand Command, was one of three special operations aimed at curbing the unrest gripping South Africa, the other two being *Eardrum* in Natal and *Phoenix* in the Eastern Cape.

During a single search operation in December, 32 found 18 AK47 rifles, ten handguns and more than 2 000 rounds of ammunition. By the end of January, 37 AKs, 22 handguns, nine hand grenades and more than 5 000 rounds had been confiscated.

The battalion's reconnaissance wing operated from headquarters at Esselen Park, conducting surveillance on hostels and individuals for days on end before specific operations were carried out. Early in February 1991, the companies moved from Alpha Base at Heidelberg and set up camp on a soccer field in the East Rand township of Thokoza. Earth walls surrounded the camp, and armed guards controlled access through the single entrance on a 24-hour basis.

Joint patrols with other SADF units were a regular feature of township deployment, and on 11 March, 32 was reunited with 1 Parachute Battalion for the first time since leaving South West Africa, when the troops provided back-up for the police during the search of an IFP-controlled hostel in Alexandra township north of Sandton.

The unit suffered its first operational casualty since moving to South Africa on 17 May, when Rifleman JA Sampaio was killed while patrolling a 'no-go' area

The province of Natal, with the different areas of responsibility for military groups 9, 10 and 27

in Thokoza. By this time the ANC's self-defence units regarded 32 Battalion as no less an enemy than Inkatha, and the feeling was largely mutual. Throughout the year the two operational groups, now known as 321 and 322 Battalion respectively, alternated township duty, despite a growing call by ANC politicians and residents of Thokoza for the unit to be withdrawn from the township.

From the end of November to the end of December, 321 Battalion was cast in the role of a guerrilla force during a military exercise, Sweepslag (whiplash), at the Army Battle School, Lohatla. Valuable lessons were taken from the exercise, and from this date on the unit formed part of the Army's Rapid Deployment Force and took part in various conventional exercises.

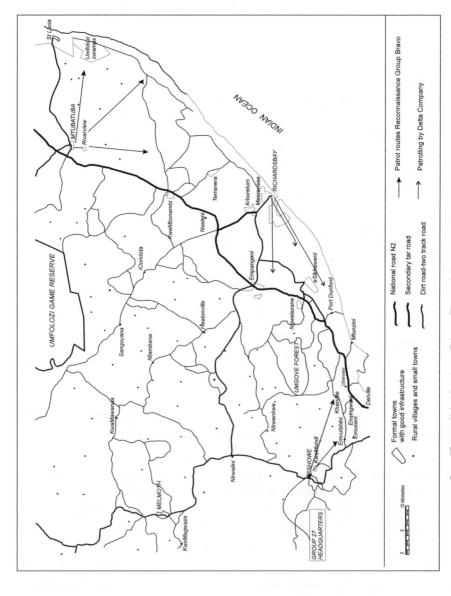

Group 27 area with headquarters at Eshowe. The map indicates the deployment destinations of the companies

OPERATIONS SABONA AND EXPOSE

With most of the unit at Lohatla, Bravo Company was deployed to Natal. Colonel Eddie Viljoen, former Officer Commanding 32, was now in command of Group 27 and had set up a communication network between his headquarters at Eshowe and the traditional Zulu chiefs, issuing them with radios to report any violent incidents. Group 27's area of responsibility covered a large rural area dominated by Inkatha supporters, who had a generally good relationship with the military.

As part of *Operation Sabona*, Bravo's second platoon was deployed around Melmoth early in December, while the first platoon was sent to Richards Bay. The third platoon set up camp at the Eshowe showgrounds as a reaction force.

Lieutenant C O'Connor's first platoon carried out daily patrols through Ntambababa, Heatonville, Eshikaweni and Inseleni, and routinely called on the local chief. The second platoon, led by Lieutenant E Fouche, concentrated on the areas around Yanguye and Nlumedi, and as part of *Operation Expose*, designed to make the military presence highly visible, the third platoon regularly called on tribal chiefs around Eshowe and on white farmers.

THE PHOLA PARK INCIDENT

During the first few months of 1992, opposition mounted steadily to 32's deployment as an urban anti-unrest force. Civilian peace monitors singled the unit out for special attention, closely watching each patrol and laying blame for high-profile incidents at the battalion's door, no matter what other military units might have been involved. As it happened, several incidents involving members of the battalion fed the growing call for their removal.

Thokoza was once again the base for 322 Battalion, which also began conducting routine patrols in the neighbouring informal settlement of Phola Park. On 28 February, one person was killed when police searched a hostel in Holomisa Park while 32 formed a cordon around the outer perimeter. Even though the dead man was found inside the hostel and nowhere near the battalion's position, 32 was blamed. Exactly a month later, shots were fired from a speeding car at a section of Golf Company patrolling Khumalo Street in Thokoza. The patrol set off in pursuit of the car, but their Buffel was unable to close the distance between the two vehicles, and when the car turned into a side road the patrol opened fire. They missed and the vehicle got away, but some of the bullets hit houses in the immediate vicinity, and the residents laid charges of damage to property with the police. An investigation turned up 25 spent AK47 cartridges at the site where the occupants of the car had originally fired on the Buffel.

By this time, armed members of Self Defence Units (SDUs), some dressed in military-style uniforms, were defiantly patrolling sections of the township. During a routine patrol in Holomisa Park, an SDU opened fire on a 32 patrol, and in the ensuing exchange a member of the SDU was killed and another wounded and handed over to the police.

After spending three months patrolling Katlehong, Golf Company was moved to Thokoza. Phola Park, some 1 500 m from their base as the crow flies, was in a state of total anarchy, and every time a patrol entered the settlement it was greeted by a hail of small-arms fire from the nearest shacks. The situation became so bad that the police refused to enter Phola Park to carry out any criminal investigations.

On 8 April, Golf Company's commander, Captain Mark Hermanson, was told by informers to expect faction fighting in Buthelezi and Dube streets in Thokoza. At 19h00 a section of 12 men and platoon leader Lieutenant Greyvenstein set off to patrol Dube Street on foot, while a second section, led by Sergeant A Mpande, moved to Buthelezi Street in a Buffel. At 20h30, the rest of the company heard automatic gunfire coming from Phola Park, but unlike the normal single shots, which they were used to, this sounded like a heavy weapon, possibly a 7,62 x 51 or 54-mm machine gun. Hermanson contacted both Greyvenstein and Mpande on the radio and ordered them to investigate.

Mpande's section arrived in Phola Park first, entering from the north at 20h45 past the Civic Association offices, which served as the ANC's headquarters. About 100 m into the settlement, Mpande stopped to ask shack residents for information about the shooting, but while climbing out of the Buffel backwards – the only way he could – he was shot in the back. His troops pulled him back into the vehicle and contacted the base to report the shooting at just about the same moment that Greyvenstein's foot patrol arrived and also came under fire. The Buffel sped off to seek help for the sergeant, while Greyvenstein and his men took cover behind piles of rubble, where they quickly found themselves pinned down.

At 21h00, Golf Company's second-in-command, Lieutenant Deon Eksteen, sent a platoon commanded by Lieutenant FR Ras to assist Greyvenstein's section, which was now coming under heavy fire. Ras and 45 men piled into five Buffels, and when they reached the outskirts of Phola Park made radio contact with Greyvenstein to determine his exact position. Ras realised that the Buffels would be at a disadvantage in the narrow thoroughfares between the shacks, so he and his men debussed behind the Civic Association offices. He instructed the drivers to take the vehicles to the soccer field south of the settlement to wait for their return.

The patrol ran towards the scene of the ambush in single file, Ras leading and Lieutenant van der Mescht bringing up the rear. Greyvenstein's section was pinned down in an alley, and as soon as Ras turned the corner into it, he saw the flash of at least six automatic weapons. As he dropped to his right knee, he indicated the target area by firing a tracer round. The platoon opened fire, and about 30 minutes later, as the opposing fire died down, both Ras and Greyvenstein fired signal flares to indicate that their troops should cease firing.

While Greyvenstein's section withdrew to the Civic Association offices, the company commander instructed Ras by radio to have his men conduct a sweep of the area to locate any dead, wounded or weapons. Stretched out over about 150 m, the troops began moving south-west towards the soccer field, but when Ras realised that the density of the shacks would make it impossible to control the line, he divided the men into groups of five, each with a section leader and radio.

From the far left of the line, Van der Mescht signalled Ras by radio that an unarmed man had approached his group and offered to lead them to the shack where the weapons used against them had been hidden. Ras joined Van der Mescht's group and followed the informer to a house, which was locked and appeared empty. The company commander gave Ras permission to break down the door and search the house. They found no weapons, but did discover a secret hiding place behind a cupboard.

For the next 45 minutes the area was thoroughly searched, but no dead, wounded or weapons were found, and the platoon returned to base at 23h00. From midnight to 03h00, Van der Mescht's section patrolled the outskirts of Phola Park. At 06h00, Ras returned to the alley where Greyvenstein had been pinned down and recovered 23 spent AK47 shells, and 175 casings from R4 ammunition. Ten bullet marks were found on the Buffel in which Sergeant Mpande had been shot. Fortunately he survived the attack after being treated at Natalspruit Hospital. At a debriefing on the night's events, Corporal Joseph and eight other members of Golf Company acknowledged that they had probably exercised undue force against some Phola Park inhabitants during the search of the shacks, and had slapped some residents who refused to cooperate. Three days later, amid damning allegations in the media, Golf Company was withdrawn from Phola Park, but it would take an investigation and a 672-page report by the Goldstone Commission (see Chapter 12) to clarify the events of that fateful night.

OPERATION EXPOSE

The Phola Park incident marked the end of 32 Battalion's deployment in urban areas, and for some companies signalled a return to border patrols. Delta Company, however, was redeployed to Group 27's area in Natal to take part in *Operation Expose*.

On 5 June the third platoon was deployed as a reaction force at Bluegum Park near Richards Bay, the second platoon was sent to the Matshana township, and the first platoon was assigned to KwaDengesa township and the University of Zululand. These were all traditional Inkatha strongholds, but radical ANC youths had begun recruiting members in these areas and tension was rising.

On 10 June, General Kat Liebenberg, Chief: SADF, paid a routine visit to Group 27. When he realised that a company from 32 Battalion had again been deployed in an urban role, he ordered their immediate withdrawal and return to Pomfret. Two days later, Delta Company was on the way back to the Northern Cape.

Slowly but surely, the ANC increased its sphere of influence in the rural areas served by Group 27. Recruitment drives and rallies were the order of the day, and it was all but impossible for military informers to infiltrate the local ANC structures and keep tabs on their actions.

On 2 November, two of 32 Battalion's reconnaissance groups were brought in as part of *Expose*. Known as Alpha and Bravo, each group consisted of three mini-teams of three members each and two offensive teams of 11 members each. They were trained and armed to take part in any action that could arise. In addition to the R5 rifle carried by each man, including the driver and medical orderly, two troops each had an SS 77 light machine gun, two had a 60-mm mortar, and two had an RPG 7 rocket launcher. Alpha Group, commanded by Captain P Eloff and Staff Sergeant G Riekert, deployed to Bizane Park at Richards Bay, while Bravo Group, commanded by Captain G Scheepers and Sergeant Major A de Abreu, remained at Eshowe.

On 5 November, various groups were sent out on specific missions. The mini-team of Lance Corporal J Paulus went to Nsingweni to carry out routine reconnaissance and observe activity at a shop owned by a suspected ANC militant. When they returned three days later, all they had to report was routine shopping expeditions.

Second Lieutenant CS Pepper's mini-team left at 18h40 on 5 November for Obanjani, 12 km west of Mtunzini, to set up surveillance on the home of a chief where an ANC meeting was scheduled to take place. The next day and night passed without incident, barring a single gunshot fired south-east of the observation post at 21h35. At 06h35 on 7 November, 15 women dressed in white shirts and black dresses moved to a gathering place just beyond the home of the chief. At 10h45, 200 people, who had arrived in buses, joined them. The meeting ended by 16h35, and for no apparent reason several gunshots were heard from different directions between that time and 18h45. Even more unusual was the sound of a large group of people passing south of the observation post at 20h35. These were troubled times and local residents did not normally walk around after dark.

At 12h10 on 8 November another 100 people met at the chief's house, leaving at 14h15. At 15h20, three children discovered the observation post, but the team leader decided not to move to a new position. At 17h20 a group of 16 youths, aged between 15 and 19 and all carrying sticks and traditional weapons, were spotted moving up the hill towards the observation post. The team leader decided it was time to leave, and by 20h40 the men were on their way back to their base.

Second Lieutenant D Beukes's team was despatched to the Emuseni area 22 km west of Mtunzini to monitor activity at a specific school. Nothing happened on the first night, and at 22h00 on 6 November the team moved to a new position 800 m away. At 09h25 on 7 November, two children spotted them, and because the operation was compromised the team withdrew back to base.

Corporal D Boshoff's team was also sent to Nsingweni to monitor an ANC rally. The first visitors began arriving at 18h30 on 6 November, and at 07h30 the next day buses brought hundreds more. By 09h30, 14 buses were parked outside the meeting ground, and by 10h45 about 1 500 people were present. At 11h45 the speakers arrived in a convoy of eight cars, and by 19h30 it was all over without a single incident having taken place.

OPERATION JAYCEE

Old comrades were reunited when 1 Parachute Battalion's anti-tank section was detached to reconnaissance group Bravo before it was deployed in the Sokhulu area on 16 November. Led by Captain Scheepers, they set up their headquarters at Umkombe Commando, Mtubatuba.

One of the consequences of the Goldstone Commission's inquiry into what happened at Phola Park was the appointment of incident monitors to report on the deployment of all security forces in Natal. Because the police and incident monitors were engaged in a crime prevention operation in the precise area where the reconnaissance teams intended deploying, they waited until 18 November. On 26 November two suspicious looking men were spotted watching the home of a local chief from a nearby plantation. The KwaMbonambi police were notified, and the two men were arrested.

The next day, information was received about an illegal firearm behind a shop known as Benade Stores. Investigation turned up not a gun but a petrol bomb, which was destroyed. Routine patrols east and south of Mtubatuba continued until 11 December, when the reconnaissance groups returned to Pomfret. Three months later, 32 Battalion would cease to exist.

12

We came, we go

RELOCATION AND DISBANDMENT

BY MARCH 1989, South West Africa was irrevocably set on the road to independence, and a year later South Africa, too, would take the first steps towards democratic majority rule. Peace would continue to elude war-ravaged Angola for years to come, but the SA Defence Force had fired its last salvo in what would ultimately degenerate into little more than Jonas Savimbi's personal vendetta against his political rivals.

Withdrawal of South African security forces from the battlefields of the Border War carried with it an inherent obligation towards those with whom alliances had been formed, especially the Bushmen and the remnants of Holden Roberto's FNLA. Unfortunately, military and government authorities responsible for incorporating these two groups into the SADF had done so with as little foresight as the police generals and cabinet ministers who endorsed the use of *askaris* – former SWAPO insurgents – in Koevoet. To those involved at the time, assurances that allies would not be abandoned to their fate would have been both a logical and honourable solution to a problem that no one anticipated having to actually deal with for several years to come.

But over the course of the conflict, such promises were inherited by a succession of commanders, and it is entirely likely that none of those who originally authorised the incorporation of indigenous groups from a foreign country into South Africa's security forces was still around when it came time to make good on the promises. As it happened, the discharge of this solemn duty coincided with one of the most tumultuous periods in South Africa's history, when one shocking revelation after another about the illegal activities of a few, relatively small covert units rubbed off on the security forces as a whole, and attempted cover-ups eroded public faith in both the integrity of the military and the credibility of the police.

Nonetheless, the Bushmen of 31 Battalion, resettled at the former military test range of Schmidtsdrift near Kimberley, and the Angolans of 32 might have expected a more equitable deal than being moved to a hostile environment in remote corners of South Africa, then finding themselves redundant within a few short years.

On 1 March 1989, Commandant Robbie Hartslief, Captain Martin Geldenhuys and Foxtrot Company travelled from Buffalo to Pomfret to pave the way for the rest of the battalion and their dependants. What they found was a ghost town, overgrown with weeds and waist-high grass, the buildings sadly in need of maintenance, the roads barely visible.

Within eight weeks the dustbowl previously inhabited by asbestos miners would be bursting at the seams, and by 1 May the costliest exercise ever undertaken by the battalion would be over. In a logistical nightmare, 11 passenger trains, one leaving every five days, would each ferry 400 people 3 000 km from Grootfontein to Vryburg, from where they were taken to Pomfret by bus. Three C130 aircraft would carry unmarried members from Omega to Kimberley, and 76 civilian trucks would each transport 30 tons of equipment to the new base. In addition, a fleet of private vehicles would carry the household goods of families to Pomfret.

The media speculated that the cost of relocating the battalion was around R32 million, but in fact the final cost was never disclosed and is not recorded in the unit's archives.

In many ways, it was as if the clock had been turned back 13 years to the exodus from Angola to Pica Pau. Nothing had been done in advance to provide enough housing for the families, and 700 of them were accommodated in ten sprawling tent towns – some for 18 months – while 800 new houses were added to the existing residential area at a cost of R30 million.

Pomfret's layout was typical of a company mining-town, with separate facilities for the various population groups, and although the SADF allocated housing in terms of rank, this happened to mirror the racial mix of the battalion. Officers were given houses in the traditionally 'white' section of the town, while warrant and senior non-commissioned officers moved into the former 'coloured' township. Junior NCOs occupied the erstwhile 'black' area, while the majority of junior leaders and troops were consigned to tents. Single members were housed in the mining compound, which was quickly organised along company lines.

Education was a priority, and three schools were quickly established: Educar, with lessons in English and Portuguese from Sub A to Standard 2; Pomfret Primary, catering for white Afrikaans-speaking pupils; and Pica Pau, with tuition in English from Standard 3 to Standard 10. Teachers from Buffalo were once again drafted into service, while the Department of Education provided additional staff and took over administration of the schools, which meant textbooks were more freely available and the system was brought in line with provincial norms.

By 23 September, when the base was officially opened by SADF Chief General Jannie Geldenhuys, all the existing houses were occupied, the church was in use, and the sports facilities were well maintained. Streets had been named for commanding officers and regimental sergeants major as a tribute to their role in building the battalion. However, neither Sergeant Major PW van Heerden nor Sergeant Major Piet Nortje had been honoured in this manner, and when asked why, current commanders were vague, eventually falling back on the excuse that neither had served 'officially' as RSM. How anyone could spend almost three years serving *unofficially* in such a high-profile post was never explained, but the omissions caused a number of former unit members to lose confidence in the ability of their successors to fully grasp the history of this unique unit, and to question their commitment in any future fight for 32's survival.

From 1990, troops not deployed on internal operations spent their time working on improvements to the base. The contrast between the thousands of trees surrounding Buffalo and the stark landscape in which Pomfret lay spurred members to introduce environmental programmes, and the first tree-planting project was launched within months. By the end of September, the tent town inhabitants could start moving into proper homes in the new development named Esperança, the Portuguese word for *hope*, which was officially opened on 14 November by SA Army Chief Lieutenant General Georg Meiring. It was only at this stage that the military authorities acknowledged that it was neither practical nor possible for families to make the 420-km round trip by road each month to do their shopping in Vryburg, the nearest town of any consequence, and launched negotiations for a SADFI branch at the base. It opened on 29 January 1991, and helped considerably to ease the plight of a community far removed from basic consumer facilities. All fresh produce, meat and milk was bought from farmers surrounding the 5 000-ha base, who were delighted to have new neighbours with money to spend.

On 21 May, members of the 32 Battalion Association visited Pomfret and attended the parade to mark the 11th anniversary of Savate Day. On 17 August, tragedy struck when Major Martin Geldenhuys, eldest son of the SADF chief, was killed during advanced parachute training at the airstrip. He had enlisted in the SADF in 1984 and joined 32 Battalion from the Infantry School at Oudtshoorn. After graduating from the Military Academy he returned to 32 in 1989, and for a while he and his younger brother, Bruwer, served in the unit together. Bruwer left the SADF in 1990, but Martin stayed on and at the time of his death was a member of 32's reconnaissance group. He was standing at the end of the runway to photograph a Dakota taking off when the accident happened. For some reason, the aircraft was sluggish and took longer than usual to become airborne. As it passed over Martin's head, he was hit by a propeller.

He had specified in his will that he wanted to be buried alongside his comrades from the unit. On 24 August, he was buried with full military honours in the cemetery at Pomfret, the first white member of 32 Battalion to be laid to rest there.

Cocooned in the Caprivi for more than a decade, the expatriate Angolans thrived on the interaction with both the civilian community and other military communities offered by life in Pomfret. One of the first social events was a *potjiekos* (food cooked in a three-legged pot over coals) competition organised by Northern Cape Command, while the inaugural concert presented by pupils from Pomfret Primary School was extremely well supported.

From the outset, the Kempton Park Town Council, which had long-standing ties with the SADF, acted as adviser on management of the town. As a result of the close ties between this local authority and the unit, 32 Battalion was afforded the freedom of entry to Kempton Park on 21 September 1991. The year also saw a visit from Daniel Chipenda, who had abandoned his FNLA supporters in 1975 and embraced the bright lights of Europe. Since 1989, Chipenda had served as Angola's ambassador in Egypt, and members of the unit regarded his arrival at Pomfret on 7 December, accompanied by a senior SADF officer, with suspicion. Although Chipenda claimed he was visiting in his private capacity, he spent the entire time trying to persuade the men to return to Angola. They would, he assured them, encounter 'absolutely no spirit of reprisal'.

Although they had not yet seen fit to inform 32 of their decision, the politicians in Pretoria had already decided by this stage that the battalion was an unnecessary evil, a problem that could prove a stumbling block on the road to negotiated democracy. Voluntary repatriation would provide an ideal solution, both from the viewpoint of the SADF, which no longer knew what to do with troops qualified to do nothing except wage highly effective guerrilla warfare, and the South African politicians, who seemed willing to make just about any concession demanded by the ANC government-in-waiting.

On 20 December the Portuguese publication *Diario de Noticias* reported the following about Chipenda's visit to Pomfret: 'Holden Roberto, once again living in the capital of Angola (as he did in 1975 after the Alvor Agreement), and who is getting ready for the 1992 electoral campaign, has opened an office in Luanda to enlist voters. The FNLA needs to fill the vacancies for cadres, and 32 Battalion would be an ideal choice as peacemaker for the movement, a source of voters, and would bring new blood into its ranks.'

Whatever the truth behind Chipenda's visit, his attempt to lure former Roberto supporters back to their homeland failed, and 32 remained intact – for the moment.

Assurances that their former opponents in Angola would not seek revenge were never tested, but the same could not have been said of SWAPO. Within the first year of Namibia's independence, the war cemetery left behind at Buffalo was desecrated, the simple white crosses marking the graves of men who died in battle kicked over and destroyed. In February 1991, Namibia's Deputy Minister of Works, Transport and Communication, Klaus Dierks, confirmed that 'an organised and wilful destruction' had laid Buffalo Base – renamed Bagani – in ruins before it could be used to resettle destitute people from other rural areas.

In April 1991 another name change had occurred, and the unit was now divided into 321 and 322 Battalion. The Support Company was also split between the two, with Sergeant van Vuuren transferred to 321 and Second Lieutenant Mark Carrington to 322. The old headquarters company became known as the Support Wing.

On 27 March 1992 the SA Army's biggest medal parade ever took place at Pomfret, with 2 015 medals being awarded to unit members. On 3 April the town of Vryburg emulated Kempton Park and bestowed freedom of entry on the unit, but the ceremony was marred by the first public signs of opposition, with protesters along the route brandishing posters demanding '32 Bn Go Back To Angola'.

Pressure was also mounting on the politicians to rid South Africa of the controversial unit, and at a parade in July 1992, members were officially informed that it was going to be disbanded.

Ironically, at least part of the reason for the unit's demise was its wider exposure to the media and general public as a result of deployment in unrest areas. For most of its lifespan, 32 was shielded from external influence, but the urban battlefields of Natal and the East Rand were fertile breeding grounds for political factions jockeying for power in the emerging 'new' South Africa, and unit members doing duty in these areas were not immune to radical agitators. For the first time in its history, 32 had to deal with internal accusations of racism and political partisanship. The media onslaught ranged from allegations of unit funds being mismanaged to specific instances of discrimination.

The unrest in Natal had reached an apex in May 1990, when 321 Battalion was first deployed around Pietermaritzburg. By September, single-sex hostels on the East Rand, mainly inhabited by migrant Zulu workers, had become the springboard for Inkatha's campaign to garner national support and shed the perception that its power base was strictly regional.

The conflict spread rapidly to townships throughout the densely populated PWV (Pretoria–Witwatersrand–Vereeniging) region, with several bloody massacres in the dead of night carried out by Inkatha militants against township residents, and running street battles an almost daily occurrence.

From the ANC side, the greatest evils were perpetrated by the paramilitary Self-Defence Units (SDUs), set up to 'respond to the grassroots demand for protection', but liberally supported and supplied by MK after the ANC officially suspended the armed struggle. By the end of 1990, SDUs were effectively controlling townships in the PWV region and Eastern Cape.

The direct links between MK and the SDUs were confirmed in the following extract from the ANC's submission to South Africa's Truth and Reconciliation Commission: 'Various clandestine units for the training and organisation of SDUs were set up, and some cadres were tasked to provide weaponry where possible ... Selected members of MK, including senior officials from the command structures, were drawn into an ad hoc structure to assist with the arming of units ... We do not have a record of MK's role in SDUs since they were not HQ controlled structures.'

On 9 April 1992, the day after Sergeant Mpande was shot in the Phola Park ambush, newspapers carried 32 Battalion's death warrant. One report, under the headline 'Midnight Mayhem', alleged that two people had been killed, 100 injured and a woman raped during 32's 'rampage' through the township the night before. One media conference followed another, but despite the fact that all members of the unit were withdrawn from the East Rand within three days, there was no respite. The situation was not helped by Defence Minister Roelf Meyer telling the media that troops had indeed overstepped the bounds of acceptable force, and that a full-scale inquiry would be conducted into the Phola Park incident.

THE GOLDSTONE COMMISSION

On 29 April 1992 the Thokoza Committee of Judge Richard Goldstone's Commission on the Prevention of Public Violence and Intimidation called the first witness at a hearing to determine why 32 Battalion had entered Phola Park on the night of 8 April, whether members had committed any offences, been provoked or were guilty of any misconduct during the time they spent there. Advocate MNS Sithole, assisted by Miss L Baqwa and Mr B Tucker, chaired the commission.

Golf Company's commander Captain Mark Hermanson, who had sent the patrols into Phola Park, was grilled for three days by counsel for the township residents over allegations of 'heavy-handed' action by the troops, why they had entered the township unaccompanied by police and the admissions of nine members during debriefing that they had applied undue force. Hermanson was unable to explain how, shortly after the operation, 'so many people with such severe injuries' had presented themselves at the nearest hospitals and clinics for treatment.

Lieutenant FR Ras, who had gone to the rescue of Lieutenant Greyvenstein's men under fire, came in for equally blistering cross-examination.

An identification parade, attended by the media, had previously been held at the Phola Park Community Centre, where a woman who accused him of raping her pointed out Corporal Joseph. The eight other unit members who had already admitted to 'heavy-handed' action were also identified. Interestingly, when Joseph switched his position in the line-up, twice, his accuser was unable to recognise him.

On 7 May the sole witness among residents of Phola Park was called to testify. John Msimango had been interviewed and photographed by the *Sunday Times* on 12 April, when he claimed to have been shot in both legs during the incident, which also claimed the life of his wife. Statements from 70 other Phola Park residents who claimed to be victims of brutality were also handed to the committee.

Msimango, who lived in Zola Section of Phola Park, testified that the shooting had started in A Section. Cross-examination by lawyers representing 32 Battalion and the Minister of Defence produced a number of crucial contradictory statements before it was cut short by the chairman of the committee.

On 9 May, Sergeant Jan Olivier, the policeman who had investigated allegations following the incident, testified that in his experience the events of 8 April had been typical of the situation prevailing in Phola Park at the time, with residents constantly goading security force patrols, taking potshots at them and at private vehicles, setting private vehicles alight and assaulting people at will. Every day in Phola Park, said Olivier, was like 'a small war'.

Residents had tried to suggest that this particular incident had been an isolated event, but Olivier was adamant that attacks on the security forces were a general occurrence. Statistics were presented to show that from 10 to 29 April there had been 13 'significant' incidents of violence in Phola Park, which had a population of 22 000, compared to six similar incidents in neighbouring Thokoza, which was home to 400 000 people. Of the 34 violent incidents in the entire Kathlehong–Vosloorus complex, with more than one million inhabitants, 13 had taken place in Phola Park.

Asked what would be likely to happen if the police entered Phola Park in search of a stolen vehicle, Olivier said there was a 'great possibility' that any police vehicle entering the township would be shot at, as had happened on numerous previous occasions, with policemen being killed.

The committee was furnished with photographs showing house No. L251, badly damaged by rifle fire, and another 16 houses, which had been hit by bullets. The house belonged to Msimango, and Olivier confirmed that the body of a woman had been found in it.

Among the most important evidence presented were the medical reports obtained from Natalspruit Hospital. Of the more than 100 people the media alleged had sought treatment after the incident, only five reports related directly to the events of 8 April.

Lieutenant Ras was recalled and asked to comment on a written statement from Prince Mhlambe, an ANC community leader in Phola Park, who stated that: '32 Battalion is the only SADF unit with which I had a good relationship, and 32 Battalion was the only unit I ever went to see in Phola Park.' Ras confirmed that he knew Mhlambe and had enjoyed a good relationship with him until December 1991, when Mhlambe left Phola Park. Since then, Ras said, 'no one' had known who was in control of the township.

The chairman of the inquiry allowed testimony from a secret witness – almost certainly an SDU member – who claimed that there were no heavy calibre weapons in Phola Park, only AK47 rifles and handguns, that no weapons were hidden in Phola Park but were brought in from Thokoza when needed, that SDU members regularly test-fired their weapons in A Section, and that security forces were legitimate targets for attack by SDUs.

After hearing all the evidence, lawyers for Phola Park residents and the ANC's regional committee argued that 32 Battalion had failed to provide any justification for the acts of violence committed. The unit was castigated for acting without police support, and the committee was asked to find that 32 Battalion was guilty of 'gross acts of impropriety' and should be removed from policing duties 'forthwith'. The advocate acting for the Minister of Defence argued that no evidence of improper behaviour had been placed before the committee, and that there were no grounds for accusations that 32 Battalion was not capable of dealing with urban unrest.

The battalion's legal representative emphasised that members of the unit had gone to investigate the source of the initial gunfire in accordance with regulations governing maintenance of law and order in declared unrest areas, of which Phola Park was one. The law courts should deal with the few members who admitted that their handling of some residents might have been 'heavy-handed' – a suggestion supported by counsel for the Minister of Law and Order and the SA Police.

In a 672-page report dated 2 June, the Goldstone Commission found that the battalion had been provoked and attacked by unknown forces, but that certain individuals were guilty of misconduct. Subsequently, a number of civil claims brought against those members were dismissed by the Attorney-General, while others were settled out of court.

Given the timing and adverse publicity that accompanied the Goldstone hearings, it is entirely likely that the announcement in July 1992 that 32 Battalion was to be disbanded was hastened by the Phola Park affair. Members of the unit were to be reassigned to 7 SA Infantry Battalion at Phalaborwa, 111 Battalion at Ermelo, 61 Mechanised Battalion at Lohatla and 1 Parachute Battalion at Bloemfontein. The end came on 26 March 1993, the 17th anniversary of the unit's birth, in the form of a massive and highly emotional parade. Founder members in particular were distraught that the era of the Buffalo Soldiers was over, and SADF Chief General Georg Meiring's speech was interrupted for several minutes when one of the early members, Lieutenant Gert Kruger, marched onto the parade ground and told the assembled troops in Portuguese and in no uncertain terms that they had been misled and let down by the South African government. It would have taken little for the troops to respond in kind, as the majority already felt they were facing a dark and uncertain future, but a group of Kruger's colleagues removed him before the situation got out of hand.

That night, however, feelings of bitterness and betrayal reached boiling point, and with the approval of the unit's founding father, Colonel Jan Breytenbach, Commandant Willem Ratte and a group of 32 veterans gathered together 30 R1 coins and placed them in a small black fabric bag made for just this purpose by Ratte's wife Zanzi. The group tried to present the bag to Colonel Mucho Delport, the last Officer Commanding 32, but he refused to accept it. Harsh words and accusations were exchanged before Major Nandes Kirsten, a serving member of the unit, defused the situation by pointing out that Delport was not the man to blame, and that he had merely carried out orders based on decisions made by the politicians.

Breytenbach and another former commanding officer, Brigadier Gert Nel, managed to calm the angry men down, but that was by no means the last of those 30 pieces of silver.

Ratte contacted Louis Bothma, a former platoon commander with 32 and an outspoken critic of what was seen as the National Party's capitulation to their former enemies, and asked him to ensure that the coins be handed to President FW de Klerk. In a letter published on 5 April in the Bloemfontein newspaper *Die Volksblad*, Bothma minced no words about his contempt for the way in which the government had 'solved' the problem of 32 Battalion. He was especially scathing about the fact that not a single cabinet minister had attended the final parade, pointing out that Hernus Kriel (Minister of Law and Order) had been in Botswana for talks with APLA, and that Roelf Meyer (Minister of Defence) was 'relaxing at Kyalami' with the ANC's chief negotiator, Cyril Ramaphosa, on the day.

Shortly afterwards, and again in consultation with Colonel Breytenbach, Bothma approached Dr Willie Snyman, Conservative Party MP for Pietersburg, who agreed to present both the bag of coins and a list of all 32 Battalion's fallen members to De Klerk in Parliament.

On 20 April, Snyman was as good as his word, but the president refused to accept the symbols of betrayal. The bag was removed by a parliamentary official and locked in a safe. Later, Bothma demanded that it be returned to him, and it was, without any problem.

Jan Breytenbach, never a man to call a shovel a spade, vented his disgust over the shameful treatment of the unit in a series of letters and articles published in various newspapers. In one particularly vituperative attack on the politicians and military leaders of the day, he wrote angrily:

The sacrifices, the battle wounds, deaths and terrible disabilities are of very little account in the minds of the president, his ministers and, it must be added, the present chief of the SADF. How can anyone in his right mind trust these morally bankrupt people ... an exceedingly corrupt bunch of manipulators to whom moral principles mean little? Our government callously throws the soldiers and families of 32 Battalion to the wolves ... [showing] a lack of understanding ... of the unique culture, *esprit d'corps* [*sic*] and pride among all men, black and white, who are serving or have served in 32 Battalion ... the most exceptional unit that ever existed in the SADF.

That disbandment of the unit was a hasty and ill-conceived decision became apparent almost at once. Relocation of members to other SADF units was a shambles – 190 men sent to 7 SA Infantry Battalion suddenly found themselves separated from their families by almost 1 000 km, as there was no housing available at Phalaborwa. Complaints were fobbed off with assurances that as soon as the men themselves had forged ties with the Portuguese members of 5 Reconnaissance Regiment, their families would be relocated. It never happened, because it is simply not in the nature of Special Forces units to go about things that way.

Similar lack of planning applied to other units as well, and within a few months most of 32 Battalion's members were back at Pomfret, where their families had remained, with no immediate prospect of full integration at any SADF base. By the end of 1994, only 300 former 32 members were serving with other units. The rest had been used to form the nucleus of 2 SA Infantry Battalion, disbanded after South Africa handed the enclave of Walvis Bay over to independent Namibia, but reactivated to accommodate what was fast becoming one of the 'new' SADF's biggest headaches. The interim solution, it seemed, was to keep the 'Portuguese mercenaries' together in one group, with most of the leader group firmly in place, as long as they were given a new name. But it was not until late 1996 that other soldiers, including members of the former liberation armies, would boost the ranks of 2 SAI.

Before and after that date, however, many of the original 32 Battalion members chose rather to quit the SADF, taking severance packages and accepting the challenges of civilian life elsewhere in South Africa, particularly in the burgeoning private security industry. Some enlisted with Executive Outcomes, the much maligned mercenary force, and found themselves fighting wars all over Africa, even back in Angola where their former enemies, the MPLA, were now their employers. Those who remained in the SA National Defence Force have fared well, some attaining the rank of senior officers.

The decades of strife in Angola claimed an estimated 500 000 lives, displaced some 3,5 million people and totally destroyed both the economy and civil society. Even though they migrated to the Caprivi as early as 1976, the members of 32 Battalion were no less victims than those who remained in Angola throughout the war, only in peacetime to face starvation and the daily peril of an estimated 70 000 landmines left behind by the various military forces. The unvarnished truth is that 32 Battalion was born of a power struggle in one land, only to perish in the political maelstrom of another.

And perhaps the most fitting epitaph for the group hailed as South Africa's finest fighting force before it was relegated to the ranks of a pariah, is a line from one of the unit's traditional songs, 'Buffalo Weya', which simply says: 'We came, we go.'

Brother remember me
ROLL OF HONOUR

IN KEEPING WITH military tradition dating back centuries, a memorial was erected to pay tribute and homage to those members of 32 Battalion who had made the supreme sacrifice. As with so much else that made this unit unique, the memorial is not only one of a kind, but was constructed of material far more representative of 32's genesis than any brass or marble edifice could ever be.

Early in 1983 Colonel Eddie Viljoen, Officer Commanding, decided that some form of monument to the fallen should be erected at Buffalo. A Citizen Force sergeant major, Horst Urbing, was assigned to scour the unit's training terrain for a suitable leadwood stump, of which one side was sliced off to provide a smooth surface on which silver plaques could be mounted as required. Erected outside the 'Palácio Regimental', the unit commander's billet, the memorial became known as the Tree of Honour. Two years later, it was moved to a new position opposite the mess, more accessible to unit members and more suitable for the holding of memorial services. At the same time, natural rock from the area was used to construct a 400-mm high wall around the tree, with sentry posts at each corner.

The first of many memorial services at the tree was held on Savate Day in 1985. When the unit relocated to Pomfret in 1989, the Tree of Honour was mounted on a marble plinth and formed part of the permanent parade ground podium. Plaques mounted on the stump itself honour only those killed in action during the Angolan war, or who died from combat wounds. Plaques set into the surrounding wall remember those who died of other causes or after the move to Pomfret. The names were updated yearly on 27 March, the anniversary of the unit's official formation.

Unfortunately, the names of those who died fighting with Battle Group Bravo during *Operation Savannah* and in other action before the unit was officially formed are not recorded on the Tree of Honour, simply because circumstances during those few turbulent months did not allow for proper paperwork. But their deaths are no less significant for the lack of public recognition.

Every man who died under the banner of 32 Battalion gave his life in service of South Africa. This was the SA Defence Force's 'foreign legion', and these are the unsung heroes of the Border War. When the men whose names appear on this Roll of Honour were killed in combat, only their comrades mourned, only their brothers in arms witnessed the sorrow of loved ones left behind.

At the going down of the sun, and in the morning, we will remember them.

1976
Rfn J Cardoso
Rfn B Domingos
Rfn M Mavuato
Lt CJ Swart
Sgt D Roxo
Sgt C da Silva
Sgt R Ribeiro
Sgt S Sierro

1977
Rfn JA Gracia
Rfn J Antonio
Rfn AG Correia
2ⁿᵈ Lt G Keulder
Rfn S Henrique
Rfn E Mukonda
Cpl E Jchikembe
Rfn S Luciano
Rfn HM Dos Santos
Sgt BA Mwonambungu
Rfn J Joaquim
Rfn R Pedro
Rfn JM Muquindla
Rfn P Paulo
Rfn J Victor

1978
Rfn A Cassamona
Rfn A da Silva
Rfn J Linhangwa
Rfn J Dumba
Rfn L Laurindo
Rfn R Augusto
Rfn A Mussungu
Rfn N Bernade
Rfn C Esals
Rfn SM Chicoto
Rfn B Caquarta
Sgt CJ Theron
2ⁿᵈ Lt AL Opperman
Rfn PP Amorim
Rfn A Zagi

1979
Rfn AM Tizondo
2ⁿᵈ Lt SW Coetzee
2ⁿᵈ Lt WA de Vos
Rfn S Mudonda

1980
Rfn J Miranda
Rfn M Yenga

Cpl CC da Trinidade
Cpl BZ Gericke
Capt A Erasmus
Capt C de J Muller
2ⁿᵈ Lt TC Patrick
LCpl AJ Falcus
Cpl EC Engelbrecht
LCpl J Kaumba
Rfn J Matamba
Rfn A Livingue
Rfn C Marcellino
Rfn B Albino
Rfn R Alberto
Rfn S Angelo
Rfn A Caliango
2ⁿᵈ Lt P van der Walt
Sgt SD Braz
Cpl M van Wyk
Rfn J Miguel
Cpl DH Grobler
Cpl MC Coetzee
Rfn J Kambinda
Rfn J João
Cpl J Francisco
Cpl K Vavala
LCpl E Sofia

Rfn A Eduardo
2nd Lt JM Muller
Rfn M Augusto

1981
Rfn A Joaquim
Rfn A Samba
Cpl J Martins
Rfn F Chameia
Rfn F Dala
Rfn TWZ Navaros
Rfn C Cabonga
Rfn D Paulo
Rfn J João

1982
2nd Lt PJS Nel
Cpl PT Steward
Cpl Y João
Cpl M José
Rfn C Evaristo
Cpl J Conroy
Rfn AP Manuel
Rfn DD Denge
Cpl M Bambi
Rfn A Haefeni
Rfn H Naikako

1983
Sgt A Mande
Rfn JD Kativa

Rfn E Kasera
Cpl GH du Randt
Rfn J Nambi
Rfn T Manganhes

1984
Cpl A Aurelio
Rfn I Malongo
Rfn J Dala
Cpl C Paulo
Rfn D Antonio

1985
LCpl L Dumba
Rfn Z Chipoya
Rfn J Fernando
Cpl MA Kinguelele
Rfn M Joaquim
Rfn P José
LCpl JE Jamba
Rfn M Muema
Rfn JA Sachilombo
Rfn A de Almeida
Rfn K Kalonga
Rfn PK Kahete
Rfn J Chihamba
Lt DG Light
Rfn B Paulo

1987
LCpl E João

Rfn D Zumba
Rfn G Antonio
Rfn K Tolosi
Rfn F Sikote
Rfn D Cassela
Cpl I Vocolo
Rfn L Njamba
Cpl B Sokola
Rfn J Gonçalvez
Rfn P Kapinga
Capt AD McCallum
LCpl MM de Klerk
Tpr MJ Kuyler
2nd Lt JR Alves
Sgt JRM Mananza
LCpl W Tchipango
Rfn C Dala
Rfn F Mauricio
Rfn EN Kapepura
Sgt AND Baptista
Tpr JR Meyer
Rfn J Pedro

1988
Rfn AN Dinu

1989
Rfn J Vimango

1991
Rfn JA Sampaio

Traditional unit songs

32 BATTALION DIFFERED from other units in many ways, one being that up to 1985 no bands took part in any ceremonial parades or functions, and no traditional military music was played on such occasions. Instead, members of the unit rendered the simple but deeply meaningful songs they had brought with them from Angola, accompanied by hearty foot stomping to emphasise a point or keep the beat.

As time passed and circumstances changed, new songs were added to their repertoire, a custom that continued even after being moved to Pomfret. Sung mostly in Portuguese, some of the words were in languages indigenous to their homeland, but each song had special meaning for the men of 32 Battalion and reflected both their feelings and experiences. It was nothing strange to hear them singing heartily as they ran from one position to another, and not a single heart could fail to be moved by the sound of their voices on the eve of deployment for battle.

Although the English translations can never quite capture the mood or pathos of these songs, they are published here along with the original words to offer some insight into the souls of these extraordinary warriors.

ANGOLANOS AVANTE

Angolanos avante	Angolans onward
Para a liberdade marchar	To march for freedom
Neste luta triunfante	On this successful struggle
A vitória conquistar	To conquer this victory
Lutar … lutar	To fight … To fight
Lutar … lutar	To fight … To fight

Nesta luta triunfante	On this successful struggle
Angola vencerá	Angola shall win
Lutar … lutar	To fight … To fight
Lutar … lutar	To fight … To fight
Nesta luta triunfante	On this successful struggle
Angola vencerá	Angola shall win

LUTAR ATÉ AO FIM

Lutar até ao fim	Fighting till the end
Lutar até ao fim	Fighting till the end
Lutaremos até ao fim	We are going to fight until the end
Combatente do Buffalo luta	Combatants of Buffalo
Caminho do Buffalo é o verdadeiro	The way of Buffalo is the right way
Andando nele sempre havemos de vencer	If you walk this way we can win
Russos e Cubanos derrotámos já	Russians and Cubans we have already won
Combatente do Buffalo luta	Combatants of Buffalo

QUERO QUERO

Quero quero	I want I want
Quero ser soldado	I want to be a soldier
Quero quero	I want I want
Quero ser soldado	I want to be a soldier
A yaya quero ser soldado	Ah, ah, ah, I want to be a soldier
A yaya quero ser soldado	Ah, ah, ah, I want to be a soldier
Visto a farda	I wear uniform
Visto a farda	I wear uniform
E toca a marchar	I start to march
Com espingarda	With a weapon
Com espingarda	With a weapon
E toca a matar	I start to kill

SOLE SOLE

Sole sole	I like I like
Sole lombeta	I like the trumpet
Sole sole	I like I like
Sole lombeta	I like the trumpet
A yaya sole lombeta	A yaya I like the trumpet
A yaya sole lombeta	A yaya I like the trumpet
Etu, etu, tubana ba Buffalo	We are children from Buffalo
Etu, etu, tubana ba Buffalo	We are children from Buffalo

ALLELUYA

Ah Ah Alleluya	Ah Ah Alleluya
Alleluya	Alleluya
Ah Ah Alleluya	Ah Ah Alleluya
Alleluya	Alleluya
Tuzali makasi	We are strong
Soki likambo ezali biso tokosalisa yo	When problems arrive we are going to help you
Biso nyoso tuzali ba solda	All of us we are soldiers
Ba solda!	Soldiers!

BISO TUKEYI

Biso tukeyi eh, eh, eh, eh	We are going eh, eh, eh, eh
Biso tukeyi eh, eh, eh, eh	We are going eh, eh, eh, eh
Botika Kuwayawaya kanga motema	Stay to look and close your heart
Botika Kuwayawaya kanga motema	Stay to look and close your heart

EU VOU MORRER EM ANGOLA

Eu vou morrer em Angola	I am going to die in Angola
Com arma de guera na mão	With my rifle in my hand
Granada será o meu caixão	The grenade will be my coffin
Enterro será na patrulha	My funeral will be on patrol

LINDA LINDA

Linda Linda Linda Linda oh o o o mama	Linda Linda Linda Linda oh o o o mama
Linda Linda Linda Linda oh o o o mama	Linda Linda Linda Linda oh o o o mama
Danger ya commando ezali koya	The danger of commando is coming
Danger ya Buffalo ezali koya	The danger of Buffalo is coming
Eh eh people sambilila Buffalo	People come to welcome Buffalo
Eh eh people sambilila Buffalo	People come to welcome Buffalo
Kombo ya Buffalo izalaka mibale zambe	The name of Buffalo cannot be two
Kombo ya Buffalo izalaka mibale zambe	The name of Buffalo cannot be two

GENERAL

General, General, General	General, General, General
Malan é general	Malan is general
Eu ouvir a dizer a direcção	I heard it said in the address
Malan é general	That Malan is general
Eu ouvir a dizer a direcção	I heard it said in the address
Malan é general	That Malan is general

General, General, General	General, General, General
Geldenhuys é general	Geldenhuys is general
Eu ouvir a dizer a direcção	I heard it said in the address
Geldenhuys é general	That Geldenhuys is general
Eu ouvir a dizer a direcção	I heard it said in the address
Geldenhuys é general	That Geldenhuys is general
General, General, General	General, General, General
Meiring é general	Meiring is general
Eu ouvir a dizer a direcção	I heard it said in the address
Meiring é general	That Meiring is general
Eu ouvir a dizer a direcção	I heard it said in the address
Meiring é general	That Meiring is general

BANANA KWIMBO

Banana kwimbo navalilalila	Our parents at home are crying
Navashinganyeka vana vavo	Who think about their children
Banana kwimbo navalilalila	Our parents at home are crying
Navashinganyeka vana vavo	Who think about their children
Tunengila Buffalo mama	We enter in Buffalo
Tunengila Pomfret mama	We enter in Pomfret

BUFFALO YETO NAWA

Buffalo Buffalo yeto nawa	Buffalo Buffalo is our home
Colonel colonel yeto nawa	Colonel colonel is our colonel
Commandante commandante yeto nawa	Commandant commandant is our commandant
Major major yeto nawa	Major major is our major
Capitano capitano yeto nawa	Captain captain is our captain
Tenente tenente yeto nawa	Lieutenant Lieutenant is our lieutenant
Samajor samajor yeto nawa	Sa'major sa'major is our sa'major
Stafo stafo yeto nawa	Staff staff is our staff
Sergento sergento yeto nawa	Sergeant sergeant is our sergeant
Corporal corporal yeto nawa	Corporal corporal is our corporal
Soldado soldado yeto nawa	Soldier soldier is our soldier
Pomfret Pomfret yeto nawa	Pomfret Pomfret is our home

WATUMALA KO KACHALO

Watumala ko kachalo	Who sits on the chair
Watumala ko kachalo	Who sits on the chair
Mangoyo oy mangoyo	That chair, that chair
Watumala ko kachalo	Who sits on the chair

Watumala ko kachalo mangoyo ya feka	Who sits on the chair of the country
Iteya, iteya, iteya	It can be broken, can be broken,
Ite yangocho	can be broken
	Be broken for nothing

ANA HE

Ana eh, Ana eh	Ana eh, Ana eh
Sisi yeto wa commando	All of us we are commandos
Ana eh mama	Ana eh mama

CATERPILLAR

Caterpillar, Caterpillar alela	Caterpillar, Caterpillar making a noise like
ya ngembo	a song
Alela ya ngembo alela	Making a noise like a song
Mama alela	Mother likes that song
Alela ya ngembo alela	Making her son like that song

MORTEIRO VINDUNDUMINO MU SAVATE

Yoyo indundumina mo Savate	What is exploding in Savate
O morteiro we	Are mortars
Yoyo indundumina mo Savate	What is exploding in Savate
O morteiro we wa kuloya	Are mortars
Katupala kuloya,	We want fire
Katupala kulo ya we	We want fire

HELENA, HELENA

Helena, Helena yoyo	Helena, Helena yoyo
Helena, Helena zuka miyambo	Helena, Helena cross the kraal
Zuka miyambo commando washala	Cross the kraal commandos are coming
Helena, Helena zuka miyambo	Helena, Helena cross the kraal

YATUKA KUNA ANGOLA

Yatuka kuna Angola	When we came from Angola
Yanate funda kiame	With our luggage
Sesesseko ankuntambula bis	Sese Seko received us
Mama mutombe mutombe yadiasila	Like we walked
Ndinga anani ese yambokela	The father of language calls us
Mama yasisa yasisa yasisa putuki	Mother, mother, mother is alive
Yalanda Holden yakumbanino	We must follow Holden till the end

YANGE JIA

Yange jia mukuloya	I am going to school
Na watata na wa mama mukulima	My father and mother went to the convent
Vajoongo yange musikola	My young brother went to school
Chifunchi china cha Buffalo	That place is Buffalo
Chifunchi china cha Pomfret	That place is Pomfret

UWA UNGENDE UWA

Uwa ungende uwa ha ha	Oh ah a good trip
Uwa ungende uwa ovala we	Oh ah a good trip
Colonel weya la wo, wela la wo	The colonel came with, came with
Commandante weya la wo, wela la wo	The commandant came with, came with
Uwa ungende uwa ha ha	Oh ah a good trip
Uwa ungende uwa ovala we	Oh ah a good trip

NBADI YAYA

Nbadi yaya, nbadi yaya umbanzange	Mbandi brother remember me
Nbadi yaya, nbadi yaya umbanzange	Mbandi brother remember me
Una yakelenge muna FNLA	Before I did not like the FNLA
Kulendiko kassi wau FNLA	Now my name is written in the FNLA
Nbadi yaya, nbadi yaya umbanzange	Mbandi brother remember me
Nbadi yaya, nbadi yaya umbanzange	Mbandi brother remember me
Una yakelenge muna kinkuza	Before I did not like the kinkuza
Kulendiko kassi wau FNLA	Now my name is written in the FNLA

BUFFALO WEYA

Buffalo weya a Cubano ukatile	The Buffalos came, the Cubans ran away
Buffalo weya ove a Russo ukatile	The Buffalos came, the Russians ran away
Da watila ai we …	If you run ah, eh …
Wabata o tungo aiwe …	You are the loser …
Tueile ai we	We came ah, eh
Tuiele tuenda ai we	We came – we go ah, eh

ANGOLA – ANGOLA

Angola Angola	Angola Angola
A pátria nossa sem Igual	Home, fatherland, matchless
A terra mãe fonte de heróis	Mother country, temple of heroes
Desde Cabinda até ao Cunene	From Cabinda to Cunene
És única és grande	You are unique, you are huge
Nós te Louvamos pátria amada	We praise our fatherland
De peito erguido é com fervor	With our hearts filled with zeal
Nós marchamos sem temer	We march without fear
Ó pátria amada!	Oh fatherland
A nossa glória!	Our glory
Angola Angola	Angola Angola
Tu vencerás!	You shall win
Angola	Angola
Liberdade e terra	Freedom and land

Weaponry, vehicles and aircraft used during the Angolan conflict

AGS 17: 30-mm grenade launcher

AK47: Soviet-made 7,62-mm automatic rifle characterised by curved magazine

Alouette: Light helicopter of French origin, mainly used for fire support, search-and-rescue and reconnaissance

AN 26: Soviet-built Antonov transport aircraft flown by Russian or Cuban pilots to supply FAPLA

APPMISR: Russian anti-personnel 'jump' mine

B10: 82-mm recoilless gun of Soviet origin

BMP 1: Soviet-made armoured infantry combat vehicle with mounted 73-mm gun and wire-guided anti-tank missiles

BM 21: Soviet-made 122-mm multiple rocket launcher, also known as the Stalin Organ or 'Red Eye'

Bosbok: Italian-made single-engined light aircraft used by the SAAF in spotter/reconnaissance role

Bosvark: Unimog adapted with armour plating and sandbags to be mine-resistant

BRDM-2: Standard Soviet-made eight-wheeled light armoured car fitted with 14,5-mm and 7,62-mm machine guns

BTR 60: Soviet-made armoured personnel carrier fitted with 14,5-mm machine gun

Buccaneer: Low-level strike aircraft of British origin with action radius of up to 1 000 km

Buffel: Mine-resistant armoured personnel carrier – workhorse of SADF infantry

C130: Four-engined transport aircraft made by Lockheed, also known as the Hercules

C160: Two-engined transport aircraft made by Aerospatiale, France, also known as the Transall

Canberra: Jet-engined bomber of British origin, dating back to the mid-1950s

Casspir: Mine-resistant armoured personnel carrier

Claymore: Anti-personnel mine that directs shrapnel at predetermined area, detonated electronically or by time fuse

D30: Soviet-made 122-mm howitzer with effective firing range of 15 km

D74: Soviet-made 122-mm howitzer with effective firing range of 24 km

DKZ B: Soviet-made single-tube 122-mm rocket launcher

Draganov: 7,62-mm Soviet sniper rifle

DSHK 38/46: 12,7-mm machine gun

Eland 90: South African version of the French Panhard armoured car fitted with a 90-mm gun

G1: 88-mm field gun

G2: 140-mm field gun of World War II vintage, also known as the 5.5-pounder, with effective firing range of 16 km

G5: 155-mm South African field gun, maximum firing range 48 km

G6: Self-propelled version of the G5

GPMG: General purpose 7,62-mm machine gun

Hand grenades: F1 RGD 5, RG 4, RG 42, M26 (South African)

Impala: South African fighter aircraft

Kudu: South African light military aircraft

M55: 30-mm tri-barrel anti-aircraft gun

M79: 40-mm grenade launcher

MAG: 7,62-mm light machine gun manu-factured by FN in Belgium

Makarov: 9-mm pistol

MI 8, MI 17: Soviet-made general utility helicopters

MI 24, MI 25, MI 35: Soviet-made helicopter gunship known as the Hind

MiG 17: Russian-made single-seater fighter and interceptor aircraft

MiG 21: All-purpose Soviet fighter-bomber and air-to-air interceptor

MiG 23: More advanced version of MiG 21

Milan: Anti-tank guided missile system of French origin, used by the SADF

Mirage F-1AZ: SAAF's main attack aircraft, built by Dassault, France

Mirage F-1CZ: SAAF's principal fighter aircraft and interceptor

Mirage III: SAAF's principal reconnaissance aircraft

Mortars: 60, 81, 82 and 120 mm

MRL: South African-made 127-mm multiple rocket launcher with 24 truck-mounted tubes firing 60-kg rockets with 22-km maximum range, also known as the Valkiri

Olifant: SA Army's main battle tank

PKM: 7,62-mm machine gun

PMD 6, PMN, POM Z: Anti-personnel mines

PPSh 41: 7,62-mm carbine

PT76: Soviet-made light amphibious tank

Puma: French-built transport helicopter used by the SA Air Force to ferry troops and supplies

R1: South African-made 7,62-mm automatic rifle similar to the British SLR and Belgian FN

R4: SADF's standard 5,56-mm assault rifle – South African version of the Israeli Galil

R5: Compact version of R4, standard issue to paratroopers

Ratel Command Vehicle: Custom-built version of Ratel Infantry Combat Vehicle, featuring built-in map tables, specialised communication equipment, air-conditioning and public address system

Ratel 20: SA Army's standard mechanised infantry combat vehicle, armed with 20-mm gun and 7,62-mm machine gun. Carries a three-man crew and nine-man infantry section. Light armour offers protection against small-arms fire, shell fragments and mine blasts

Ratel 90: Anti-tank version of standard ICV, armed with 90-mm gun, effective up to 1 200 m

Ratel ZT3: 127-mm missile-carrying version of standard ICV

RPD: 7,62-mm machine gun

RPG 7: 40-mm anti-tank/anti-personnel rocket-propelled grenade of Soviet origin

SA 2: Soviet-made surface-to-air missile with 40–50-km range and 18 000-m ceiling

SA 3: Soviet-made medium altitude surface-to-air missile with 29-km range and 15 000-m ceiling

SA 6: Soviet-made guided missile with 60-km range and ability to lock on to aircraft at altitudes from 100 m to 18 000 m

SA 7: Soviet-made portable, shoulder-launched surface-to-air missile

SA 8: Soviet-made short-range surface-to-air missile system mounted on BRDM-2 armoured car

SA 9: Gaskin surface-to-air missile system

SA 13: Successor to SA 9, mounted on PT76 tank with 8-km range and 4 000-m ceiling

SA 14: New generation SA 7 with 4-km range

Sabre: Customised Land Rover with armoured plates fitted on both sides and mounted 7,62-mm machine gun

Sagger: Anti-tank missile system

Samil 20: Two-ton cargo and personnel truck

Samil 100: Ten-ton cargo truck

Seminof: 7,62-mm carbine of Soviet origin, also known as the SKS

SS 77: South African machine gun that replaced MAG or GPMG

Stinger: American-made portable shoulder-launched surface-to-air missile

SU22: Soviet-manufactured attack and close support aircraft

Super Frelon: French-manufactured helicopter, the largest in use by the SAAF until early 1980s

T34, T54, T55, T62, T65: Soviet-built main battle tanks

TM: Anti-tank mines

Tokarev: 7,62-mm pistol

Unimog: 4 × 4 troop carrier manufactured by Mercedes Benz

VZ 23/24/25/26: Various models of 7,62-mm carbine of Czechoslovakian origin

VZ 52: 7,62-mm assault rifle of Czechoslovakian origin

Withings: Mine-resistant recovery vehicle built on 6 × 6 truck chassis

Wolf: Mine-resistant vehicle built on Unimog chassis and in use until early 1977

Ystervark: Self-propelled anti-aircraft system mounted on a Samil 20 chassis with mine-resistant hull and armoured cab, armed with a single-barrel 20-mm gun, operated by a three-man crew

ZU23: Soviet-made radar-controlled 23-mm light anti-aircraft gun with vertical range of 2 500 m

ZPU 1: 14,5-mm anti-aircraft gun

57-mm anti-tank aircraft gun of Soviet origin with effective range of 1 250 m

76-mm divisional gun of Soviet origin with effective range of 1 000 m

103-mm rifle grenade (South African)

106-mm recoilless gun – SA Army's secondary anti-tank gun

Glossary of foreign and military terms

2IC – second in command

APC – armoured personnel carrier, designed to protect troops while being transported into a combat zone

Area operations – carried out to clear a specific region of enemy personnel, support and shelter

AWOL – absent without official leave

Bigpack – canvas backpacks containing everything a soldier needs on patrol

Black is Beautiful – black cream used to camouflage exposed skin of white/light-coloured troops in the bush

Bombshell – sudden dispersal of troops under fire, each man heading in a different direction to regroup later at a pre-designated rendezvous point

Border control – operations aimed at combating illegal immigration or securing international frontiers to prevent enemy personnel, supplies or equipment from entering a country

BRIL – Brigada de Infantaria Ligeira (light infantry brigade deployed for counter-guerrilla operations)

BRIM – Brigada de Infantaria Motorizada (motorised infantry brigade equipped with heavy weaponry such as artillery, tanks and anti-aircraft systems, deployed in conventional warfare)

Browns – nutria battledress of SA Army

Call sign – identifying name or number allocated to a patrol for use during radio communication

Casevac – evacuation of wounded, usually by helicopter, from battlefield to nearest hospital

Chana – Owambo word for clearing

Chest webbing – ammunition pouches attached to harness, worn across a soldier's chest

Chopper – helicopter

COIN operations – counter-insurgency measures

Contact – exchange of fire with the enemy

Cutline – 460-km strip along the northern border of Namibia, cleared of vegetation in terms of a 1962 agreement between South Africa and Portugal

Echelon – combat element's logistics and support vehicles

Escudos – monetary unit of Portugal and its former African colonies

FCP – forward command post

Firefight – exchange of fire following 'contact'

First-line ammunition – ammunition for personal/portable support weapons carried by each soldier at start of deployment

Group – specific area of military responsibility in South Africa, for example Group 9

Gunship – Alouette helicopter fitted with 20-mm gun positioned to allow firing through open door

HAA – helicopter administrative area, normally close to tactical headquarters, where helicopters refuel and wait for operational orders

HE – high explosive

HEAT – high explosive anti-tank

HQ – headquarters

Kimbo – Angolan word of Portuguese origin for village or settlement

Klepper Kayak – collapsible two-man canoe made of canvas and vinyl mounted on lightweight wooden frame

Kraal – collection of huts occupied by local population in the bush

Laager – protective circle of vehicles

Lay-up – safe hiding place in the bush where troops can wait for optimum operational conditions

LMG – light machine gun

Local population – civilian and usually indigenous inhabitants of an operational area

MAG – light machine gun made by FN, firing 7,62 × 51 NATO belted ammunition

Makorro – wooden boat made by hollowing out a tree trunk, used by indigenous people of northern Namibia and Angola

MBT – main battle tank, in South Africa the Olifant

MCP – main command post

MRL – multiple rocket launcher

Napalm – incendiary substance made of thick jellied petroleum that burns at up to 1 000°C, used in bombs and flame throwers; first used by America during World War II

NCO – non-commissioned officer

ODP – local militia in Angola

Parabats – paratroopers

PE-4 – plastic explosives

PF – Permanent Force (full-time SADF members)

Quartel – military barracks

Ratpack – food packs issued to soldiers in the field, each containing sufficient rations for a 24-hour period

Recce – specially trained member of a reconnaissance unit or Special Forces operator

Rev – attack-designated target, usually a base

Ripple – salvo of 24 rockets fired simultaneously by multiple rocket launcher

RSM – Regimental Sergeant Major – most senior non-commissioned officer in a unit

Shona – used by the Owambo tribe of northern Namibia to denote grassland or savannah

Tac HQ – tactical headquarters, usually a tented operations room manned 24 hours a day, from which movements in the field are controlled

Timo Line – road 1 000 m south of and parallel to the border between South West Africa and Angola

White phosphorous – incendiary agent commonly found in hand grenades, mortar and artillery rounds and smoke bombs

Yati Strip – one-kilometre wide strip of land between the Timo Line and Angolan border, barred to all but military personnel

Bibliography

THE INFORMATION IN this book is based almost entirely on official records preserved by the South African Department of Defence's Documentation Centre. The recollections of former 32 Battalion members about certain events have been verified by the relevant documents. However, the author also consulted a number of books and newspaper reports as part of his background research. Those who wish to learn more about South Africa's recent military history would do well to read the following accounts:

Breytenbach, Jan, *Forged in Battle* (Saayman & Weber, 1986)
—— *They Live by the Sword* (Lemur, 1990)
—— *Eden's Exiles* (Quellerie, 1997)
Bridgland, Fred, *Savimbi – A Key to Africa* (Macmillan, 1986)
—— *The War for Africa* (Ashanti, 1990)
Dempster, Chris, and Dave Tomkins, *Fire Power* (Corgi, 1986)
Els, Paul, *We Fear Naught but God – The Story of the South African Special Forces* (Covos Day, 2000)
Geldenhuys, Jannie, *A General's Story – From an Era of War and Peace* (Jonathan Ball, 1995)
Greef, Jack, *A Greater Share of Honour* (Ntomeni, 2001)
Hamann, Hilton, *Days of the Generals* (Zebra Press, 2001)
Heitman, Helmoed-Romer, *The South African War Machine* (Bison Books, 1985)
—— *War in Angola – The Final South African Phase* (Ashanti, 1985)
—— *The South African Armed Forces* (Buffalo Publications, 1990)
Lord, D, *Fire, Flood and Ice* (Covos Day, 1998)
Marks, Bernard, *Our South African Army Today* (Purnell, 1977)
Moorcroft, Paul L, *Africa's Super Power* (Sygma/Collins, 1981)

Paul, Matthew, *Parabat – Personal Accounts of Paratroopers in Combat Situations in South Africa's History* (Covos Day, 2001)

Pimlot, John, *Guerrilla Warfare* (Bison Books, 1985)

Potgieter, Herman, *The South African Air Force – The Poster Book* (Struik, 1987)

Potgieter, Herman, and Willem Steenkamp, *Aircraft of the South African Air Force* (Woolworths, 1980)

Report of South Africa's Truth and Reconciliation Commission, Volumes 2 and 3 (TRC, 1998)

SADF Review (Walker-Ramus Trading Co, 1989 and 1990)

SADF Yearbook (Edupress, 1985)

SADF Directorate Public Relations, *Still Champions – South African Defence Force 1912–1987* (Walker-Ramus Trading Co, 1987)

Spies, FJ du Toit, *Operasie Savannah Angola 1975–1976* (SADF, 1989)

Stander, Siegfried, *Like the Wind. The Story of the South African Army* (Saayman & Weber, 1985)

Steenkamp, Willem, *Border Strike – South Africa into Angola* (Butterworth, 1983)

——— *South Africa's Border War – 1966–1989* (Ashanti, 1989)

Stiff, Peter, *The Silent War – South African Recce Operations 1969–1994* (Galago, 1999)

UNITA, *Identity of a Free Angola* (Unita)

Van Wyk, A, *Honoris Crux – Ons Dapperes* (Saayman & Weber, 1985)

Index